BEFORE I F

James Mason ... the
British and American ...
years. Here he looks back on a career which
spans such famous films as *The Seventh Veil*,
Rommel – Desert Fox, *North by Northwest*,
Pandora and the Flying Dutchman and *Lolita*. He
has played opposite Judy Garland, Margaret
Lockwood, Ann Todd, and Ava Gardner and co-
starred with Cary Grant, Kirk Douglas, George
Sanders and Peter Sellers.

Before I Forget

AUTOBIOGRAPHY AND DRAWINGS BY
JAMES MASON

SPHERE BOOKS LIMITED

A SPHERE BOOK

First published in Great Britain by
Hamish Hamilton Ltd 1981
Published by Sphere Books Ltd 1982
Reprinted 1989

Reproduced, printed and bound in Great Britain by
Cox & Wyman Ltd, Reading

ISBN 0 7221 5763 0

Sphere Books Ltd
A Division of
Macdonald & Co (Publishers) Ltd
27 Wrights Lane, London W8 5TZ
A member of Maxwell Pergamon Publishing Corporation plc

For Clarissa, Morgan, Portland

CONTENTS

The author's thanks are due to Kaye Webb for enabling us to reproduce the drawings published first in *Lilliput* and to the National Film Archive for help in tracing film stills.

PART ONE

1/Huddersfield

My purpose in writing this book was to get things out of the way. Anyone who has lived a rather full life may find, even while he is still quite young, that his mind is so stuffed with funny things that have happened to him that he wants to make a neat pile of them and put them to one side. If the writer is getting on in years he is in danger of slipping into anecdotage and may already be repeating the same story to the same friend two or three times in the course of one evening. And it is reasonable to hope that when one has put a lot of his material between the covers of a book one need never refer to it again and so avoid becoming the club bore and have a nice, clear space for all the new adventures, projects, theories and jokes that one continues to collect in the vivid present.

I would have been so happy if my father or my mother had stumbled upon a good reason for setting down an autobiography because now I feel properly ashamed of myself for knowing so little about them. For so many years I did not bother to find out and then suddenly they are no longer around to answer questions. And so I am entitled to assume that, later on, not only my son and daughter but others too may wish to pose questions and now that I have written the book all I shall need to say is you'll find your answer in the chapter titled *Stratford Ont.* or whatever.

When I started the project I happened to be rehearsing a play in New York, so I thought that perhaps a blow by blow description of our preparations might supply a lively, action-packed first chapter. It turned out to be a very long chapter and certainly not lacking in action; for instance it would be hard to top the scene in which a member of the cast threatened to leap out of a ninth storey window if the producer did not release him from his contract, but the reader on finishing the chapter would have known not much more about the autobiographer than when he began, especially since the play lasted no more than three weeks on Broadway.

I had thought that I would leap merrily from one phase of my career to another with little regard for strict continuity, but then it struck me that the reader might prefer to be told where I was born and how one thing led to another in chronological order. There was one drawback. Just about the time that I had ploughed through Waterloo Road/Dublin and Beaconsfield and was half way through Olleberrie Farm I realised that if I went on like that indefinitely the book would be too much for the strongest stomach. In terms of weight, I mean. And it was not difficult for me to choose an appropriate finishing line, since my career has, up to this point, fallen neatly into three Acts. Act I covered my stage and screen acting until I decided to go to California. Act II covered some sixteen years in America. And Act III started with my return to Europe in 1962 or thereabouts. By way of a curtain to Act II there was a notable film called *Lolita* in which I played a part. This eased me back to Europe because although in every other way it was an American production it was actually shot in England. The book would end, I decided, with *Lolita*.

I mention this because it will act as a warning to any prospective reader who might open this book or – more rashly still – even buy this book with a view to finding out what it was like to be working with Lynn Redgrave or Anthony Quinn or Sam Peckinpah or Warren Beatty or Raquel Welch or a heap of others who were to crop up only in my Act III. Maybe that is how the book should have been advertised. 'This book contains no mention of Raquel Welch.' Too late now.

*

4

My father, John Mason, was a textile merchant who had been born, lived and died in Huddersfield, an industrial town in the West Riding of Yorkshire, as people of my generation will continue to call that section of the map.[1] The manufacture of generally high class textiles is its principal industry. Or was. Maybe that has changed too.

My father's father, George Simpson Mason, travelled in textiles and had earned a name for himself as an exceptionally good and Christian gentleman. And my father's maternal grandfather was that John Wilkinson whose warehouse was a prominent feature of St. George's Square opposite our fine railway station. The firm was called 'John Wilkinson & Son' and in it a place was found for my father when he left school at the age of sixteen. It was now run by the 'son' whose name appropriately was 'Johnson'. My father's first job was to spend a winter in Lausanne and learn French, since export trade with the French speaking countries represented a large part of their business. I assume that it was in Lausanne that he became the dapper, well groomed man of the world one sees in photographs taken of him at the time of his marriage. In Lausanne also he broke a kneecap playing soccer.

In 1905 he married Mabel Hattersley Gaunt. This must have been quite a catch, for my mother was terrifically well educated.

Her father, J. Shaw Gaunt, had sent her to a high class boarding school in London where she set about preparing herself for a life of culture, until the death of her mother rudely transported her back to Huddersfield to keep house for her father and two brothers.

Once married to my father, she was destined to start looking after another family of men, her husband and three sons.

The lady trained for a life of elegant gentility had to settle for one of masculine encirclement. This became a dominant

---

[1] Under the Local Government Act of 1972 the boundaries and even the names of certain English counties were altered by the whimsical Edward Heath, who was then Prime Minister.

theme in the more plaintive moments of her later life, though there is no knowing if she was aware of the entrapment to a point of resentment during her early married life.

The eldest son was Rex Linton Gaunt Mason, born in 1906. Then came Edward Colin in 1907, followed by me, James Neville, in 1909. I think that the Neville had a literary or historical significance for my mother. Linton was a name that frequently cropped up in my father's family. The Edward must have been a salute to the reigning monarch.

Though I had no standard of comparison, the world I encountered when born seemed to me to be sensational. I did not see much of my father for a while, but my mother was attentive and loving. And there was a heroic little old nurse. I don't suppose she was really very old but how was I to know? She was older than anyone else there. And I don't remember any incidents that caused everyone to think of her in heroic terms. She was small and dominant; I suppose that's enough. But also I am told that my mother was won over by her initiative and her thriftiness. An example of initiative was her habit of carrying a bundle of old newspapers, some of which she could stuff inside our outer clothes if the weather suddenly became cold. Also there were a cook and a maid and a gardener who came two days a week.

We lived in Croft House Lane in the house into which my parents had moved at the time of their marriage and which gave the lane its name. It clearly antedated all the other houses in the lane, built later to accommodate the population growth caused by the Industrial Revolution.

In the older section of Croft House there was a large low ceilinged room which we called the washhouse and since there was a stone sink and a 'copper', it was indeed used for the household washing; but it was in fact an old brewhouse. Above was what we called the barn, with a huge loading door opening onto the fresh air some ten feet above ground level. During our early winters the floor was covered with shallots, bulbs from the garden and the tubers of dahlias. Adjacent to the washhouse were a mysteriously unused kitchen and pantry and cellar, then the kitchen proper and the pantry which were in current use and a place called Maude's back room, indispensable for dumping muddy boots and cleaning them. On the other side of a baize-covered swinging door was the living section of the house on two floors, with a bathroom halfway up the stairs which featured a noble arched doorway with stained glass panels. And then, just below the ground floor level, was the strong room, which got its name from the iron bars which criss-crossed its windows and those of the bathroom directly above. A previous owner had been a collector of 'stones' which had presumably been accommodated on the fine mahogany shelves which lined the room. The collector had also distributed in the garden large, interesting stone urns; guarding the front door were two beautiful marble lions.

My brother Colin recalls that the mysteriously unused rooms mentioned above had in fact been occupied during the first year or two of my parents' residence by a married couple who worked for them. The husband became very ill and lay in bed all day in the 'kitchen'. He made up his mind that he was going to die in spite of my father's patient attempts to talk him out of this defeatist attitude. 'Nay', said the sick man, 'the wife 'as made mi funeral supper already.' My father expressed dismay. 'But ah've tricked 'er!' said the sick man with a wink. 'Oh? How did you do that?' 'Ah've etten it all up!' Thinking that he was asleep the wife had improvidently stowed the funeral supper under his bed.

The newer section of the house, consisting of the dining room, the drawing room and the two principal rooms upstairs had the stern classic look which suggested 1870 or thereabouts. All these four rooms were rather long and dark, which further upset any member of the family who had reason to be depressed at any time.

Nothing very dramatic or colourful imprinted itself as a first memory. I retain a clear crib's-eye-view of the night nursery, and I remember being very fond of a short,

Japanese, quilted dressing gown and perhaps it was at the same time that my favourite toy was a small Japanese battleship. I admired its lines. And there was a fine bear called Big Teddy.

But it was not until after 1914 that the imperishably memorable toys became part of our daily lives, the lead soldiers and their accoutrements. Every action of the First World War was fought again on the linoleum covered floor of our nursery and in the air space immediately above it.

Resulting from our growing up process the heroic little Nana left the scene to make way for a governess. The first did not stay long enough to play an important role; her successor did. The part she played was that of not only the most unforgettable character in my early life but also the most influential.

This was Ada Frances Daft, a farmer's daughter from Shouthall, Nottinghamshire. She came into our lives in 1913. We had our early seaside holidays at Filey on the East Coast of Yorkshire. But in the autumn of 1914 Scarborough, the next town down the coast, was bombarded by the German Fleet. August 1913 must therefore have been our last summer holiday at Filey. After that we switched to the West Coast. That last year at Filey was marked by the encampment nearby of five thousand soldiers. Children of today would not be impressed by such an event since they are likely to see soldiers killing each other practically every night on television. But at that time soldiers were known to us only in the form of toys. Here then were *five thousand* living breathing marching soldiers, and in *khaki*. That was novelty enough for most of the grown ups but for Miss Daft there was another thrilling detail. The men were Sherwood Foresters! This was a famous Nottinghamshire regiment, and as a Nottinghamshire patriot Miss Daft was second to none.

So, from this summer Miss Daft looked after us in every way until each of us in turn went to boarding school. And even after that she stayed on because she had made herself

8

not only beloved but indispensable. Also by this time the two-person staff of one maid and one cook was reduced to a single 'cook-general'.

She was the scenarist of our war games on the nursery floor. The soldiers were all the product of W. Britain; a firm which had for many generations supplied British children with painted soldiers of truly British quality. Each birthday and each Christmas brought reinforcements. Sometimes the soldiers were simply taken out of their boxes and arranged in the form of an impressive parade. But more often they were lined up in battle order and exposed to artillery fire.

Colin had a French 75, a piece that was receiving a lot of publicity in the early stages of the war. It fired tiny wooden shells. Rex had a fine howitzer. And there was also a cannon which fired matches. You put your unused match in the breach, below which burned a tiny spirit lamp. After a moment or two the match exploded and was jet propelled towards the enemy ranks causing negligible damage. This was a point in its favour because there was another cannon which fired a metal shell, activated by a spring, which caused irreparable casualties. You could reinforce a fractured leg with a match stick, if you had the skill and the patience, and send him back to the front, but that was not our sort of war. My soldiers at least would be kept well out of that kind of harm's way. Rex had a Royal Army Medical Corps horsedrawn ambulance and there were some of those neat looking WW I nurses. Aeroplanes figured only in the form of magazine illustrations which would be pasted into scrapbooks along with photographic reportage from the newspapers which we had cut out and coloured in varying shades of khaki and blood. I was particularly fond of the German plane with the bird-like wing tips. It was always being shot down in flames.

When the weather was favourable the war moved into the garden. If we scraped below the topsoil we came immediately to a soft clay. Digging into this was no great problem and we fashioned for ourselves a trench and

9

dugout with shell-proof roof of criss-crossed, turf-covered branches. I use the phrase 'no problem' loosely since I cannot remember lending much of a hand's turn myself. And would it be disrespectful to number one brother Rex, to wonder if Sam Kaye, the gardener, may have given a hand? In my mind I see a trench about twelve feet long and four feet deep.

Rex was what they call a born leader. He had the rank of colonel in these outdoor war games, Colin was a sergeant and I was a private, but unlike real life privates I was spared the hard work. Indeed I cannot remember actually taking part in any of our acts of aggression. And aggressive we certainly were. The boundary of the territory which we defended was the high stone wall which separated the garden from Croft House Lane. This was breached by the front gate, through which Rex and Colin made punitive sorties. Adult men were frequently identified as German spies, though seldom exposed to physical violence. The worst that one of us would do was furtively to approach the German spy from the rear and step smartly on the tip of his walking stick, and thus bring it crashing to the ground. This was followed by a hasty retreat to previously prepared positions. But the real enemy were the boys of the neighbourhood.

Rex and Colin were armed with hand grenades. Some were the same eggshaped objects which are still favoured by our hijackers. But during World War I they also used a grenade which sprouted a short handle, intended to make them easier to throw. All our grenades were of course made of our handy dried clay. And the handles were carnation sticks from the gardener's stock. Our side arbitrarily decreed that the use of stones was a breach of international law, which, if accepted by the other side, would have effectively disarmed them. Aside from the occasional rapid sortie through the front gate, our men pitched their grenades from the top of the wall or from the coalhouse roof, an advantageous position in the back yard. Colin was to my memory our only casualty, a direct hit with an enemy stone. Colin was injury prone.

Shortly after this, pressure from the home front brought hostilities to a close. Nevertheless my mother, perhaps more than anyone, encouraged the military fantasies since she equipped us with smart khaki uniforms and conscripted us for charity concerts. On stage we marched and counter-marched and rendered 'It's a long way to Tipperary' for the benefit of the Red Cross, for the National Society for the Prevention of Cruelty to Children and other good causes.

The garden was not a permanent war zone. It was a perfect hide-and-seek ground and also on a more serious level a cricket ground. Kaye, the gardener, was a considerable cricketer. How considerable there is no telling. We know that he was a close friend and neighbour of Percy Holmes who for many years opened the batting for Yorkshire (Holmes & Sutcliffe). And Kaye in reminiscent mood was heard to say that George Hirst and himself were once the two greatest Yorkshire players. But no independent witnesses were found to bear this out. My father bought us a practice net which was set up on a corner of the flat lawn at the bottom of the garden. And so Kaye introduced us to the mysteries of bat and ball. I learned how to keep a straight bat but little else since at my age there was no point in wasting a lot of time on me. When I went to our first boarding school I was given my big chance and blew it.

Impressed perhaps by my style they put me in the second eleven to play against a neighbouring school. The first ball that I received bounced off my bat unimpressively in the direction of square leg. With the next I was bowled out. I was trying to find excuses for myself as I walked off the field. Arriving there I heard these words snarled at me by the master in charge of the event: 'Playing back to a half volley!'

I felt deeply injured. It was all very well for this man to snarl at me, but no one had *told* me which balls I was supposed to play forward to! This was the inauspicious

11

start to a zero athletic career. Colin, by contrast, was a natural athlete. He had a good eye and perfect coordination. It was a pleasure to watch him on the tennis court. I always wanted to have a dirty mark dead centre of my lawn tennis racket instead of those smudges around the edges. But there was no mistaking Colin's racket. Under Kaye's tutelage he was a natural medium slow bowler, and he fell into a temporary disfavour when he came back from school with pretensions to fast bowling. As an adult he was to become a really terrific field hockey player. To our leader, Rex, glory was to come on the rugby field and in the boxing ring.

There was a lot of work for Kaye in our garden – the flowers, the vegetables and the endless pushing of the heavy mowing machine. He was slowed down at one point by heart trouble and we, being innocent of all medical knowledge, misinterpreted his predilection for sitting out much of the afternoon in his special chair in the washhouse. From Kaye's chair issued a fund of stories, some taller than others. And then he became so sick that he could no longer leave the little house in Quarmby where he was presently to die. We visited him and sat around the bed, our eyes stinging with tears. We had been very lucky to know such a man. We soon realised that he was irreplaceable.

Miss Daft was irreplaceable too, but we were not to know that until long after she had gone. No sudden death took her away but a gradual phasing out. First there was the nursery and the games and her reading aloud. Everyone at the beginning of that war was knitting. Sister Susie was sewing shirts for soldiers. But with our lot it was socks and gloves and Balaclava helmets. And Miss Daft was the champion. She knitted at an amazing speed and could pay attention to half a dozen other matters at the same time. At a certain hour of the evening she was into her knitting and reading aloud routine which continued long after the demand for Balaclava helmets had receded. I have sometimes found myself blaming Miss Daft for the fact that I have always been a slow reader. For I was still listening to Miss Daft reading stories out of *Chatterbox*, *The Boys' Own Paper* and *The Captain* at an age when I should have been destroying my eyesight with tome after tome of Charles Dickens and Sir Walter Scott. But in the hours when nursery became classroom she made me want to learn. She was a really good teacher. I went to my first boarding school a few weeks before my tenth birthday and I was already comfortably into Latin and algebra. The classroom relationship dwindled with each of us in turn but she still had us heavily on her hands during the holidays and in every way she was a great help to my mother and in at least one way to my father. The hens.

At the beginning of the war my father started constructing encampments in three separate areas of the garden. Three houses, with covered scratching run adjacent, and what must have amounted in all to about two hundred yards of chicken wire fencing. Also there was a wired-off section in the barn and several of those movable runs affording protective custody for mother hens with chicks. Dyson Iredale, the plumber, helped my father with the original construction but my brothers and I became a permanent maintenance crew. We handled feeding, fence-mending and cleaning the houses, under the supervision of my father, of course. Miss Daft was a member of this crew and also the chief egg collector. She could tell you the laying record of each hen. Whenever a hen clucked to announce the laying of an egg, Miss Daft would rush out to the most likely henhouse hoping to be in time to identify the emerging egg layer.

For our summer holidays in 1915 my parents chose Barmouth, in what is now Gwynedd, where we stayed in a rented house near the beach a little further to the north. To get to the beach we had to cross the railway line at a miniature station called Llanaber Halt. I can no longer visualize the house but I have a clear view of the beach itself which was of rather large pebbles, in sharp contrast to the one at Filey which had been of a delightfully muddy sand, an ideal material for the construction of castles amid a system of communicating mudways. I confess that my memory of these contrasting beaches has been reinforced by snapshots. My father was handy with a camera, so is never to be seen in these holiday scenes. I am sorry that he did not capture Miss Daft in her bathing outfit which featured long black stockings, because this is another image that is no longer with me, though Colin with the advantage of two years' seniority still retains it. I don't believe that Miss Daft would have allowed my father to snap her when she was outfitted for her daily dip. She was shy and I wonder now to what extent she appreciated my father's teasing. He was not a man who would overdo it, but there were several ideal set-ups which clamoured for repetition. For instance there was the distribution of additional brandy when the pudding was served on Christmas Day. There may have been in the pudding itself and the sauce that accompanied it a minimal dose but not enough for even a child to be aware of; so my father would go round the table with the bottle of brandy and anoint each adult's helping with enough to give it some character. This was a cue for Miss Daft to protest that she never touched alcohol. My father would then insist that she hold her fork inverted over the pudding so that the tiny drop he poured would be evenly distributed. 'Say when', he added. For some reason the 'when' took a long time coming. My father would draw attention to this and never failed to raise a laugh. Further protestations and a giggle now from Miss Daft.

Then there was the ever successful 'A soldier got drunk' routine which kept repeating itself during our seaside holidays. My father was not responsible for this one. His non-appearance in family snapshots was not due only to his being the man behind the camera; half the time he was not even there. Whereas my mother and Miss Daft and my brothers and I enjoyed a spread of four weeks at the seaside, my father seldom allowed himself much more than a week.

My cousin Evelyn was married to a man called Francis Bull whom we liked very much because he had a fund of stories and songs and tricks and could play the harmonium in our lodgings. One of his tricks came in very handy when we were out for a long walk. Each person in turn had to recite the following with a steady beat: 'A soldier got drunk and he packed up his trunk and he left . . . left! And it served him jolly well right . . . right!'

The trick was to be stepping with your left foot when you said 'left', and with the right foot when you said 'right'.

None of us caught on to it at once and there was much merriment. Then one by one we would realise that if you started by synchronising the word 'soldier' with your left foot and the word 'served' with your right, the lefts and rights would automatically fall into place. All except Miss Daft, who, in spite of her superior intelligence, never got it. And so it became an annual joke. One of us would say 'Do a soldier got drunk, Miss Daft!' 'No, you know I can't.' 'Go on, Miss Daft, you'll get it this time.' The giggles, the protests, but finally like a good sport she would allow herself to become our butt once again.

After the one summer at Llanaber – or was it two? – we switched to a little town called Nevin (Nefyn) on the northern surface of the Lleyn peninsula, the part that reaches out towards Ireland balancing Anglesey on its wrist. Here was a beach neither of mud nor of pebbles but of good yellow sand. And there were cliffs and rock pools and a fascinating range of scenery against which the drama of the drunken soldier was played hilariously but not exclusively. Someone carried the thermos flask while others took turns with the little picnic hamper which held the salmon and shrimp paste sandwiches and the ginger biscuits. After tea the afternoon became a nature ramble, with Miss Daft once more playing the leading part. A lot of good walking was already the rule in Huddersfield and it had not taken her long to turn us into dedicated nature students. But North Wales was more lavish with its

15

wonders than the Fixby woods had been. Here there were marvellous things to look for even if we never actually found them. Take the death's head hawk moth for instance. Some hawk moths we captured, if not as moths then as caterpillars which we took home and, by supplying the diet they favoured, hoped successfully to see through their life cycle. We never passed a potato patch, but a few moments were snatched to search for the death's head caterpillars which were known to feed on them. But it was not just moths and caterpillars, it was flowers and birdsong and trees and hermit crabs and sea anemones that were identified and admired. One of Miss Daft's major triumphs was the pursuit and discovery of some grass of Parnassus at Edern. And she knew how rare it was already. Now its name is familiar to all who have studied with dismay the recurring lists of threatened species.

The sad thing is that Miss Daft made her exit from our lives without the least demonstration. She left when we were all away at boarding school. Colin and I were always inclined to drop a brief tear at a parting. But there were no tears for Miss Daft and, God knows, of all partings this was one that rated a tear or two. But during his teens the human male is at his most selfish. We were all in our different ways becoming involved in our school activities and during the holidays we were getting to know not the neighbourhood kids with whom we had waged war but the children of my parents' friends. A social life was beginning to stir.

So, during one of these holidays Miss Daft was no longer there. She was with another family remote from Huddersfield. But it did not occur to any of us to write her a letter. And it was not as if we had not learned how to write letters. But we had not learned what letters were for. To us they represented a child's duty to correspond with his parents when away from home. Two or three years later we were told that Miss Daft had died. So we never saw her again.

2/Windermere

In series we went to a preparatory school at Windermere called the Old College. It was a small private school, and the word 'preparatory' implies that for a period of some three years the pupils were 'prepared' for entry into a 'public school' which was, of course, an equally private institution.

Windermere is in the English Lake District, famous for its scenic beauty and heavy rainfall. At this time there was a high percentage of women among the teachers since the war was less than six months over and the heads of State were currently drafting a Peace Treaty at Versailles. Being used to Miss Daft and my mother and the maids at home and having reached my father only in strictly limited areas I found comfort in this female majority and was prepared to be scared of the few male teachers. In the event I was justified. The head master, Mr Raikes, was now in semi-retirement because his son and heir had recently returned from Burma where he had been serving with His Majesty's Armed Forces. By some he was called Captain Raikes, by others Mr Marcus. I was plain scared of the old man, Mr Raikes, and as for the Captain, I could not have told you at the time that it was dislike that I felt because I was lucky enough to have had no similar experience in the past. But if, as an actor, I were now asked to play the part of Captain Marcus Raikes he would turn out to be quite dislikeable. Apart from Mr Raikes and the Captain the only other male members of the staff at the time of my arrival were Mr Lythgoe, the music teacher, and Mr Mallinson who filled in occasionally, his regular employment being with the local Grammar School. Apart from his face,

17

which I can see quite clearly, the only thing that I remember about him was his nice wife who further inflamed our passion for nature study.

Before I checked into the school my brothers had spoken with some awe of a person called Al who was the school matron. And so it was with an equivalent awe that I anticipated my first meeting with this character. Although I had been told that her name was Al it came as a surprise when I heard the boys address her by that name. The first few times that I tried, it came out as 'Sir'. She seemed to expect instant and articulate reactions, which with me did not come easily. I put her down as a bully and watched my Ps and Qs.

She was a buxom local woman with a ruddy complexion, said to be a butcher's daughter and a particular pet of old Raikes. Certainly much more of a pet, it would appear, than Mrs Raikes who was seldom visible and who lived in a cottage near Keswick in what I later identified as Beatrix Potter country. Boys were invited to spend the weekend with her in this cottage, two or three at a time. I was so privileged myself on one occasion and can testify that it was a dreamland. There was a lovely babbling brook with sticklebacks in it. And there was the sheep dip, the first and last I ever saw. Yes, she was a fine old girl, a retired valkyrie.

But Al Carruthers was the reigning power, and she turned out to be not too bad. An effort was being made to improve her image and in my second year at the school we were given to understand that we all must call her Miss Carruthers. She could still put up a terrific barrage when she wanted to. I remember an explosion one day when we were in the dining hall eating kippers. It seemed to her that we needed a lesson. We were leaving too much that was edible on the sides of our plates. She picked on my plate as a staging area for one of her demonstrations. 'Look at all this good stuff that you're leaving. It's good, it's crunchy, that's the best part. And look at all that good skin!' And so on. I recognised that she had a case because

18

there were indeed a number of slobs around who handled their food with a minimum of efficiency. But it seemed unfair to haul me into her act since at home to show a clean or 'Yorkshire' plate after eating was a mark of distinction and I was well on my way to earning it. Later I was to earn the additional credit of being 'a good trencherman'.

'It's a pity to let all this good food go out,' my father would say plaintively when offering second helpings. He knew that he could rely on my cooperation. But I could never quite match up to the standards set by Al Carruthers when it came to eating kippers, which, incidentally, are still among my favourite foods. I liked the food they gave us at that school although, yes, it could be said that the porridge was sometimes lumpy. But there was no substitute for the scrambling of powdered egg. This may come as a surprise to those who learned to despise the powdered eggs of World War II vintage. But it is true my taste buds reacted positively to those offered immediately after the First World War, just as they relished the tinned salmon kedgeree which was another Old College speciality. And by way of elevenses during the mid morning break there were slabs of bread and margarine thinly spread with 'Marmite', one per boy. But they would run to a second slab of bread and margarine without the 'Marmite'. So, if one's taste leaned in that direction, one could obtain the second slab before eating the first, then by pressing together the upper surfaces of both one would end up with two slabs with 'Marmite' of lesser proof.

Of the female teachers, or mistresses, the most popular was Miss Strout, a sturdy, good natured party and pretty. She was the kind one could talk to and she did not condescend. She was unruffled when once or twice I was demonstrably guilty of absentmindedness in class. She was teaching arithmetic and during a period when we were all supposed to be intent on a written exercise I suddenly became aware that she and all the boys in the class were looking at me.

19

'What did you say, Mason?' she said.

'I said something?'

'Did you say Tostig?'

'Oh ... Did I?'

'Yes, Tostig, it sounded like.'

'Well I was thinking of Tostig. But I didn't know that I actually said it.'

'Well, try thinking about your sums!'

'Yes, Miss Strout.'

Scattered laughter from the other boys. And we all resumed our studies.

(As every schoolboy knows Tostig was killed at the battle of Stamford Bridge in ten sixty six.)

During my second year at the Old College two or three masters were added to the staff. These included a Mr McGlaslyn who committed an unforgivable faux pas. As a teacher and a mountain climber – for that was his pastime – he was beyond reproach; his offence was that he married Miss Strout! And he must surely have known that we all adored her.

Miss Strout's close friend during pre-McGlaslyn times was a teacher called Miss Davies who was tall, capable and generally respected although she lacked the charisma of Miss Strout. In her I am introducing my first critic. She was perfectly all right as a teacher and she lacked the opportunity to criticise my work as an entertainer; it was as the judge of a photographic competition that she struck me down.

The evidence came to light five years ago when my father died and brother Rex inherited the gruelling task of sorting all letters, documents, photographs, account books, cheque stubs, newspaper clippings and clothes and old boots, toys and flotsam which he had accumulated in the past seventy years. Rex and his wife Halo subdivided this booty and some quite surprising items fell into my hands. There were my letters home, a few books from my schooldays, programmes of forgotten concerts, my entire collection of toy soldiers and – this was a big surprise – the actual photographs which I had submitted in that long ago contest adjudicated by Miss Davies.

I had acquired a Number Two Folding Brownie for my eleventh birthday, and became a keen photographer so far as a strictly limited budget would permit, making good use of the small dark room that was available at school. I started with the daylight prints which ended up in those attractive shades of sepia which nowadays we so dearly cherish, and then proceeded to printing by artificial light which was only slightly less simple. My work was not of the daintiest but at least I had mastered the basic techniques and thought myself ready for competition work.

We had to submit four prints, mounted; just contact prints since we had neither the equipment nor the skill to make enlargements. At that time colour photography had not reached the general public although in many a backroom the boys were grappling with it. In photographic stores one could buy the materials with which to 'tint' one's black and white prints. This appealed to me instantly, and so, although colour was by no means specified in the rules of the contest, submissions turned out to be palely hand-tinted. Here are the descriptions of my six subjects and Miss Davies's comments:

Description	Marks	Comment
1 A DISTANT GULLERY A flock of seagulls perched on a rocky headland. *Simple rectangular 'mask' giving the print a neat white border.*	20/25	COULD BE CLEANER.
2 NEVIN BAY A conventional view of this attractive bay with the Rival mountains in the distance.	22/25	AN EXCELLENT EFFORT. YOU COULD HAVE CLEANED UP THE PRINT WITH A MOIST RAG – VERY GENTLY – AFTER MAKING

Rectangular 'mask'.		SUCH A MESS WITH THE MOUNTANT. ALL MARKS LOST WERE BECAUSE IT WAS DIRTY.
3 ST. BEUNOS CHURCH, CLYNOG An interior of this Welsh church featuring the wooden screen. *For this a 'mask' with rounded corners was used.*	16/25	AVOID MASKS WITH ROUNDED CORNERS. VERY FEW PEOPLE CONSIDER THEM TASTEFUL.
4 THE SWALLOW FALLS A view of the famous falls of BETTWS Y COED. *For this it had seemed appropriate to use an oval 'mask'.*	11/25	OVAL AND FANCY SHAPED MASKS ARE AN ABOMINATION

I am surprised that she did not scoff at my tinting.

This was my first encounter with a critic. I know that she was not really a critic, she was a prep. school teacher who had probably volunteered for the chore of adjudicating the work of a handful of juvenile shutterbugs. But she fell into the traps which beset the professional critic. Taste is a tar-baby with which a wise critic does not grapple. On other grounds, Miss Davies had a valid cause for complaint. The artist was messy; he showed lamentable lack of mucilage control.

Prizegiving, which the parents were invited to attend, took place midway through the summer term. It included Sports events and the Concert. As a participant in the midsummer sports I was nowhere.

There was always a place for me, however, in the Concert. The semi-retired Mr Raikes prepared the show and staged it. It consisted of music, instrumental and vocal, speeches, written by Mr Raikes, and a short French play the author of which, according to the programme, was Miss Rathkins, a nice woman who taught French. But in effect it remained strictly Mr Raikes's show.

On a Sunday at the beginning of the summer term of 1919, in the Library after Evening Prayers, Mr Raikes turned the meeting into what theatre people refer to as a casting session. He picked on one or two of the smallest boys and briefed them as follows: 'I want you to imagine that some of those boys at the other end of the room are fooling. You have to shout at them and tell them to be quiet.'

Three or four boys made pitiful attempts to comply. They were dismissed. Then he came to me. There was no need for him to repeat his instructions, I went straight into my act. 'You fellows down there, stop fooling!' I screamed. 'If you fellows don't keep quiet, you'll all be kept in!'

Mr Raikes laughed in a manner which suggested that I had passed some sort of test. And it transpired that my 'effort' – one of several diminutive speeches to be delivered by diminutive new boys – was to take the form of a funny story about a passenger on an ocean liner who stuttered badly especially in times of stress. As he happened to be the sole witness of a dreadful accident, he rushed up to the bridge and tried to report the accident to the captain.

Waving frantically towards the ocean, he worked his stutter into total unintelligibility.

'If you can't say it, sing it!' said the captain.

So to the tune of 'Auld Lang Syne' the passenger sang:
'Should auld acquaintance be forgot and never brought
    to mind,
The blooming cook fell overboard
And is twenty miles behind!'
Gratifying applause.

The summer term over, Rex left for Marlborough College, his chosen public school. I had been hitherto referred to as Mason tertius. There being now only two of us, Colin became Mason major and I Mason minor. And for the following year's concert I had a part in the French play. This was one of a series, all set after World War I in the Island of Guernsey in the English Channel. The

23

Islanders all spoke French with the exception of the central character Johnny, an English Tommy. My role in 1921 was that of a local woman called Odette, some of whose chickens had been stolen by bad neighbours. Since no one in her village would help her to straighten out her problems, she had recourse to an ancient ritual peculiar to the Island of Guernsey. It somewhat resembled the old Roman formula 'Civis Romanus sum', meaning 'I am a Roman citizen and as such I claim the right to be tried in Rome.' Paul of Tarsus did this, remember? In Guernsey anyone in a serious fix could still claim the right to have his or her case heard by the highest tribunal in the land.

So, in the role of Odette, I cried 'Haro, Haro, a mon aide, mon Prince', this being the traditional formula.

Fortunately for the parents the playwright did not pursue the case right through to a hearing in the presence of the twentieth century equivalent of Haro, for at this point the redoubtable Johnny with the infallibility of a William S. Hart took charge and reached a settlement that made everyone happy.

But that was not the end of the matter for me. These plays went on just like a modern television series, except that each year there had to be a change of cast. And so it came about that in 1922 the full glory was to fall upon me. I inherited the role of Johnny and the obligation, in lieu of Haro, to aid yet another victimised Guernseyite.

After my performance I felt fairly smug. I would have achieved a total smugness only if I had heard or read somewhere that I had 'brought the house down'. When Mr Raikes had, in fact, occasion to refer to my performance, what emerged was a somewhat backhanded compliment. I had been experimenting with my new pen-knife on the top of the table behind which he usually sat. Sure enough his attention was ultimately drawn to this new disfigurement.

'Who did this?'
Silence.
(*Finally*) 'I did, Sir.'

'Who's that?'

'Mason, Sir.'

'Come here, Mason. Take a look at your handywork ... It's all very well being the funny man in the school play but it's time you had a little more sense, Mason.'

He blew me up unmercifully.

On the printed programme of The Old College Concert I had the satisfaction of seeing my name twice. Besides in the play, at the top of the programme one read:

	Orchestra
Violins:	Mr Raikes, Miss Nowell, G. M. Wild, J. A. E. Hemingway, C. D. Smith, C. Crossthwaite, P. G. Cumming.
Violoncellos:	Mrs Longmire, A. I. Haythornthwaite.
Piccolo:	J. N. Mason.

Others learned piano, cello and violin. For me it had to be the piccolo. A heavy-set man with a chestnut coloured cavalry moustache came at regular intervals to teach me, without marked success. I wanted very much to play the piccolo and later the flute: I already had an instantaneous interest in anyone who played the instrument. Such a one was Mr Kirkbride who taught us carpentry.

We three brothers all took carpentry as an extra. It reassured my father that we would at least be able to lend him a useful hand around the house. But it was especially good fun for us because Mr Kirkbride's workshop lay almost a mile away from the school and there was no supervision other than by Mr Kirkbride himself. We felt easy in his place. Rex was particularly good at carpentry and when the term was over always brought home some splendid trophy. I was more interested in Mr Kirkbride's flute which with a little coaxing he would bring out and give us a tune. He would not let me play on his good flute, I was only allowed to handle one of the rather broken down specimens which needed to have the pads on their keys restored or suffered from some other respiratory ailment.

My father must have given me too much pocket money or else I was unnaturally careful in the handling of it. At any rate I found myself with ten shillings still unspent and with this offered to buy one of Mr Kirkbride's unwanted instruments. The offer was accepted with what I should now recognise as indecent haste. Mr Kirkbride knew a good sale when he saw one.

I spent two weeks of the ensuing holidays trying to coax a decent tone from my acquisition. But the huskiness was there to stay. I spent the following two weeks making the rounds of the pawnshops trying to get rid of the thing. Having no case for the instrument I got Miss Daft to let me have one of her long black stockings now beyond repair. The flute broke down into three sections and the black stocking seemed to me to make a handy container. But the family laughed at me and my round of the pawnbrokers became a saga which retained currency among them for years to come. I never thought it very funny.

At Marlborough I played in the military band and the school orchestra but by then I was aware that I would never shine as a flautist. I sometimes find myself wishing that I had had as a teenager the determination and application that came to me later. Oh, well, I could never have become a threat to James Galway. I never touched a flute with any seriousness of purpose from the time I left Marlborough. But that does not prevent me from regarding it as 'my instrument'. My footsteps falter when I pass a musical instrument shop knowing that there is a wood wind instrument in there that I long to put my fingers on. In fact all over the house there are drawers where tin whistles, ocarinas, recorders and potentially raucous Eastern reed instruments silently secrete themselves, evidence of the occasions when I have succumbed to the lure of those magical shops.

Reverting to the Old College, the midsummer prize-giving day and the concert were all very well but not to be compared with the joy of getting to know the world outside which my parents' visit made possible. They stayed for the few nights at a charming hotel at Bowness called The Old England. It had a lovely garden which sloped down to the lake close to the jetty where the steamers put in. I don't remember seeing a motorboat on Lake Windermere at that time although I am sure that they were not discouraged since they had not yet learned to make a nuisance of themselves. My mother, leaning from a second floor window, could still speak to me in the garden below without raising her voice. Aural pollution was in its infancy. There were expeditions by road and on the steamers to one end of the lake or the other, but best of all were idle afternoons in canoes and rowing boats. We fished for perch too, but I read that pollution has now taken care of all those that we failed to catch. I also read that The Old England fell into the hands of Charles Forte.

There comes a moment when a boy, having reached a certain age and having passed the entrance exam, is supposed to be prepared for his public school. Some never are, but they don't find that out until later. I on the other hand was ideal public school fodder in the sense that boarding school life had so far given me no cause to moan. I did not feel in any way frustrated. I did not mind sitting in a classroom being taught whatever they had to offer. I got on with boys and teachers alike. There were no end of things one could enjoy without making inordinate demands. And it was not even necessary to explain to oneself or anyone else just what was supplying the joy. Could one explain the sound of a summer evening when the sun did not sink until nine o'clock and one wandered around the fringes of the playing fields carefully sidestepping the cow pats? Could one separate in one's mind the things that were worth writing home about and those that were not? On one such evening I and a couple of friends were playing a simple game of throwing a ball from one to another. I ran to retrieve a bad throw and, as I stooped to pick up the ball, a cow tossed its head in my direction and ripped my short trousers, bruising me slightly. When I returned home at the end of the term, my mother found these torn pants in my trunk when she was unpacking.

'How did you split your shorts?' she said.

'Oh that was when the cow tupped me.'

My mother had good reason to feel affronted, not because my trousers had been torn but because of my failure as a correspondent. Though I dutifully wrote my letters home, they would always, after an elementary summary of my scholastic or athletic achievements and a weather report, finish up with 'There's no other news so I'll close now' or words to that effect. My failure to report such a sensational news item as being tupped by a cow became, to the increasing dismay of the protagonist, family legend for years.

3/Marlborough

Virtute Studio Ludo

At Marlborough one was obliged to study and play with virtue. Team games were obligatory, rugby football in winter, hockey in the spring term and cricket in summer. When the weather was so foul that it was impossible to stage these games we were sent on long runs or 'sweats', as they were called. And somehow time was found for many other optional athletic activities, such as boxing, gymnastics, fives and fencing. Overall discipline in the school was strict, the climate could be savage and the heating was sub-standard. But, during my time at least, there was not much bullying and the tough or 'hearty' element did not always have things its own way. The scholastic level was high, always among the first three or four of the Public Schools.

It had been founded in Mid-Victorian times and its terms were especially advantageous to the sons of parsons. Thus Anthony Blunt, for instance, was a 'Foundation Scholar', being one of the sons of the vicar of St. John's, Paddington.

There were 'In-College Houses' and 'Out-College Houses'. There were three or four of the latter which I gather somewhat resembled the country houses of the well-to-do, and it was there that the better-heeled parents placed their sons. I never saw the inside of one of them but always assumed that they had all the comforts of a goodish hotel. On the other hand the In-College Houses could fairly be described as stark. As a further preparation for the serious grind of public school life, there were junior Houses where the pressures were less rigorous. In my time there was a total of about seven hundred and fifty boys in the school.

After I had served a short stretch in a 'Junior House' called Barton Hill I was to proceed to an 'In-College House' called 'B-1'. While still at Barton Hill, I suffered my first and only caning. I felt that I had been a victim of a miscarriage of justice and this hurt me because I was instinctively a cautious Isaacs. The caning, hereinafter referred to as 'beating', was administered by the Junior House equivalent of a prefect or monitor. (It is funny how when writing and thinking about the distant past strange expressions come to mind along with a lot of other junk. I just caught myself writing 'cautious Isaacs'. Where did that come from? Some Jewish father who was proud of his son for possessing this sterling quality?)

One often reads nowadays of the extravagance of the 'fazing' rituals in American private schools sometimes allegedly leading to a neophyte's death. A sort of fazing was practised in English public schools but not to the point of extreme personal danger, certainly not in either of the Houses to which I was attached. All right, I was lucky.

I was particularly lucky at Barton Hill because the fazing there was a breeze. A concrete staircase which went up to the third floor provided the most perfect banisters for sliding down. Just the right angle to permit a spine chilling acceleration but not steep enough to make it really death-defying. The average performer could brake slightly at the turn by momentarily grabbing one of the iron uprights just behind him, but the expert managed to manipulate the turns with his arms folded throughout. It was a treat to watch the champion come down. The modern equivalent in public life would be Stenmark doing the special slalom.

No more of Barton Hill, and practically no more of the entire public school scene, because I feel that everyone has read so many accounts of it from former inmates. In the case of Marlborough I can refer the reader to *Prelude* by Beverley Nichols or *Summoned by Bells* by Sir John Betjeman.

The architectural nucleus of Marlborough College is a very handsome Queen Anne building which at one time was a well patronised inn on the Old Bath Road. As such it was the setting of a novel by Stanley Weyman called *The Castle Inn*. As one of the school buildings this is now called 'C' House.

In front of 'C' House is a large courtyard surrounded for the greater part by Victorian buildings of a similar red brick. Near the main gate is a beautiful chapel by Bodley containing decorative panels by Burne-Jones. In my day one of the brick buildings was the vast Dining Hall, rich in wooden beams and atmosphere. Four years ago I found myself driving through Marlborough with my wife Clarissa. It was during the summer holidays and we were free to roam at will. A major surprise awaited me down where the Hall used to be. It had gone. In its place was a modern building, an assembly plant you might think for chrome and plastic furniture which would not be out of place in Boreham Wood or Slough. I noticed too that the doors on the front of the Memorial Hall were now of a bilious yellow. This was also a disappointment because I had happened to be at the school when the building was completed and proudly inaugurated. The architect Newton had had the doors painted a forceful green which somehow invigorated the whole of that classic facade. One could rationalise this happy effect by reminding oneself that on an ancient Greek building with a similar frontage the bronze doors would be green with age.

To compensate, there was one visible improvement, and one that must have affected many an old Marlburian in the same way that bulldozing the old Hall had affected me. The trees had gone! I mean those referred to in one of the school songs as 'The Lime Trees' Double Row'.

This double row of lime trees used to stretch from the front door of the 'C' House to the main gates, effectively bisecting the court and blurring the vista from the point of view of one entering the gates. So now one has a clear view of this fine building. All that remains to be done is to plant a tall coniferous hedge in front of the new dining hall.

Another interesting building has been removed since my day, something called Upper School. In spite of its great size it was tucked away behind the front buildings so that you could not see it from the courtyard. Thus the casual old Marlburian stroller is less likely to froth at the mouth when he learns of its destruction. It was like something from Dickens. Very weird. It was again a huge raftered hall and constituted the daytime quarters of all the boys who belonged to the In-College Houses up to a certain level of seniority. It was furnished with rows of benches and desks at which we worked during 'prep', that is to say the evening period given over to those studies which had to be done before the following day's classes. To my recollection the heating came from two large fireplaces on one side of the room. If I am wrong and there was a vestigial heating pipe along the other side, its effects were not felt. What I remember most clearly about this great barn was the extraordinary ritual which preceded 'prep' every evening.

Upper School must have provided living space for about a hundred and fifty boys. Security was in the hands of four captains who spent the preparation period sitting around one of the two fireplaces in large wicker chairs. This small group of superior beings would, on a point of honour, enter the room on the dot of the particular hour at which prep was to begin. Any boy who was out of his seat at the moment of their entry would be caned, for the captains had a licence to inflict corporal punishment. In the case of any untidiness in the room, however, the fags or junior boys would be ordered to clear it up without incurring any punishment except of course the loss of time which should have been devoted to their work.

This was how the game worked. The four captains chose eight others of equal seniority to share with them the privilege of sitting round the fire. This group was called 'Big Fire', the pattern of whose behaviour was similarly dictated by honourable conventions. They created each evening a state of maximum untidiness prior to the

32

entrance of the captains. They made huge structures of piled up benches and tables and anything that could be moved. Someone would 'keep cave' (pron. cavey) while all this was going on and when the captains were seen approaching the perpetrators would hurry to their seats. Very often one or more of them would be caught away from his seat and at the end of prep due punishment would be discharged. The untidiness was often so massive that, after clearing up, the fags would have little or no time left for study.

My brother Colin contributed energetically to this form of entertainment. I admired his dare-devilry. Many beatings which he earned in the cause of sport or tradition or something he cheerfully sustained.

The Public School system is for ever being criticised for various aberrations, but for beaters and beaten alike the corporal punishment was never thought of as a major aggravation. Incidentally beatings were seldom inflicted by the housemasters, almost never by the headmaster. We had a housemaster, George Turner, who was admired by all. Reputed, perhaps loosely, to have been the youngest British officer in World War I to have held the rank of major, he may well have been one of the smallest. He was referred to as Little George but no one made fun of him. He had dignity without pomp and at suitable moments one could reach his sense of humour.

In spite of all his good qualities he once caused me a big disappointment. I had been number one on the list of those who had passed the entrance exam for my year. I was therefore placed in a form mysteriously called 'Removes' halfway to the top of the school. In my second year I was in 'The Hundreds' which was the last step on the ladder before one passed over into the various 'Fifth' forms which in turn led to the 'Sixths'. At this stepping off point one had to decide in what subjects one wished to specialise; one could proceed into the Classical Fifth or the Maths Fifth or the Modern Language Fifth etc. I wanted to specialise in modern languages. I also fancied history. Up to this point at Marlborough my classes had not included French or German and I already entertained romantic ideas about mastering French, especially because my father had made himself practically bi-lingual and because when he spoke of his travels in France and Belgium he made it sound as if they had provided the happiest times of his life.

But no. It was not to be. At one time my father seriously discussed my future with George Turner. It became clear to George (we usually dropped the 'Little' when referring to him) that my father was willing to see me through the University in the hope that at the end of it I would be fitted for a profession which would offer a healthy pension at the end of it. George assured my father that I was a good scholar and that I could undoubtedly find a place in the higher echelons of the Civil Service; not the Home Civil perhaps but certainly the Indian Civil. It followed therefore that I must continue my study of the classics.

My father accepted George's assessment. As for my learning French what good would that do? The last thing he wanted was to have to find a place in textiles for yet a third son. Rex by this time was already off in Lausanne learning French so as to follow in our father's footsteps if not in his firm, and a year later Colin was to follow the same route.

This happened to be a very bad period. Nineteen twenty-six, the year of the General Strike, was on its way. My father was alarmed by the state of his trade. Customers on the continent of Europe were falling behind with their payments and my father was trying to open up new markets in South America. He did not travel there himself but later on he thought of Colin as a possible emissary and, after Lausanne, sent him for six months to Madrid to learn Spanish. My father had enough to worry about without my creating problems. And so, temporarily at least, I was to be labelled Indian Civil Servant and to go on studying Latin and Greek.

But it was a let down. I had a sneaking suspicion that

George had overrated my scholarship. A year later the form master of the Classical Fifth, whose name was C. A. Emery, also known as 'The Drain', glanced at my Latin composition and remarked 'Nice fellow, but no scholar!' One remembers these little tributes. He added, 'But to be a good cricketer and play the flute is something!' He himself played the flute and, like myself, was prejudiced in favour of fellow flautists. As for cricket I happened to have noticed on the previous day that he was strolling past the cricket grounds at the precise moment when I made a nice 'cut' to the boundary. Even I had been impressed by it. Fortunately he had not lingered long enough to see my middle stump go shortly afterwards.

Another master whom I must mention was called A. C. B. Brown (a.k.a. Sweaty B.). The 'Sweaty' came from the fact that he suffered from a high blood pressure, to alleviate which he went for a daily four mile walk up on the downs to the north of the school. Every afternoon he was to be seen striding back past the playing fields, looking neither to right nor to left, his red face aglow. Boys who went to his rooms for any sort of private tuition reported that he had excellent taste in cream cakes. But he has found his way into this writing only on account of two of his better known observations. Asked to name the two things he most liked, he said, 'Trains and pretty women'. And the two things he most disliked? 'God and cricket'. Like many persons inclining to fat, he had a rather high pitched voice, the perfect instrument for the brisk aphorism. He made a study of Bradshaw's Railway Guide and had a masterly knowledge of all the latest schedules of the then diverse rail services of the British Isles. When there was a school holiday he would carefully select an itinerary and treat himself to a long day in a train.

While George Turner was still our housemaster, he organised periodical house concerts. These were mostly singsong and we threw ourselves into *Turmut-hoeing*, *The Golden Vanity*, *D'ye ken John Peel*, *The Lincolnshire Poacher*, *Green grow the Rushes*, easy folksy stuff.

35

But the most popular performer was George himself. He gave credibility to some extremely unlikely folk songs such as the one about Moppety Moppety Mona, and *The Berkshire Tragedy*, which we took with the utmost gravity. But his most moving performances were of *Lord Randall* and a Hungarian song called *Mohacs Field*.

This last one dates from a time when the Hungarians had been savaged by intruders. The singer moans about the fine stallion which he used to own (the song is sometimes called 'Had a Horse'), but 'the sheriff took him in the name of Law'. Similarly his house had been burned down and his wife had been abducted. After each item comes the reminder 'But no matter, more was lost at Mohacs Field'. George gave this with a simple and powerful delivery which was very effective.

The song came back to my mind at the time of the Russian invasion of Hungary in 1956. I sent for a copy of the music and thrust it into the hands of Harry Belafonte with whom I had just been working on a movie, suggesting that he sing it should there be a charity concert in aid of Hungarian refugees. And I am sure I could have persuaded him if we had remained together in the same continent. But he went one way and I went another. He would have sung it very well.

But George did not remain with us as Housemaster of B.1. The Headmaster, Dr Cyril Norwood (a.k.a. 'The Yellow Peril'), moved on to another post and George was elected to take his place. E. H. Dowdell became our Housemaster. From then on we had less personal contact with George, though he delivered sermons in the chapel at the beginning and end of each term and read one of the lessons in the services on Sundays. The other lesson was read by the Heads of the houses and I got to do this when Mr Dowdell promoted me to that position in B.1. I was influenced by George's style almost to the point of mimicry. The performer in me definitely took over at the lectern.

I never had a chance to disport myself in a play at Marlborough since the only ones staged were put on by the

French Society, membership of which was limited to boys studying modern languages. John Hunt, later the famous mountaineer, and his younger brother Hugh, who took to the theatre, scored in plays by Molière.

At this point the performer in me had not the least thought of going on the stage when he left school. But there were plenty of indications that I liked theatre. My maternal grandfather, a cosy old party with a stubby white beard, tended to visit our house on Sunday afternoons. We boys were smart enough to realise that the thing to do was to be hovering around at the moment of his leave-taking for then he was likely to slip his hand into his pocket and bring out a small paper bag of toffees which we would receive with a chorus of thank you grandpas. We would then share the spoils. When I went away to school, he took out a subscription on my behalf for something called *The Children's Newspaper*, which was delivered to me regularly for the three following years and which I read with pleasure and pride.

But once I got to Marlborough and the thing pursued me, I started to feel a fool unwrapping *The Children's Newspaper* in front of my oh so grown up fellow students when it was delivered.

So I wrote to my grandfather suggesting he should spare himself the expense now that I was sort of beyond all that. When he very kindly asked if I would like some other periodical instead, I immediately replied, yes, *The Play Pictorial*. This was a shiny monthly which gave summaries and photographic illustrations of all the latest West End shows. Thus in 1925 I picked up the reflected glitter of *White Cargo, Rose Marie, No, No, Nanette, The Farmer's Wife, The Last of Mrs Cheyney* and *The Rat*.

My only visit to London prior to the arrival of *The Play Pictorial* had been for a three hour scramble around the British Empire Exhibition at Wembley. The wonders which it offered had somehow disappointed me. But now *The Play Pictorial* argued that London might one day deserve a second visit.

37

4/Cambridge

I went up to Cambridge in the autumn of 1928. My college was Peterhouse, one of the smallest in the University but also the oldest, having been founded in the year 1284.

I read the Classics because I was going to become an Indian Civil Servant. My tutor was Paul Vellacott; my director of studies Bertie Hallward. I had to attend only a limited number of lectures, one of them incidentally given by J. T. Sheppard of whom we shall hear more later. There were not enough rooms within the College to provide accommodation for all the students, and so during my first two years (out of three) I had lodgings in the town not far away. The landladies were programmed to make sure that we checked in each night by ten o'clock except in the event of a special dispensation.

The sense of freedom was exhilarating. I realised that Cambridge was to offer me, thank God, time and space in which to read and think about my circumstances and to figure out just who I was to be. There was of course the assigned work that had to be done. I found, too, that I had an urge to become a rowing man. A book that I had read persuaded me that rowing could have a mystical and aesthetic appeal. So I was to spend two years responding to this appeal until my third and last year came around and then I thought 'What am I doing here, wasting all this time? Aren't there better things I might be doing?' As it turned out, there were.

But it was a gratifying waste of time, especially at the time of Bumping Races. The River Cam is too narrow to allow boats to race alongside one another. So they line up one behind another separated by a distance of about a boat's length. There is a rubber ball on the prow of each boat and the object of the game is to bump the boat ahead. This having been achieved the two boats affected draw aside to the river bank and that's it for the day. Next day the victorious boat replaces the one that was bumped. The races continue for four days, at the end of which period your boat may have advanced four places. If you are a member of a crew that performs this feat, you are entitled to an emblazoned oar, which you can hang on your wall if you have the space. I belonged to two such Peterhouse crews. If I had thought that I had a chance to make the Trial Eights for the University Crew I might well have persisted through my third year and missed a lot of good reading.

Cambridge introduced me also to a type of theatre which I had never thought existed. In fact it did not exist or, at least, had not taken root anywhere else in England other than at the Festival Theatre in Newmarket Road. It was the plaything of Terence Gray, an Irishman who had chosen to learn his craft in Paris rather than in the British Theatre. As I have indicated, I was especially raw as a theatregoer, being not familiar even with the most conventional offerings of the London Theatre. The first thing I had ever seen was *Aladdin* starring Lupino Lane in the role of Pekoe. We were taken to see this pantomime as a family treat in a huge theatre in Manchester. Lupino Lane was a fantastic acrobat and in the course of one routine he was reported to perform one hundred and thirty somersaults or pratfalls.

Henry Baynton had visited the Huddersfield Theatre Royal with his Shakespearean repertoire. I was considered too young to attend, being only five at the time, but my imagination was fed by Miss Daft's replay of one of the tragedies. (Was that a dagger that she saw before her?)

Otherwise my experience was limited to the Theatre Royal with such plays during the school holidays as seemed to my parents to deserve our attention, mostly touring thrillers and musical comedies, and, of course, we never missed the Theatre Royal's very own Christmas Pantomime.

So it was a jolt for this provincial boy to visit the Festival Theatre for the first time. In the lobby there were usherettes got up like eighteenth century gentlemen with green satin suits and powdered wigs; a Festival punch was being served in the bar, which was decorated in a style evolved from the work of World War I camouflage artists. There was a novel feature in the printed programme itself. For the benefit of those who had neglected to study it before the lights in the auditorium were lowered the relevant page opened up in such a way that you could hold it up against the stage lighting and read the information without difficulty, the lettering being transparent on a black background. The stage had a slight thrust with three or four broad convex steps leading down to the level of the front seats. At the back of the stage was a curved cyclorama upon which Klieg lights would play with appropriate colour and wattage during the performance. The two or three productions which I saw during my first year at Cambridge exhibited a uniform grimness of purpose. German expressionism had clearly made its mark during Mr Gray's formative years as a stage director. The décor was simple and odd without necessarily being functional. In a production of Shakespeare's *Henry VIII*, for instance, we found the monarch sitting in a garden swing, and most of the characters uncomfortably got up as playing cards. The company and director were only in their proper element when they chose to present Ernst Toller's *Masses and Men (Massenmensch)*. I was impressed by this new theatricality, but not persuaded that any great discoveries had been made except perhaps the Klieg lit cyclorama.

I had not even been to many movies either, before I went up to Cambridge. The only film I remember having been taken to *en famille* was a newsreel which illustrated British tanks in action during the war. There had been photographs in the newspapers but this was the first filmed evidence that our tanks actually performed the wonders claimed for them. In order to catch this important footage we had to sit through a feature film which was much more fun. I never knew its name but it told the story of an unfortunate lady who became in some way overfriendly with a very wealthy business man who took advantage of her in a way which led to her feeling sorry for herself and lonely. It was one of those nice silent dramas which changed colour in accordance with the mood of the drama or the time of day.

The heroine found work in a factory which by pure chance belonged to the very wealthy business man. The factory was working overtime – we knew that because the exterior scenes were blue at this point – and the owner made a tour of inspection. When he spotted our heroine a surprising look of hatred spread over his face. Was there some reason for him to fear her? Surely not. In the event we saw him carelessly – or intentionally? – toss his cigar butt into a pile of shavings. The factory is on fire. The screen goes red. Pandemonium. Our girl cannot find the way out, she claws at the window, she coughs pitifully. She faints. But not for the first time. Afterwards we always referred to this film as *The Fainting Lady*. I described it recently to Kevin Brownlow, but he has not yet come through with an identification, though he thinks he has seen bits of it.

At Cambridge everything was different from what I had known before, even the films. The talk was different, the jokes, the food, the ideas, the teaching, all were new, all different. As I opened up to receive and to respond to it all my suspicions on one point became certain knowledge. I was not going to become that Indian Civil Servant. British rule in India was being made to seem as unattractive as the notion of myself shaping up as a pukka sahib. So towards the end of my second term I told Paul Vellacott of my decision to give up reading for the Classical Tripos. What did I propose to read then? I said that I intended to become an architect and had heard good things about the Architectural school. He pointed out that the first year's examinations would necessarily take place in June and

41

asked me if I thought that I could do the entire year's work in the one remaining term. I said there would be no problem. He put no obstacles in my way and I signed on as an architectural student.

My new director of studies would now be H. C. Hughes, a practising architect who was also a fellow of Peterhouse. Of course architecture was the career for me. Why had I not thought of it before? Perhaps I was lucky that it had taken me a long time to make up my mind, for had I reached my decision before coming to Cambridge, it would have been more sensible and probably more economical to have sent me to one of the more firmly established schools in Liverpool or London. The Cambridge school was fairly new and was not yet known to have hatched any notable talent. Yes, I was lucky.

So I worked hard enough to handle the first year's examination and then went to Henley Regatta as a 'spare man' for the Peterhouse eight which was entered for the Thames Challenge Cup. It would actually be true to say that I rowed for Peterhouse in the Henley Regatta if I wanted to big-note myself. There was another spare man beside myself and the two of us were entered in the race for the Pairs, not to be confused with Double Sculls. As the Peterhouse Pair therefore we practised every day until the day of the first round when we were quite easily beaten. So we relaxed and got drunk, my fellow spare man and I. His name was Harry Gulland and the only good thing that came out of this Henley episode was the firm friendship that we established. The drunk took place at the Marlow Summer Fair, just down river from Henley. At the moment at which intoxication peaked I found myself on one of those chairs which are flung out horizontally by a relentless centrifuge.

Gulland and I abstained from monumental drunkenness after this experiment. But we fell together into another sort of trap. For me at least it was the first of a series of similar traps to which I became susceptible, the sum of which was to alter the course of my life.

Gulland told me that a Greek Play was about to be

produced, the *Bacchae* of Euripides. It seemed that once in every three years the University Football Club for some reason financed the presentation of a Greek play. The leading parts were allotted to the current crop of Greek scholars, e.g. A. B. Cohen, who was to play Dionysus. Gulland suggested that it might be a lark to apply for a job in the chorus since we were both familiar with the language, and we were accepted. On the higher levels of the production many dazzling talents were involved, mostly Kingsmen. Perhaps it was not the University Football Club but the King's Football Club (if there was such a thing) who footed the bill; at any rate there was a Kingsish air about the thing. George (Dadie) Rylands produced and Donald Beves, another fellow of King's, played a stout Citizen. Dennis Arundell, a fellow of St. John's College, had gathered certain airs from Handel's operas and neatly matched them with the words of the chorus, thus supplying a musical score. Boris Ord was the conductor and among those responding to his nod was that nonpareil of oboeists Leon Goossens. Decor and costumes were by Humphrey Jennings, a man of many talents who later made a great name for himself as a maker of wartime documentary films. He died young and has become a cult figure.

The chorus in the *Bacchae* consists of gloomy Argive ladies. We did not get to do much singing or speaking since most of that was done by one or other of four soloists who had the best possible credentials. Mostly we grouped and regrouped in one part of the stage and then in another. Though what we did could hardly be described as dancing, we were at least objects of choreography. Humphrey Jennings's contribution, deriving from Magritte and early Dali, was of a severity not far removed from what one had been exposed to at the Festival Theatre. The Argive ladies had white faces relieved only by a vertical dab of crimson on the lips, harsh black wigs, squared off skirts and blouses. We were a stunning chorus line.

Somehow I got the impression that I was a success.

Whenever a gesture or movement was assigned to an individual rather than to the group, I seemed to be the one who got to do it. I was, you might say, the leader of the chorus. It was partly this special prominence, partly just the fact of showing off on the stage, certainly a far cry from being the funny man of long ago, that gratified my vanity. Somewhere in each unlikely chorus line pants an ego equally confident of success.

I did not join the ADC or any of the other acting societies because conscience kept reminding me that I was at Cambridge to study. Conscience however must also have been influenced by monetary considerations because during my third and last year I allowed myself to be inducted into two productions which called for a considerable expenditure of time without having to pay membership dues.

The first of these was Purcell's *Fairy Queen*, an expensive production and I still don't know who paid for it. In 1692 Henry Purcell supplied the incidental music to this anonymously rewritten version of Shakespeare's *A Midsummer Night's Dream*. Most of the original play was still there but the vogue for masques had made it desirable to insert musical interruptions, thus leading to an 'English Opera' style.

Dennis Arundell, who had overall responsibility for the production, cast me as Oberon. Since he lacked a stage manager and since I, having worked in a chorus line the previous year, was now a man of experience in the theatre, he asked me to take on this job as well. I was not keen but, thinking that it might teach me something, I said yes. But I realised at once that I was not at that time a person to whose instructions others were likely to jump and that I was quite capable of forgetting something of vital importance such as giving orders for lights to be switched on or for the curtain to be raised. Also I knew that stage managerial responsibility would paralyse me as an actor. I therefore looked for someone to whom I might depute authority without fear of failure. Such a one was

Chapman who had been a student of unusual assiduity at Marlborough and so well prepared for following a prompt book and pressing a button on cue. Chapman came through with full marks. During rehearsal when people came up to me with problems, I would listen and say 'umm' then turn to Chapman and say, 'Did you hear that, Chapman?' and he would nod and there would be that little problem taken care of.

Wherever in the text of *A Midsummer Night's Dream* Purcell and the anonymous lyricist had come to a point which could reasonably be interpreted as a cue for song, a series of stately scenas had been introduced. As an extreme example, a very grandiose one was introduced at the end of the play when, after the clowns' command performance of *Pyramus and Thisbe* has been sent up by the courtiers, Oberon takes over as master of ceremonies and introduces a spectacular Oriental Act. The original production happened to coincide with an early explosion of chinoiserie.

A talented girl called Elizabeth Vellacott was our stage designer. Her oriental design for Oberon's spectacle resembled a willow pattern plate. On a given cue Oberon would raise his hand and behold, the lights would go up on a glorious plate-shaped vision with arched vermilion-coloured bridges, loaded with singers in Chinese costume.

To lead up to this effect Oberon, accompanied by Theseus, Hippolyta and Puck, moved to a position left of stage down by the footlights, making it possible for a curtain to drop immediately upstage of them so that the stagehands could get on with the big change of scene. Actually it was two curtains. The front curtain (call it A) framed a huge plate-shaped expanse of gauze which looked solid so long as the lighting was coming from the front of the house and so long as there was either no lighting on the stage itself or it was effectively masked. In our case the masking was effected by an opaque curtain B which was dropped immediately behind curtain A. As Oberon and his group's ensuing conversation could not be made to last longer than a minute and a half, this was the maximum time allowable for the big scene change behind us. In any professional theatre a stage manager, without benefit of special machinery, would insist on at least two or three dress rehearsals for such a change. There was no chance for this in our case since the scenery had emerged from the carpenter's shop only on the very day of the first of our two public performances.

Enter Hymen, God of Marriage and principal singing part in this scena. The role was taken by an auburn-haired young singer called Hamlin Benson. Our Miss Vellacott ordained that at the moment when Hymen was scheduled to burst into song he should appear slap-bang centre-stage really looking like a golden God. To achieve this effect a large drum was to be constructed and placed atop the large, practical vermilion-coloured bridge. There again gauze would be trickily employed, so that at the beginning of the scena the drum, illuminated from the front only, would be poised looking perhaps like an outsize sunflower. On the given cue a spotlight would come up *inside* the drum and there would be our brilliantly illuminated baritone. On paper it was a nice idea.

Work in the carpenter's shop fell behind schedule. Ideally this great drum of a sun should have been constructed by metal workers, one would think, but no, the carpenters had accepted the responsibility and it began to take on ghastly shape. It was enormous all right, and the front of the drum which should have appeared as a perfect circle presented more the outline of some crazy polygon. It was the last item of scenery to be completed; the rest of the décor was in order, and the fact that we had no time for an overall dress rehearsal caused no serious dismay, since the Oriental transformation was the only tricky operation.

By the time when the sun drum was carried towards the stage I had practically faded out as a stage manager. However, I could see at once that someone had made a gross miscalculation which an alert stage manager might have anticipated. The New Theatre at Cambridge was without benefit of the usual large scenery door; the only way in was too small for our drum. Only the fraction of an inch too small, but enough to cause an *impasse*. We looked helplessly at one another. Since it was too late to start work on a new drum we calculated nothing more could be lost if we made a gigantic effort to push it through the door against its will. As the stage hands applied their weight the stage manager in me checked out and Oberon took over completely. As I turned away I heard the drum groan.

It was time for the curtain to go up. I nodded to Chapman, who pressed the button which lit the cue light, which caused the man to pull the rope which raised the curtain and we were on our way. Miss Vellacott's scenery and costumes stood up well to public scrutiny. The actors played their parts adequately, the singers sang, the fiddlers fiddled and Chapman did all the right things. No happy, relaxed actor I, however, for I was all too well aware that the moment would soon come when almost anything might happen.

The clowns had done their fooling and I, Oberon, engaged Theseus in conversation, drawing the small group down towards the footlights. A slight thud behind me reassured me that curtains A and B had been lowered: simultaneously all hell broke loose as the stage hands back there attacked the scenery.

It is disconcerting for the inexperienced actor to be playing a scene in front of a drop; it seems incredible that the audience cannot hear that terrifying din, the pushing, the shoving, the bumping, people shouting, it seems, at the tops of their voices. I did not hurry my words. Would the one and a half minutes be long enough? Our dialogue finally petered out, the transformation must now be complete and it is for me to speak the cue line which will reveal the mammoth Oriental spectacle.

The noise back there should have stopped but there were still some thuddings and scrapings, and now there were more voices, hushed and urgent. Well, what the hell, take a chance. Hoping, I suppose, that everything would magically be in order and that curtain B would gently rise on a blacked-out stage and that with my gesture the lights would come up on our breath-taking Willow Pattern tableau, I raised my hand and uttered the cue. I wanted to close my eyes but no, I had to look; after all I was the stage manager.

Curtain B had *not* been raised. As I looked, it started to go up, but not on a blacked-out stage. The work lights were fully on. The principal elements of the scenery were in place but the singers were not. They were scattered in disarray about the stage and, dotted among them, were several stage hands in their cloth caps. Their hands were raised in an attitude of defence and their eyes strained in a single direction. And there was a sight indeed. Hamlin Benson, Hymen, was in position on the crest of the big vermilion bridge. He, too, raised his hands defensively and with good reason, for immediately above him, suspended by a rope, was the carcass of the great drum. The plan had been to superimpose it onto him after he was in position, for there was no other way to get him inside it. They had been in this process of superimposition when a final buckling took place. The people on stage now realised, one by one, that they were no longer invisible. The cloth-capped stage hands ran off stage in a crouching attitude, as if that helped; the singers jockeyed for position and Hymen, the benign Marriage God, reluctantly faced front, pretending that he was unaware of the tortured carpentry that threatened him from above ...

Never again did I risk stage management. But I made one final appearance as an amateur actor at Cambridge. I have mentioned J. T. Sheppard whose lectures I had attended and who impressed his audience with his wit and his erudition. Now he was to produce Webster's *The White Devil* for the Marlowe Society and I was asked to play the part of Flamineo.

Sheppard's expertise made of this another extraordinary experience. He was able to reveal a wealth of historical and literary references in the text which I would have walked straight by unawares. We rehearsed in odd moments over a long period but even so I never got to be quite sure of all my lines in the last act, a circumstance which made me writhe in what must have been a most unnatural manner as I listened to the voice of the prompter. But it seemed that the audience didn't notice anything, and my acting was acclaimed.

The Marlowe Society devotes itself to the production of plays of the Elizabethan era and is, very sensibly, anonymous; that is to say the actors participating were named neither in the programmes nor in the attendant publicity. Thus anonymously I received the best reviews in my stage career up until April 1979 in New York. W. A. Darlington of the *Daily Telegraph* went into fits about me. Well, let's not exaggerate; at least he gave me a very flattering review, the like of which I never received from him when I became a professional.

In my second year at Cambridge a theatrical event of major professional importance had taken place. A new company had settled into the Festival Theatre. At the head of it was Anmer Hall. Among the actors were his wife Gillian Scaife, his son David Horne, an excellent young leading man called Robert Donat and, even more interesting, the young Flora Robson. But it was the new director who gave the season its unique quality: Tyrone Guthrie.

The first production was Pirandello's *Six Characters in Search of an Author*. It was the first time that I had encountered an exhibition of acting of which I never questioned the reality. It was something which had been prepared by actors and director in such a way that the bizarre events were happening as if for the first time in front of one's eyes. And it was this man Guthrie who knew how to bring about such miracles. I saw practically all of the year's productions and observed how he had captured the style and the mood of each author's work, whether it was the levity of Oliver Goldsmith, the audacity of

Pirandello, the nervous tension of Ibsen or the pawkiness of James Bridie. It was good to see Guthrie in person from time to time. There was a friendly outrageousness about him as unconventional as it was unpretentious. Guthrie made a curtain speech after *Six Characters* and appeared as an actor in *She Stoops to Conquer* and in *Tobias and the Angel*. He was perfectly cast as the Angel in this, being six foot four and loaded with Celtic whimsy.

So here was something happening that made the theatre appear fascinating as much to one sitting in the stalls as to the actor on stage. Only during my second year did this wonderful thing happen, for in my last year the theatre reverted and offered us what seemed to be an extension of the Terence Gray regime. But to make up for a falling off in that direction, I became enmeshed in something called the Film Society, the purpose of which was to exhibit films from the Continent of Europe. They were not necessarily avant-garde but they were all so unlike the regular American and British product that they were, by our standards, uncommercial. One could thus be entranced by such films as *Siegfried*, *The Battleship Potemkin*, *Turksib*, *The Student of Prague*, *The Cabinet of Dr Caligari* and *The Passion of Joan of Arc* without having to forgo one's abiding interest in Clara Bow.

In the final architectural examination three of us qualified for first class degrees, Peter Megaw from Peterhouse, John Grace and myself. Geoffrey Webb, one of our lecturers, informed a friend of mine that the only one of us that 'God blew through' was John Grace, who was indeed a real artist. I do not know what became of him. I had not been at all worried about the outcome of the written examinations dealing with building technique and art history, but when it comes to design, one can never be sure how the examiner will react because, once again, there's that old question of taste.

I had discovered however that the examiner was likely to be Edward Maufe who was very much in demand in England at that time, especially for anything ecclesiastical, e.g. Guildford Cathedral. Our assigned design was for a church hypothetically to be constructed in the county of Essex. Although we were all that time somewhat under the spell of Le Corbusier, who would no doubt have described a church as a machine for worshipping in, I thought it wise under the circumstances to eradicate such dangerous thoughts and put myself as best I could into the mind of Maufe.

I wish now that I might have had the opportunity to build that church in East Anglia. But at that moment in England churches were not proliferating. In the architectural periodicals there were illustrations of lots of quite ugly modern churches in Germany or Holland, but our English ugly modern was appropriately restricted to new Underground stations or Lex garages. Maufe had the pick of the churches and in the field of domestic architecture inertia was the order of the day.

And the day was located halfway through 1931, the year in which Japan was starting to invade Manchuria, the second British Labour Government fell and was replaced by a National Government under the leadership of Ramsay MacDonald, Gandhi was proposing an all-Indian government and the whole world was in a state of chassis in the words of Sean O'Casey's Paycock.

In the summer of 1930 I had spent a few weeks in Germany. At the end of one happy day we gathered on the waterfront of a little town on the Ammersee in Bavaria. There were going to be fireworks that night, but before the sun went down a small plane flew over and we all looked up and watched it. Some people were laughing. A word was spelled out on the underside of the wings. That must be what they were laughing at, I thought. The word was HITLER. I asked my friends what the word meant. They laughed and said that he was a political rabble rouser in Munich. It shows how little attention I had been paying to the newspapers, I had never heard of the man.

The year that I switched from Indian Civil Servant to Architect both Paul Vellacott and a spokesman for the

Royal Institute of British Architects had written to my father reassuring him that undoubtedly I would find employment in an architectural firm after my three years at Cambridge although for qualification as an Associate of the R.I.B.A. I would need to study for a further two years. But we were in a decade in which events were hurtling past us at a frantic speed. Why, in the following year 1932 this Hitler's party was to become the largest in the German Reichstag, a fact which did not seem to worry us much at the time. But the situation in the British building trades was changing with an equivalent speed. It was racing to a standstill.

I was now convinced that only divine intervention could get me a job. There were no strings for me to pull, divine or otherwise. For two months during the previous summer I had worked as an unpaid 'Improver' in the office of Professor Worthington in Manchester, but only because George Turner, an old friend of his, had put in a good word for me. Now I would be unlikely to land a job on the lowest rung of the professional ladder since I did not regard meticulous draughtsmanship as my forte. And even if I got such a job it would mean that I would have to study at night school for the final exam for my A.R.I.B.A. To press on without the job was unthinkable, because I had no intention of causing a further drain on my father's purse.

5/London 1

Peter Megaw and I, both strangers to London, took a room in Oakley Street which leads down from the King's Road to the Albert Bridge in Chelsea. The room cost us only ten shillings and sixpence a week. There was a bathroom we could use just down the corridor. Slot machines supplied hot water and gas for the radiator and cooking ring in the room. My capital amounted to about £25 of which £21 had been given to me by my father for my twenty-first birthday the previous year. My plan was to make this last until I earned some money of my own and proved my independence.

Megaw was not much more secure. But proof of independence was not of such vital importance to him, and he fully intended to press on with his architectural career or in some way make use of the knowledge he had acquired. In the event he was to become an archaeologist. He also had the advantage of a working brother's presence in London. This was a source of comfort to him and, as things turned out, of some service to me.

I knew almost no one. Indeed I had to screw up all my courage to write a little note to Sir Edward and Lady Hilton Young to remind them that I had stayed at their house in Norfolk on the invitation of Peter Scott who was a Cambridge friend of mine and the son of Lady Hilton Young. Although Peter was not in London at the time, they graciously, if rather rashly, invited me to lunch at their house in Bayswater Road. I found myself rather heavy going during that luncheon, the more so as the meal proceeded, since Sir Edward, while abstaining himself, opened a half-bottle of Sauterne for me. It made me feel quite woozy as I walked back across the Park towards Chelsea.

And that was the extent of my own previous acquaintance. From then on I had to latch onto Peter Megaw's. I learned that the brother shared a semi-detached house in Neasden with some friends who also worked in that part of London. It was their practice, Peter told me, to have a party once a month so that they could all relax and let their hair down. The guests would bring extra liquor and spend the night, so that it became something of a mating party. Most of the mating couples were firmly established, in some cases even to the point of being married.

So this was Bohemia, not quite what I had imagined but it would serve. Indeed I liked all these new people, and among them I found a real actress, the first I had ever met. So the evening was not to be a total loss. From the actress and from some of the others present I obtained the names of theatrical agents and producers whom I should approach. Approach? Just call on them and ask for an appointment. Hmm. And what about the old lady across the river, have you tried her? Who's she? Lilian Baylis at the Old Vic. And you might do worse than to read the advertisements in *The Stage*. What's that? It's a trade paper that comes out every week, you can buy it anywhere in Soho.

The party took a long time to peter out to a general sleepiness. There being no odd girl out for me to mate with I found a rug and a cushion and tried to sleep in an isolated corner. It should have been easy enough because it was summer and in fact I was sleeping on the floor in Oakley Street – Megaw enjoyed the comparative luxury of a camp bed. We had two kitchen chairs and a table made out of an old tin and plywood tea-chest topped by my drawing board. At the party headquarters in Neasden I could not sleep. I thought it best to sneak out of the front door and walk to Chelsea.

Anybody contemplating such a walk should be warned that it is a matter of nine miles as the crow flies, and that nowadays even at three o'clock in the morning the streets will be heavy with the smell of burned petrol and the silence frequently shattered by the all night articulateds, but at that time it was quite pleasant.

The best way to learn a city is to walk. I walked to and from the West End practically every day, not that there was often any professional excuse. But there was a constant search for the impossible restaurant which would meet my budgetary demands and also satisfy the taste buds. One shilling and sixpence per head was our target. There was an Express Dairy just off Sloane Square which gave good nutrition for the price but zero for the taste buds. A 'Dining Room' towards the far end of King's Road encouraged high hopes; a good helping of rather gristly meat but the gravy did it a disservice. The best buy was to be found in a Chinese restaurant in Dean Street about twenty yards beyond Old Compton Street. Three course meal including tea, all in, for one and six.

Breakfast and lunch we did for ourselves in the room. Elementary stuff, nothing more complicated than scrambled egg or a pancake. I had been impressed by something that I had eaten in a Munich Stube, called Bauernfrühstück. My rendering of it consisted of corned beef and potatoes cooked together in a frying pan with an egg broken on top. Porridge for breakfast, bangers occasionally and the odd apple or orange.

Sometimes I managed to insert myself into the office of an agent or theatrical producer. They were friendly enough but unhelpful. They all came around to asking me about my past experience and they were equally unimpressed by my triumphant appearance with the Marlowe Society at Cambridge. The ritual answer to this was 'I hope you will come back and see us when you have had some professional experience.'

Aside from my letters to these theatrical characters I wrote to newspaper editors recommending myself for the post of Architectural Critic whenever and if ever they should have need of one. Some replied politely, but in the negative.

I could think of no other sort of job to invent for myself.

I was advised not to bother The Old Lady across the river because by now she would have selected her entire cast for the coming season at the Old Vic and was holding no further auditions. I started buying copies of *The Stage* every week and studying the advertisements. I was discouraged when it became obvious that most of the talent required was for concert parties or some other sort of travelling revue, and that applicants should have their own Dinner Jackets and Tap Shoes. A tap dancer I was not.

The cheapest form of entertainment that I could find was to explore London by tramcar. At that time one could buy a sixpenny ticket and travel by tram throughout the day. A large part of me was still the Architectural Student and I found this a highly satisfactory arrangement. Before World War II Christopher Wren's city churches were mostly still intact plus a number of others by Nicholas Hawksmoor and John Vanbrugh. All had to be inspected. On a Sunday it would be walks in the park and perhaps a cheap seat in that cinema in Shaftesbury Avenue which alone specialised in the Continental films which I fancied. There Brigitte Helm made herself known to me, and Gerda Maurus. And there was that haunting French silent version of *The Fall of the House of Usher* ...

As summer turned to autumn I began to get a little nervous about my budget. At the outset of my London residence I had sometimes treated myself to a Sunday lunch that cost more than twice the basic one and sixpence. In the luxury price range a French restaurant in Old Compton Street was my favourite. The menu, written in squiggly French, was reproduced by the old fashioned device which seemed to make use of violet coloured jelly. That was not its only appeal; the cuisine was excellent. But now a halt was called to all such extravagance. More often the expensive meal of the day would be a meat pie at the coffee stall in Sloane Square, or a hot saveloy.

Towards the end of October the Word came to me in the form of a letter from a producer whose advertisement in

The Stage I had answered. He asked me to come for an interview at a rehearsal room in Soho. I attended the rendezvous with flagging optimism and within a quarter of an hour was hired. I had told them about my lamentable lack of experience but they seemed not to be interested in all that. I was apparently in good health and I suppose what could be called a personable juvenile. I say 'They' because I was clearly in the presence of a team. When I started rehearsal I learned a number of things about them. The producer's wife was the leading lady. The producer's partner was the leading man, whose wife also played a major role.

It was to be revealed later that the team could be said to include the stage carpenter who also happened to be the stage manager and played the part of the Court Doctor.

Before giving my nod to the deal I had to be told what it was. They called it a 'Co-operative Venture'. This meant that the salary which they agreed to pay me would not necessarily find its way to my pocket each week; it would depend on our receipts at the box office. Some weeks they might decide to withhold part of our salaries and make them up to us when we came to London. London? Yes, it was a prior-to-London tour that they were planning. After the Christmas season they would open at the Scala Theatre in London.

The one thought in my mind was that after my first job I should be able to introduce myself to all those agents and producers and brag about my experience in *The Rascal*. That was the name of the piece. An actor with this one thought in mind does not quibble about the fine points of his deal. Three pounds a week was to be my basic salary, subject of course to co-operative deductions.

The producer was also the author of the play and had high hopes of success. His advertising campaign would lean heavily on his claim that 'this play which was condemned by the Lord Chamberlain can now be seen without the alteration of a single line of dialogue'. Unfortunately his 'advertising campaign' was not likely to stretch further than a placard outside the theatre and half an inch in the local newspaper and his boast about the Lord Chamberlain would hold little excitement for the prospective customer as soon as the word got around that it was a play about Rasputin and the Russian Imperial Court which had been cleared by the simple device of changing the names of all the characters. Thus instead of the Czarina of all the Russians, we had as one of our principal characters the Czarina of all the Tintalians. The actress who played this role was a pretty woman with a retroussé nose and a figure that would have been just right for Dick Whittington in a Christmas Pantomime.

Her husband was the producer's partner and thus played the part of the sinister monk Karelin – the new name for Rasputin. He spoke with his native North Country accent and, further to show the audience what a crude fellow this Karelin was, he spat a great deal. He was tall and impressive looking.

When the play still purported to be about the Russian Imperial family it had indeed been put on in a provincial theatre and had been immediately banned by the Lord Chamberlain because it concerned certain real characters who were not only still alive but of a litigious disposition. Prince Yousoupoff who plotted and was the leading perpetrator of the murder of Rasputin had given endless trouble to MGM in Hollywood when they had set about making a film about the same historical events. They finished up with a very tame version featuring the three celebrated Barrymores.

The part that I played was that of Prince Yousoupoff himself though for the duration of our exploit he was billed in the programme as the Grand Duke Ivan Maritzi. There were two other actors, unrelated to the management, and one other actress, named Carey Stephens. All played members of the Tintalian nobility and, as the plot developed, of the anti-Karelin conspiracy.

I should love to possess a copy of this play. I never even read the full script since we were issued with 'sides'. The words of each actor's part were typed on half sheets of paper, each speech preceded by the last half dozen words of the previous speaker, so that one could memorize one's cues as well as one's own speeches. These pages were roughly bound together. By the number of these pages or sides an actor's relative importance rose or subsided. I did not have a vast number of sides although both romantically and homicidally Ivan Maritzi was deeply implicated.

The play opened at the Theatre Royal, Aldershot, the garrison town about 30 miles from London. We gentlemen had to supply our own wardrobe which in my case was an unadorned dinner jacket. The two unrelated noblemen wore orders, presumably from their own theatrical stock. The ladies were not by any means overdressed, and the scenery looked as if it had been shunted into many a railway siding. We were to find out that it actually belonged to the stage carpenter. That was his stake in the enterprise. The management supplied pistols and ammunition for all who turned to gun-play in the last act, but any other hand props were the actors' own responsibility.

I had to have a horsewhip with which to flog Karelin at the curtain of Act 1. I had little difficulty in obtaining a short stock but the lash presented a problem. Since I had to flog Karelin as if I meant it I could obviously not use the real thing made of leather, but one of the more experienced members of the cast told me that plaited wool would be an effective substitute. It would make a convincing sound and look like the real thing but not actually hurt the actor who had to be on the receiving end. For some reason I left it to the last minute but was not worried because all I needed to complete the job was a piece of string to attach the lash to the stock. I had even put on my make-up and my dinner jacket before starting my hunt for the string. I learned to my surprise and dismay that no scrap of string was to be found backstage at the Theatre Royal, Aldershot. Stagehands, electrician, carpenter, none could help me. The stage doorkeeper, glancing up from his evening paper, recommended that I go round to the front of the house to the manager's office; he could be counted on to find me some string. I took his advice, since life without that piece of string would not be worth pursuing. Making myself as invisible as possible I went to the front entrance, received instructions from the doorman to go up the main stairs, move around the back of the dress circle as far as I could and there I would find the manager's office.

The manager was in his office and had no difficulty finding a piece of string. I was afraid that he might have been put out by the sudden appearance of a tense and overmade-up young actor, but he took it calmly almost as if it was just what he would expect from our group. The producer however was looking even more tense and over made-up when I reappeared backstage. And I was the cause of it, or so he said. Didn't I know that for an actor to go round front when dressed and made up for a performance when the audience were already taking their seats was the most unprofessional thing he could do? I chose not to argue the point and expressed fairly sincere contrition. I had in fact been embarrassed by the need to go round front to borrow a piece of string from the manager and now I knew what such a misdemeanour was called. Unprofessionalism.

I knew that I was tense to a degree that I had never experienced before, but I did not know that I was over made-up until Carey Stephens told me. In the dressing room which I shared with the stage carpenter and the two unrelated noblemen I had been so excited by the act of putting on my own make-up for the first time that I had wanted to blurt it out to them.

'Do you know something? This is the first time I ever acted in the professional theatre!'

'Go on, you must be joking!'

'No, it's true! It's the first time I ever put make-up on!'

'Well I never! And we all thought you were so experienced!'

Some such fantasy conversation was going on in my

head while I fumbled with my brand new sticks of Leichner's grease paint numbers two and nine and the thinner sticks of carmine and lake and a touch of yellow for the high lights.

There was a real call boy and he was now shouting 'Orchestra and Beginners please!' Before the curtain rose there was no sign that any audience was present out there in front, no anticipatory buzz, but the producer, who had been peeking through a hole in the curtain, reported on an encouraging note, 'About half capacity I should say'. That was not what it looked like to me when I found myself on stage a few minutes later.

The flogging scene seemed to work all right, but in the second act one of my lines caused a sound that I took to be a raspberry. I put that down to bad manners on the part of the person who blew it. More serious was the laughter which greeted one of my exit lines: 'I shall not rest', I said, 'until this outrage has been avenged!' Then came the laugh. Not the entire audience, just a small group of young people seemed to think it was funny. When I reported to Carey she grinned and said that it might be a good idea to dispense with the gesture; I was aware that I made a gesture, indeed I had planned it rather carefully. 'What's wrong with it?' 'Oh nothing', she said, 'it just looks as if you're pulling a chain.'

Later, the producer said the manager had said 'they' liked the show, and everybody acted as if all was well. But on a subsequent evening the same week a terrible thing happened. In my great whipping scene, the thong of my horsewhip fell off after the first two strokes. I was left with nothing to beat Karelin with but the short stock. I now had to *pretend* to strike my adversary with this useless weapon. He acted up splendidly, seeming more terrorised than ever by my onslaught, and I felt that the grin which was beginning to spread across my face as the curtain fell might have been dangerous. Karelin would have had a perfect right to turn and abuse me, so I was relieved when he took it quite calmly as if he had known many worse disasters. Much more had been lost at Mohacs Field.

In spite of this I received my full salary of £3 from the company secretary when Friday came around. When things started to go wrong with our enterprise Carey and I found that the company had made a curious arrangement with the secretary when he was taken on. They told him that money would be passing through his hands and that it was customary for a person holding a post of such responsibility to give the employer a deposit of ten pounds as security. As that happened to be the sum of his life's savings, he was able to accommodate them. He was a shy young man who had not yet emerged from the pimply stage.

On the Saturday we were given our railway tickets to Tiverton and were told that we would play there for only three days. And where would we be playing during the second half of the week? We would have three days free and the whole of the following week we would be playing the Theatre Royal, Bath, an excellent date.

Tiverton is situated in a rural area of Devonshire. And rural life was evidently in just as bad a shape as industrial life. The theatre in which we played was more like an old drill hall; inactivity at its box office was an established condition. It was not only our play that the locals wished to stay away from but several companies which had preceded us had met with similar disdain. We kept running into out-of-work actors stranded at Tiverton and lacking the wherewithal to buy their tickets home. The only cheerful thing in the town was the cider. But you could not rely even on that since it was so strong that one could unwittingly cross the borderline from cheerfulness to despair.

On the Friday I walked to the theatre hoping to find the company secretary and my salary. But there was no one. No local staff, not a trace of our company, not even the scenery. Aha, I thought, so now it has happened to us! I met Carey on the way back to the lodgings. The producer himself had dropped by with railway tickets to Bath for her and myself. No money.

I had enough money left from my first week's salary to meet the modest demands of my Tiverton landlady. So next day we went to Bath and settled in for what was to be a really nice week. The exterior of the house where I found lodgings recommended itself on a point of style and thus made up for the draughtiness of the interior.

Other good things included the theatre itself, one of the oldest in England, and the elegant eighteenth-century splendour of the city. One could have spent many weeks there without tiring of the pleasures it offered. Our staple diet was hot faggots and peas with a glass of Guinness.

But certain members of the company were not so easily satisfied. It did not sit well with the two unrelated Tintalian noblemen that they had touched no salary the previous week. The management kept them in line with the hint of increased benefits at the end of the current week. But when Friday came there was only one pound ten shillings in my pay packet. I do not know what theirs contained but it failed to satisfy them; they decided to confiscate the management's typewriter and the leading man's evening trousers and hold them to ransom. Since no settlement was reached after the two shows on Saturday the cast was suddenly short of two noblemen. The poor secretary was talked into taking over the smaller of the two parts and an unemployed friend of the management was urgently summoned from Blackpool.

And so to Bilston, a manufacturing town in the Midlands, not far from Wolverhampton. Employees in several of the big factories had recently been laid off. The few weeks before Christmas are always thought of as bad for business in the theatre but not always for this reason. It must have been the fourteenth of December when we opened in Bilston. Business was negligible throughout the week. At first we had all thought that the management was just outstandingly stingy but now it was clear that they were actually running out of money. One symptom was the strict rationing of ammunition. It detracted from historical authenticity to see Karelin fatally riddled by a mere half dozen pistol shots. Even we knew that a demijohn of poison and enough bullets to decimate a regiment had been spent on the operation before the seemingly superhuman Rasputin finally succumbed as he was stumbling across the frozen river Neva. And on the Saturday it became ridiculous. By that time we were down to a mere two or three – not for each assassin, but two or three for the entire gang. At the last of these performances, when I had spent my one bullet, I heard myself say BANG BANG. Now with the theatrical style that we were emulating this was simply not in keeping. In other schools, the Berliner Ensemble for instance, you might get away with that sort of thing but in Bilston's pre-Christmas season 1931 I knew that this was not quite the thing. But I did not giggle, as well I might, and the producer did not give me a tongue lashing as well *he* might have done.

One tiresome embarrassing thing bothered Carey and myself. We both liked the young company secretary whom circumstances had forced to become an actor. Having got through his first performance without mishap he looked quite happy, almost preening himself. Carey, who was a good natured tease, suggested we write him a fan letter and together we plotted this dastardly deed. We strung together the sort of phrases that we thought that a Bilston teenager might use, ending with the suggestion that she wait for our secretary at the stage door after the show on Saturday night. By that time the show was washed up. At some time during the day we had all been given some token payment. I had received fifteen shillings and been told someone would come round to my lodgings on the Sunday morning to pay the balance. As it happened, foreseeing disaster, I had lived so thriftily that my entire expenses for the week came out at little more than the fifteen shillings. It worried us that on top of everything else this poor boy was to hang around at the stage door waiting for our phantom fan. And when, if ever, was he to recover his ten pound deposit?

But in spite of our concern for him I confess that we let the whole stage door scenario slip from our minds until a good half hour after we had left the theatre. We hurried back and, sure enough, he was there casually lighting up another cigarette. We said we were looking for him because we wanted him to have some supper with us. He seemed to think he had an appointment with someone. It took quite a little time, but we finally managed to persuade him to stand up this bit of local goods whoever she was. So we took our last little meal together in the sad town.

The next day no one came around to settle with our landladies. The management, I was soon to hear, had left by an early train. No provision had been made for the stage manager or his scenery, or the secretary or Carey, or for the replacement from Blackpool who had nobly served the get-rid-of-Karelin conspiracy the whole week. Carey was at that moment trying to make contact with the Church Aid Society, a charitable organisation which specialised in rescuing abandoned actors. She knew that I had from the beginning craftily saved just enough money to buy a railway ticket to Huddersfield. I was not to worry about her, she said, because although she also had enough to get her back to London she intended to stay with the left-overs until the Church Aid Society came to their aid. She'd see me in London, she added.

I gave a report of my professional activities to my father, but only in rather superficial and strictly practical terms. I had to mention that I was slightly worse off now than when I had signed up for the job. This was something that my father would understand, since things were bad enough in his own line of business. And I wished to convey the hint that a further handout would be welcome as soon as the Christmas holidays were over to enable me to get back to London and start over. This was, I believe, the last bite that I was to put on him. Twenty pounds. And I truly appreciated it because I knew how he felt about 'The Stage'.

The Christmas of 1931 came and went. All the rituals

were duly performed. The stories and the jokes and some favourite decorations were dragged out of the cupboard. And there was still that exciting moment after our evening dinner when the front door bell sounded. 'That must be the choir.' My father went out and welcomed them all into the house. The men and the boys of the choir of Holy Trinity Church lined up in the corridor which led from the vestibule to the staircase, thus separating the dining room from the drawing room. We settled snugly and listened to their friendly, well drilled voices.

'That was wonderful, we enjoyed it ever so much', 'You were really in good voice tonight', 'Happy Christmas', 'Happy New Year', and so on, and my father discreetly slipping a previously prepared envelope into the hand of the leading chorister.

And the next day, being Boxing Day, if the weather was not too miserable we'd go and watch the Northern Union Rugby match at Fartown, or Colin would be involved in a hockey match – and Rex? In 1931 he was not yet addicted to following the local pack of beagles over the moors. That would come later. Sufficient for this year and the next were his final seasons of gentleman-style Rugby which he still played with so much heart.

Which might well leave my father and myself to entertain each other. Some work to be done in the garden? Or, perhaps better still on a day like this, we'd join my mother in front of the fire in the drawing room and play a few hands of bezique or piquet. And I would concentrate either on the game we were playing or on my future involvement in the strange career I had got myself into.

6/London 2

If I had known more about the theatre in the United States in 1931 I would have recognised that there was one aspect of theatrical life there which might well have made it more appealing than the London Theatre. And this was the fact that in the States showbiz is one and indivisible. In England on the other hand, the barrier of class, which exists in all areas of our life, also rears itself in a slightly different form even in the life of the theatre. It separates legitimate theatre from musical comedy, music hall and concert party; Shaftesbury Avenue from Charing Cross Road; you might almost say Theatre from Stage. Nowadays the lines have become blurred by the confusing emergence of television and films, though it could very well be said that the BBC lies on one side of the line and ITV on the other.

But in those days the line was very clearly marked, especially since the prevalent style in the theatre of the West End of London was that which was exemplified by the acting of Gerald du Maurier. It was drawing-room comedy at its crispest and most elegant. One of the unfortunate results of this was that access to the legitimate theatre had become extremely difficult for any young aspirants whose manner of speaking was less than refined. Actually this was the reverse of the phenomenon that was to take place in the fifties and sixties when a touch of any sort of local accent was to be the thing, and the unfortunate young man who was cursed with a 'Public School' accent would find it hard to get a job until he learned to disguise it.

This was not a problem which affected me; I only

mention this basic English set-up because, happily for me, my friend Carey Stephens was one who straddled the borderline. Most of her experience as a performer had been Charing Cross Road, but she was equally at home in Shaftesbury Avenue when working as secretary, producer's assistant, casting manager and other chores connected with legitimate theatre. Having worked for a long time as a certain producer's assistant she had become bored and, feeling that a touring job might give her a nice change of environment, had offered her services the previous year to the producer of *The Rascal*.

When I returned to London after Christmas she had already spoken about me to several of her friends. There was one producer of whom she had high hopes. This was Jevon Brandon Thomas, son of Brandon Thomas, the playwright, who wrote *Charley's Aunt*.

Jevon Brandon Thomas made an annual practice of presenting something called the Brandon Thomas Seasons which he booked into three or four of the most popular resort theatres during the summer months. Carey assured me that in a few weeks he would start planning this year's repertoire and putting his Company together. I was to write reminding him that she had spoken to him about me. She gave me the names of two or three of her acquaintance to whom she had recommended me, but she did not think that they had any specific plans at present.

So I wrote to Jevon Brandon Thomas expectantly, and to the others less so. I rented another room for myself in Chelsea, dropped in on some of those agents and producers to whom I had introduced myself the previous year and told them all about my experience in *The Rascal*. In spite of this they were not enormously friendly.

I hung around doing nothing for what seemed like an inordinate length of time, though, to my inexpensive distractions, I now added an occasional seat in the gallery at the Old Vic Theatre. This was one of the seasons in which Ralph Richardson was the leading man. It was wonderful the way the audience lapped up everything he did, and with good reason, for there was in him an endless supply of virility and boisterousness which could warm the coldest heart in his audience. I saw him as Faulconbridge in *King John* and as Ralph in *The Night of the Burning Pestle*. He was the first actor of stature that I ever saw.

Finally I received a note from Jevon Brandon Thomas inviting me to an interview. I showed up on time, I explained about myself with becoming modesty, we exchanged warm comments about Carey Stephens, he suggested a salary which I accepted without argument, and so I was hired.

Our leading man was Wilson Barrett who had worked with Brandon Thomas in previous seasons. The two of them knew each other's methods and needs so well that stage direction could be reduced to an exchange of grunts, not that either of them could ever be described as inarticulate. They constituted a bright and enthusiastic leadership. The middle aged women in the troop were Kitty de Legh and Deirdre Doyle and there was an impressive middle-aged character man, Stephen Ewart, who excelled in what might be called C. Aubrey Smith or Lionel Barrymore parts. There was besides myself another utility juvenile, Leonard Sachs, and an ingenue called Patricia Hayes; Brandon Thomas himself also acted in many of the plays. These constituted the permanent company. Others were added or subtracted according to the exigencies of casting when a new play was introduced into our repertoire. For instance, after our initial six weeks in the Bournemouth Pavilion we moved to the Pavilion at Torquay and at this point we introduced *Private Lives* which called for a leading lady who could reasonably be expected to get away with the Gertrude Lawrence part. She came in the form of Agatha Carroll who was tall, svelte and attractive and did very well.

But that was later. The play with which we were to open in Bournemouth and was to be rehearsed in London when I joined the company was *Old Heidelberg*. Brandon

Thomas had a romantic attachment to this because its original production had been contemporaneous with that of *Charley's Aunt* and its author, R. Bleichmann, had been a close friend of Brandon Thomas senior. In a later reincarnation it had become the well known sentimental operetta called *The Student Prince*.

In its original form it was already quite sentimental enough. The story concerns a German Prince who, absorbed into the student body at the University of Heidelberg, sheds his princely demeanour and falls in love with the innkeeper's daughter. In the last act the idyll is shattered by news of his father's death and the young man's reluctant acceptance of Royal responsibility. I loved it. And I particularly loved Patricia Hayes who played the innkeeper's daughter who was probably called Heidi. She was the most talented of the troupe but there were not many impressive leading parts for her since she was young and tiny. The best that she had to do during the season was that touching waif in *The Constant Nymph* which had been created in the original London production by Edna Best.

It seems to me that we played six weeks in Bournemouth, three or four in Torquay, two in Eastbourne and three finally in Brighton. Our best times were the weeks in Bournemouth and Torquay. This had something to do with the weather and a great deal to do with the fact that we were still preparing new productions at that time and that the vibrations that emanated from Brandon Thomas remained optimistic, whereas at Eastbourne and Brighton he seemed to be thinking perhaps more about his own future plans. Although I never enquired about our business returns I could at least detect that the Brighton audience was not responding with the warmth that we had picked up in Bournemouth and Torquay.

I should have been happy if the season had been extended indefinitely. The work was all so new that the importance of the parts which I was given to play mattered very little, though there was some gratification when I

70

found myself with more sides than my fellow utility juvenile Leonard Sachs. By the end of the season the company had presented *Old Heidelberg, The Torchbearers, The Skin Game, The Great Adventure, The Constant Nymph, John Ferguson, At Mrs Beam's, Private Lives, The Queen was in the Parlour*. Looking back on these, I am not reminded of any role in which I could have imagined that I was distinguishing myself. To be sure I rather fancied myself as the son of the Northern Irish farmer in *John Ferguson*, but somehow I find my eye always travelling eagerly back to *Old Heidelberg* in which along with a group of local young men suitably attired as German students we churned out the schmaltzy accompaniment for the events that were taking place centre stage. As we sang 'Gaudeamus' and 'Tannenbaum' I was using the sentiments that had been in rich supply when we had sung 'All Aboard' and 'Auld Lang Syne' at the breaking-up concert at the end of each year at Marlborough.

Non-working hours were passed happily in the company of Patricia Hayes and Leonard Sachs and later, when she joined the company, with Agatha Carroll the svelte. Leonard had travelled much further in his life than I had, having been born in Johannesburg. With an unexpected enthusiasm he could drag us to matinees at the local music halls where he would admire such artists as G. H. Elliott, the chocolate-coloured coon, or to cinemas where they were playing some film of a kind which, left to myself, I would probably never have seen, such as Jan Kiepura in *Be Mine Tonight*. My tastes at the time were far from catholic.

When Brandon Thomas wound up the season he did not, as it turned out, throw us all out of work. Indeed he was most helpful in the setting up of another touring repertory company. He had a very nice and efficient stage manager called Billy Bell who aspired to be a producer. So now that the Brandon Thomas Seasons were closing down for the year, Bell saw that his moment had arrived, and assembled a company almost identical with the one now being released to rehearse a repertoire of Nöel Coward plays. The essentially summer resorts would be given a miss, but otherwise we would aim for many of the dates which Bell had visited in the past with other companies.

Nöel Coward himself quite properly insisted on withholding his approval until he had seen us in rehearsal. So he appeared one day at the rehearsal room in London, The Master himself, accompanied by the indispensable Lorn Loraine. They came in quietly and talked for a while with Bell who then presented Wilson Barrett and Agatha Carroll who proceeded to run through one of the scenes from *Private Lives*. I was cast in what may legitimately be referred to as the Laurence Olivier part and was relieved when I was told that they would not be getting to do any of the scenes that I was in.

The tour was peculiarly unsuccessful. Bell and Wilson Barrett were taken by surprise since Coward's was thought of as being a magic name at this period. Nineteen thirty-two was the year of his *Words and Music*. He was at the peak of his creativity and, though it was not staged in England until later, he also wrote *Design for Living* at this time. But his contribution must have been the only good thing about the year. Provincial audiences were certainly not in the mood for light comedy and perhaps the plays themselves were not ripe for revival. The theatre in general was going through bad times and in London there was a new vogue for 'Twofers', two tickets for the price of one. Bell went one better, or so he thought. He offered two plays for the price of one.

Coward plays were never very long and on a point of time it was not unreasonable to expect an audience to sit through two of them. If not for the audience, it became rather a strain for the actors, especially on Saturdays and the midweek matinee days when we had to rattle off four of them. And so we petered out. I was most distressed, not for my own sake so much as for that of Billy Bell, who took a terrible beating financially. He and his wife were such nice people; the next time I saw them, they were selling second-hand books in the lane that runs past the Albery and Wyndham's Theatres between Charing Cross Road and St Martin's Lane. I hoped then and I still hope that they were into something that gave them infinitely more satisfaction than touring a Repertory Company, even one endorsed by the most glittering figure in the English Theatre.

So back to London. This time I found my room in St. George's Drive, Pimlico. It happened to be quite ghastly. I had not been able to find one in Chelsea in my price range and Pimlico had been associated recently with a newsworthy event which appealed to the Vie de Bohème fantasy which was still my companion. The Rector of Stiffkey (pronounced Stewkey) had disgraced himself by keeping company with a low woman in a modest room in Pimlico. He had been drummed out of the Church and at the time that I established my toe-hold in Pimlico I do not think that his melodramatic demise had yet taken place. Figuring that he could sink to no deeper humiliation and recognising there was no form of desirable employment for one of his notoriety, he allowed himself to be exhibited as a side show freak in Blackpool. People paid to see him sitting in an open fronted barrel. The exhibition moved from one resort town to another until it ended for him in Skegness, where a circus lion killed him.

But for me, Pimlico provided no great fun. Smoked sprats at threepence a bunch figured almost too frequently in my diet. In one direction, however, my social life took a turn for the better. Pat Hayes and Sachs introduced me to The Interval Club in Dean Street; this offered a comfortable meeting ground for all of us who were in any way connected with the theatre and a very good lunch with a choice of basic main courses such as steak and kidney pudding and cottage pie. The woman who ran it, a Miss Fawcett, was a perfect saint and an excellent administrator into the bargain.

Resting in Pimlico did not last for long. I was accepted by Michael MacOwan as a member of the Repertory

Company of which he was to be the producer in Hull. He had a good name, having done well as an actor before he switched to directing. The only thing, however, about the project that did not please me enormously was that once more the leading man was to be Wilson Barrett. Now, he was a nice man and we had had very good relations in the other companies but he was pre-eminently the leading man, not the kind who every so often would take on a character part or a supporting role. If it turned out the same way with the Hull Repertory, I had a feeling that I might not be there for a long stay. A girl in the Nöel Coward Company had told me about this time that she was going to work in a Repertory Theatre which was about to open in Croydon. The resident producer was to be Henry Cass whom we had both met when he had caught our *Private Lives* when we had played Malvern. Joyce Wodeman had been playing the other secondary part in that play. So now, with the idea of preparing an escape route for myself, I asked her to let me know the moment there appeared on their schedule a play which might conceivably need an extra man like myself.

Gerald Savory was an actor in the Hull Company. In the opening production, *The Prisoner of Zenda*, he played the part of Rupert of Hentzau while I played the less rewarding role of Fritz von Talenheim. But after that nothing very interesting seemed to be coming along for either of us and, to relieve Gerald's boredom, he asked MacOwan to let him at least select music for the entr'actes. Permission having been granted, I joined him in this enterprise. Now, feeling that he was on a winning streak he pressed his luck to the point of persuading our producer that he should find a showcase for himself and me and thus relieve the pressure on Wilson Barrett who was working non-stop on these exhausting leading parts. We changed the programme every two weeks which was not so bad as changing each week. But even so, Savory said, Wilson Barrett deserved a break. To our great surprise MacOwan bought the idea and the next thing we

74

knew was that Gerald and I were to play the leading parts in *The Importance of Being Earnest*.

It was a disaster. Here was another play that was not really ripe for revival. Hitherto all revivals had presented it as a contemporary work. Now it was time for producers to treat it as a period piece, and one of them was MacOwan. But he went too far and encouraged all of us to act in a highly stylised manner against scenery which also made no concessions to reality. Fortunately by the time this disaster had run its allotted fortnight, with minimal encouragement from the audience, I had received a message from Croydon which suggested that a retreat from Hull might be timely.

Joyce Wodeman reported that Henry Cass was making a very good name for himself and that his productions were rapturously received by the local community. And being so close to London, young actors who had already achieved some standing in London were eager to work there. For instance Alan Webb's 'Hamlet' had been a great success and highly praised by the London critics. But, apart from revivals of well tried successes with an occasional classic thrown in, Cass was known to have several new plays lined up for production. All of this sounded most enticing. There would be the possibility that one of the new productions might transfer to a theatre in the West End, though this in itself was not my aim at the moment. All I wanted was to find an opening in some company which did not have a permanent leading man to swallow up all the good parts. In fact I was reacting to poor Wilson Barrett rather more plaintively than the circumstances justified, for I can think of four plays that we did in Hull which did not offer outstanding parts for the leading man. There was *The Lady from Albuquerque*, the ill-fated *Importance of Being Earnest*, then Eugene O'Neill's *Moon in the Caribees*, in which no-one could pretend that the role of Smittie is necessarily a rewarding one; and finally there was a new play about Robert Louis Stevenson in which I was allotted the not entirely insignificant part of Lloyd Osbourne and there was none for Wilson Barrett because a more famous actor was imported to play the role of R.L.S.

This play was called *Tusitala*, and, if not very good from the spectator's viewpoint, it was at least an exciting event for those of us who shared the stage with the famous actor in question, John Laurie. I had progressed now to the point of acting with a widely recognised pro who at this time had already appeared in every play by Shakespeare, the great leading parts in many of them. He was a Scotsman and very much in tune with the spirit of Stevenson. His total familiarity with the character gave his performance a credibility and emotional strength which reached a peak in the scene leading up to Stevenson's death. Returning from the balcony from which he has been gazing at the night sky, 'A wonderful night of stars!', he says and, a moment later, collapses. A milestone in my life, if not in the history of the theatre. It was a treat for Hull and as an additional bonus Laurie gave them a special solo performance in which he replayed many of his best Shakespearean bits. It was not surprising that his favourite, judging from the number of excerpts, appeared to be that play about the Scottish king which is of such ill omen that proper theatre folk are at pains to avoid quoting from it or even mentioning the title.

My retreat from Hull was not so much motivated by an urgency to reach the West End as by a modest desire to find a spot for myself in a theatre with a bracing climate. I had been told by the old hands that an actor should stick to the provinces for as long as ten years, if need be, to gain the experience and maturity that would assure him success in the West End. This would have made complete sense before the era of Gerald du Maurier. Now the rule was losing its validity.

In the vague hope of a friendly reception at the Croydon Theatre, I handed in my resignation at Hull and made my rounds of the 'Rooms to Let' notices in Pimlico. I settled into one which was only marginally more comfortable than the last.

Since I was gambling anyhow, I can't think why I did not try to find something equally cheap in the vicinity of Charing Cross Station where the trains for Croydon are most commonly found. Joyce Wodeman must have given me a great build-up since Henry Cass's welcome was warmer than could have been justified by his having caught the Nöel Coward Company's *Private Lives*. At least so I thought. Almost at once I was offered parts in two of his coming productions in quick succession. The first was a new play about the Abbé Prévost, the author of *Manon Lescaut*, by Helen Waddell, a lady of letters, whose novels and belles lettres had a large and loyal following. The play read much better than it played. She showed how the man's personal agonies were closely related to those inflicted on his fictional hero by the troublesome Manon. Hugh Miller, angular and intense, served our authoress with great distinction. Though everything took on the air of truth when he spoke it, the scenes themselves had little dramatic substance.

Several revivals followed. These included one in which Joyce Wodeman and I played elderly father and mother of the young protagonists. We painted out our eyebrows and lips and hatched on our faces a survey map of wrinkles and highlights, topping it off with an overload of powder on the hair. Young actors always do this even when the 'elderly' parts they are playing are likely to be only in their late fifties. Neither of us racked this up as a great success.

Then came the new production which Cass may have had in mind when he hired me since a number of young men were needed in the cast. The play was *Gallows Glorious* by Ronald Gow. It was a dramatisation of the famous raid on Harper's Ferry in West Virginia, carried out by the abolitionist John Brown. For the purposes of this play only four of John Brown's sons were on display. They were played by myself, Richard Warner, Norman Claridge and David Steuart. Mrs Brown was played by Susan Richards, the elder daughter by the beautiful Nancy Hornsby, her suitor by Clifford Evans, and the younger daughter by Nova Pilbeam. Here was another new play that read well, but it also had some very powerful scenes and we, on our side of the footlights, felt that it played beautifully. But the great thing that it had going for it was the presence of Wilfrid Lawson in the role of John Brown. I was able to feel that for the first time I was participating in a great event. I know that the event I am talking about was only a play and that commercially it was not even a very successful one. But I know also that what is listed as a great event in the mind of an actor is very different from what is listed in a playgoer's. Wilfrid Lawson's greatness pervaded the entire play but it was at its most powerful in the scene in the Browns' farmhouse immediately prior to the raid. It was a briefing similar to those that became so popular in post World War II movies in which Spencer Tracy explained their mission to a roomful of pilots who knew that some of them would not come back. But this being a scene which dealt with a more remote historical event the briefing advanced one further step emotionally and culminated in John Brown's leading us into The Lord's Prayer.

This was quite a little triumph for the Croydon Repertory Theatre. A London management desired to transfer our production to the West End. We were all elated. I was able to throw my weight around in the Interval Club as if I were now a West End actor. After a reasonable length of time had elapsed to allow for preparations to be made in the chosen theatre, we assembled again to re-acquaint ourselves with the play and make whatever adjustments were needed for the larger stage on which we would now appear. Also there were to be minor changes of cast. For instance there was the part of a negro preacher. In the modest circumstances of the Croydon Theatre this had been played effectively by a young character actor called David Marsh (a.k.a. David McCandlish), but for the West End the management persuaded the director to turn him in for a genuine black. There were at that time hardly any black actors around town. One of the few was Ernest Trimmingham, who was renowned not so much for his acting ability as for the fact that through the length and breadth of Charing Cross Road everyone knew him. Unusually tall, often affecting a swallowtail coat, he was a character. He was cheerful, goodnatured and willing but after a little while the management persuaded Cass to try to find David Marsh again. For reasons unexplained he proved the more believable preacher. Later in the same year I was to move to an address in Endell Street where, in a room at the very top of the house lived Trimmingham, so we enjoyed a lengthy meeting-on-the-staircase relationship and became friends that way.

John Brown provides me with an excuse at this point to make a giant flash forward to 1960, when John Kennedy won the Presidential Election in the United States by a dubious margin over Richard Nixon. During that year I had occasion to renew my acquaintance with Brown. This time our drama was for television, not live, nor yet filmed, but on tape. Hitherto theatrical productions which had been taped were restricted to the studio because they had not yet learned to splice video tape, so each act had to be recorded in its entirety. They could not even splice in the commercials.

If an actor blew his lines or some other technical error was made during the recording, they had to stop, go back to the beginning and start over. But now the great day had arrived when we needed no longer to go back to the beginning and start over, because the technicians had learned to splice video tape. Think of the joy. Think of the freedom.

One of the virtuoso television directors at the time, Sidney Lumet, was assigned to *John Brown's Raid*. Although he had already made a successful film of *Twelve Angry Men* he had not yet peaked in this medium and still thought of himself principally as a television man. I had already happily worked with him and now he was to be the first to take advantage of this great new development, splicing video tape. Lumet and his producer realised immediately that they were no longer restricted to a studio. They could shoot the scenes anywhere they wanted to. So why not at Harper's Ferry? Great idea. Everyone was excited, including myself who had been hired for the part of John Brown.

We rehearsed, as for a television play, in a studio in New York for ten days. Since it was the first time I was to play a historically established American character I struggled hard to produce an acceptable accent for one who was born in Ohio and later moved to Kansas. The script was good, Lumet communicated his euphoria to the entire team and it gave us an enormous sense of achievement to stage each sequence exactly where the events actually took place. There was at first some doubt whether the lighting equipment that we had brought with us would be enough. But Lumet was reassured on that point as soon as he saw the results of the cameraman's work. A large truck contained all the recording equipment, complete with the line-up of monitor screens, and the consoles that one expects to find in the director's booth at a television studio. 'We're running through some of the sequences we have taken,' says Lumet, 'I want you to see how they look.' Our cameraman is quite brilliant, he goes on, every frame is like a still by Dick Avedon. I went inside and what I saw was beautiful, just as he said.

When the devil heard Lumet speaking with such confidence he knew instantly where to strike us: in the splicing department and in the lighting department.

A play written for television had always demanded meticulous timing since any overlap into the period dedicated to the sponsor's message was unthinkable. But the ability to splice the tape relieved us of that keen sense of timing and, when our drama finally went out on domestic television, I could not help observing that a lot of good material was missing, and dramatic urgency was never successfully established. It may be that more commercials had been introduced at the time of the transmission than had been initially bargained for. Either way, something was now missing that had seemed very compelling when we had first watched a run through of the material we had shot at Harper's Ferry.

In the United States or in any other country where the viewer's concentration is to be fractured by a remorseless intrusion of commercials, the television writer must take into account the frequent interruptions, and protect his play from jarring breaches of continuity. In the case of our John Brown saga the writer had prepared a splendid effect for an interruption point which would be the equivalent of the curtain of Act I. One of John Brown's raiding party, a white boy, is posted at the railway station, where no incoming trains are expected until the early hours of the morning. Shortly before this a railroad man is liable to show up on the platform. The boy is instructed to challenge him, and when the man halts and raises his hands he is to be escorted to the baggage room and locked up. And if the man does not halt? Then the boy will challenge him a second time and if he still does not halt, then the boy must fire. So now, after a certain tension has been built up in the preceding scenes, we come to the boy in the railway station and see his attention suddenly alerted by the appearance of a man at the far end of the platform which he is guarding.

The boy calls, 'Halt'.

The man continues on his way, seeming not to have heard him.

'Halt, or I fire!'

The man turns his head momentarily towards the boy but does not stop walking.

The boy fires and the man falls. The boy, scared, runs towards the man who now lies face downward, motionless.

The boy turns him over with his foot and reveals ... *the man is black!*

Now in view of the fact that the aim of John Brown's raid was to expedite the abolition of slavery, we had all agreed that the irony of this scene at the station made for a

81

particularly effective curtain. So what went wrong?

The show was taped in black and white. In spite of our belief that the lights supplied had been quite adequate and that our cameraman had used them superbly, the images we saw on our screens were obscure. A viewer like myself who was determined to see the show through to the end would screw up his eyes and suffer patiently. But I could almost have cried when we came to the railway station scene. When the white boy turned over the body of the man he had killed so that you could see his face, you could not for the life of you tell whether it was white or black!

If Lumet's work was in a sense victimised by technological progress, Ronald Gow's *Gallows Glorious*, a decidedly better piece of work, was the victim back in 1933 of nothing more mysterious than disappointing box office returns at a time when many better known plays were doing just as badly. During the time of our re-rehearsal I felt the sting of Lawson's uneven temper which took me by surprise when we were on stage running through one of the scenes in which Brown was supposed to be briefing his sons and his daughter's fiancé. He suddenly stopped in the middle of a long speech and turned on me – 'I can't go on if you are going to behave like this!' he fumed. Now what had I done? Nothing really, I thought, though it was true that I had an inappropriate grin on my face. 'Look, I didn't do anything. That's all I have to do in this scene – just stand here and listen to you and . . .' – 'You had a silly grin on your face.' He turned to a group who were in one of the boxes watching us. 'I'm sorry but I can't go on.'

My instinct for self-preservation prompted my response to this, at least I think that that is what it was. I know that if we had been rehearsing quietly among ourselves I would just have shuffled my feet and said that I was sorry. But now I felt impelled to put up some sort of a defence because of the presence in the stage box of two big men in the West End, Albery and Tennent. I thought it would be better to go down with all guns firing, and so, with an air of injured innocence which I felt quite sincerely, I explained that if I had not been totally 'in' my part during the foregoing rehearsal it was because I construed this rehearsal to be strictly a matter of refreshing our memories and adjusting our movements to the dimensions of the larger stage. And the smile on my face was a simple reflex action since Lawson, tracing our projected itinerary on the map which was spread on the table in front of him, had said something like: 'We shall proceed along this road into Maryland' at the precise moment when his index finger was jabbing insistently at Lake Erie. Lawson and I continued yammering at each other until Henry Cass materialised on stage and quietly drew us into the wings. I shrugged an apology while Cass attended to the unruffling of Lawson.

We were at the Shaftesbury Theatre, which was destroyed during World War II. It was half way between Piccadilly Circus and Cambridge Circus on the right hand side going up. Lawson's voice, for all its oddity – sometimes the source of merriment among critics – was powerful and unique. Later on, after Lawson had died, my liking for both Peter O'Toole and Albert Finney increased enormously when I found that they both could imitate that voice to perfection.

I never appeared in a play in the West End or on Broadway but it closed within three months. In London they generally held on for three months precisely, like this one. I could not kid myself that Oliver Brown was an attention-getting part, though I made the most of my death scene in Act II.

During one of the many periods when my presence was not required on stage, they allowed me to provide mood music in the background by strumming a guitar and crooning 'Water Boy' in what I intended to be a deep dusky voice. But apart from this the outstanding plus in my balance sheet for this engagement was the acquaintance of Wilfrid Lawson. But towards the end of the run another was added. A totally unexpected visitor came round after the show to see me. It was Tyrone Guthrie, the man whose work I had so much admired during his season at the Festival Theatre at Cambridge. I supposed that he was doing the rounds of the West End Theatres, because, as it turned out, he was about to assemble a cast for the coming season at the Old Vic. He said that he would like me to audition for him.

7/Waterloo Road

When I was at Cambridge I put myself up for a reading competition. I did not win, but was placed second or third. I was a badly disciplined reader, inclined to gabble away without letting my eyes scout a sufficiently long distance ahead. Back at Marlborough I made something of a fool of myself the first time that I read a lesson in House Prayers. Since we were allowed to choose whatever passage took our fancy, I made sure that for my first go I would choose something bizarre enough to make some of my audience break up. So I chose the passage from the Book of Proverbs which opens with the words, 'There are four things which are little upon the earth but they are exceeding wise'. I was going to read it with perfect solemnity, and indeed I did so, but I ultimately spoiled the effect by stumbling over a couple of words and breaking the tempo. The house master was not in the least irked by my choice of material and merely insisted that in future whenever it was my turn to read I should come to his study for a preparatory run-through.

A minor stumble of the same sort brought me down at the reading contest at Cambridge, just when I thought that I had got the best of the piece of Shakespeare they had thrown at us in the final round. It was Claudio's famous speech from *Measure for Measure*. 'Ay, but to die and go we know not where; to lie in cold obstruction and to rot,' etc. When film actors have played one of their little scenes and are not completely satisfied with what they have done, they tend sometimes to go on rehearsing it to themselves although there is no way that they will get the chance to shoot it again. So it was with my reading of 'Ay, but to die

. . .' It became like an old friend whom I had let down in some way. And then I picked up a faint rumour which said that *Measure for Measure* was likely to be on Guthrie's programme for his season at the Old Vic. I knew then what I should choose for my audition piece. I would make amends.

When you have crossed Waterloo Bridge you may ignore the pile of concrete on your immediate left and press on in a southerly direction. There is shortly afterwards an agreeable church in the classic style, then, opening up on the right hand side is a grand confusion of approaches to Waterloo railway station, and if you glance to the left you will notice a turning and at the junction facing you stands the modest classic frontage of the theatre you are looking for. With certain important differences it was the same Waterloo Road that I walked down one day in the summer of 1933. But first, as I was actually crossing the bridge itself I stopped long enough to take in one of the most beautiful panoramas in Western Europe, the view towards the City where at that time only half hearted attempts had been made to clutter the skyline, and it remained low enough to allow a number of the old church steeples to assert themselves as well as the silhouette of St. Paul's. At the southern end of the bridge there were unremarkable buildings on the left and only dim terrace houses on the right, on the ground floor of which were some shops where you could buy rubber goods or get yourself tattooed. Then there was a church on the left followed by a confusion of entrances to Waterloo station on the right, but on a scale far less grand than now, and across the road was the Old Vic.

So I reported to the stage door and the porter showed me how to reach the stage, in a corner of which other hopefuls waited for their names to be called out. Guthrie and half a dozen others were sitting in the stalls and gave us all a polite hearing. He himself came round afterwards and spoke to us individually. I do not know what he said to the others but I was invited to follow him to his office where we were to discuss my salary. Well, it was not much of a discussion, he just said rather diffidently that all they could pay me was eight pounds a week and I, not seeing this as an offer to be diffident about, said that that would be quite enough, thank you. So I was in.

A great deal has been written about Lilian Baylis, the dedicated lady who had inherited the Old Vic from her aunt Emma Cons, the creator of what had been in her lifetime a centre of uplifting and temperate entertainment for the needy. Lilian Baylis had been true to her aunt's lofty aims and had converted the theatre into a temple of Shakespeare. She was a religious lady and had the habit of consulting her maker when there were complicated problems to be sorted out. It had been her policy during the years immediately prior to 1932 to develop a team of actors who had been virtually unknown before they came to her theatre. Gielgud and Richardson had made their names at the Old Vic. But now, in spite of the enormous appeal of these two during their occupancy, the lady had come to the conclusion that a change of policy was needed. Perhaps the inclusion in the company of an actor who had already become celebrated in the world beyond Waterloo Road. And it seems that the finger of her god had pointed to Charles Laughton.

And it was the finger of Charles Laughton that had pointed to Tyrone Guthrie. Laughton had elevated tastes, was au courant with developments in all areas of artistic activity. No young director was a figure of such outstanding promise as Guthrie who now proceeded to throw together a strong cast topped by Flora Robson, Athene Seyler, Ursula Jeans, Elsa Lanchester, Roger Livesey, Dennis Arundell, Morland Graham, Frank Napier, Ernest Hare and bottomed by Marius Goring and myself. Occasional visitors during the season included Leon Quartermaine, George Curzon, Clifford Evans, Sam Livesey and Barrie Livesey. In addition we had the use of all the students in the Old Vic Dramatic School which was administered by Murray Macdonald. They were a nice group and keen as mustard but no great talent loomed up

Charles Laughton as Tattle in
Love for Love, *1933*

among them during the current season.

By the time we started rehearsal for the first production I had installed myself in a room in Endell Street, Covent Garden. It was close to Bow Street, in fact I had to walk down Bow Street to get to Waterloo Bridge on my daily walks to my place of work and back. My room was quite large with the customary gas fire and gas ring for cooking and it had a lavatory with a sink. For more extensive washing I had to walk up the street a hundred yards or so to get to the Holborn Public Baths. The most unattractive feature was the jellied eel shop next door. I never made terms with the smell of it.

The heavy guns, that is to say Laughton and Flora Robson, were not brought out for the first production of the season which was *Twelfth Night*. One got the impression too that Guthrie himself did not turn out in full strength and this may have had something to do with the casting of one of the principal women's parts. Mrs Maynard Keynes (Lydia Lopokova) had been entrusted with the part of Olivia. To us, the junior members of the company, this occasioned some surprise. Unfortunately, I never got to know what was going on behind the scenes during this season. I should like so much to have been privy to all the discussions between Laughton and Guthrie for instance, and I would have appreciated a little high level gossip from time to time. Thus I cannot now explain why we found Mme Lopokova in our midst. In earlier life she had been a ballerina in Diaghilev's Russian Ballet, had danced for instance The Lilac Fairy in *The Sleeping Princess* and with Massine the Can Can in *La Boutique Fantasque*. In 1925 she had married Maynard Keynes, the financial wizard of King's College, Cambridge. The fact that she had danced with the Vic-Wells Ballet in the 1932–33 season still did not quite explain, to me at least, her emergence now as a straight actress and later appearances she made at other theatres.

She was tiny and dainty and her oddity was certainly consistent with a lady of exalted position in Illyrian society and perhaps it was the formality of the dancer that stayed with her and prevented her agreeable personality from showing itself. The stage was at its liveliest when occupied by Athene Seyler (Maria) and Roger Livesey (Sir Toby Belch). I played the negligible part of a gentleman attending on the Duke, called Valentine and thus practically invisible. The costumes were rather pretty and the 'architectural permanent setting' designed by Wells Coates made its first appearance. This was intended for use in all the Shakespearean plays that we were to put on. We all felt that the season started seriously with *The Cherry Orchard* which followed. It seemed to me that it was beautifully staged and perfectly cast.

Lopakhin	Laughton
Ranyevskaia	Athene Seyler
Vera	Flora Robson
Anya	Ursula Jeans
Trofimov	Dennis Arundell
Simeonov-Pishchik	Roger Livesey

Firs	Morland Graham
Epihodov	Marius Goring
Yasha	James Mason
Dunyasha	Barbara Wilcox
Governess	Elsa Lanchester
Gaev	Leon Quartermaine

All of us managed to be happy, even the critics.

On the evening of our dress rehearsal I had a conversation which I must report simply because it was the only one in which our much-admired leading actor gave me what could be called professional advice.

It was while we were waiting for our entrance in the last act of the play.

'Why do you put all that muck on your face?' he said.

'You don't like my make-up?'

'No.'

At this time I was distinctly make-up happy. The part of Yasha was that of a valet who had accompanied Lyubov Andreyvna (Ranyevskaia) to Paris where he had learned to dress stylishly and to see himself as a lady-killer. In my mind's eye Yasha was a person who looked like Leonid Kinsky, one of those dazzling character actors who were beginning to appear in the Hollywood films of that time. He had exactly the right looks for playing your Bolsheviks with ideas above their station. These looks included pronounced cheek bones and slanting eyes. So I had emphasized this with the contents of my now well stocked japanned metal make-up box. The face that I had put on was very pale with strongly marked hollows and high lights.

'Well', said I, 'I saw the character as having a rather sallow foxy face like this ...'

'There is nothing that says that he was not a perfectly good looking young man. And your own cheekbones are quite Russian enough. Look, you are very effective in the part and you are not bad looking so you should take advantage of that.'

I was not feeling very happy about having my make-up criticised.

'And there are a lot of people', he went on, 'who will be seeing you in this play, like Frank Joyce, my agent, and Alex Korda. It would be just as well if you looked your best.'

'Yes, I see what you mean ... Er, thank you.'

Next came *Measure for Measure*, which again made everyone happy. Well, I don't know ultimately how happy Guthrie was with my contribution in the role of Claudio. I had been accepted for the company presumably because I had at the audition given an adequate rendering of Claudio's torment in face of death, but poor Guthrie had to spend a long time getting some life into my act. Flora Robson who played Isabella must have been very bored having to be my feed during these extended rehearsals. She was excellent, of course, and so was Laughton who made an extremely credible Angelo. Roger Livesey scored, as they say, in the part of the Duke, but the great success of the production was due to Guthrie's shrewd handling of our permanent setting and the choreography of the large company consisting of over twenty speaking parts and thirty or more nuns, citizens and soldiers. The stage, so effectively filled, and the constant sense of movement were further served by the austere costumes of bold elementary colours that had been designed by John Armstrong who was then one of the leaders of the English chapter of the school of surrealism and incidentally a friend of Laughton.

Then came *The Tempest* as if to douse any exalted notions of our own importance which might have been kindled. This production brought little joy, least of all to the critics. Possible exceptions may have been Livesey as Caliban and Morland Graham as Stephano who, together with an actor called Lawrence Baskcomb who was enlisted as Trinculo, constituted a ribald and happy looking group.

When I had first heard them talk about it, Guthrie was to give lavish production value in the style of a Victorian pantomime and Elsa Lanchester was to make her entrances and exits on a wire in the manner of Peter Pan. I drew an imaginary sketch of her wired up to this end. But the project had suffered a surprising sea change by the time we started to rehearse. No longer the air lift for our Ariel, gone were the pantomimic transformation scenes, all was reduced to surrealism at its most arid. For lack of any means of checking, I will stand by my original assumption that Laughton was to blame for this conception, since his friend, John Armstrong, was put in charge of décor and costume. It seemed to me that if décor was to take on a dreadful simplicity they might just as well have remained faithful to the Wells Coates permanent set which theoretically was to have served all Shakespearean purposes. But then I realised that there was a practical reason for not using it. Vic-Wells was a twin operation. In principle ours, the theatrical company, resided at the Old

Elsa Lanchester as Ariel
(eventually played without benefit of wires)

Vic Theatre in Waterloo Road while the opera company and the ballet company were based at the Sadler's Wells Theatre in Rosebery Avenue. Indeed these were our respective headquarters, but both companies traditionally played spells in both theatres. Some of our theatrical productions escaped this ritual. But *The Tempest* had to play at the Wells and later on so did our *Henry VIII* and this called for handier scenery than our permanent structure.

No matter the reason for it, our setting for *The Tempest* was reduced to an unhelpful simplicity. Nothing could have been more easily transportable than the few simple elements with which we were provided. There was a sky cloth without even the cotton wool cloud that Humphrey Jennings had allowed us in Cambridge for our *Bacchae*; then there were three rectilinear flats on each side of the stage in solid greens and yellows edged with fringes of raffia; and finally there was a small greenish baseball pitcher's mound close to the centre of the stage. For Guthrie to create a fantasy in this desert was surely asking too much. If a modern director were to take it on he would undoubtedly cram the arena with musical and lighting effects. Well, Dennis Arundell did provide excellent and provocative music but not enough to cause a ripple in the prevailing flatness. But there was another serious handicap which slowed us down. Laughton could not find the 'key' for his performance.

It was about this time that Guthrie came to recognise that Laughton had none of the hallmarks of an experienced professional; rather he was a brilliant amateur. He was, I would say, a method actor without the bullshit. He knew his Stanislavsky but was in no way bogged down by the jargon and the mystique that the word method now conjures up. In his search for a personal, emotional identification with the matter at hand he would ask too little of his intellect, preferring to leave it to his intuition. To find a 'key' was his 'open Sesame'.

Everyone knows the story of his preparation for the

delivery of an emotional speech in the attempted film of *I, Claudius*. Before each 'take' he is said to have retired to his dressing room and listened once again to a recording of the abdication speech of Edward VIII. Then brimming with emotion he would rush out and give an ever richer rendering of the tricky material.

Laughton as Prospero

When attempting to bring to life his Prospero, his key was even more elusive. And it was not so much the pursuit of an emotional condition as of an identity. It eluded him to within a few days of our opening. Then suddenly he got it and it took a most surprising form. He had commissioned a beard from his film make-up artist and, lo, the moment he stuck it on he knew that he was there. He had got it! Thereafter he was happy, or seemed so. In certain scenes he was very impressive, as when he quietly and slowly mounted the pitcher's mound and said:

'Ye elves of hills, brooks, standing lakes and groves;
And ye, that on the sands with printless foot
Do chase the ebbing Neptune and do fly him
When he comes back.' etc.

I had to play Prospero at a children's matinée. These
matinées were a regular feature of the Vic and the Wells.
Remember, Lilian Baylis was public spirited to a fault.
There was no segment of the community that did not have
some access to the culture that she was vouchsafing. And
she was untiring in her efforts to coax others to underwrite
her generous gestures. This note appeared in the
programmes:

FREE SEATS – AT THE OLD VIC ONLY
Owing to the generosity of the *Sunday Pictorial* twelve
people (in a special queue) will be admitted without
charge to the Vic Gallery, at all except special
performances, or on Saturday, first night or last nights.
Please bring this kindness to the notice of those who
could not otherwise afford to enjoy the performances.

On the occasion of the children's matinées the stars of
the show were allowed to take the afternoon off. The
practice seemed rather undemocratic to me but it was a
firmly established one. I was not by any means panic-
stricken when I tackled Prospero but I was aware
throughout that I was performing a difficult task quite
ineffectively. Having put myself into his boots I had all the
more respect for Laughton for winning through on the
strength of his presence and his magic beard. And his
severest critics could not take those away from him. At the
very end of the season there was some sort of a special
performance – was it for Shakespeare's birthday? – which
incorporated an act from *Measure for Measure* in order to
display favourably the ensemble work of the full
company. By this time the Laughtons had gone and once

more I was called upon to take over the Laughton part (this was an act in which Claudio did not figure). It was much easier, largely, I suppose, because I was swept along by the lively participation of all the others. But the children's matinée had been by no means easy. This did not however prevent me from becoming in later years wedded to the idea of making a film of *The Tempest* with my friend Michael Powell. As a matter of fact I am still passionately wedded to that notion. But that is another story.

Before I leave *The Tempest* I should mention that Elsa Lanchester, without benefit of wires, made a strangely interesting and angular Ariel. Livesey as Caliban remained resolutely human, but Lanchester far from it. She looked like a lively and attractive mayfly. She was very slim and had at her disposal a rather dotty look which worked to her advantage in certain roles. She had used it effectively in the part of the German governess in *The Cherry Orchard*.

The last work on film that Laughton had performed before coming to the Old Vic was *The Private Life of Henry VIII*. (In fact he took us all up to Elstree one day to have the film run for us before its release. We were impressed by the film and also by our importance for having been so invited.) Therefore since Henry was not only in his mind but also expectantly in the minds of the public, it was thought appropriate that Shakespeare's version be included in our season.

To me the most memorable feature of this production was the enlistment of a strange actor called Robert Farquharson to play the part of Cardinal Wolsey. Tyrone Guthrie carried around in his head an unusual casting directory. It was loaded with persons of unique personality and strange talent, many of whom were not even professional actors. Farquharson, however, was known to have acted professionally and to have drawn attention to himself in a revival of Shelley's play *The Cenci*. Otherwise all we knew of him was that he lived in Florence.

Naturally I could not know how telling his performance was from the point of view of the audience. But to us backstage his personality came through weird and strong. Mine was the part of Thomas Cromwell and therefore I had quite a nice little scene with him. Clearly he did not think so highly of my performance as I did on this unique occasion, and in the middle of the scene when his back was momentarily turned towards the audience he pulled a fierce face and muttered something under his breath. I believed that he was saying 'Hurry up', and this offended me. True I was not playing so important a part as he, but was I not entitled to use my own judgement? And sometimes his own Macready pauses seemed to be going on for ever. On account of this episode I was inclined to agree with some of the junior members of the company who insisted that there was something evil about the man. Christopher Hassall, who was one of our student actors and was soon to become well known as a poet, testified that during one of the performances when the courtiers were solemnly dancing at the king's behest, a gob of spittle from the mouth of Farquharson – he was inclined to spray the occupants of the front row of the stalls – had landed on Hassall's upper lip, and that on the following day an ulcer appeared on the very spot. It was decided too that the man had a certain boyish look which was inconsistent with his advanced years. Another Dorian Gray? And finally it was said, again by Hassall, that they could hear him every night before the performance reciting a strange rune in his dressing room. So, just as we had suspected, he was into Black Magic! But the next day's bulletin let us down badly. Hassall had listened to the rune more attentively. There was no longer anything mysterious about it. It was a vocal exercise. He was intoning the words 'M.A.A.A.AKE F.U.U.U.ULL U.U.U.USE O.O.O.OF YOU.OU.OU.-OUR NA.A.A.A.A.SA.A.AL CA.A.A.VITIE.IE.IES'. This dissipated some of the man's mystery but he continued to repay study.

Laughton and Robson were exactly as impressive as one

expected them to be but the play is not out of Shakespeare's top drawer.

It was during the run of *Henry VIII* that Guthrie discovered that a certain voice coach happened to be in London and recommended that all those with vocal problems take advantage of his presence. He had performed wonders with Guthrie's own voice, he assured us. His speaking voice was clear and strong and we asked him what sort of a problem he had had. Oh, said he, he had not consulted the coach about his speaking voice; it was his singing voice that had given him trouble.

Laughton rehearsing
Henry VIII

And we now learned that his favourite fantasy featured himself as a fabulous baritone spotlit on the stage of the Palladium spellbinding his audience with a repertoire of Irish ballads. 'I have a very powerful voice', he said, 'but unpleasant.'

Solid Yorkshiremen like Laughton and myself were also surprised to learn that this man of theatrical genius was at this point in two minds whether he should press on with his career as a director or drop it in favour of managing the family estate in Ireland. In later years he allowed himself to be lured from his life's work in the theatre by the notion of establishing an Irish jam factory, which ended in disaster.

By now we have reached February 1934. This was the year of the Reichstag Fire in Berlin and the foundation of the Falangist party in Spain. On the other hand Prohibition was repealed in the United States and Roosevelt had introduced the 'New Deal'. Meanwhile at home important events were taking place, like our next production at the Old Vic, which was *The Importance of Being Earnest*. At least I had the part of Merriman, butler, whereas Marius Goring had no part at all. Merriman can do nothing very much since he is only there to announce visitors to the Manor House, Woolton. I had hoped that I would qualify for Lane, manservant, who appears in the first act and has quite an enlightening conversation with John Worthing. Hopes having been dashed I sought ways of making something rewarding out of Merriman. It became an exercise in the application of crêpe hair. I developed a walrus moustache of great distinction. This at least attracted the attention of a critic who wrote in his paper, 'In what English home of this type would you find a butler wearing such a moustache?' I had not actually visited any English homes of that type, but I did not grasp that as an excuse for my lamentable ignorance of English custom. Heavens, I should have known that butlers are born clean shaven and must so remain. Once I had discarded my moustache my interest in the play flagged to such a degree that I failed not once but on two separate occasions to be on the spot to announce the arrivals of such important persons as Flora Robson (Gwendolen) and Athene Seyler (Lady Bracknell).

Livesey scored again as John Worthing, an outsider named George Curzon was enlisted for Algernon and the

Laughtons were extremely good as Canon Chasuble and Miss Prism.

Bracketed with *The Cherry Orchard*, the outstanding success of our season was *Love for Love*, the Wycherley masterpiece. Whereas the classic and impeccable production of *The Importance of Being Earnest* came a few years later when John Gielgud produced it at the Globe Theatre, I do not believe that our *Love for Love* has been surpassed, not even by that excellent production at the Old Vic when Olivier played Mr Tattle and Lynn Redgrave played Miss Prue in 1965.

In 1934 theatrical pioneers were still exploring new ways of making the Restoration playwrights acceptable and attractive to an audience of the twentieth century. Guthrie was one of those pioneers, whereas thirty years later the work had been done and our society had reverted to a set of morals which would have been par for the era of Charles II.

In the thirties the Lord Chamberlain still had wide open eyes and ears. There is a line in *Love for Love* the retention of which would, it was thought, have brought us to an almost embarrassing degree of disrepute. And its removal caused no serious side effects, though I still do not know if it was Guthrie or the Lord Chamberlain or the old lady herself who prescribed the operation. The doddering scientist Foresight, in attempting to smear Mistress Frail and prove her a witch, alleges that she has 'an unnatural tit under her left arm'.

Roger Livesey played the salty character Ben but, not content with just our regular Livesey, Guthrie brought in two more. Barrie Livesey played Valentine Legend, Sam Livesey, their father, played old Sir Samson Legend. There were good parts for all of us. I got to play the servant Jeremy, which made me feel that I was a member of a winning team. Lawrence Baskcomb coaxed a serviceable cockney accent out of me.

Now there remained only for us Shakespeare's famous bad luck play. But I have to put on record that our production of it sprang no immediate disasters, unlike the one that was produced a few years later at the Vic which coincided with the old lady's death.

Ours was not thought by many to have been a success. There were those who were unwilling to accept Laughton as that warlike opportunist. Swordplay did not become him, I have to admit, nor did the Scottish kilt, since he was always a little tubby and our kilts were worn with a simple rough jerkin, and short socks only; there were no picturesque skean dhus or other accoutrements such as are commonly favoured by Highland roosters. But there was a spookiness about this driven man that many found fascinating, and a shrewd handling of the language. A little later, after the season was over, we trooped along to Bush House for a radio performance. Here Laughton spoke with an even more evident relish. It was a foretaste of the Laughton who during World War II was to entertain the American troops by endlessly reading great gobbets of the Bible.

Once more in this our final production Roger Livesey triumphed in the part of Macduff. Laughton's friend Alexander Korda was a frequent visitor throughout the season and shared his admiration for Livesey, at least to the point of giving him a good part in their next film, *Rembrandt*. Livesey played the part of a beggar whom Rembrandt brought in from the streets for use as a model.

Later in the year 1934 Korda also hired me for a part in a film. This was one called *The Return of Don Juan*, the star of which was Douglas Fairbanks Snr. It was based on a whimsical notion of Robert Sherwood's, to the effect that Juan owed his fame and success as a lover as much to the expertise of his sales talk as to his physical prowess. Repeated scenes illustrating his somewhat corny approach accounted for much of the fun. Fairbanks was not quite the actor to play this, since the butt of this comedy was not unlike the image that he had created for himself in the great days when he and Mary Pickford had been the world's sweethearts. He still liked to invite society friends down to the studio and re-enact a scene in which the need to escape from an irate husband caused him to dive through a glazed window. The boys who were working on the film would know that he had this in mind whenever they saw the window being wheeled onto the stage. The society visitors were duly impressed by this display of amazing acrobatic skill and remained so even when the boys of the stage in an effort to spoil his act picked up fragments of broken 'glass' from the floor and started to suck them. It was a sort of candy.

But by the time when this sort of fun was taking place in one studio (the old British National Studio at Elstree) I had been fired. Mine was the part of a youth who, assured that he can take on all-comers as a swordsman, tries to beat Don Juan's record as a cocksman. It turns out that he can't even make it in the first category and an irate husband runs him through. Since there is no one around to identify the corpse it is assumed that it belongs to the notorious Don Juan. Thus, later on when the real Juan, in the course of a pass, tells the girl that he is Don Juan, she just laughs at him. If everyone believes that he is dead, how is poor Juan to prove that he is alive?

So I played the young man for a few days. I got very little assistance from Alexander Korda who was himself directing the film. The unit dawdled until the maestro showed up. In a way this was a blessing, because Georges Perinal, a favourite of Korda's, was the lighting camera-man and he was not one to be rushed. It would be after half past ten, when Korda appeared behind a cloud of expensive cigar smoke. He bade us a brief, friendly good morning, sank into his director's chair and further screened himself behind *The Times*, which held his interest rather more than the film sequence to which he was expected to give his attention. We dragged ourselves through three unexciting days, at the end of which an aide of Korda's called David Cunningham drew me aside and suggested we have a little chat. So I padded after him and had it. What he wanted to say was that they had decided that I was miscast for the part. Oh. But I was not to worry because there would be other little parts later in the filming and even if they did not represent as many days' work as the one of which I was now being deprived they would respect my contract. Oh. It was just a matter of miscasting, I was to understand, it was something that happened all the time.

My contract had been for seven days' work. Having read the script I knew that there were no other suitable 'little parts' which I would want to play. I recognised that in this case 'miscast' was an euphemism for 'lousy' and that the gentlemanly Messrs Korda and Cunningham preferred the euphemistic treatment to the cut and thrust of a few harsh words with an actor's agent. So I matched their gentlemanliness by forgoing the pay that would have accrued from sitting out the balance of my contract and started looking for a job elsewhere. Although I knew in my heart that I must have been totally inadequate in the part, that did not stop me being terribly hurt when in an unexpected manner this truth was thrown at me by someone other than myself. As I was walking up Shaftesbury Avenue I ran into an attractive young woman called Joan Gardiner who was one of the young Korda stars and who later married Zoltan Korda. 'Oh', said she, 'I was so sorry to hear that you're no longer in the film.' (Pause) 'But never mind, I remember how terrible *I* was my *my* first film.' I saw the film when it was completed and my part was played by an actor called Barrie MacKay, and very well indeed, for he had a nice way with comedy.

But before this unfortunate false start to a movie career I acted in another West End play in the late spring of 1934, shortly after our season at the Old Vic. This was *Queen of Scots* by Gordon Daviot (the author of *Richard of Bordeaux*), directed by John Gielgud. This ran no longer than had *Gallows Glorious*. Those concerned with the production were disappointed and surprised. There had been many reasons to expect a fair success. *Richard of Bordeaux* had run for over a year and had made Gielgud the supreme star of the London Theatre. The Queen in our play was played by Gwen Ffrangcon-Davies whose reputation was at its peak and the part of Lord Bothwell was played by Laurence Olivier who had not yet by any means peaked but was already a star with a big following. I believe now that the story of Mary should be handled only with extreme discretion. I do not know of any British dramatist who has succeeded with it. It tells of a series of defeats culminating in deep tragedy. The only character who in a sad way scores is she who remains in the wings, Queen Elizabeth of England. Mary's story, like John Brown's, is the stuff of Grand Opera.

I contributed what I fancied was a 'clever double'. There was a large cast of characters and many scene changes. Consequently I was not the only one who had to play more than one part. My two parts were those of the Earl of Arran, an hysterical young suitor of Mary, and a French valet called Paris in the service of Lord Bothwell. They were quite good parts.

The best thing about the engagement that my memory has to offer was the backstage social scene. Two very nice women, Peggy Webster and Mercia Swinburne, played the Queen's two ladies-in-waiting and had much off-stage time on their hands. This they put to good use in the form of never failing refreshment for those others whose appearances on stage were brief. These included even Olivier, since Bothwell dominates only the second half of the story. Not only was Olivier well placed in the English theatre but he had already enjoyed a taste of success in Hollywood. He was genial and friendly and provided the best entertainment in our group. But of all the stories they told, only a personal anecdote from the much loved Felix Aylmer has a place in a history book like this.

As a young man during World War I he had served in a minesweeper off the coast of Scotland. He told us that he had been on the bridge with the captain one night, and the captain had told him long stories about his peace time adventures with the fishing fleets. He was a talkative good-

Gwen Ffrangcon-Davies as
Queen of Scots, *1934*

natured man and finally he had paused and said to Felix, 'And what was your line of work before the war started?'

'Oh, well, sir, I was-er-an actor.'

'What was that?'

'I was an actor, sir.'

That was the end of the conversation. And the captain did not address young Felix for over a week, merely throwing a grim, disapproving glance in his direction from time to time. Then one day when of necessity they were standing beside each other on the bridge the captain turned to Felix, fixed his blue eyes on him and said:

'Paintin' yer face to make the people laff at ye!'

Not long after the play had closed and I suffered the indignity of being sacked from the *Don Juan* film, I was asked by John Gielgud, who had directed *Queen of Scots*, to play Rosencrantz or Guildenstern in his forthcoming production of *Hamlet*. This was to be a commercial undertaking and since he had already gained enormous kudos from playing Hamlet on two occasions at the Old

Vic it seemed to me that it might well run forever and I would have but a slender chance to rise from the ranks of R & G. In spite of my enormous admiration for Gielgud, I was now in too much of a hurry to wish to settle down and learn it the slow way. I wanted some experience in playing leading parts. If only I could get myself into one of the superior provincial repertory companies, that would be the thing.

8/Dublin

One of my friends at the Old Vic with whom I kept in touch was a girl student named Valentine Richmond. She told me that she had got herself a job at the Cambridge Festival Theatre as assistant stage manager. Also, knowing that I too was looking for a good repertory away from London, she told me that she had mentioned this to an Irish actress called Betty Chancellor, and had learned from her that there was to be renewed activity at the Gate Theatre in Dublin. I was given the name of the key man at that Theatre, Hilton Edwards, and wrote to him boasting of my vast experience. I received an encouraging reply. The first production of the new season was to be *Julius Caesar*, he said, and there remained many parts still to be cast, from Brutus all the way down. My return ticket and living expenses would be guaranteed no matter what part I ended up with; but what he was really looking for was a Brutus. So off I went.

The history of the Gate Theatre has been magnificently covered in *All for Hecuba* by the late Micheàl Macliammoir who was the partner of Hilton Edwards. They had started the Gate Theatre in 1928. So they were now beginning their seventh season, powered by an encyclopedic knowledge of world drama and a bubbling enthusiasm. They had called it the Gate Theatre by way of homage to Peter Godfrey who had founded the Gate Theatre in Villiers Street in London. Godfrey, Hilton Edwards and Terence Gray had all originally been animated by a spirit of avantgardism and the stage of the Dublin Gate had groaned under the weight of Toller and Karel Capek. But it had a considerable advantage over the earnest minority theatres in England in that the principal serious theatre in Dublin was firmly established as a folk theatre, Irish plays for the Irish. This was the Abbey Theatre, the great and lively days of which were at this time only a memory. There were two commercial theatres in the city, the Gaiety and the Olympia. Respectable companies bringing commercial successes settled for a while at the Gaiety, while the Olympia played Music Hall and, as Christmas approached, pantomime starring Jimmy O'Dea and Noel Purcell.

Now the Gate under its energetic leadership had levelled off at an easy-to-take, slightly above mid-brow level. Micheàl Macliammoir was the star, let there be no doubt about that, but other actors were encouraged to shine, at least for limited periods. During the previous season the great Orson Welles had been so encouraged. As all serious Orson Welles watchers have learned, he represented himself on arrival in Dublin as a young man who was winding up a cultural tour of Ireland in the company of, perhaps in those days even on the back of, a donkey. He told Hilton and Micheàl that he was some years older than he actually was and listed an impressive number of Shakespearean roles in which he claimed to have appeared as a professional actor. They were to learn later that it was actually at his school that he had played them. Just as they were now looking for an actor to play Brutus, they had been at the inception of the previous season looking for an actor to be acceptable in the role of the decadent and powerful Duke in Feuchtwanger's *Jew Süss*. And here he was. True he was younger than the age specified by Feuchtwanger but he was so perfect in all other details that no one was likely to quibble. During the summer of 1934 Hilton and Micheàl had visited this prodigy in the United States and they had exchanged views on the subject of Shakespeare's *Julius Caesar*, which Welles was to produce with spectacular success in New York in 1939 and with which The Boys, as people referred to them, were to open their impending season.

Hilton Edwards, Dublin, 1934

The theatre was run by a triumvirate. The third partner was Edward, the Earl of Longford who was the brother of the present peer, the beloved Lord Porn. Edward, our Earl, contributed to the set-up a devotion to Ireland's history, culture and native crafts, some financial aid and a friendly presence in the front of the house; also, juxtaposed every night with his wife Christine, a friendly presence in the fourth row of the stalls. A partnership of three seldom lasts for ever but during its initial period, which happily included our season, the theatre rested securely on this tripod.

Micheàl was a real artist of many facets. He was a good writer and an excellent stage designer. I got to know first of all the actor, the man with the splendid voice, and inevitably, soon afterwards, the stage designer. The set which he gave us was simple and extremely practical. It might not have served other minded directors, but he knew his Hilton's intentions and capabilities. He also knew what the two of them could do with their limited lighting resources. The theatre was quite small. It was to be found in an attractive Georgian building called the Rotunda, at the far end of O'Connell Street, next to the Hospital. A capacity audience was about three hundred. The stage was reasonably broad but so shallow that it was often difficult

109

for the actors to squeeze from one side of the stage to the other behind the scenery. There was not enough height to allow scenery to be 'flown' nor was there ever the possibility of constructing a permanent set on two levels, a trick which producers of Shakespeare's plays were already re-learning. But there was no problem that Micheàl would not find an ingenious means of overcoming.

A young man called David Basil Gill was a powerful Cassius, Coralie Carmichael was Portia, Ria Mooney was Calpurnia and Hilton Edwards was Julius Caesar. The actors constituted a lively and effective team. On his first appearance, before and after his athletic bout, Micheàl as Mark Antony was costumed in leopard skin and looked like something from a painting by Alma Tadema. The central section of the play belongs to the actor who plays Antony; Micheàl constructed a glorious thing of it, and was appropriately applauded. To my surprise I was also very well received as Brutus, not only by the public but by the critics too.

Micheàl wrote in his book, *All for Hecuba*: 'In London we engaged a young actor called James Mason, whose icy English smile froze my heart, but whose Brutus, in spite of a passionless voice, I admired immensely.'

Much as I love Dublin I think that it is a city that breeds bitchiness. Well, that is the way it seemed to me in 1934 and I see no reason for it to have changed. And I truly mean it when I say that I love Dublin. It is just the right size for a city, neither too big nor too small. You have a good idea of what is going on in every corner of it. Apart from the regular contingent of saints and scholars which the constitution demands you also can find any number of colourful politicos, eccentric artists, sports of every complexion, con men and boozers. What more could one ask for? I mention bitchiness because I still believe that the only rational explanation for the good reviews which I received was that the writers felt an impulse to tease the man who had been the unchallenged star of the Gate since its inception. And I'll bet that my explanation coincided with Micheàl's.

In spite of the fact that I did not entirely believe my own press reviews, they gave me a dose of what I needed at that time; they engendered a particle of self esteem, they made me feel that I was welcome and encouraged me to enjoy myself.

I was sorry to find that the Abbey Theatre Company was touring the United States at that time and that the Theatre itself was temporarily occupied by a second rate company who were attempting an international repertoire, so that I never got to see the classic Abbey Theatre stock in trade performed on its own ground. But there was a large number of writers and other gifted people who had a close relationship with our theatre. There was Denis Johnston who had already written two of his best plays, *The Moon in the Yellow River* and *The Old Lady Says No*. He was then married to Shelah Richards, the actress and stage director, and she in turn was the aunt of the then very young Geraldine Fitzgerald. There was eccentric writer and amateur economist Francis Macnamara and his friend the lovely Iris O'Callahan who from time to time played small parts at the Gate. And there was Terence de Vere White, the critic and novelist, and our own Lord Longford and his wife Christine, who was perhaps the most entertaining of the lot. Both the Longfords were playwrights and fed the Gate with occasional material. Later during the present season we performed Lord Longford's *Ascendancy* and during one of the previous years they had done the same author's *Yahoo*, in which Hilton Edwards had had the fun of playing Dean Swift.

Hilton was provided with the same sort of fun, but funnier, in one of our productions which followed the successful *Julius Caesar*. He played Sir John Brute in Vanbrugh's *Provok'd Wife*. Micheál and I played the swaggering restoration fops whose respective characters corresponded with their given names, Constant and Heartfree. Hilton had the best of it. He was a good actor and being one of the bosses he had the advantage of being able to cast himself in whatever role took his fancy. If he had pursued a commercial acting career in London the

111

roles he played would have been more strictly in keeping with his appearance. He was a Londoner and when he started his career he had the suggestion of a cockney accent, which coming out from under a big nose gave people the impression that he was an East End Jew. He tells us that he spent a lot of time apologising for not being Jewish.

As a Christmas show we did the Victorian melodrama *The Drunkard*, in which Micheàl played the Drunkard himself, looking just the way Jack Yeats might have painted him. Thereafter we delivered H. I. Hsiung's *Lady Precious Stream*, G. K. Chesterton's *Magic*, a nice version of *Wuthering Heights* which had been written by Ria Mooney and a Mr Strauffer and in which Ria played the part of Cathy, and, finally, *Othello*.

While I was having the time of my life in Dublin, some interesting things were going on at the Gate Theatre in London, which was now very different from the temple of modernism that Peter Godfrey had mounted in one of the arches of the railway bridge which springs from Charing Cross Station. It was being run by a producer called Norman Marshall whom I had first met at Cambridge. Marshall's standards were just as high as his predecessor's but less lofty. It was a 'club' and people could not buy tickets at its Box Office unless they were members. The great thing about a Theatre Club was that the Lord Chamberlain could not reach in and exercise rights of censorship over the plays that were produced in it. Worthwhile modern plays, especially those from foreign parts which would have run into censorship problems if presented in public theatres on a point of moral or political content, found an invaluable haven in these Clubs. Plays were often being presented under the auspices of a Club even in a regular public theatre on a Sunday where normally the law forbade Sunday performances. The Theatre Club was a blessing for producers, playwrights and members alike. I had seen Norman Marshall just before leaving for Dublin and he had said that he would let me know if there was to be a good part for me in any of his future productions. Now, after a rewarding time in Dublin, as our season approached its conclusion, I wrote to Marshall to say that I would soon be back in London, and almost at once he told me that he was soon going to present a programme made up of short plays that Laurence Housman had written about episodes in the life of Queen Victoria. No such play could obtain a licence for public presentation because it was against the law to produce a play featuring a member of the Royal Family within two generations of the Reigning Monarch, who at this time was George V. Only in a Theatre Club was Victoria fair game. And the part for me? Why, Prince Albert of course! Didn't I think so? This was not by any means an official offer, just a conversation between friends, but it seemed to me to be more than adequate reason to hasten home. The conversation took place while I was playing Cassio in *Othello*. I told Hilton Edwards my promising news from London, and he said that I should feel free to leave whenever I wanted, provided that he had time to find someone to replace me. A good actor named Fred Johnson was instantly available and ready to take over within the week, and I found myself already regretting my haste. I had of course made a sensible practical decision but I hated to say goodbye to such friends and such a city.

Myself when young

113

But I did. And the funny thing was that another Prince Albert had stolen a march on me. Norman Marshall greeted me warmly when I showed up at his theatre in Villiers Street, and could not wait to tell me about his discovery being just as aware as I was myself of the non-binding nature of our previous discussion about Prince Albert. The name of the young man he had found was Vincent Price, who had studied in Germany, could speak with a German accent and whose voice and deportment instantly suggested Saxe Coburg Gotha. 'Oh good,' I said. Pamela Stanley was to play Queen Victoria. She would be wonderful. Good. I saw the play when it opened and they were both excellent.

I must, it seems, have kept a firm grip on most of the salary I had been paid in Dublin since there was nothing else coming in until quite late in this year 1935.

At the Lyric Theatre a play called *The Dominant Sex* had been enjoying a long run. In celebration of this a party was given on the stage of the theatre by the cast, the principal members of which were Diana Churchill, Ellen Pollock, René Ray and an actor called Richard Bird. I was taken to the party by some friends who had been invited by Diana Churchill. After we had been there for some time René Ray, whom I had not previously met, introduced herself to me and said that there was a gentleman who wanted to meet me and could she bring him over? I said yes, and she skipped away and came back with the man whose name was Al Parker; then she skipped off and left us together.

Mr Parker, who was American, did not waste time with small talk, he got right down to the subject which interested him and that was me. One of his first questions was, had I ever been in movies? I said no. There was no point in telling every stranger I met about my short career with Alexander Korda. In describing our meeting later Al Parker was in the habit of saying that I looked at him as though he had peed down my leg, which always puzzled me not only because of the strangeness of the expression

114

but also because I had assumed that I had been on my best party-going behaviour at the time, genial, affable, polite. It was true, though, that I was not used to Americans and maybe, yes maybe, a touch suspicious. He encouraged me to tell him about my acting experience and I had no difficulty in supplying all relevant details. Then he said that if I had no objection he would like to make a screen test of me and gave me a brief account of his present activities. He was, he said, in the process of making a series of films for the American Company, Fox, and on behalf of this company he and his associates had taken over a small studio at Wembley which was now known as the Fox British Film studio. Were there any scenes from plays in which I had appeared that I would like to use for my test? It didn't matter, he'd find a scene from one of the films which he had made. But first he would like me to work on some scene of my choice and if I came to his office, we could work on it together.

All this was done. Reverting again to Mr Parker's later descriptions of our early encounters he was in the habit of saying that I had come to his office and read the scene I had chosen and that I was *terrible*. This again puzzled me because if I had been that terrible he would surely have given me a hint in his reaction, even though refraining sensibly from coming down too hard on me. Anyway it was decided in quick succession that he would give me the film test and sign me up for a long term contract. This brought his partner into play. He was a man called Ernest Gartside who could be described as the executive producer of all the products that they were making at Wembley. According to this contract my salary was to increase each year until it reached an unimaginable largesse (very little by modern standards) and the parent company, the Hollywood Fox, would be entitled to pick me up and transport me to Ultima Thule. Another person whom it called into play was my agent.

While I was at the Old Vic, Charles Laughton introduced me to his agent Frank Joyce, of the firm Joyce and Selznick. This was a Hollywood outfit which had recently opened an office in London. Myron Selznick's name was to become even more legendary than that of Frank Joyce in Hollywood. The story goes that Herman Mankiewicz, whose Hollywood career was never a smooth ride, complained to Myron Selznick, who was his agent, that he was asking too high a salary for him – say two hundred thousand dollars per assignment. Slamming the top of his desk Selznick is said to have replied 'Even if it keeps you out of work for the rest of my life, I'm going to get you that two hundred thousand dollars!' Sounds crazy but I, knowing Hollywood, believe it.

I never saw this Selznick, though I met his brother David the producer when I went to Hollywood, by which time Myron was dead. And I only saw Frank Joyce once or twice prior to my being fired by Korda. He had then settled back in Hollywood and had been replaced by another American in the London office with which my own contract was still in force. When Parker was in the process of signing me up for Fox he asked me for the name of my agent. He then contacted this new man at the agency whose name was Harry Ham and asked him to discuss the contract on my behalf.

'What's the name of this actor?'

'Mason. James Mason.'

'Never heard of him.'

'He has had a contract with your firm since the beginning of last year.'

'Never heard of . . .'

'Well just look him up in your books! I'll call you again tomorrow!'

Parker slammed down the telephone in disgust. It was my first genuinely Hollywood experience.

The Hollywood options were of no great interest to me. But I was keen to have some experience in films because I thought it was such a wonderful medium, though I was still not seduced by what Hollywood was offering us. And Al Parker himself did not attempt to make a case for its way of life. Indeed as I could best piece together his story he had been a victim of the factionalism which has always been rife in that area. He said something to me at this time which may be regarded as an essential Hollywood truism.

'When they put the Indian sign on you, you're finished.'

Al was quick to recognise my unplumbed naivety and I thought that he took pleasure in making my eyebrows go up. For instance when he would talk about these guys who, when they went to a party in that town would drop a coca cola bottle into a pocket of their pants to make an impression on their partners when they danced, could he be serious?

His own story went something like this. He was a New York actor. When the need for actors on the West coast was clearly no longer limited to cowboys and comics, Al Parker responded to the call along with his friends Douglas Fairbanks and John Barrymore. Very early on he made the grade as a director. His best known film was *The Black Pirate* starring Douglas Fairbanks, a landmark in film-making, since it was the first film ever to be made on two strip technicolor throughout its length. He was also the first director to give an important part in a film to Rudolph Valentino. He was riding high and had taken time off for a trip to the Far East in the company of the Fairbankses and Jack Pickford, Mary's brother, when the crash of 1929 came along; so he was hardly in a position to withdraw his money from his tottering bank or whatever the smart people in New York were doing to save it from going down the drain. But worse was to come. When one faction superseded the one to which he belonged in his studio, his option was not taken up and he was out. Although, as things finally turned out, Hollywood did very well during the depression, it gave way to a characteristic panic during the early stages. For a while things did not look good for Parker. But then his friend Winfield Steeham offered him a job directing tests, which he accepted on condition that after the first year he be given a directorial assignment on a feature film. And it was during his tenure of this contract that Parker came to England to make tests of actors whom he considered suitable for roles in the upcoming production of *Cavalcade*. The idea then came to him that Fox should have their own studio in England for the manufacture of British made films and so fulfil the obligation imposed by the new British Quota regulations.

Prior to 1933 a 'Distributors' Quota' had already been in force. Distributors of foreign product were obliged to handle a certain percentage of British product. But the new regulations applied equally to the exhibitors. British films actually had to be shown in all cinemas for a given number of hours per day. Many production companies, reacting to this in the most pragmatic manner, manufactured 'quota quickies' of such low quality that they were fit to run only during the morning when the cleaners were at work. No matter the quality, it was in the interests of all the American companies to make or acquire some British footage which they could offer for rental along with their own product.

But Al Parker being a true movie maker was not the one to approach the matter cynically. Fox British films were to be the very best that they could turn out for the strictly limited budgets that the home office allowed them. Parker wanted to make a little masterpiece of each of his pictures but it was not with the intention of re-establishing credit in Hollywood, it was just because he was a professional who loved movies. Once he had settled down in England he had no intention of facing the Hollywood jungle again. He spoke with the greatest affection of the friends he had known in New York and had a soft spot for the showbusiness glamour of that city, but he had no wish to go back there either, except for the briefest of visits.

So this was the man who 'discovered' me. Movie stars were always being discovered in those days, and Parker had some impressive credits as a discoverer. Top of the list were Valentino and William Powell. Many others followed. Now he was discovering me. This process extended even to giving advice on hair styling – would it be a good idea to shave back your hair line at the sides? I didn't know. Would it? And your eyebrows should be plucked a little here ... and here ...

One day, walking down the street, he said:

'I think you should change your name.'

'Oh.'

'Yes.'

'Er what do you suggest I change it to?'

'Yes, well, I think that JOHN Mason would look good.'

'Why is that?'

'Well ... there is a well-known critic in New York whose name is John Mason Brown. If your name were John Mason the people would feel that they had heard it some place before. They'd get to feel familiar with your name much more quickly.'

I was not impressed by this reasoning.

The first film was called *Late Extra*. There was already in Hollywood a trend favouring stories of crime in which the really smart work of detection was done either by a cub reporter or a private dick, rather than by the regular forces of law and order. I was the cub reporter. The News Editor was the superb Alastair Sim. A large reward for the information leading to the arrest of the bad guy is offered by our paper, and this tempts a lady reader to come forward hopefully and get shot for her trouble, but not before Jim Martin has arrived and taken down her statement. He then tracks down the bad guy and the thing ends in a blaze of fisticuffs. Parts were found for Cyril Cusack, Michael Wilding and Donald Wolfit and our leading lady was Virginia Cherrill who only quite recently had played opposite Charlie Chaplin in the best feature film he ever made, *City Lights*.

As a beginner at this class of work I was inclined, when making an exit, just to drop out of the side of the frame as if tugged. Al drew attention to the fact that when a person leaves a room he invariably *looks* where he is going. So on such occasion he would drive this lesson home by repeating like a military command 'Look . . . Turn . . . Go!' There was not much else that my first film taught me. I was repelled by the thick yellow make-up we all had to wear at that time. The sound recordist had difficulty with my sibilants. He noticed that one of my lower teeth sticks out more than it should and persuaded me to lodge a piece of chewing gum or other foreign body behind it in order to correct this fault. But when I worked in a different studio the problem stayed behind at Wembley.

The different studio just referred to found itself at Walton-on-Thames where I was employed by an outfit called George Smith Enterprises whose quota pictures were priced more reasonably than those of Fox but still not down to the level of 'quota quickies'. Also the shooting schedule was shorter. My first at Walton was called *Twice Branded*. This done, I returned to Wembley for Al Parker's next, which was called *Troubled Waters*. Once more we had Virginia Cherrill as leading lady, ever more glamorous since she was shortly to become the Countess of Jersey. A rather good actor, Raymond Lovell, played the heavy and otherwise the cast contained less promising talent than had the cast of *Late Extra*. There was a new young cameraman who was good looking and a popular man in the unit. His name was Roy Kellino.

Raymond Lovell

120

None of us ever knew precisely how long one of Al Parker's films would take to shoot. The studio manager thought that he knew, and so did Ernest Gartside. But that meant that they were conversant with the schedule, the printed listing of what scenes would be shot on which days, and what would be the total number of days. But the relevant schedule was one that existed only in Al Parker's mind. As shooting advanced from day to day our director would become progressively dissatisfied with the scenario from which we were working. He could not stop himself making the little improvements which occurred to him. In fact he began to shoot 'off the cuff' as we used to say. The term is not much used nowadays since once the modern film has surmounted the first hurdle and, by some miracle, become fully financed, then the budgetary restraints are negligible, and the director feels free to improvise. But in those days budgets and schedules were sacred, especially if you were in the quota film game. So Al's habit of shooting off the cuff did not go down very well with the production staff. They would try to extract some information about latest script changes from the continuity girl but she was usually equally in the dark.

The problem was that Gartside and his aides only allowed a minimal break between the termination of shooting on one film and the first shooting day of the next. So finally desperate measures were called for and Gartside or an aide would tell Al that at the end of the following day his sets would be struck, whether he had finished shooting in them or not. In such a case Al had no choice but to continue shooting throughout the night and throughout the following day until the wrecking crew came in.

This situation had arisen during the last two days of *Late Extra*. We were at it for thirty-six hours with no more than a short tea break from time to time. We, the actors, had the best of it because in normal times we seldom need to be constantly on the alert. There are those periods for instance when the cameraman is arranging the lighting for the next scene and uses the actor's 'stand-in' to move

121

around and stand or sit or lie down just as the actor himself will have to. Also, in the case of this actor, he had to take time off to shave.

And now *Troubled Waters* had already shot several hours overtime even before the threat had become really serious. When we knew that this was going to happen all who had wives to prepare their evening meals would telephone to say they would be late. On each such occasion Kellino's wife had received the news with mounting exasperation. And on the final most exasperating occasion she decided to descend upon the studio some time after midnight and throw such dark looks at Al Parker that he would feel obliged to call it a day. I had heard them talk about this wife of Kellino's. She was, they said, the daughter of Isidore Ostrer, big man in Gaumont British; she was one of the much publicised baby stars under contract to Gaumont British and had even played an important part, that of Süss's daughter, in the lavish production they had made in 1932 of Feuchtwanger's *Jew Süss*.

And now on this particular night she was on view at our humble studio. Someone pointed her out to me. 'That's Pamela Ostrer', he said. She was standing in the vicinity of Al Parker who nevertheless remained unruffled. She was darkly good looking, slim and simply dressed in an outfit that had an expensive look. I did not get to talk to her that night, but not long afterwards the people in whose house I was staying said they were having a party and was there anyone that I wanted to ask? I said I would like to ask Roy Kellino our cameraman, and when I spoke to him on the telephone I suggested that he bring his wife if he wanted to. She did not appreciate being invited on this not-that-it-matters basis, she told me later, but she came along to the party just the same and it was an easy evening. I had invited her in this over-casual manner to cover up the fact that I was much more interested in having her turn up at the party than Kellino himself. I got to see quite a lot of them after that.

122

I made another film at Walton-on-Thames which was a little better than the previous one. It was called *Prison Breaker*, a story that concerned the difficulties of a young man who had been gaoled for breaking the law in the interests of the Secret Service and of one of his colleagues in the Service who felt that the least they could do was to help the poor fellow break out. It was quite a sensible little effort directed by a man of cultured tastes named Adrian Brunel.

Then back to Wembley for my third film with Al Parker, *Blind Man's Bluff*. It was the story of a man (Basil Sydney) who was struck with blindness, but whose eyesight after a while began to return. He made a snap decision not to confide in anyone, not even his wife (Enid Stamp Taylor); I should say least of all to his wife, because it occurred to him that it might be rewarding to make a study of her conduct while she imagined that he was still blind. When all was revealed, she found herself in a heap of trouble. Other parts, less interesting, were played by myself, and by Al's latest discovery, Barbara Greene.

Just as I was beginning to fear that the movie world had no more to offer than an endless alternation of Wembley and Walton a new American materialised in England. No one knew anything about him but his advertised intention was to make a big film of the English classic *The Mill on the Floss*. Soon I was being paged for the part of Tom Tulliver. It was clear that my immediate employers, Fox British, had loaned my services to George Smith Enterprises for the two films which we had shot at Walton, and so I had no hesitation in asking that they loan me out again for this big project. Unfortunately the request synchronised with the completion of Al's plans for his next Fox picture; I was to play his young hero and he did not want to relinquish me. I had not expected this display of possessiveness. I pointed out to him that *The Mill on the Floss* represented a great opportunity for me, I would be moving into the world of *big* pictures. Hadn't he read the list of important actors and actresses who had already been signed up for it? Frank Lawton, Victoria Hopper, Geraldine Fitzgerald, Fay Compton, Griffith Jones, Sam Livesey, J. H. Roberts, Mary Clare, Athene Seyler, Amy Veness, Felix Aylmer, Eliot Makeham, William Devlin, Ivor Barnard, David Horne, O. B. Clarence, Cecil Ramage?

That's pretty good, isn't it, I said. But the fact that I was wound up about the bigness and importance of this opportunity came over to Al as an unwarranted belittling of the work that he was doing for me. I realise now that he must have been deeply insulted. I should not have treated this proud man as if he was a mere mass producer of quota films, even if at this stage of his career it was true. Next time I saw him he announced sulkily that he had recommended the deal to Gartside, on condition that he, Parker, be allowed to handle the negotiation. So it was settled. He discovered an actor called Donald Tidbury to replace me as his leading man and persuaded him to change his name to Donald Grey.

About this time my old friend Leonard Sachs told me that he and his friend Peter Ridgeway had found a charming little intimate musical play by a Hungarian writer, Ladislav Fodor, which they intended to present at the Arts Theatre on two successive Sundays under Theatre Club rules; since there was a part for me, would I like to read it? Most decidedly I would. They did not yet have all the money they needed and had no leading lady; perhaps I would be able to think of someone.

I read the script and it registered as Hungarian and cute, words which at that time were almost synonymous with 'good'. So I said to Leonard Sachs that a young actress, Pamela Ostrer, had done some work in films and had been very well received in *Jew Süss*, but that I did not know if she had ever acted on stage nor if she could sing. I said it might be worth his while to talk to her, and if she liked the idea, he might even talk her into putting up a little money. She evidently came through with a contribution – it was not an expensive show – and we were into rehearsals the following week. Those members of the public who were advantageously seated attested that Pamela sang her number very prettily. I also sang in one – or was it two? – of the numbers and particularly enjoyed, in the course of the one that I remember, being allowed to make lightning sketches on big blocks of paper that were pinned to the walls of the set. (We were all supposed to be artists living in garrets.) The experiment was considered quite a cute little Hungarian style success, though not to the point of giving Sachs and Ridgeway much of a leg up. But by sheer grit they made it as impresarios not long afterwards. They opened a sort of beer hall-cum-entertainment-parlour overlooking the vegetable market in Covent Garden and called it *Evans' Late Joys* which became very popular and gave birth to Leonard Sachs's ineluctable Music Hall Act which will survive us all.

Roy Kellino had told me that in his opinion Pamela was not overloaded with acting talent. This did not stop me from undertaking several theatrical ventures with her during the next two years. We even wrote a couple of plays together, the first of which, *Flying Blind*, was performed at the Arts Theatre under Theatre Club rules once more. A young man called Martin Solomon financed the offering and even submitted it to the Lord Chamberlin with a view to putting it on commercially. We were surprised to learn that we were guilty of a shocking indecency. The play, a light comedy, dealt with a relationship between an airline pilot and a married woman – although it would have made no difference from the point of view of the Lord Chamberlain if she had been unmarried. She had a teenage sister who had no illusions about what was going on between the two and kept ribbing her. Now this was construed by the Lord Chamberlain as an instance of voyeurism. Nowadays this has become a practically universal foible but at that time it was a minority fad. I had to have someone explain to me what the word meant.

Nigel Balchin, who was a Cambridge friend of mine, wrote a play for us called *Miserable Sinners*. He was to become an enormously skilful novelist but I don't think that he ever wrote a really good play let alone a successful one. Perhaps ours was the best of them. Pamela and I also made a quick trip to Dublin to appear together in a version of Jane Austen's *Pride and Prejudice*. She played Jane quite effectively to Betty Chancellor's excellent Elizabeth. By this time the triumvirate had come unstuck. Half the year the Rotunda was occupied by Hilton Edwards and Micheàl Macliammoir, the other half by Lord Longford who presented our *Pride and Prejudice*.

Somewhere along the line we also appeared in a play at the Q Theatre in London called *A Man who has Nothing*. It was about a young crazy man, just crazy enough to make him interesting. It was directed by Gabriel Toyne and one of the actresses was Maire O'Neill, whose name in print seldom appears but to be followed by the words 'the sister of Sara Allgood', which must have been very boring for her, to say the least. True Sara Allgood was the more famous – had she not appeared in films in Hollywood? – but Maire was a darling and a very moving actress too. In one scene she had to try to lull the crazy fellow to sleep, and she came out with a lullaby that I never heard before nor since:

There was an old woman went up in a blanket
Seventeen times as high as the moon
Where she was going I couldn't imagine
But in her hand she carried a broom.
Old woman, old woman, old woman, says I,
Where are ye goin up so high?
To sweep the cobwebs off the sky
And I'll be down tomorrow bye 'n' bye.

Eventually Al Parker saw to an appropriate loan-out arrangement so that I could work in the great production of George Eliot's *Mill on the Floss* with that impressive cast of actors and actresses. The director was Tim Whelan, an American with Hollywood experience. We worked at a studio called Sound City which was in the grounds of a mid-nineteenth century country house at Shepperton in Surrey. It had extensive grounds with ancient trees overhanging a versatile piece of water which could be dressed as a lake or a river depending on the exigencies of the plot. In later years the studio acquired several grand new stages and changed its name to Shepperton Studios. But in 1938 it was plain old Sound City and the piece of water served as the River Floss on one of the banks of which the set department constructed an attractive mill with, elsewhere on the estate, further segments of convincing Olde Englande. Our producer, John Clein, ran into financial difficulties as the shooting proceeded. Payments became unpunctual, which is something that Hollywood technicians cannot stand. Thus Tim Whelan was the first to protest and when it became clear that a sound economy was unlikely to be restored, he walked out. We took our directions thereafter from a series of replacements, one of whom was the film cutter. Another was an elderly American whom Clein had found and who had directorial experience; there was no doubt about that, but one wondered how long ago his last assignment had been, using as he did the jargon of the silent era. 'Jimmy,' he said to me one day, 'in this scene you just have to walk out there and when you are in the middle of the stream, you pause, turn towards the camera and *read your title*.'

No one else in the cast or crew followed Tim Whelan's example and I do not know how many of them received their full pay. I do know that Fox British was paid for the loan of my services and that the film was finished and released and reviewed, and about fifteen years later showed up on American television. It was not very good.

Another film that I made in 1936 was *The Secret of Stamboul*, an assignment that took me on a short visit to Istanbul – so short indeed that there was no time for the most modest demands of tourism. I hardly got beyond the architectural ingenuity of Santa Sophia and a lasting taste for yoghourt. Back at Sound City, the studio in which once again I found myself, the film became a source of mounting pleasure. The director was one of the Hungarian contingent whose invasion had been spearheaded by Alexander Korda. This was Andrew (Bundy) Marton. The film being based on a book by Dennis Wheatley called *The Eunuch of Stamboul,* it was no surprise that the leading part was that of the eunuch and called for the services of a character actor. This was Frank Vosper who was just about to terminate a very successful career on stage. He played the part with a bald wig – it was not yet obligatory for film actors to shave their heads when affecting baldness – with a high pitched mysteriously accented voice and lifts in his shoes. He was not the only one to tower over me. The worst offender was the one who played my constant companion in the film, Peter Haddon. It was a real pleasure to act in scenes with Kay Walsh and not only because she was petite. During my last scene with her as we were waiting for the camera to turn she said suddenly, 'Hasten Mason fetch a basin.' Then she apologised, 'I just had to say it. I've been holding it in all through the picture.' Other than in this isolated instance she was a bright and witty petite lady. On the other hand Valerie Hobson who had top billing in the film, tended to croon when we were waiting for the camera crew to organise themselves. She was rising rapidly as a film star and had a crooning voice that had been endorsed by Bing Crosby himself. She had been to Hollywood already and sung on his programme. In the book called *The Films of James Mason,* which I lean on as a source from which to quote critics' opinions, I find that the *New York Times* man had this to say, 'A foully acted British thriller. Biologically and cinematically speaking, the film is still in the egg-laying stage.' I am glad that I did not read this in 1938. I might have been deeply hurt.

In the same year I appeared briefly in a film of some distinction called *Fire Over England.* I played the part of a bearded young English spy in the employ of Philip II of Spain. He was killed in the first reel of the film at which point the Earl of Leicester, played by Leslie Banks, thought it would be a crafty idea to cause a thoroughly loyal young man (Laurence Olivier) to grow a beard, masquerade as the dead spy, penetrate Philip's court and come back with some good secrets. As can be seen, mine was a vitally important role, but after one day's and one night's shooting it was all over.

I appeared at greater length in something called *The High Command*. The little Ronald Colman moustache which had made a tentative debut in *The Secret of Stamboul* was allowed to emerge again. Having not read the *New York Times* review of *The Secret of Stamboul* I thought it had served me well in that film in spite of its distressing habit of breaking continuity from one day to another.

My record up to this point was not so bad as it looks if you take into account the dwindling condition of the British industry itself. In the following year, 1937, it dwindled almost to extinction.

Not long after we had made our film Frank Vosper took a trip to the United States and on the return journey somehow found himself in the sea. The coroner thought it unlikely that he had jumped or squeezed himself out of a porthole but it was not known that anyone had pushed him, so the coroner brought in an open verdict, commenting 'it is impossible to say from the evidence how he got into the water'. For me the event took on a grisly complexion because the make-up man on the film that I was making at the time that this sad event took place had been consulted on a point of identification, when the body was finally washed ashore. And so he possessed a photograph of it and did not hesitate to show it to the occupants of his make-up chair. So this was the untimely finale to the career of Frank Vosper, the poor man.

The great Alexander Korda was feeling the pinch again. By his unique wizardry he had raised enormous amounts of money to build Denham Studio and to subsidise his imperial plans. Once more we had a movie giant whose aim was to capture the international market, and once again financial embarrassment was at the studio door. I took it upon myself to write one of my pompous letters to a movie magazine called *Picture Show*. Grandiose film making had been attempted in the early days of Elstree, quickly followed by a Gaumont British assault when the studio at Shepherd's Bush had been opened up and Ostrer had put Michael Balcon in charge of production with an eye to the world market. Next came Korda with his dreams of glory and his expensive Denham product such as *The Four Feathers, Knight without Armour, The Shape of Things to Come*, which were not only less good than we had hoped they would be, but were also falling short of their targets in the United States and elsewhere. The latest Korda shortcoming must have prompted my letter. In it I said, 'But if we are to compete seriously with Hollywood, we shall do so only by improving the standard of our cheap unpretentious films, forgetting our extravagant endeavours to capture the world market with super productions. The cheap film should have as much chance of a world release as any colossal masterpiece, provided that sufficient attention is paid to the story and the writing of the dialogue and the casting of the small important parts.' I offer this quotation only because in this at least I can prove myself consistent. This is a song that I have sung with many reprises, and not only when J. A. Rank attempted world conquest immediately after World War II.

The only scraps that I was able to pick up in 1937 were in *The Return of the Scarlet Pimpernel* made by Korda's company, London Films, and in my final Fox British effort called *Catch as Catch Can*.

Our Scarlet Pimpernel was Barry K. Barnes, Lady Blakeney was Sophie Stewart and the whole of the long cast was well selected and probably reasonably well paid. My own criticism of the film was that it suffered much in the same way as recent James Bond films. Just as the latter have become one special effect after another, so our

Pimpernel was one disguise after another. And such elaborate disguises! They would have got the same effect with much less trouble if they had substituted other actors in their entirety, and just dubbed in Barry K. Barnes's voice on the occasions when he was all set to go into his act but in the meantime chatting with Sir Andrew Ffoulkes and other chums.

Our director was called Hans Schwartz. One day I asked him what he would be doing when he had finished work on our film. He said, 'I shall go to New York and settle down there until the film comes out. Then I shall take my choice of the offers that will come in.' I worried about him when I read what the *New York Times* man had to say: 'Same old Guillotine Square,' wrote he, 'same old aristocrats dying with incredible grace, same old extra women knitting and cackling obscenely as the heads fall ... same old British melodrama laid on with fine British unrestraint. Credit is due to both the director and cast for betraying so few signs of ennui.'

The last of my Fox British quota films, *Catch as Catch Can*, was directed by Roy Kellino, his first directorial assignment. The screen play was by Richard Llewellyn who not long afterwards came through with a memorable and best-selling novel, *How Green was my Valley*. In my book the film's existence was justified because it had a part in it for Margaret Rutherford. Not much of a part, but there she was, the great lady herself.

Interspersed with this film activity were the minor stage appearances, some of which I have mentioned. But there was one stage appearance that could almost be called major. At least it was a regular West End production with the healthiest prospects. The play was *Bonnet over the Windmill*, the fifth play by Dodie Smith. The preceding ones were *Autumn Crocus, Service, Touch Wood* and *Call it a Day* all of which had enjoyed success. Dodie Smith was a virtuoso of the common touch, but she had evidently mislaid it while writing *Bonnet over the Windmill* ... We had all enjoyed reading the play and were surprised when it did not attract enough public support to justify extending its run beyond my statutory three months. Having had several years to think about it I would now suggest that it failed because it was about theatrical folk and that in this area a writer is almost bound to fail unless he reduces his subject matter to the level of a back-stage success story. There was a tiny area in our play where the common touch might have taken over successfully but it did not occupy sufficient playing time. This was the chance encounter after many years of an actor, who has now become an actor manager in Shaftesbury Avenue, and an actress from Charing Cross Road, who as aspiring juveniles had shared some tender moments. These parts were nicely played by Cecil Parker and Ivy St. Helier. Unfortunately much more playing time was accorded to the carryings on of the young people. I myself was cast as a not very successful playwright, besotted by the sort of earnest young actress character who, on the stage as in life, can be abysmally boring; the realistic playing by the young actress who took the part did not make it less so.

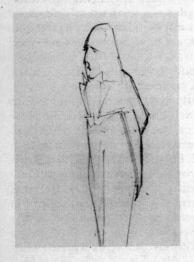

Cecil Parker in Bonnet over the Windmill, *1937*

Willie Douglas Home, who had not yet become the excellent playwright we now know, was, in the role of one of the young theatre folk, the best of company both on and off the stage. I am beholden to Cecil Parker, who played the actor manager, for having opened my eyes to an invaluable technical aid. He was much admired for the lively tempo in which he handled passages of light comedy. One of us must have asked him how he came by this particular skill. He pointed out that you must never come to a full stop. You may stop speaking, yes, and you may use pauses as much as you like, but you must always be thinking already of your next action or the next thing you are going to say. In a conversation, for instance, in which more than two are involved, it may often happen that while you are still speaking to 'X' you will already be looking at 'Y' to whom you will be addressing your next thought. He said that he had picked this up when as a young actor he had worked with the celebrated Charles Hawtrey. Everyone thought that Hawtrey worked with terrific speed, but Parker, having observed him, knew that it was not a question of actual speed; one got this impression only from his way of setting up an unbroken continuity of thought. I have found that this hint can be of the greatest service to playwrights and screen writers as well as to actors.

While there was still no reason to suppose that *Bonnet over the Windmill* would be anything but a smash hit, I was setting in order, strictly for my own enlightenment, the shoulds and shouldn'ts of an acting career. So as to keep up his spirits, an actor should play only in limited runs. Enough of this commercial madness of running a play until its life blood is squeezed out of it. Repertory theatres were okay but better still would be the repertoire system such as was practised in the state theatres and municipal theatres in most of the countries of Europe. Not only would such a revolution be a blessing to the entire acting fraternity, since I could not believe that there was an actor alive who would willingly choose to stay in a play throughout a seemingly endless run of a commercial success, and I knew that I myself would die of boredom if it ever happened to me. And the funny thing was that, as if to punish me for harbouring such portentous thoughts, I was never in a commercial success in the theatre. Later on when I had become an habitual movie actor people would look at me with a kind of pity since I was not involved in the *real* acting that was practised in the live theatre, it being generally held, especially in England, that it was only here that an actor could achieve stature. To a certain degree this was also the thinking in the United States, and a movie actor who felt that he was less in demand than was healthy would go do a play in New York. If the play was a success he would be discovered afresh by Hollywood and his movie career would roll along nicely for a couple of years.

Portentousness would have become me better if I had in early years managed to get myself into a notable success. Having not done so, I was understandably shy about saying that I found the practice of doing the same thing night after night *boring*. It seemed to me to be comparable with singing the same song night after night instead of having it mechanically recorded and marketed in the form of a handy disc. When notable actors (like the Lunts) would claim that they could go on improving their performances through three or four hundred repetitions I would politely nod my agreement but without crediting these improvements and variations with an enormous value. After all in many cases the most memorable performances come on a first night, and this is partly due not only to the special helping of adrenalin available on that occasion but also to the sustenance drawn from the really important work that has gone into the preparation of a role during the period of rehearsal.

Earlier in 1937 I had had my most exciting and rewarding experience on stage up to this time. This was the revival of Robert Sherwood's *The Road to Rome* which was presented by Ronald Adam at the Embassy

Theatre at Swiss Cottage. It was a timely revival and went down so well that they transferred it to the Savoy Theatre in the West End. Here for the first time my name appeared in lights above the entrance.

Robert Sherwood was one of the great satirists who flourished in the United States before World War II. The lightness of touch with which he handled serious material made him unique. Not that that there was anything serious to the point of solemnity about the subject matter of *The Road to Rome*; but it was something that a student of history could take seriously along with the modern elegance of its dialogue. Sherwood tries in the play to supply an acceptable reason for Hannibal's decision after his easy victory at Lake Trasimene for not moving in for the kill and taking Rome before the autumn of the year gave way to winter. To this end Sherwood has the wife of Quintus Fabius, the Roman leader, make her way to Hannibal's camp and in the course of a long and intimate scene persuade the Carthaginian general that there are things in life that he might find more rewarding than non-stop conquest. Ena Burrill was the actress who played the part of this Roman lady with wit and sex appeal. Aubrey Dexter as Quintus Flavius and David Tree as Hannibal's brother Mago were excellent. As always we thought the thing would last at the Savoy Theatre. But it did not. On one of the early nights I was having supper after the show at the Savoy Grill which at that time I took to be the most glamorous activity of which a human being was capable. And to top it off, the very leader of this glamour world was sitting at an adjacent table and invited me to come and sit beside her for a moment or two. Yes, Margot Lady Oxford and Asquith, no less, endorsed my ascent to stardom with a bouquet of fine words now forgotten.

In this year many people were already getting out of England and going to America. Business men seemed to be equipped with the kind of antennae that enable them to pick up the threat of war more quickly than average folk who are alerted only by the strange behaviour of the business men. At this time the theatres were feeling the pinch and the film industry even more so. Fewer and fewer films were being prepared for production in the studios. So it seemed to the Kellinos and myself that there was only one thing to do about it – to make a film of our own. This from a strictly professional point of view was one of my more sensible decisions.

9/Cookham Dean

We went to Wengen in Switzerland for a few weeks just after Christmas of 1937. It was here that Pamela and I wrote the first draft of the script of the film which had the working title *Deadwater*. The writings that we did together were almost invariably based on an 'idea' which made a vertical take off from the top of her head. None the worse for that since among film people it has always been accepted that a story to be good movie material must be one that can be written on the back of a postage stamp.

On take-off, Pamela's idea ran as follows: Farmer's nagging wife kills farmer's devoted dog. Farmer kills wife. Farmer runs away and takes to the woods. Girl in trailer offers shelter. Convinced she has no suspicions, farmer accepts. Girl is writer, but farmer finds hidden manuscript which betrays fact she has been writing about him. Farmer runs away again, runs from populace now armed with shot guns and is killed.

So now we dreamed up the devices that would humanise the stark operatic simplicity of this yarn. We gave the wife a brother who was our farmer's only 'hand'. It is this surly individual's negligence which causes a cowshed to be burned down. This brings about the firing of the hand, increased work load of the farmer and terminal moodiness of wife. Terminal, I say, because it causes her to take it out on the dog. She shoots the poor beast with the family shot-gun. For the farmer this is the last straw, since the dog happens to have been his only friend. So we have the farmer march into the farmhouse while the camera remains outside and travels over its surface guided by the angry voice calling 'Martha!' in one room after another,

137

then suddenly whipping to the front door from which the wife frantically and silently makes her escape, followed shortly afterwards by the husband who now carries *the gun*. Hold on empty screen. Then the sound of a gunshot. Another. Then silence again. In the best tradition of the silent screen much of our action was to take place off screen or in the dark or in remote long shot.

We accepted the fact that our effort must perforce be more of a silent than a sound film. The money which the three of us pooled for the making of the picture was £4,500. At this time you could buy five dollars with your pound but it was not much with which to make a feature length movie. We had decided that recording sound while we shot would be out of the question and since we would be able to afford to do no more than one day's post-synchronisation in a studio we must limit our dialogue to fragmentary essentials.

The central part of the story which involved the girl writer who lived in a trailer was at once the least credible and the one which most stoutly resisted our quasi-silent treatment, but we did our best. Our favourite bits went into the final act. The farmer having now become a hunted person, his trials took on a likeness to those of a hunted animal. He hides at one point in a barn. He sees plain clothes policemen cross-question first the farm hands and then some members of a foxhunt whose hounds have led them to the same group of buildings. Our fugitive, glancing around the barn where he is hiding, finds that he is not alone; in the straw not far away crouches the fox. They both manage to evade their pursuers as they run from the farm. It becomes after that one of the manhunts when all the local men band together and arm themselves as best they may since the hunted man is known to have a revolver (which had belonged to the lady in the trailer) and stretch a dragnet over the area. Now we introduced our analogy with a hunted stag. Shot and wounded, our fugitive runs on regardless. As the camera pans him along the side of a rough gorge, we discover that his course is taking him straight towards the sea. He staggers into it and swims as far as his remaining strength will carry him. The End.

When we felt that we could do no more with our scenario Roy Kellino took a hand and put it into a proper technical shape with appropriate headings to each scene and every *cut to* and *dissolve* and *fade out* in its right place. Being an experienced cameraman with already the eye of a director, he was able to see how some of the narrative points could be made in strictly visual terms.

Actually we were obliged to start shooting one sequence before the script had reached its ultimate tidiness. Often film makers whose scripts included hunting sequences had shot them in summer months when the leaves were on the trees and in most cases got away with it, because though there might be many in the audience who felt there was an unusual look about such sequences, only a minority realised that it was leaves that did it. The foxhunting season starts on November 1st and terminates in mid-March. We were not going to fall into that trap.

So we went to work in early March, having assembled our basic equipment and crew, which remained equally basic throughout the seven months that we devoted to the project. Roy Kellino was director and principal cameraman as well as being one-third of the production team. The assistant camera operator was Ossie Morris. And that basically was it. I had a chauffeur at the time called Fisher; he and I humped the equipment around much of the time as did also Ossie's younger brother, Reggie Morris, who was the 'loader' on the camera crew when he showed up but he was not with us all the time. We also had a casual continuity girl named Jo Harcourt who was working legitimately in a studio most of the time but would tidy up for us at week-ends making what sense she could of our chaotic documentation. The camera itself was something of an antique which Kellino borrowed for the duration. There were many out of work cameras in London at that time. In order to cut down on the price of film stock we bought 'short ends'. At that time the reels which were most commonly used in a proper commercial operation contained one thousand feet of film. Again in the proper commercial operation, in order to avoid too frequent reloading they would often leave a fair length of usable footage in each magazine. These were the short ends that we could pick up for a reasonable price. Extra time spent on reloading was not one of our problems. Since we seldom shot indoors we used no electric lights, only 'reflectors' which we made ourselves. Thus we made great demands on sunlight which during an English summer can often be in short supply.

We found the farm for our hunt sequence in Essex and in the same district a foxhunt whose members were willing to make themselves available for our shooting at a modest price, since their presence was required for one day only. On the same day we were lucky enough to get a usable long shot of a local fox making his way at speed across one of the fields close to the farm. This was, of course, not the same fox who posed for the close-ups. We located a 'drag hunt' in the neighbourhood of Windsor, having learned that for the purposes of the drag the excreta of a real fox were needed. They would wrap the excreta in a sack which a horseman would drag after him through the countryside which the huntsmen, hounds, and members of the hunt would then work. So they had this adorable fox who owed his survival to his talent for satisfying this unusual demand. We were lucky because in many parts of the country a sack charged with aniseed would do the trick, but this must have been a really top class drag hunt who were satisfied only with the real thing.

Having got this sequence in the can we now relaxed for several weeks while reconnoitring for locations on which to shoot the main body of our story. We found a farm not far from Marlow on the Buckinghamshire side of the river, which seemed to us to be just about the right size and was owned by a Farmer Morris who was accommodating and helpful. The next essential was an extensive wooded area where the trees were all coniferous. We expected to be shooting only in the summer and early autumn but we saw that we would need a background which would tie in with the wintry look of our foxhunt sequence. Our conifers would look exactly the same summer and winter and we found just what we wanted quite close to the farm. There was an endless expanse of beautiful scenery in this district which could serve all purposes except the final sequence at the coast.

We rented a serviceable furnished house in Cookham Dean which we made our headquarters. A wonderful maid called Violet Taylor worked in the house and had bullied its owner into allowing her to remain with it as a human fixture, since she had her own cat who would not have taken kindly to being asked to move out. Our party brought three additional cats to join him. I, having come up in the world, had a flat in Marylebone High Street which I shared with two cats, and Pamela brought along her Siamese.

Ours was similar to your average film making operation except that we had all the time in the world. During periods of persistent sunshine there was a sudden feeling of working under pressure because we wanted to shoot as much as possible while the weather lasted; each working day was extended to the last flicker of usable light. When the sun refused to shine there was usually some sort of construction work to be attended to. We built the cowshed that had to be burned down. And a fake front entrance had to be constructed on the side of the farmhouse where none existed. It was really like making an elaborate home movie and it was something that could never be attempted again because after the war every little job would need to be performed by union labour. In 1938 Equity was for the first time insisting that we all become members. I remember Richard Goolden's shocked reaction to this proposal when he was rehearsing for the part of Sir Andrew Aguecheek in our production of *Twelfth Night* at the Old Vic. At about the same time Roy Kellino and his friend Bernie Knowles, who both worked at the camera department of Gaumont British Studio, were lending their weight to the formation of the Cinema Technicians Union (now the A.C.T.). Nowadays, especially in the United States, it would be the simplest thing in the world to build a stockpile of fascinating and original films created by enthusiastic and reasonably gifted small groups if it were not obligatory to share the work with numerous well paid operatives. And this is the reason why, given the opportunity, I will always support and encourage the practice of film making on a strictly amateur level. The technical side of film making gets easier every year, and in the commercial world the content of film making becomes more and more restricted by the fancied requirements of merchandising. The intelligent and cultural future of films is in the hands of amateur film societies. At least that is one of my pet theories. Another is that it is the work that counts rather than the results. The work that we put into this small project is a memory that I cherish. The follow up was practically non-existent, as we shall see. But it could have been worse.

Once our farmer had met up with the girl in the trailer many of our sequences illustrated their travels from one place to another. In a normal commercial production many of the shots involved would have been done by back projection. That is to say we would have placed the car in front of a screen onto which film of the moving background was being projected. But since this was not feasible economically we set up a camera on a structure which we had built over the radiator of the car to photograph us as we were driving along on actual road. The bulk of camera and operator was an obstacle that made driving extremely hazardous. Besides having the virtue of cheapness the scenes were also more realistic when photographed this way.

We had only two regular supporting actors, and they were with us only throughout the early period when we were shooting at the farm. William Devlin played the surly farm hand who was fired for the negligence which caused the burning of the cowshed, and who after the murder of Martha came nosing around and found the grave in which the farmer had buried her. We did not have to worry about him when the time came for post-synchronisation, since he had no words to say. A very good actress who had served in the Hull Repertory Company with me and had more recently given a splendid performance in a production of Aristophanes' *Lysistrata* at the Gate Theatre in London, Sylvia Coleridge, played our nagging Martha, and this was undoubtedly the best performance in our film. All the other small part actors that we employed were either local amateur talent or were professional friends whom we coaxed down to Cookham on the assumption that a spot of acting in our quasi amateur production was a small price to pay for 'a few days in the country'. One of those who swallowed our bait was Peter Coke who had been with me in *Bonnet over the Windmill*.

So the summer ended. We said goodbye to Violet Taylor and her cat, Tich, and successfully disposed of the little old two-seater car that we had used in the film to go with the trailer. The purchase price had been £15, and we now sold it again for £20. The caravan itself we had rented from Denham Studios where it had in slightly earlier life had the distinction of being used as the mobile dressing room of Robert Donat during the filming of *Knight without Armour*. The Kellinos had also acquired at second hand the Ford station waggon which had been the 'camera car' during production. When Kellino had shot one or two additional close-ups of Pamela (supposedly inside the trailer) in their apartment in Dorset House, he returned the camera to its owner and turned all our footage over to the cutter, Fergus McDonnell.

Based on some strange notions in our heads, we had originally called our story *Deadwater*. None of our friends reacted to this title with any enthusiasm, but it never occurred to us to change it until one evening at Ascot. Isidore Ostrer, the father of Pamela and of Gaumont British, was one of a set of five brothers. The other four had

Maurice Ostrer, 1942

been given various jobs in the organisation in a descending scale of responsibility. For present purposes we shall not descend lower than Mark Ostrer who was the big public man, while Isidore, the only brain of the group, remained discreetly in the background. Mark was the one whose photograph, together with that of his good-looking American wife, frequently adorned the pages of the shiny magazines as a result of attending all important premières, entertaining visiting celebrities from Hollywood and being a landmark at the Savoy Grill, the Ambassadors, the Four Hundred and other 'In' places of the period. In the summer he would occupy a grand house at Ascot, and, since that was not out of reach from Cookham Dean, Pamela saw to it that we were acceptable extra guests at his Saturday night dinner parties. Kellino and I were rather scruffy guests and Mark with his air of good natured bonhomie would refer to us as the Dirt Track. (Dirt track motor-cycle racing was still in vogue.) I never got to know him well enough to find out if he really was good humoured. We told his guests about our activities, and noted the usual reaction when we mentioned the title of the film. '*Deadwater!*' repeated Leonora Corbett, and added an expletive that could be transcribed as yeuhchk.

'Do you have to call it that?' 'Well, no, we just thought it was rather a good name … Moody.'

'I don't know about moody. But it would certainly keep me out of any cinema … Wait a minute, what did you say was the name of the novel that the girl in the trailer was writing? The manuscript that the murderer discovered?'

'*I met a Murderer.*'

'That's it!'

'That's what?'

'That's your title! *I met a Murderer*!'

Leonora Corbett was a very good looking woman, tall and elegant. She had appeared briefly at the Cambridge Festival Theatre during my final year. I thought she was gorgeous. And witty too. And at Mark's house at Ascot whenever she accepted a dinner invitation, she was the queen. So we changed the name of our film to *I met a Murderer*. Mark did not register a great interest.

Other events of some importance were taking place behind our backs. Most of these were related to the activities of Mussolini and Hitler, which led up to the signing of the Munich Pact. Everyone was holding his breath and since war was expected, things came to a sticky standstill. At this time our composer should have been adding the final touches to the score of *I met a Murderer* and making preparations for the recording sessions. But there was no point in going on, people were saying, and it was not at all easy for Kellino and myself to persuade them that there was every point in seeing our work through to the end even if it were to prove a bitter one. And wasn't anyone concerned about our enormous financial investment?

Munich was signed and Eric Ansell completed his score, the musicians were called and the music track was recorded. And now there remained the one final process, the dubbing session, at which the dialogue track, the effects track and the music track are recorded together onto a single strip of film. Unfortunately we ran out of money just as the session ran out of time. Every time I saw the film

145

I was deeply embarrassed by the loudness of the music, while lots of things that I did in it as an actor embarrassed me much more.

Now that the film was completed it was only natural that Pamela would wish the Ostrers to see the result of our efforts. They had not been asked to contribute a penny to the making of the film but the least she expected was that they be willing to distribute it for us or give it a good showing in their theatres. I never knew which of them, if any, deigned to sit through a running of the film but they ran scared, as if in some way there was a danger that they might be contaminated by us. Up to this point I have mentioned only two Ostrer brothers, Isidore, who had the brain, and Mark, who was comfortable in white tie and tails. There was David, the oldest, who was married to a mid-European wife and was allowed to look after foreign sales. He looked like an unsuccessful Ruritanian pretender in an UFA film. Then came Maurice who was Isidore's shadow and lastly you got Harry who, having been a school teacher, became the literary department at the studios. The five of them had one opinion and one brain.

During these pre-war years they controlled the Gaumont British Studios at Shepherd's Bush and Islington, General Film Distributors, one of the two permanent giants in the British Industry (the other being what is now known as E.M.I.), and similarly one of the two major blocks of cinemas in the country. After the war this whole empire was to become the property of J. Arthur Rank, but that story can wait. What Pamela got from her family connections at this point was a general turning of the back. Very well, we decided; we shall find ourselves another Distribution Company, and started running the film for representatives of these companies.

It is hard to believe this in retrospect, but the Ostrers could not stand the idea of *anyone* being allowed to see it. They acted as if they were afraid that people in the industry would sneer at them. It was not easy even to get these others to look at our film, let alone make a distribution deal with us, because the men in Wardour Street would naturally be saying to each other if the Ostrers won't distribute a film in which Isidore's daughter is involved, it can't be worth looking at. In spite of this there was a newly formed distribution company which was willing to make a deal with us, and a fine bunch they turned out to be when the crunch came a year later; but in the beginning they handled matters in a proper professional manner. They even got a fragment of satisfaction from the Gaumont British Group, insofar as we were given a first run booking at the Marble Arch Pavilion which ranked as a West End house and, starting at a later date, September the eleventh 1939, we were to be allowed a general out-of-town release in seven or eight other Gaumont British cinemas.

Once we had actually made the film, I was aware of having become painfully available. Some money in the till would help. In a later segment of my career my friend Sidney Lumet introduced me to his special use of the phrase 'Call your agent'. When the last shot of the last sequence concerning a given actor has been done, Sidney may say, 'That was your call-your-agent shot'. 'What?' 'You can go call your agent now.' In my present case, my call-my-agent shot was long past, but was I forever to go on calling whoever was in charge at the Selznick office? The original bum who had not known that his office represented me when Al Parker first called, had been replaced by the nice Cecily Pape, and she had been joined and later superseded by the nice and capable Englishman, Cecil Tennant, but they had never broken any fresh ground for me nor shown the least interest during the months taken up with *I met a Murderer*. On the other hand was there any other agency on whose mercy I wished to throw myself? The most successful and best known outfit was one called O'Bryen, Linnit and Dunfee, but they were too terribly West End for me.

For my quandary relief arrived from an unexpected

source. Al Parker reappeared. He had been so cross with me for wanting to go off and work in *The Mill on the Floss* instead of his next film at Fox British that he had not exchanged a word with me for two years. But if all film production was coming to an end, there was no longer a need for quota pictures, and so the Fox British company had gone out of production. It then occurred to Al that the right spot for a man with an unusual talent for spotting talent in others was the agency business. Roy Kellino rang me one day to say that Al had asked him to convey this information to me and to say that he would much appreciate it if I were to become one of his first clients. I knew at once that such an alliance would work very well for both of us. Our good relations were instantly restored and we started something that was to last without tears or sweat until his death in 1974.

Al Parker in my opinion was the perfect agent. Some may think that that is not a very nice thing to say about a friend. Some people regard agents as the scum of the earth. And it is true that some of them can easily be mistaken for something like that. But then that would be true of quite a lot of actors and producers too. A friend of mine who was in show business, American style, told me that once his father, when handing out free advice to his young son, had warned him against making a friend of a policeman, a newspaperman or an actor. Why was that? Because the first two never forget who they are and will take advantage of anything you may say in their presence. And the actor? The actor is never quite sure who he is today nor who he will be tomorrow, so how can you trust him?

The thing about agents is this. Success as an agent is seldom compatible with a totally loyal friendship with a client. By way of illustration I have only to think of any of the agents through whose hands I passed in California. They were stuck out there, the poor slobs, they made their living there, and consequently it was in their interest to cultivate relations with the most important people in the business, the ones from whose trade they might best profit: the big producers. Very useful to manufacture a cosy relationship with important talents also, but if you had to choose one or other and if you had a head on your shoulders, you would choose the bosses. The artists were transients, most of them would outstay the span of their popularity; the bosses were permanent. Oh, of course there are exceptions to this rule and one of them was William McCaffrey, who broke the rule because he had started out as a booker for the big vaudeville chains and because he was a man of Broadway and wished to stay that way. He was the only one that I happened to know, other than Parker, whose loyalty to his client was total. Parker himself made enemies in most of the British studios almost as soon as he was firmly established.

I can think of one other agent of this calibre, whose name is Maggie Parker, who was Al's wife and for the last six years has been his widow. At the time of *I met a Murderer* she was a young actress who had only recently arrived from Australia. In the following years, as Margaret Johnston, she became recognised as a leading West End actress. In the last two or three years of Al's life she started to look after his business for him and in due course took shape as a formidable agent in her own right. By formidable I mean that potential employers knew that they could not expect her to lower her guard and allow them to take advantage of her clients. An infectious serenity pervades her office.

My principal activities in 1938 and 1939, apart from *I met a Murderer*, were a play called *Sixth Floor* which came to the St. James's Theatre and left again in rather a hurry, and a fair number of appearances in the newborn television medium. If ever I mention such activities to friends in the United States, I lose credibility because over there television remained undiscovered until after World War II. They probably had some splendid pioneers in this field whose faces will appear on postage stamps in due course but they refrained from making international noises about their achievements. In Europe on the other hand everyone knew about Scotland's very own genius John Logie Baird, the first demonstration of whose invention had been given at the Royal Institution as long ago as January 1926. The German post office had started television broadcasting in 1927, using Baird's system. And later in the same year the BBC also used it when it started its television service. But when I took to the game myself, I knew no one who possessed a receiving set; one's friends could catch the results only if they had an entrée into Broadcasting House or knew the owner of a set. There were very few.

It was a weird sort of fun to participate in these broadcasts. They were transmitted from Alexandra Palace, a grandiose complex constructed in the late Victorian era shortly after the marriage of Edward, the Prince of Wales, and Alexandra, the Princess from Denmark, as a staging area for Trade Exhibitions. Now in it was an area rather untidily equipped as a primitive television studio. The live broadcasting of television plays was of its nature very rough on the actors' nerves. But in later years at least one operated in an atmosphere of silent regimentation, free from distracting technical activity. But in those days the technicians wandered around at will. They wore white coats like laboratory assistants and the cameraman, often equipped with the kind of pointer that a lecturer might use, would indicate to the electricians the movements and adjustments of the lighting equipment that he deemed necessary as the action proceeded.

An actor named Henry Oscar was playing an important part in one of these televised plays. His concentration was beginning to fragment when he became aware that the camera was relentlessly dollying towards him to capture a big close-up. The camera was not alone, it was accompanied by the lighting cameraman still indicating adjustments with his pointer. As the camera settled on its prey, the only words, it is reported, that Oscar could find to say were, 'Oh, God, these men in white coats!'

I witnessed the de-stabilisation of several of the actors with whom I worked and I despaired of a happy resolution of the problems endemic in live television acting. In 1947 I spent an evening in New York in the company of John Royal who was a very big man in NBC. He was excited and at the same time alarmed by the prospect of presenting something which was to be called Theatre Guild of the Air. Did I think that the actors would be able to remember their lines? Mindful still of the experiences in Alexandra Palace, I could not reassure him. His colleagues, he said, had thought of a solution. 'Is that right?' I said, 'I'd really like to know what your solution is.' 'It is quite simple,' he said, 'you get the actors to pre-record the dialogue, then all they have to do at the time of transmission is to mouth the words in synchronisation with what you have recorded.' 'Interesting idea,' I said.

The surprising thing was that this never became a major problem in United States television. Of course actors forgot their lines occasionally just as they do on the stage. But all those young soldiers who had fought in World War II were the beneficiaries of something called the G. I. Bill of Rights which gave them access to a period of free education, which for many took the form of immersion in a Television Academy. So a new generation mastered all the techniques required by television, and since it was the only form of acting they ever had attempted, there was no other acting with which to compare it. So they had none of the fears which assailed veteran stage actors facing the red eye of the television camera. And what a wonderful generation these young men proved to be. Though it is hard for anyone familiar with the current television scene to believe, the early days of television in the United States were really exciting. There was adventure for the young directors and even some freedom. The top movie directors of the sixties were already limbering up in the live dramas and anthologies of television of the fifties, men like Sidney Lumet, Johnny Frankenheimer, James Roy Hill, Bob Mulligan, Franklin Schaffner.

Reverting to Alexandra Palace, the plays in which I participated that come to mind are Molière's *L'Avare* (*The Miser*), in which Henry Oscar played the leading part very well and without for one moment yielding to his fears, Priestley's *Bees on the Boatdeck* and Denis Johnston's *The Moon in the Yellow River*. Johnston himself directed this and it was a thrilling event. He was to have an ever widening experience in the new medium. At the time of my above-mentioned conversation in New York with John Royal his name came up as a real expert to be imported from the old world for the production of one of the first features that would appear on the Theatre Guild of the Air. This was the Northern Irish play *John Ferguson* by St. John Ervine. When Johnston took charge, the dialogue was not pre-recorded by the actors!

The more important ingredient in my life during 1939 was patiently waiting in a pile of cans preparatory to its promised release in the month of September. And in the meantime *I met a Murderer* was permitted to unroll itself briefly for its showing at the Marble Arch Pavilion. This happened in the month of June and lifted our spirits. A certain brainwashing had been effected by its hostile reception by the brothers O. *Was* it really something that would bring shame to the brothers? The newspaper reviews reassured us. They treated it like a proper film! The first newspaper that I opened was *The Times*. Since I do not now have the newspaper in my hands I cannot guarantee the accuracy of these measurements, but the review of *Marie Antoinette*, starring Norma Shearer and all that, which had emerged at the Empire Cinema, Leicester Square, was reviewed in a matter of four inches, whereas *I met a Murderer* scored a full twelve inches. The serious papers all treated it with respectful admiration, while the cheaper papers could find little in it to titillate their readers.

My last professional activity before Europe fell apart was two or three days' rehearsal for a television production of Somerset Maugham's *The Circle*. The producer was Val Gielgud. I played the 'Anyone for tennis' young man and my opposite number was the enchanting Dorothy Hyson.

Other contemporary rehearsals included Mussolini moving into Albania and Hitler into Czechoslovakia, and prior to this General Rommel had been privileged to lead the German armour into Austria, and terror bombing had been practised at the expense of Guernica and Nanking.

Towards the end of August it was thought sensible to cancel further rehearsals for *The Circle* and in due course the Germans marched into Poland; their then friends, the Russians, marched in from the other side while administering a side-kick at brave little Finland.

By the time Prime Minister Chamberlain told us that we were at war with Germany we had all been supplied with gas masks because the German Luftwaffe would soon be dropping poison gas on us.

At this point in our lives many of my contemporaries volunteered for the armed forces. My brother Rex was already programmed since he had been an officer in the Territorials since way back. His battalion was now switched on to active service. Colin also without hesitation signed on for the Royal Naval Reserve. My own war record on the other hand maintained a consistently low rating.

In the early and middle thirties when Hitler was starting to make a bad name for himself and people were first saying that we were going to end up in another war, I rejected such an idea. I had read so many books which dwelt on the horrors of World War I, seen plays and films which so effectively conveyed the message that war is hell, that there could be no chance of such a turn around in public feeling that would allow us to drift into war, no matter what sort of a bogey man Hitler would turn out to be. Even before the Hitler threat made itself felt, I had a recurring personal fantasy. Come another war, I had said to myself, I shall use it as the starting gun for a life of adventure. Young men of my generation in their late teens had often found jobs as able bodied seamen or as assistant pursers and taken off on the first leg of an intercontinental adventure. I had assumed that the assistant pursership would be hard to get since I had no useful connections in Fyffe's Bananas or other such fleet owners. And I was not at all sure that I could qualify as an A.B., but the fantasy never left me for long. For instance I had toyed lovingly with it at the moment when I was ousted from my job in *The Return of Don Juan*. It offered a timely alternative to Rosencrantz or Guildenstern. But now that an even more suitable moment had arrived, my circumstances had changed somewhat. I was no longer the carefree bachelor. Technically I was a bachelor, yes, but morally – if that is the right word – I was married to Pamela Kellino. Since it would not be feasible to circumnavigate the globe with Pamela tucked under my arm, I must adopt a new war strategy. Mutual protection must be the aim. We would do whatever was desirable or even obligatory under conditions of war but the bottom line was that we would stick together until dragged apart.

War, as I saw it, was a pale horse ridden by mankind and accompanied by pestilence, death, famine and other horrors. The operative word was mankind. Pestilence, famine, earthquakes etc., when unaccompanied by the pale horse, usually qualified as acts of God, but war was strictly manmade. I assumed that everyone else saw the matter in similar terms but most other men of all ages were obliged to participate because they had a keener sense of duty to their community or to King and Country than I. I knew that I had a sense of responsibility but I found little trace of anything that could be described as a sense of duty.

A sense of duty to my parents, if any, would not have known what to do with itself at that moment because we were hardly on speaking terms, it having been discovered that I was living with a married woman. I did not feel that I would be effectively looking after them by joining up. Just as I most certainly would not have been looking after Pamela if I had joined up.

Community then? No sense of duty to community? Well, I did not feel that I had a community other than the

fraternity of actors, each member of which was traditionally, if not a vagabond, at least a free-wheeling individual.

How about King and Country? It was a phrase one never
heard except in times of war and had by association lost
some of its power to stir. And, much as I liked our royalty,
the word Country had sometimes become confused with
the more dubious words Nationality and Empire. In my
earliest childhood I may have been stirred by the words
'red on the map' which illustrated the vastness of the
British Empire, but the feeling did not survive my
schooldays.

So, during the period of the so-called phoney war we
observed the changing conditions. After Mr Chamberlain's
declaration of war the first knock that we suffered
personally was the immediate closing of the cinemas. We
were all going to be gassed in the air raids, remember, so it
was inadvisable to allow large numbers of people to
congregate in theatres and movie houses. This stoppage
lasted for the first six weeks of the war. The money that we
had made from the showing of *I met a Murderer* at the
Marble Arch Pavilion had been scarcely enough to pay the
laboratory what we owed them, and so we had looked to
the returns from the general release of the film, scheduled
for the first week of September, to refund most, if not all, of
the cost of production, the £4,500 odd. If we had been more
optimistic we might have assumed that a little later, as
soon as the threat of air raids should dwindle, an
alternative release date would be arranged by our
distributing company. Luckily we were not such opti-
mists and so avoided what would have been a considerable
disappointment. Without consulting us, our distributors
went ahead with their own little plan. Since they had
possession of several British films, including ours and one
made by the Boulting Brothers called *Pastor Hall*,
obviously the smartest thing that they could do was to
pack them up and sail with them to New York. The
negative of *I met a Murderer* went down somewhere in the
Atlantic as a result of submarine action, but not the

distributors, who arrived in New York with a dupe negative or a 'Lavender print' or whatever was needed to have the film shown in New York. They must have done quite nicely out of it since the reviews were excellent.

The live theatre was restored to life sooner than the cinema. Touring companies shuttled around the country and then, more tentatively, the West End resurrected itself. I went out on tour with the first of ENSA's dramatic companies. Our repertoire consisted of a whodunit, *I Killed the Count*, and a nautical melodrama called *Eight Bells*. We played in both real and make-shift theatres situated in garrison towns or large encampments of the military. Just as we were not fully prepared for theatrical activity in this novel form, neither were our audiences. They were receptive when they were numerous enough, but since theatre-going was not yet a habit with most of them we had to be satisfied with scattered applause at best. One night in a converted gymnasium in Aldershot we counted only five in our audience. Raymond Lovell and I started to incorporate into the set dialogue a few exchanges with these lonely individuals, and so made friends with them to the point of suggesting that they might have a better time if they joined us backstage for a few drinks. For that night at least we were a hit.

Among the Hungarians now rampant in London, the principal was Gabriel Pascal of whose background I knew nothing, except that he was said to be a gypsy and/or a former cavalry officer, and, still more important, that he had already produced in England the film version of Bernard Shaw's *Pygmalion* which had been beautifully directed by Anthony Asquith and played by Wendy Hiller, Leslie Howard and Wilfrid Lawson. And, without having checked, I would bet that it was more successful than any of Alex Korda's films since *The Private Life of Henry VIII*. Anyway, Pascal's most valuable asset was his ability to enchant G. B. Shaw and to succeed (where bigger producers had failed) in acquiring the film rights of his plays seemingly at will. So now, the reactivated trade papers told us, he was to have a go at *Major Barbara*, a much more difficult piece than *Pygmalion*. Since I subscribed to no trade papers, this news was passed on to me by Al Parker, who further informed me that Pascal wanted to see me and that it might be a good idea to read the play if I was not already familiar with it. Robert Morley and Wendy Hiller were to play the Undershafts, father and daughter, and I was being considered for the part of Adolphus Cusins. Pascal wished to test me on film.

I duly familiarised myself with the play, which makes fascinating reading, and concluded that it was not likely to have a strong popular appeal as a film. Also it had been announced that Pascal himself was to direct as well as produce, which drained one's confidence even further. Still it was an important role in a more important production than any in which I had appeared up to this point. I saw it as my big chance. I went to see Pascal who

Contract-signing session, 1941

could hardly have been more friendly. However he made it clear that he was not going to give me the part without having tested me, and the trouble was that his cameraman who by now should have arrived in England from the United States was holding things up. He could not make a movie test of me until he arrived. But he had an idea . . . (pause)

'Yes, what was that?'

There was this wonderful still photographer, Sasha, the man who invented the Sasha flash – did I know him?

(The Sasha flash was the forerunner of the regular flash bulbs which we would all come to know only too well in the years that followed. It was a biggish, clumsy looking bulb containing what looked like a crumpled handful of aluminium foil.)

'Yes,' said I, 'I know him . . . So?'

So Pascal thought that it would suit his purpose just as well if he took me through certain scenes in the play and Sasha would keep popping off these flash light shots of me.

I thought it was a perfectly ghastly idea, but since I did not wish to create problems, I said that the arrangement would suit me fine. I wanted to play the part of Adolphus Cusins, so I made up my mind to go along with any crazy notion he might come up with.

The character of Adolphus Cusins in the play is a professor of ancient Greek who is in love with Barbara, one of the daughters of Andrew Undershaft, arms manufacturer. Since Barbara has become a major in the Salvation Army, Adolphus pretends an interest in her work and beats the big drum in the band. The dialogue, which concerns itself chiefly with the contrasting moral attitudes of Undershaft and his daughter, flows on amusingly to be punctuated sparingly by Adolphus. When Barbara finds that the very existence of her shelter is being guaranteed only by large monetary contributions from a leading distiller of whisky and her arms manufacturing father, she quits the Army and inclines to

Undershaft's credo that the good wages and the comfortable living quarters that he offers his workers amount to a more effective saver of souls than her shelter. She and Adolphus end up contentedly in one of his workers' cottages. Whereas in the first half Adolpus is something of a Greek Chorus, in the second half he is technically speaking, more of a feed.

I offer this outline only to stress the absurdity of this projected test by flash bulb. Adolphus is an observer and one who participates in the action only insofar as the mating process demands. Since Pascal's sense of urgency did not allow time enough for me to learn the lines assigned to Adolphus in the play, all that Sasha would actually be doing would be photographing me in natural dead pan as Pascal described a selection of scenes to me. So at one moment I would mime beating the drum, at another I would be acting laughter, at another acting gravity. The results must have been truly awful. According to Al Parker, when John Barrymore, whom he frequently quoted, was asked his opinion about a certain actress's performance, he replied 'She has only two expressions, laughter and constipation'. And this, I am sure, would be an equally apt description of Pascal's test of me. Although he kept up his gypsy cavalry officer style of cordiality till the conclusion of our session he followed it up with no overt demonstration of intent to sign me up. So I pressed on with my professional life as best I could.

I found myself rehearsing a play by the novelist A. J. Cronin called *Jupiter Laughs*. It was decidedly not bad, but it fell short of handing out the kind of frisson that emanates from the boldly true or the truly artistic. It was to have opened in the West End, but now, since France had fallen and bombs were once more expected to be dropped on our cinemas and theatres, that area was sinking back into another period of inactivity. So we set off instead on a tour, which started in Edinburgh, then proceeded to Glasgow and several cities in the North of England. Our producer was the gifted Claude Gurney who had

159

sensibly taken in marriage Nancy Hornsby, the beauty of *Gallows Glorious*.

Shortly after our opening I learned that Al Parker and I were not yet rid of Gabby Pascal. (From now on we shall refer to him as Gabby.) I had sent to Al copies of some very good reviews that I had received. Like a good agent but without any encouragement from me, Al had shown these to Gabby who reacted as if I was his own personal discovery and the only actor who was fit to take on the role of Adolphus Cusins; he insisted that I go down to London at once to be given a genuine screen test. I disdained this invitation since I was not keen to reappear on the Gabby Pascal show and in any case I was now committed to appearing in *Jupiter Laughs* wherever the management could find a stage for it. In the event the tour did not last very long because many of our bookings had been in the manufacturing towns in the Midlands which were already getting attention from the Luftwaffe. Our potential audiences therefore were likely to stay home and become increasingly addicted to Arthur Askey, Tommy Handley and the other radio favourites of the time. During the latter part of our engagement Parker informed me that Gabby had signed up a young actor called Andrew Osborn for the role of Adolphus Cusins and that the cameras had started to roll.

When Pamela and I returned from the tour we rented a cottage in Taplow near Maidenhead and waited for the next thing to happen. We wrote another play together and Pamela made some progress as a solo novelist. A couple of years earlier one of her sisters had written a novel about a sequence of romantic events which she had imagined taking place in ancient China. Pamela had told her that she thought she was making things unnecessarily difficult for herself by writing about people and times of which she knew nothing; she should write about the life she knew. To prove the point, in spite of having had no previous experience of authorship, she dashed off a piece of writing which could reasonably be mistaken for a novel and which was based on the adventures of herself and her sisters when they lived as teenagers in the South of France with their mother. It was rough stuff but though when she submitted it for publication she collected a number of rejection slips, the tone of a couple of the publishers' letters encouraged her to press on. The hit novel of this period was a shocker called *No Orchids for Miss Blandish*. If it was just a question of shocking people, Pamela figured, she could write a best-seller. So in a very short time she had a book accepted and the curious thing was that, so far from shocking, it was taken very seriously even by some of the well-placed critics. It was not a best-seller, but it was worth her publisher's while to treat with the greatest respect the three further novels that she went on to write before the war ended.

While we were at Taplow, Gabby Pascal came back into my life. He rang me up and told me that he was sending a special messenger down to our cottage bearing a copy of the script of *Major Barbara*. He said that he had stopped production because he had decided to re-cast the role of Adolphus Cusins. His voice was that of a man dogged by misfortune, victimised by false friends, sideswiped, booby-trapped, the lot. And he ended his recital with the unforgettable words, 'Jimmy, we have made a great mistake!' *We*? Where did he get that 'we'?

He was sure that I was going to like the script, and would let me know in due course when he would want me at the studio. Pamela and I enjoyed reading the script. But what was even more pleasurable was the glow that accompanied the awareness of one's sudden importance. As a final smart move before yielding to catastrophe, the French High Command had recently selected a new commander-in-chief of all its forces. This was General Weygand, whose prestige and experience, we were assured, were to be the salvation of France. Even so had Gabby turned to me in his hour of need. My ever increasing experience and my prestige, if any, were now to save *Major Barbara*, Gabriel Pascal, Denham Studios and the reputation of Bernard Shaw. I knew exactly how General Weygand had felt when they came knocking at his door. Gad, the responsibility.

After a week had passed I began to wonder what would be Gabby's interpretation of the phrase 'in due course'. After two weeks I came across an interesting item in the gossipy section of one of the daily papers. Gabriel Pascal, it informed us, had recast one of the important roles in his current film production *Major Barbara*. The part of Adolphus Cusins was to be played by Rex Harrison.

Such are the ups and the downs. It was not as if my encounter with Gabby could figure on the balance sheet as a disappointment. Though it is true that every young or youngish actor thinks of this or that as 'my big chance', to me this was just a further escalation of my 'increasing experience' referred to above. And it made us laugh a lot because on previous occasions I had received earfulls of bullshit only from the small time entrepreneurs who had nothing better to hand out. Gabby had style.

10/Beaconsfield

It was time for me now to register for military service. While we were still occupying the house in Taplow I received notice that I was to go to an office somewhere in Maidenhead and fill in the required forms. So I did as I was asked and made it known that I wished to be accepted as a conscientious objector. There seemed to be no alternative for me since I had no intention of being enrolled in a group of armed men whose job would be to kill other young men similarly drafted from another country. And since I was not going to shoot people or drop bombs on them it was patently unfair that I be employed in the manufacture of their bullets and bombs or in any other way aiding or abetting those who were doing the killing.

I had to wait around for quite a long time before facing a tribunal. We all had to submit written statements in which we explained why we thought we should be regarded as conscientious objectors. Not being religious, I could not claim that I was forbidden to take up arms by the rules of my Church. It seemed that Christians who were devout enough to attach importance to the commandment 'Thou shalt not kill' were the ones most frequently listed as genuine conscientious objectors. Those who did not plead religious motivation were usually directed to non-combatant service and stricken from the register of conscientious objectors.

It did not seem to be of any great importance whether I was on the register or not. I knew what my conscience would allow me to do and what it would not. I knew that I was not going to kill any poor slob just because he had been struck by war just as we had and because his country was a member of a different team than ours. It was not that I was responding to the religious injunction 'Thou shalt not kill'. I could imagine a variety of circumstances in which I would be prepared to kill someone. And I knew that, if I were shoved into uniform and a gun placed in my hands, I would be more likely to point it at anyone who proved to my satisfaction that he deserved to be shot no matter which uniform he was wearing. I wonder if there is a list somewhere of Generals, Sergeant-majors and other ranks who have been wiped out in this way.

The other thing that I wrote about in my statement was my abhorrence of war as an accepted means of settling international economic and political differences, institutionalised war in fact. I abhorred the glib acceptance in wartime of a totally alien code which we would quite properly condemn in the intervals of peace.

The tribunal had heard it all before and predictably wiped my name from the register of C.O.'s and directed me to non-combatant service. We were allowed to appeal against these verdicts and I did so on the grounds that a pacifist could not be directed to non-combatant service because it was not the act of killing he was objecting to so much as any act which contributed to the war effort. Appellants had also to furnish letters from two character witnesses, the more distinguished the better. I obliged with letters which I extracted from two Cambridge professors. One of these expressed friendly feelings towards me without suggesting that he shared my views, and the other was very far from being a good reference, but I submitted it just the same in the hope, I suppose, that the tribunal would not bother to read all these letters. This letter was from Paul Vellacott who said, as I recall, that he had never been in charge of a student whose interests were so exclusively concentrated on himself and his prospects. I was really surprised that I had shown up so badly. Whether they read the letters or not they had no compunction in shooting me down in flames.

While waiting on these proceedings I toured with another play. Once again the management had planned to open in London but changed their minds when the bombing of the city was suddenly stepped up. The play was called *Divorce for Christobel* and aimed at being funny more than anything else. The divorce laws which prevailed in England during this epoch gave rise to a lot of jokes and this was one of them. The only way to obtain a divorce was to prove that adultery had been committed by the marital partner. Therefore if a husband and wife sincerely wanted out from their marriage although adultery had nothing to do with it, they were obliged by the law to stage an adulterous charade, the evidence of which would later be produced in court to prove that one or other of them had committed the only act that could make him or her a respondent in divorce. The evidence did not need to stipulate that the allegedly guilty party had been caught in the act, it was enough for him or her to have been seen, scantily dressed (pyjamas or nightdress would do) in bed but out of wedlock. I had at this time figured as a co-respondent in a divorce suit. A sensible and good-natured maid who had worked for the Kellinos had agreed to stand up in court and testify that she had entered the bedroom of the Kellinos when the master was away and had seen me sitting up in bed dressed in pyjamas beside Mrs Kellino who was dressed in a nightdress, a scene which we staged expressly for her benefit. I remember the twinge of hurt pride which was occasioned by a headline in one of the trade papers which read: Pamela Ostrer Divorced, Actor Named.

Another common ploy was for the husband to take a room for a night in a hotel in Brighton and pay for the services of a lady who would slip into a nightgown and join him in bed long enough to allow a preordained witness to enter the room and find them there together.

In the second act of *Divorce for Christobel* the hero, who has made a rendezvous with a professional co-respondent,

165

is shown into the hotel bedroom. Shortly afterwards a lady with overnight bag enters the same room. The hero has every right to assume that this is the lady he has hired for the night while the lady, for a complication of reasons which we don't need to go into, assumes that *he* is the professional co-respondent who has been hired for *her*. Endless fun ensues.

My leading lady, who was in fact the star of the show, was Frances Day, a big favourite in the London musical comedy scene. This may have been her first straight play. She was a good sort and could put over a number saucily and with skill. A cue for song was found for her in our second act, rather to my surprise, and she would regularly launch into 'All the things you are', a current hit from America.

Before setting out on this tour, which incidentally did not last very long, we had moved from Taplow to a small house in Beaconsfield, which had large grounds in which it was our plan to set up something that would qualify as a small-holding. Just as my notions about war emerged from what I had read and been told about World War I, Pamela's ideas were the direct offspring of *Gone with the Wind*. Already she had applied herself to growing radishes in various locations, in none of which we had stayed long enough to sample the crop. Now at Beaconsfield things were going to be different. We would grow enough vegetables to keep our neighbours well supplied. And in no time at all we had caused to be built an enormous henhouse and stocked it with Rhode Island Reds.

I had no idea what the military authorities would decide to do with me. They would presumably 'direct' me to non-combatant work in the Forces, which I was not going to accept. Then, I supposed, they would arrest me and send me to gaol. Or, if they were short of space, they might urge me towards some civilian work in factory or farm. I would decline the factory but accept the farm, if it came to that, though at first I should of course try to sell them the idea that my small-holding was going to be a worth while venture. In the meantime, while we waited for the knock on the door or whatever form my call was going to take, the thing to do was to keep busy. So I planted these vegetables and encouraged the hens and continued to do some acting on the side. Pamela's routine was much the same except that instead of acting she was writing novels.

As the period of waiting extended itself I took a job in a film called *This Man is Dangerous* which was to be shot at Welwyn Garden City. It was a little thriller which turned out to be immensely popular when released. It introduced me to a nice director, Lawrence Huntingdon, a talented Czech actor, Frederick Valk, and a very beautiful leading lady, Margaret Viner. About a week after the shooting finished I married Pamela Kellino by courtesy of the Registrar of births, deaths and marriages in the town of Amersham.

A most unfortunate thing happened during this ceremony. I am sure that there are many cases of one of the protagonists being moved to hysterical laughter during a register office ceremony and even, though I hesitate to suggest such a thing, during a church ceremony. The oddity of our happening lay in the surprising form of the marriage lines themselves. We had chosen Amersham because it lay on the route between Beaconsfield and Welwyn where the film was being shot. I had stopped at the register office and found the little registrar sitting at his desk behind which hung a large map of the local graveyard. Had I wished to register a death he could easily have swung his chair around and pointed to available burial plots. But the purpose of my visit was to find out what was needed to be done to effect a marriage. He said that I should satisfactorily prove that I was a bachelor and that, since my intended was a divorced woman, I must supply documents that would establish this. Also, said he, I should, when the time came, bring along a couple of witnesses.

So it was arranged that we forgather in his office on

167

February 12th 1941. I have always had difficulty in remembering dates and this was no exception. I thought that I had licked the problem later when I discovered that this was also George Washington's birthday. But then I always got to asking myself, was it Washington's or Lincoln's. I can now say with assurance (having checked) that it was Lincoln's.

So on this date we trooped into the office, Pamela and myself, accompanied by her mother, her sister Diana and Carmen Flemyng, who were to be our witnesses. The little registrar was a mumbler and I had neglected to study the script, so when he said to me, 'Mr Mason, repeat after me, I call upon these here present', I did not immediately understand what he had said and asked him to repeat it. I caught the distressed looks of my friends and simultaneously realised what the man had meant. I said hastily, 'Oh you mean the witnesses... I call upon these here present...' And he completed the line 'to bear witness etc. etc.', and we continued evenly with the dialogue for a while. But I had been destabilised by the incident. I was like an actor on stage who is afraid that something else may go wrong. And it did. Among the things that he was asking me to repeat was, 'I take thee, Pamela Helen Gislingham, to be my lawful wedded...'

'Excuse me,' I said.

'Yes?' he enquired, scowling.

'Would you mind very much if I said "I take thee, Pamela Helen Kellino"?'

He looked at his script and, sure enough, Roy Kellino's name had been accurately copied from what had appeared on the divorce papers. Roy Gislingham *orse* Kellino. I assumed that the funny looking word *orse* was an abbreviation for otherwise.

The registrar now looked deeply unhappy. This was a new turn up for him. I felt that I had to say something.

'Everyone calls him Roy Kellino. I don't believe anyone ever called him Roy Gislingham, except perhaps when he was christened. And certainly no-one ever called Pamela by that name. I would feel much more comfortable if I could say Pamela Helen Kellino.'

Gislingham was indeed the legal family name of the Kellino family. Previous generations of Gislingham had been circus folk and they had dreamed up this fancy name Kellino, thinking it more appropriate for their line of work. In the circus it was traditional to switch to a vaguely Italian name, just as in ballet Russian names were favoured.

By now even my witnesses were frowning at me and Pamela had started to nudge me.

'No,' said the little man firmly, 'you will have to say Pamela Helen Gislingham.'

The appearance of this comical 'Pamela Helen Gislingham' in the marriage ritual took me completely by surprise. From this point on I was destroyed. Helpless explosions of laughter punctuated the rest of the scene. I was not popular, I can tell you. But we were married.

An impresario called Jack de Leon, who before the war had run the little theatre at Kew Bridge where *A Man who had Nothing* had been offered, now decided that the moment was ripe for a West End presentation of *Jupiter Laughs*. There was a lull in the bombing. I was allowed to stage it myself but I stuck largely to the general plan already established by Claude Gurney in its previous outing. Leueen McGrath, who had been our previous leading lady, was now replaced by Mary Bryan, indeed it was an entirely fresh cast who opened at the New Theatre in St Martin's Lane (now called the Albery). I was already committed to this when suddenly I was wanted for another film to be shot at Welwyn. This turned out to be another very popular little item. Called *The Night has Eyes*, it was an effective and rather original thriller, with Wilfred Lawson, God bless him, in the cast. It introduced me to Leslie Arliss, one of the only two directors with whom, throughout the length and breadth of my career, I have had cross words.

The coincidence of the revived *Jupiter Laughs* and *The*

Night has Eyes took place during the dark months. Early morning there was a dark and sometimes foggy drive to Welwyn, later the drive from Welwyn to the West End and finally back to Beaconsfield.

Deborah Kerr in Hatter's Castle, *1941*

Pamela kept her eye on the hens and the vegetable plot made few demands during the winter season. No sooner had I finished *The Night has Eyes* but I was hired to take part at Denham in a film adaptation of A. J. Cronin's novel *Hatter's Castle.* Robert Newton played Brodie, the Hatter, and the cast was also graced with the presence of Deborah Kerr, Emlyn Williams and Beatrice Varley. The producer was one that none of us had encountered before, I. Goldsmith, who was most anxious about the spectre that was beginning once again to haunt the producers in our industry, the American audience. It was rumoured that the American ear was not receptive to any sort of

British accent. Some tattle-tale assured Goldsmith, whose own accent betrayed a Mid-European origin, that we, the cast, were using a variety of Scottish accents. So Goldsmith implored us to desist; else how could we penetrate the American cinema? So we toned it down to a point at which no one could accuse us of speaking English English and at which neither Goldsmith's ear nor even his tattle-tales could pick up a trace of our guilt. Actors were inclined to think that if there was a good script and if they did a job that was as near perfect as their talents allowed, then everything else would fall into place; the better the job, the more easily marketable. Others did not see it our way. Three years later, when the war was over, the big powers in the American industry came trotting to Europe to make deals and there was much laughter at the expense of poor Spyros Skouras, the President of 20th Century Fox, who had occasion to lecture the assembled heads of the British industry on how to make films that could be well received in the States. I was not an ear witness to this address and do not know his exact words. But his eloquence on behalf of well-spoken English proved irresistibly funny when voiced in his own formidable Greek/American accent.

Robert Newton, who played the part of the paranoid hatter, carried the show, and once he had studied, prepared himself and committed many of his lines to memory, lines written with a Scottish lilt to them, it was too much to ask him to shake off an accent that had been on his mind already for several weeks. But I believe that he tried to oblige Mr Goldsmith in response to his nagging. 'But, Robert', Goldsmith would say, 'the others aren't speaking Scotch. Mason here is speaking quite naturally.' 'Oh no, he's not', replied Robert, 'it's just that you can't hear it. He's too crafty for you.' Whether he managed to play the part as he had wanted or not, Robert was magnificent. He had come into a run of success which started with the role of the colourful sinner who had thumped the Salvation Army Lassie (Deborah Kerr) in *Major Barbara*, a film that for the greater part was short on action, and carried him through his wildly eccentric Pistol in Olivier's film of *Henry V* and the Gully-Jimpson-like painter in *Odd Man Out*.

It was about this time that I made an interesting discovery which affected my working life. Before undertaking my last two film commitments I had been asked to apply for a 'deferment of call-up' and did so. No matter what form my call-up was to take it was necessary to make sure that I would not be snatched away during the period of shooting. But the discovery was this. The film industry was deemed to have national importance and we who worked in it, no matter what we thought we were doing, were deemed to be sustaining the national morale. Consequently the same rules applied to us as to those who worked in other similarly placed industries, and one of these rules decreed that anyone occupying a position of importance in the industry who had been over thirty when he had registered for National Service could apply for a deferment of call-up so long as his services were in demand. So, it seemed I had become a reserved individual, provided of course that the demand was kept up.

Noël Coward contacted me when he was preparing to film *In Which We Serve*. There was evidently a leading part in it which he wanted me to play, but before offering it to me he wanted to meet me and have a talk. So I suggested that he come to the house in Beaconsfield which was convenient for him, being not many miles from Denham Studio where much of the preparation for the film was taking place. So one afternoon he showed up, accompanied by his friend Joyce Carey, the actress.

What he wanted to know was why I had not joined the armed services. So I told him at some length first of my determination not to get involved in killing conscripts from other countries, not to take any part in the mutual bombing of civilian populations. It might seem to him and to others who were like minded that I was one of those who wished to have their cake and eat it but, no matter what others might think, I had made up my mind either to help produce food or carry on doing my normal and, I thought, quite harmless work.

In other conversations about the individual's wartime obligations there was always some participant who would argue that if one worked on a farm one would be helping the war effort by contributing to the food supply; similarly anyone involved in entertainment was arguably bolstering the national morale. Indeed one was forced to the conclusion that, no matter what one did, one would inevitably be helping one side or the other. For instance, if one ended up in gaol, one would be helping the enemy because food and manpower would be expended on the upkeep of a useless individual. And if one chose to commit suicide this would distinctly help the allied cause since it would mean one less mouth to feed. Once I even heard myself lying to an old friend who had innocently asked if it was true that I was a conscientious objector. It was not that I expected to be criticised or put on trial, but I just did not want to have to go through the predictable rigmarole with her. For a moment I was afraid that I would hear a cock crow.

With Noël Coward there was no call to get involved in all of that. I told him my feelings about war as an international sickness for which a remedy was so rarely sought. In peacetime when governments and individuals might reasonably be expected to treat a problem seriously, they were more interested in selling each other tanks and torpedoes with which to prepare for the next outbreak. I also suggested that a nation like ours should have the same sense of responsibility about the welfare and problems of other nations as of our own.

He asked me then if I had travelled much. No, said I, my experience was limited to rather brief spells in Belgium, France, Switzerland, Germany and a few days in Turkey.

He said that he had travelled a great deal and that, with a little more experience, I too would learn that the British way of life was well worth protecting. He did not say 'well worth fighting for' because I now learned that he was not asking me to put on a uniform with intent to fight. He just wanted me to endorse Britain's war effort, to make the gesture and thereafter get leaves of absence which would permit me to carry on with the work for which I had some skill.

No one has ever faulted Coward's patriotism and he was always helpful and protective towards members of his profession; sometimes, they said, he could be didactic, but there was no finger-wagging during our conversation.

On a point of common sense, Noël could perfectly well have given me the job if he thought I was right for it. But it can be said that during the war Noël pursued two coincident careers. He was the playwright-actor-song-writer whom we had learned to love, and he was the propagandist who throughout the war had hitherto devoted himself to boosting morale throughout the Empire, a labour for which his patriotic fervour made him ideally suited. For the proper conduct of *In Which We Serve* he was wearing both these hats. And he had my entire sympathy if he thought, as I supposed, that the propaganda value of his film could well be marred by the presence in the cast of such a well-known civilian as myself, a failed conscientious objector at that. I was sorry to have missed working with the Master.

The next time I met him was on one of the stages at Denham Studio when I was working with Michael Redgrave in the film version of Robert Ardrey's play *Thunder Rock*. 'Ah yes', said Coward, 'he plays the part of Charleston, doesn't he?' And as he said the name his feet echoed it with a few steps of the synonymous dance.

In 1942 I worked in several other films beside *Thunder Rock*. There was *Alibi*, a thriller which had a not very credible pre-war Parisian background and in which the villain, played by Raymond Lovell, was a night club clairvoyant. There was also *Secret Mission*, a name which in my mind is coupled indelibly with that of its producer Marcel Hellman. And there was *The Bells Go Down* which constituted my only contact with what was to

174

become artistically the most distinguished workshop ever to be part of the British film industry. I am referring to the Ealing Studio whose boss was Michael Balcon and whose principal star in its heyday was Alec Guinness.

Marcel Hellman had no difficulty in talking me into a second film, *They Met in the Dark*, because the earlier one had seemed to be such a smooth operation. But it was only later that I learned that the cause of this was the insistence by its director Harold French that Hellman never appear on the stage when he was rehearsing or shooting a scene. He had learned on a previous occasion that Hellman's presence led to dissension.

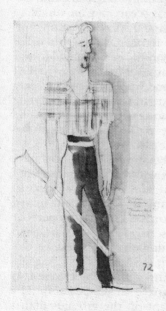

Michael Redgrave in Thunder Rock, *1942*

Hellman had taken on a new director called Karel Lamac, a refugee from Czechoslovakia whose command of English was less than perfect. Hellman, a Roumanian,

175

had however already been resident in England for a number of years, so took advantage of his seniority in residence to lecture poor Lamac. 'Karel', he would say, 'you are a foreigner, you don't understand these things.' There was no limit to the little ways in which he managed to aggravate the director's feelings of insecurity. He interfered on the set and gave directorial advice at every turn. I was particularly sorry for Lamac when he inadvertently got a big laugh with a comical misuse of English. When the assistant director says 'Roll 'em' and the camera begins to turn, the 'clapper boy' springs into a position in front of the lens and 'claps' the board on which the names of the film, the director and the cameraman and the number of scene they are about to shoot are inscribed. The director then says 'Action' and the actors do what they have to do. One day when the assistant had said 'Roll 'em' and the cameras had begun to turn there was a long pause. The director looked around and finally said in a loud voice, 'Where is the boy with the clap?' He said it quite innocently and everyone hooted with laughter. Lamac was embarrassed because he knew that Hellman would not like people to laugh at the expense of his director.

Meanwhile I was annoyed with Hellman because I could not stop myself arguing with him. Argue with the director, yes, if necessary, but not with a producer. In those days the producer was a person who it was hoped would raise enough money, acquire a literary property or original screenplay and the services of a director, who then should be left to work unmolested, unless he was likely to spend all the money too quickly.

But even before the shooting started there were two areas in which he had provoked me unbearably. His backers had criticised the script on the grounds that it was too English. And it was not as if they were Americans themselves; they merely believed that, to crack the American market, the actors must learn to talk sloppy. So Hellman hired some sort of American publicity man to eradicate a few pronouns and insert a few apostrophes, and then went around telling everyone that this well known American writer had done wonders and that the script was now superb. He was the first and last producer with whom I fell into a silly argument about script changes. Thereafter I discussed improvements with the director only, and if we saw things the same way the producer would know nothing until he saw the rushes, at which time, if we were lucky, he would not notice the difference.

Hellman also had a very successful method of annoying both Tom Walls and myself. Our contracts were for the run of the film. Small part actors were paid by the day. When there was a sequence in which several such actors took part, Hellman would knock himself out to make sure that each daily rater's work would be finished in the one day. Very shrewd you may say. Yes of course it was, but Walls and I would arrive at the crack of dawn, get made up, perhaps shoot one 'master' scene before settling down in our dressing rooms and not get to work again until he had eliminated his daily raters. By the time they got around to shooting Walls and me at the end of the afternoon we would have run out of gas.

And how right Harold French had been to insist that Hellman never appear on the stage. It was there that he exasperated most. He would annoy Otto Heller, the cameraman, by asking him what was the 'source of light' represented by the way he had grouped his lights. Heller was a real artist and he was not used to being asked how and why he achieved his effects. Hellman bothered me mostly with his excessive attention to my turn out. He would come up to me and adjust my tie just at the moment that I was readying myself to start one of the scenes. The sum of his annoyances was such that I was obliged to seek relief with a hitherto untried technique. If he tried to catch my eye or to address me, I just pretended that he was not there. As an aggravating presence Hellman no longer existed.

177

But I became aware that he always treated his crews with consideration and that Al Parker liked him and this weighed very much in his favour, so that in the last forty years a sort of mutual affection has burgeoned.

I was shortly to appear in a film called *The Man in Grey*, a landmark for Gainsborough Pictures and, I suppose, for myself too. But even before *The Man in Grey* was shown to the public I had the shock of my life when Peter and Hope Burnup insisted on visiting me in Beaconsfield because they wanted to be the first to tell me that the English edition of something called the *Motion Picture Herald* which they edited had polled me as England's most popular actor. This was because these movies in which I had been appearing had collectively enjoyed such enormous success.

Pierre Rouve

I must add the titles of two more films which were made on the ascending or descending foothills of *The Man in Grey*. One of these was *Candlelight in Algeria*. It concerned the successful efforts of a British officer and an American girl covertly to pave the way for General Mark Clark's historic secret landing in North Africa. This not only proved popular in the home market but, like many other films that were made in England during this period, notably *The Man in Grey*, also rang the bell in a number of European countries after the Liberation. Forever afterwards, while the generation who saw them still breathes, people in Italy have smiled at me with the look of true movie lovers, and after a pause, breathed the words, 'il Huomo in grigio!' I can't say that I remember anyone having breathed the words *Candlelight in Algeria* in any known language as I approached but I have it on good authority – Pierre Rouve, with whom I became professionally associated in later years – that in one year in the late forties it was the most popular film in Bulgaria. Rouve was Bulgarian and he knew. I said it might be a good country for us to go make an independent production. 'No hard currency', he said, shaking his head, then added as an afterthought, 'If you'd like to be paid in tobacco, they could do that', 'And it's good', I said. I had yet to exhale my last puff of cigarette smoke at the time. I could not understand why people continued to smoke the stuff that came from Virginia or Rhodesia when they could so easily enjoy the superior flavour of that emanating from the Balkans. But then, when and if I should come to possess this valuable bulk I'd have to spend a fortune on an advertising campaign.

Speaking of Bulgaria I am reminded of another film which belonged to this group. *Hotel Reserve* was based on the early work of Eric Ambler which had made us sit up and take notice of him when it was published in 1939. Its relationship with Ambler was its only claim to distinction, and the longer we worked on the film the more distant that relationship became. As a book it had been called *Epitaph for a Spy*. Heaven knows what made them swap such a strong title for one so feeble.

11/Shepherd's Bush

I always figured that the Gainsborough Girl was in her prime in the few years before the Second World War. But most aging folk would regard the period from 1942 to 1946 as her heyday, for it was then that an extremely successful programme of movies was churned out, mostly period pieces featuring Jean Kent, Patricia Roc, Phyllis Calvert, Margaret Lockwood, Stewart Granger and myself.

The product of the earlier period, 1935 to 1939, was happy and honest and the very stuff of good movie-making. It includes some peak Hitchcock, some up-and-coming Carol Reed, some splendid scripting by Launder and Gilliatt. I think of *The Ghost Train* and *Sunshine Susie* with that adorable Renate Muller. The actors who answer the recall most promptly are Will Hay, Graham Moffatt, Moore Marriott and the Crazy Gang; yes, and Jack Hulbert, of course, who was in *The Ghost Train*; and Naunton Wayne and Basil Radford insist on being remembered. They all happened in what might properly be defined as Period Three, because Gainsborough had already been going for a long time.

The founding fathers were Messrs Michael Balcon and Victor Saville, who threw their energy and pioneering spirits into the British movie business in the early Twenties. Saville was related by marriage to C.M. Woolf, who had abandoned the fur trade in favour of motion picture distribution and was doing well. Thus Woolf was persuaded to allow Balcon and Saville to handle, as an agency, the Midland distribution rights of the movies which Woolf controlled, such as the early Tarzan adventures and the Harold Lloyd comedies.

Strengthened by other useful alliances, they became bold enough to form their own production company. Their first big success was *Woman to Woman* starring Betty Compson. The next landmark was *The Passionate Adventure*, for the production of which they rented Islington Studios.

Their staff now included men who were later to become big names in the British movie scene: Harold Boxall, who later became Alexander Korda's general manager; George Gunn, who rose to be Britain's leading expert on colour photography; and, in a junior capacity, Alfred Hitchcock. Clive Brook and Victor McLaglen had been launched as stars.

Islington Studios were bought from Paramount by Balcon, Saville and their associates for £14,000. And the films made there may be regarded as the corpus of Gainsborough Period One. Madeleine Carroll emerged as a star, and Benita Hume, and, a very big name in those days, Ivor Novello.

In 1927 Novello and Mabel Poulton were in the original production of *The Constant Nymph*, directed by Adrian Brunel. On this unique occasion the Queen's Hall and full symphony orchestra, with Novello acting as conductor, were hired for a silent film. In the same year the British film industry came under the protection of the Quota Act. Also an important new character, Isidore Ostrer, entered the scene. Period Two was about to begin.

Ostrer acquired cinemas, took C. M. Woolf on to the board of the newly formed Gaumont British Picture Corporation, bought his distribution company, floated Gainsborough Pictures as a public company, took over the little old 'Glass house' studio in Lime Grove hitherto the property of the Gaumont Company and sold a substantial share of the Corporation to William Fox of Fox Film Corporation while adroitly ensuring British control of the total operation.

He also put Michael Balcon in charge of all ensuing production from both the enlarged and modernised Lime

Grove Studio and the Gainsborough Studio in Islington. Of the films made during the lush years that follow it is difficult to be dead sure which were made for Gaumont British and which for Gainsborough. A safe rule is that the more pretentious were Gaumont British because Ostrer and Balcon were having a big romance with the UFA studios of Berlin, enlisting squads of German technicians for service at Lime Grove and dreaming of world conquest for their films, thus anticipating the later fantasies of Alexander Korda and Mr Rank. No-one at that time could charge Gainsborough with pretentiousness; light-hearted stuff for the domestic market was their speciality. Balcon continued to rule the two houses until he joined MGM in 1936; this was the cue for Ted Black to take over as head of production and Period Three to begin.

I picked up a lot of inside stuff from Pamela, who had been involved since early days. She was the boss's daughter and, as Pamela Ostrer, had become a baby star employable in both Gaumont British and Gainsborough productions. Thus I got to know not only the name of the girl, another baby star, who posed as the Gainsborough Girl on the trademark (Glynis Lorrimer), but also learned something of the power struggle that reverberated along the 'Polish Corridor' at the Lime Grove Studios.

Isidore Ostrer, the dexterous and imaginative tycoon who put together this impressive complex, supported by his brothers and C. M. Woolf, came to own the largest chain of cinemas in the British Isles. Again, in partnership with C. M. Woolf they controlled the most important distribution company and the greatest production resources, though this may well be contested by Associated British Picture Corporation who then ran neck and neck with the Gaumont British interests as they do now with the Rank opposition.

The name of J. Arthur Rank, a big man in flour, was first mentioned in connection with motion pictures in the late Thirties when he financed several inexpensive film productions. A church-going man, he chose subjects which were uniformly wholesome.

As soon as World War II got into its stride, the shrewd J. Arthur Rank bought up almost everything that was going in the way of theatres, studios and distribution companies, notably those which had belonged to the Ostrers. In the latter years of the war the British film industry was surprised by its own boom and those contributing to it were surprised to find that they were now working for J. Arthur Rank and that at the beginning of every one of their movies there was the likeliness of an ex-heavyweight champion boxer pretending rather awkwardly to strike a large gong.

In the circumstances the Gainsborough Lady retained her identity remarkably well. Though subordinate to the man with the gong, she continued to show her face until movie-making at Shepherd's Bush was discontinued in 1949.

Gainsborough's good period, as I choose to call it, came to an end in 1939. The resources of British film production were put at the disposal of the Ministry of Information. We were to be informed, instructed and encouraged but not necessarily entertained. But the state of war was soon found not to have checked the British public's movie-going propensity, and so such commercial companies as still had studio space at their command once more set their cameras rolling.

When war broke out in September 1939, Ted Black called everyone on to the set at Islington and told them that there was to be no more production at the studio because, in the event of an air-raid, the huge power chimney was likely to collapse and crush everybody. The filming of *Band Wagon*, an Arthur Askey vehicle, was halted. The following week it was resumed at Lime Grove, where Gaumont British Productions had petered out.

A glance at the list of films made by Gainsborough in 1940 and 1941 suggests that the management decided to play it safe. Thus it rented the studio to 20th Century-Fox for two splendid films by Carol Reed, *The Young Mr Pitt*, which glorified Britain's reaction to the threat of invasion in 1795, and *Kipps*, and 'escape' romance of impeccable style. As for Gainsborough's own product the management leaned heavily on Arthur Askey, the nation's cherished comic. Although Maurice Ostrer was an executive this programme must be regarded as a continuation of Ted Black's innings which started in 1936. But in 1942 an entirely new-style programme was initiated with the production of *The Man in Grey*, new enough to suggest a shift of power among the executives. Although the studios now belonged to Rank, there was a powerful lobby of Ostrers and Ostrer retainers. Harry was there in charge of the Story Department and among the credit titles there appeared on every film the unusual caveat 'In Charge of Production – Maurice Ostrer'. I used to worry about this a lot at that time. How can M.O. be in charge of production when we all know that Ted Black is the boss? I would ask myself.

Let us suppose, however, that Harry Ostrer, who presumably spent his days rifling through the library, was the one who discovered the master work of Lady Eleanor Smith titled *The Man in Grey*. It need not have been Harry who made the discovery. It could have been R. J. Minney, an omnivorous reader who had once been the editor of the *Sunday Referee*, an organ that had been the property of Isidore Ostrer at the time when I. O. thought that his opinions should be made available to a wider public than his own family. Minney was now a producer at the studio. No matter which of them made the discovery, it is at least known that the Ostrer pack were very high on the subject, and with good reason.

Although I. O. had no official position in the Gainsborough scheme he lent spine to any attitude that M. O. might choose to adopt. I believe now that the success of Gainsborough's 'escape' movies represented a victory for the Ostrers. They were fortunate in the fact that Ted Black ran an extremely efficient operation and that their own taste was well suited to the requirements of the time, and thus they have been unable to repeat the success in different circumstances, but at least we must concede to them this one personal victory in the production field.

In return for being awarded the role of bad Lord Rohan in *The Man in Grey* I gave options to the company to use me on specified terms for a further five films. My willingness to sign a multiple contract, which is highly distasteful to me, was earnest of my own faith in the commercial potential of Lady Eleanor Smith's novel. There was nothing about it that I could actually bring myself to like, and I had no clue about how I could do anything with a part so monstrously nasty as that of Lord Rohan. I allowed myself to be beaten by the problem at the outset. To make matters worse, I had worked with Leslie Arliss, the director, on a previous film and had failed to establish a happy relationship. We just could not get along with each other. Angered by my own inability to cope, I wallowed in a stupidly black mood throughout and since my own imagination had contributed nothing to the Lord Rohan who appeared on the screen, I have to conclude that only my permanent aggravation gave the character colour and made it some sort of a memorable thing. The extraordinary success of the film made me even more cross, since I could claim none of the credit.

During this period I was making a bad name for myself, partly because I was a compulsive tease and partly because my experience with producers had made me regard them as natural enemies. It was not until I worked with Sydney Box in 1945 that I learned that one could make friends with a producer. Sparing only Ted Black, whose record I respected, I acted with uncalled-for hostility towards all the top brass of Gainsborough. I somewhat respected R. J. Minney because he could read and write, but he was tainted by producership. To me producers were men who polluted the artistic aspirations of writers, directors and actors; who responded only to the promptings of vulgar men in Wardour Street; who were bad sports and bad losers.

Of the films covered in the multiple contract referred to above, I served in only four. After these I had a terrific stroke of luck. The company failed to pick up the options for the two further films by the date specified in the overall contract, permitting me thus to be once more a free agent.

Stewart Granger shared my feelings about the bosses, but was forceful and resilient and deservedly became the Gainsborough Girl's pride and joy.

I had gone, in the spirit of curiosity, I suppose, to the press showing of *The Man in Grey* and found myself afterwards at the customary free-drink session beside C. A. Lejeune, who was the best film critic we ever had. 'This is an occasion worth celebrating,' said she to the company at large. 'It is not often we have the privilege of attending the birth of a great new star.' A pause and a sip, then, 'This young man Stewart Granger, isn't he marvellous!' And she went on from there. As I have said, I had no illusions about my own contribution to the film, but somehow I failed to enjoy Miss Lejeune's little talk.

The Man in Grey mode was sustained most faithfully in the following hits: *Fanny by Gaslight*, with Granger and myself, Phyllis Calvert, Jean Kent; *The Madonna of the Seven Moons*, with Granger, Peter Glenville, Phyllis Calvert; *Love Story*, with Granger and Margaret Lockwood; *They were Sisters*, with Phyllis Calvert, Dulcie Gray, Anne Crawford, Peter Murray Hill and myself; and finally *The Wicked Lady* with myself, Margaret Lockwood, Pat Roc and Jean Kent.

If I ever see *The Wicked Lady* advertised on TV I make a point of watching it. The part I played in it was rather small and for this reason there was a clause in my contract which prevented the producer, who happened to be Minney, from cutting anything out of my scenes without my approval. Thus when, during the editing, he found himself wanting to snip a fragment from one such scene, he was obliged to run the film for me and point to the proposed excision. At the end I was surprised to hear myself saying: 'Oh, I don't think you should cut anything from *my* scenes. It was the long stretches between my appearances which seemed to drag.' I am sure that Minney was not surprised, since my anti-producer attitude must already have persuaded him that I was a cad.

They said at the time that the late Queen Mary frequently asked for the film to be run for her at Marlborough House, but I have no means of verifying this report.

The Wicked Lady acquired international notoriety on account of the 'cleavage' exhibited by Margaret Lockwood and Patricia Roc. The Production Code of America was very fussy about the way ladies dressed at the time, and no film could be released on a profitable scale unless it was granted a seal of approval.

Mr Rank's public relations officer deftly took advantage of the situation and it was widely publicised that the film was to be re-cut for American distribution and that where it was not possible to substitute shots taken from an angle which showed less cleavage, scenes were to be enlarged by optical printer so that the offensive anatomy was no longer visible in the frame.

The nice thing about show business is that success cannot be computerised; the know-it-alls know nothing. The know-it-alls at Gainsborough glanced at me pity-ingly when it became known that I was to play a part in a film which had been dreamed up and modestly budgeted by Sydney Box, who was known only as a producer of documentaries. But the film was *The Seventh Veil,* which became a huge success in all the world's markets, including that of the indomitable United States. Box himself became the pet of Arthur Rank and was given Gainsborough. The know-it-alls, who now included myself, thought: 'Aha, now we shall see something'; but, surprisingly, nothing very sensational came out of Gainsborough from that moment on.

Ted Black had left the company in 1945; Maurice Ostrer ceded to Box in 1946, taking Minney with him. The redoubtable Leslie Arliss had got a job with Alexander

Korda. Patricia Roc and Phyllis Calvert worked again for Gainsborough after sorties to Hollywood, and Margaret Lockwood, who remained under contract to Rank, made one more film under the new management. But the mixture was not as before. Something was missing, perhaps the Gainsborough Lady's naivety, which had been her special quality.

In 1949, on the completion of a film ironically entitled *Don't Ever Leave Me*, the Lime Grove Studio fell to the BBC, and the lady vanished.

12/Olleberrie Farm

I always construed the studio's failure to pick up its option for my services in two further pictures as a friendly closing of Ted Black's eye. And it certainly did not stand in the way of further engagements being offered to me as a free lance. One of these was their projected film to be based on the life of Paganini, the astonishing violinist who flourished during the period of Napoleon's conquests. They had not yet completed their script when they spoke of this to me and I had at the time only an elementary knowledge of his career; nevertheless I welcomed it as a demanding venture for all of us. So, until they had a script to offer me I would concentrate on the basic need, a familiarity with the instrument. I rented a violin and bought myself a bow and, thus accoutred, set out with Pamela on one of our periodic expeditions for ENSA. Patrick Hamilton, the author, himself rehearsed us in *Gaslight*, his famous melodrama. Pamela played the part of the Manninghams' maid. I leave the name of the actress who played Mrs Manningham unmentioned because our relations were none too good and I confess to having aggravated them by practising the violin in my dressing room which was next to hers during the period between matinée and evening performance wherever we went and sometimes even in the intermissions. Justifiable homicide is the worst she would have got, had she done me in.

So when we returned home the script of *Paganini* was sitting on top of the pile of mail waiting to be read.

It was just one of those deep disappointments. All my imagining had concerned itself strictly with the professional and politico-social history of the man. I should have known that they would concentrate on his alleged love life. But I was no longer under contract to the company and was therefore not obliged to accept the role. A pity about all that wasted violin practice. Never mind. At least I did not need to waste the bow. With a loving note I sent it to Stewart Granger who *was* still under contract and would be obliged to inherit. And, although he seemed to get as much fun from a spot of producer-baiting as anyone I ever worked with, he was deeply conscientious and had a load of theatrical talent. He should have made himself a producer and/or director, preferably working with other actors since it is almost never that an actor can direct himself. You have to be such a tough trader, so crafty to get away with that. I can think of only one such, a character with whom I was to grapple in later years.

It is not true that *all* the films that were perpetrated by our gang were big hits. I can think of one which I have always assumed must have been quite a flop. And the blame must be shared by myself and R. J. Minney and Bernard Knowles, the director. Knowles deserved his share because he had never got over *Citizen Kane* and still thought that it was a shortcut to success if one had the actors play immensely long sequences without any intercutting or covering shots. In *Citizen Kane* the director could afford to do this because Herman Mankiewicz had devised one strong situation after another. Knowles was not the only one to misapply the technique. The great Hitchcock fumbled with it twice (*Under Capricorn* and *Rope*).

This was *A Place of One's Own* and the truly original story was written by Sir Osbert Sitwell whom no one is going to blame for anything. Minney was handling it with unaccustomed tenderness. He had even hired the brilliant Rex Whistler to do the designs. When I read the script – it was not submitted to me – not only did I enthuse but I even asked that I might be permitted to play the role of the elderly retiree in the story, Mr Smedhurst. And this is

Osbert Sitwell, 1944

where Minney and I earned our share of the blame. He said
yes.

Of course it could have turned out a failure even if the
most suitable actor in the world had played that part. But
the reactions of the top brass at the studio did nothing to
allay my own feeling of guilt for having volunteered my
services. In any case it was not that I was incapable of
turning my hand to a character part, it was just that I had
amassed what I always realised was an absurd degree of
popularity, and the fan population wanted me to appear
only as some heroic young lady-killer; or better-still, lady-
basher.

I was receiving now an enormous fan mail, much of
which I read. And there were frighteningly large numbers
who, having seen me play mean roles on the screen,
assumed that I was equally mean in my private life. I am
sure that I have many tiresome habits but beating up

J. M. in Sitwell's A Place of One's Own, *1944*

women does not happen to be one of them. I was rather cross that I had already been typed as a heavy on the strength of only two roles which were at all intimidating. No, make that three or four. It started with the moody individual in *The Night has Eyes* who was thought to have been shell-shocked during the Spanish Civil War and thus to have developed a sort of moon madness which caused him to strangle animals of various sizes as every full moon came around. The script compelled the audience to expect the strangulation of Joyce Howard, who played the part of an innocent, if nosy school-teacher. But it turned out in the end that he too was totally innocent and was the victim of a conspiracy on the part of Wilfrid Lawson and Mary Clare who ended up, quite rightly, in a bog on Dartmoor. Innocent, you see. Next time up I played the Marquis of Rohan in the triumphant *Man in Grey*, who was surely more sinned against than sinning. After all, Margaret Lockwood had planned the death of poor Phyllis Calvert and therefore could one not say that horse-whipping was too good for her?

Then there was Lord Manderstoke in *Fanny by Gaslight*. No contest here. Manderstoke was rotten.

Then there was the character I had played in *They Were Sisters*, for whom there was no accounting. I mean the writer had had such a busy time setting down all the most colourful events in the lives of all three sisters *and* their husbands that he had neglected to supply motivations. The critic on the *Sunday Express* wrote: 'I wish Mr Pertwee, author of this screenplay, would tell me how he accounts for the villainies of the husband, Geoffrey, played by James Mason as though he were suffering from a succession of Victory hangovers. There is absolutely nothing to motivate Mr Mason's viciousness. He is flung on the screen as the husband of one of the three sisters who drives his wife to suicide, loathes his own son, snubs the servants, threatens his own sister when she interferes, and behaves generally with incredible caddishness. Why? It will never be known.'

I never consulted Mr Pertwee himself, but when an actor has to try to make real a character who has been only roughly sketched by those responsible for the screenplay, then he has to work twice as hard filling in all the details of the character's background so that at least the actor himself is convinced of his reality and can react automatically to the motivations he has invented. So here you had a character, I informed myself, in which an innate three hundred and sixty degree hostility had been exacerbated by careless eating habits.

So perhaps they had a right to think of me as an actor who habitually played heavies, but I did not wish to spend my life avoiding the bad name that could accrue from this practice. 'Are you really like that?' 'Do you treat your wife in the same way?' wrote the fans. I realised that this was an occupational hazard, something to be taken reluctantly in one's stride, and perhaps be converted into an innocent source of merriment.

So I wrote a little facetious article and called it *Yes, I Beat My Wife* and offered it to that nice little magazine, *Lilliput*. The first member of the editorial staff who glanced at it promptly tossed it aside but fortunately Kaye Webb, another member, spotted it and thought it worth publishing. It was a poor thing but I had supplied a couple of sketches to go with it and was glad to see them in print. Also I was glad to make the acquaintance of Kaye Webb who was to become a star in the publishing world and at that time was on the threshold of her marriage to the great black and white artist, Ronald Searle. She published two more of my articles, one called *I Hate Producers* and the other was about Joe Breen and the American Film Production Code. As an extracurricular activity the writing of such articles had almost replaced the writing of pompous letters but sometimes the one led to the other.

In October of the year 1944 Michael Powell made one of

'Yes, I beat my wife'

his most attractive films, called *I Know Where I Am Going*. He had asked me to be in several of his films but for one reason or another I had never been free at the right moment. And now he offered me a part in this one and since it was the best of his scripts that I had read I wanted very much to be available and indeed Al Parker had practically agreed on a contract when a point came up that made the project unacceptable. It was simply that Pamela and I constituted a mutual protection society; it was our war aim to stay together and, if necessary, be demolished by the one bomb. We knew that the film was to be shot on the island of Mull, off the West Coast of Scotland. Powell now let it be known that we would live in camping conditions – hutments, cottages or tents and that although we would never be shooting beyond a radius of thirty miles from Tobermory, the largest town on the island, we could not use its hotel accommodation because no transportation would be available, except what was specifically required for the actual shooting.

Michael Powell

I pointed out that in the month of October the light would not be enough to allow us to shoot before 10 a.m. nor after 5 p.m. so that we would have a daily period of seventeen hours in which no shooting would take place. All right, even if I myself had no personal means of transportation, they would surely need to get the film that had been shot during each day to the port of Tobermory, and surely, that being the case, Pamela and I could cadge a lift. But Powell would not budge. I think that he was not very keen on overloading his unit with wives or husbands who were there strictly as passengers, a view which I already respected, though on this occasion the one-bomb principle blocked my co-operation. There are two reasons for mentioning this film in which I played no part. The experience enhanced my admiration for the man as an artist and as an eccentric. But even more important to me personally was the fact that the ultimate failure to get together with Powell threw me into the ranks of the temporarily unemployed. I was thus free to accept work a little later in what turned out to be the most successful film of my entire career, *The Seventh Veil*.

This film was the brain child of Sydney and Muriel Box, who, before the war, had applied their talents, separately or as a team, to writing one-act plays. In 1939 he founded a company called Verity films which produced more than a hundred documentary and training films for the War Office and Ministry of Information. In the final years of the war their interests veered towards feature films.

Sydney had been asked to make a documentary about the rehabilitation of shell-shocked soldiers and had been studying the recent application of hypnosis and truth-disclosing drugs employed with the aim of effecting a cure. Hearing of this, Muriel, according to her own account, exclaimed, 'What a wonderful film could be made showing these techniques applied to the rehabilitation of, say, a famous dancer or violinist or what-have-you!' Sydney agreed and suggested that she rough out a story on those lines.

Together they developed a screen play in which Francesca, the central character, was a mixed-up concert pianist, a rôle to be played by Ann Todd. Their story was put together with great skill and much flashing forward and backward but in a way that enlightened rather than confused. In chronological order the principal events were an initial trauma caused during her childhood by a teacher who struck her fingers with a cane; loss of parents and adoption by Nicholas, an austere music lover; a flirtation with a young dance band leader, causing unnaturally possessive guardian to whisk her to the Continent, there to continue her musical training until ripe for her debut; further incitement of guardian's jealousy by attentions paid to his ward by noted painter. It has become clear by this point that guardian is decidedly neurotic. Now it is he who thwacks her fingers with his cane as she is running through Beethoven's Moonlight Sonata. But this is topped by an automobile accident in which her hands take another beating; she attempts suicide by jumping into the Thames, is rescued but is now reduced to such depression that she has lost even the power of speech.

Cue for our psychiatrist and his hypno-therapy. When she has been straightened out, the authors tease the audience with the question – to which of the four established men in her life will she show a sign of love? This worked especially well since the writers changed their minds dramatically at some point of time between their first completed screenplay and their ultimate. I had read the first screenplay at a time when they were not offering me a part in the film because I was unavailable. At this time the role of Nicholas, the guardian, was seen as a straight Svengali figure and the actor they had first chosen for it was Francis L. Sullivan, the portly actor who was later to be so sensational as Mr. Jaggers in *Great Expectations* and the Beadle in *Oliver Twist*.

Likewise in the original script, once her cure had been effected, our concert pianist was to have made a bee line for the dance band leader. In the ultimate script the lady chose

Nicholas, her cranky guardian. This in my opinion was a winning stroke. It made for an unexpected and strangely romantic dénouement. In fact it converted a modest experiment into an international hit.

Muriel Box's autobiography *Odd Woman Out* surprised me with an item about J. A. Rank of which I was totally ignorant; and since I was to acquire the reputation of being resolutely anti-Rank, I think it is only fair that I repeat what Muriel has to say of the part he played in the financing of the film. It seems that the Boxes had undertaken to put a new picture into production at Riverside Studio by October 1944 or to forfeit the space reserved for them. The script was sent to Rank's General Film Distributors for consideration and read by the Board of Directors but failed to get an unanimous verdict on its merits. Arthur Rank however ignored their views and, according to Muriel Box, spoke out as follows:

'I gave this script to my wife to read and she said how much she liked it. So I read it myself and I agree with her. It's original, a jolly good story, and I propose to go ahead with it – and that's final!' There was no more to be said.

If super stars had been invented in 1945, that is what Ann Todd would have become as a result of the great personal success that she scored in *The Seventh Veil*. She demonstrated an interestingly ambiguous personality. We saw a scrubbed urchin behind whose little-girl attractiveness there was a hint of danger.

After his years at Gainsborough Sydney Box retired to Perth in Western Australia. I suggest that if he has the time and inclination he give a thought to the marital life of Nicholas and Francesca. He would find it an interesting challenge. Sydney had the air of a baby rogue elephant, in the most flattering sense. When he paid his daily visit to the set where we were working his beaming presence gave the impression that for him each new day was a new adventure.

The career of Compton Bennett also took off impressively. He was honoured with a contract at MGM in

The Seventh Veil *as J. M. saw it*

Hollywood and had his name attached to an outstandingly successful picture, *King Solomon's Mines*, before returning to England.

As for myself I became, thanks to the Boxes, a piece of merchandise distinctly worth bidding for in Hollywood. Not long after we had completed the film I got the impression that Americans looked at me in a new way, but it was not until I actually travelled to America at the end of 1946 that I came to realise how sensational that success had been and indeed just what value was attached to the incidence of success in the United States.

One of Sydney Box's first acts when he came to power was to suggest to me that if there was any film subject that I wished to produce myself there would be no problem finding finance for it. Pamela and I decided that we could write a very nice scenario about the Brontë family with a special emphasis on the character of Bramwell, the gifted but unstable brother of the sisters Charlotte, Emily and Anne. We even offered what we thought was a suitable title, *The Upturned Glass*, which along with a full statement of our intentions was duly announced in the Trade papers. But our choice had been ill-timed for almost at once we were confronted by advertisements in these same papers of the forthcoming release of a Brontë film which had just been perpetrated by Warner Bros. I have never seen the film, so I have no right to use such a word, but naturally we felt frustrated, and I was especially irked since, being a Yorkshireman from the West Riding, I had a proprietary feeling about an area which included Haworth as well as Huddersfield. The Warner Bros. film was called *Devotion* and the girls were played by Olivia de Havilland, Ida Lupino and Nancy Coleman.

Our production had even been scheduled for a given date though no actual physical preparations had yet taken place. All we now lacked was a story to go with the title we had announced and to settle into the studio space already allocated. So we wrote a new script. This time it was about a brain surgeon whose wife mysteriously falls out of a window. But did she fall or was she pushed? The surgeon plays private detective, finds out who the pusher was and exacts his revenge. The story was acceptable more on account of its form than of its substance. It was accepted as a proper film, was nicely reviewed and I for several years drew quite a lot of additional money as a result of my .participation in the profits. The writing of the script was credited to John P. Monaghan, more than a little inaccurately, since his contribution was not in fact very large.

Monaghan was an American captain with whom we had first become friends when he was stationed in Salisbury at the time when we were playing *Gaslight* there and my rented violin was being tortured. We had kept in touch with Monaghan until the European war was over and learned of his wish to become a writer. He was not originally due to be 'separated' or released from the American army in England but we suggested that he inform his authorities that he intended to study writing in England and he would therefore appreciate it if his separation were effected in England. Officially therefore he became our writer and indeed he did some writing for us but he was generally more effective as a fixer, occasional driver and a telephone handler who was programmed to say no; also transportation officer and public relations officer. He was employed by us to carry out one or more of these functions from the time of his 'separation' until November of 1946 when we set sail for the United States aboard SS. *Queen Elizabeth*, and spasmodically thereafter.

When the war in Europe ended we sold the house in Beaconsfield complete with hens, henhouse and vegetable plantation and moved into one near King's Langley which by some previous owner had been given the attractive name of Olleberrie Farm. This had a lovely garden with some judiciously placed trees. The bottom of the cultivated garden yielded to a somewhat neglected apple orchard while almost in the middle of the lawn was a handsome elm. Closer to the house on a paved terrace was a beautiful prunus or decorative cherry which bloomed shocking pink and which seemed especially stunning because directly behind it, if looked at from the correct angle, were two tall wild cherry trees which bloomed a big white cloud. But during the year of our occupancy the weather seldom permitted the full enjoyment of this great garden.

It was not a very big house nor even very expensive but it was the background for our new lives as the internationally sought after movie star and his clever wife. Even before the glorification that followed the American release of *The Seventh Veil* I was sought after in the sense that men who represented Hollywood power came marching to our very door, men like Spyros Skouras for instance who came blatantly bearing gifts and offering a fantastic contract with 20th Century Fox which would permit me to visit Hollywood at their unlimited expense and then, having taken a look at the studio and considered the films they were going to offer me, I could make up my mind whether to stay or return to England. Among the visitors also was the famous Hedda Hopper who wished to present me with an award on behalf of *Picturegoer* magazine. She had a big hat and endless badinage.

I was also receiving vague attentions from J. Arthur Rank, not personal attentions, but as the owner of General Film Distributors and of the largest chain of cinemas, he was constantly negotiating with producers other than those at his Gainsborough plant, where incidentally Sydney Box had not yet taken over, because our success in America had not yet peaked. Pamela and I were actually in Wiesbaden when word first filtered through to us that customers were lining up round the block in all the American cities where *The Seventh Veil* was playing. Intent on taking a closer look at these Americans who were liberating Europe with their Hershey Bars and their silk stockings and their disarming ways, we had moved in on the Entertainment Section of the American Red Cross.

We had prepared several sketches for ourselves as a

means of bringing merriment to the exhausted GIs whose only wish was to be sent home to be 'separated'. It did not work out just like that. The two sketches which were our own creations were never put to the test. One was a peculiar Japanese joke and the other was a little bit of fun based on the premise that an eminent Shakespearean actor was with his partner about to embark on excerpts from *Othello*; a Red Cross Lassie would announce that unfortunately the female partner was down with the flu and could not appear, at which point another Lassie (Pamela) would pop up in the audience and volunteer to substitute as Desdemona since she knew the entire play by heart. Rollicking fun would ensue. But through no fault of our own, we got no further than the Olympia Theatre in Paris with our third sketch which was an abbreviated version of a duologue by Molnar about the same sort of husband and wife team that the same playwright had used as characters in *The Guardsman*. Our act was a segment of a variety programme catering, it was hoped, to the tastes of the soldiery, most of whom would rather have passed the evening in Pig Alley (a.k.a. Place Pigalle). If they had not racked up enough 'points' they were liable to be shipped off to the other war which was still going strong in the Pacific. I don't believe that we did much to cheer them up. In the event it was decided that, instead of touring from place to place in a 'cinemobile' as had been originally intended, we should proceed to Wiesbaden and initiate the production of plays in the severely damaged Opera House.

I staged Robert Sherwood's *The Road to Rome*, with which I was familiar, having chosen an excellent group of amateur actors and technicians from among the now stationary US Personnel (Pamela played Ena Burrill's part), and topped that with a never-to-be-repeated play of our own called *Made in Heaven*. The greatest pleasure that accrued to us from the ARC Mission was our temporary association with the actor John Buckmaster, who was cast in the rôle of a comic English nobleman. An elegant, good looking blond Englishman, he had been extremely popular on the West End stage in the thirties. Being now a naturalised American he found himself among the soldiery in Wiesbaden and hence, to our great delight, in our play.

It was getting cold in the theatre, being already early November when we opened *Made in Heaven*. Our bombers had destroyed a large section of the front of the building during the later stages of the war and one of the proscenium curtains had been hung over the gap to keep the light out rather than the cold. The bottom of it was about a foot off the floor and the November gales caused the whole thing to billow like a sail. The time of the action in our play was supposed to be summer and through the French windows of the stage set could be seen the likeness of a typical English herbaceous border. But the actors' breath was also distinctly visible when we spoke. We outstayed our welcome, not as far as our new colleagues and the audiences were concerned, but our superior officers in the ARC decided to wrap up our section of the entertainment effort and had ordered us home some weeks before we actually left.

We had not intended to go rushing off to the United States so soon after the war, but now we changed our minds. This was partly because the Americans managed to make an awfully good impression on so many people including ourselves. The role of daredevil liberators became them.

A second consideration was Hollywood's magnetic attraction for Pamela. In the South of France that she had known there had been some kinship with Hollywood. On the Côte d'Azur there still is. And then there was that exposure to the Hollywood élite at her uncle Mark's table.

But I had something else in mind when I found myself leaning towards the Hollywood experiment. I had a clear sense of my own status in the English entertainment world. I knew always on which step of the ladder I stood. All the time that I spent pursuing the available projects in England I had always been keenly aware of the stars who were at any given moment more attractive to a producer than I was. Laurence Olivier, Rex Harrison, David Niven, Michael Redgrave, Richard Greene, Trevor Howard etc., etc. I would encourage myself by saying 'Ah but this film is not nearly good enough for Laurence Olivier or Rex Harrison. And Niven and Richard Greene are doing other films which I have read about in the *Kinematograph Weekly*. And Redgrave is going to do that play... etc.' I knew the pecking order. I also knew that in spite of the grand boasts about future British products that might be attributed to J. Arthur Rank, the number per year of good British films could be counted on the fingers of little more than one hand. Flukes like *The Seventh Veil* were rare. Therefore the good films would correspond exactly with the number of our good directors, none of whom at that time, thank God, was likely to be coerced into making a film which did not accord with his own taste. So each year one could reasonably expect:

One film by Carol Reed
One film by David Lean
One film by Powell and Pressburger
One film from Launder and Gilliatt
One fluke
One film by Anthony Asquith.

That makes a total of six. And that would be a very good year. Since of these directors I had worked only with Anthony Asquith who, I was sure, would prefer Trevor Howard any day, I thought it more than likely that I might have to go on knocking myself out in an unbroken line of banalities, whereas the Hollywood people were liable to be much more impressed by my highly touted popularity; I would extend my range, have a wider choice.

Also there had been a wild sophisticated wit in many of the pre-war films and plays from America which had not yet been matched by anything that we had attempted in England. Actually a turnaround was taking place without my knowing it, for in the late forties and throughout the fifties British films were to become wittier and American films were to become less so. But at the time when Pamela and I were bringing our momentous decision to the boil, I was powerfully influenced by thoughts of James Thurber, Robert Sherwood, Dorothy Parker, Preston Sturges, George Kaufman, Moss Hart, Herman Mankiewicz and many others.

So it was a definite tilt towards Hollywood that we registered when we came back from the Wiesbaden Opera House and we hastened to discuss it with the only American of my acquaintance who had Hollywood connections.

His name was David E. Rose and I believe that I had met him for the first time during the production of *Hatter's Castle*, he being the head of the British limb of Paramount Pictures, the company which distributed that film. It may indeed have been he who caused the producer I. Goldsmith to bother Robert Newton about his runaway Scottish accent. So between 1941 and 1946 I met the man frequently. I guess that he was the smoothest American that I had met before I went to the States and found that they were in plentiful supply. He wore very well-cut suits and shirts and showed good taste in his choice of neckties. He was also an extremely well-shaved man. I went once to his office in mid-morning and was shocked to find that he had not yet shaved, but this was in later days when our mutual cordiality was wearing a little thin.

'I know that you cannot think of going to Hollywood now,' he said to me on various occasions during the course of the war, 'but if you should ever want to make the move, just say the word and I should be only too happy to arrange a contract for you with Paramount.' I thanked him and assured him that I would do just that.

And now, it seemed, the moment had come. We had made our decision, and this charming man was going to see that we be translated to Hollywood in the most prestigious and profitable style.

Trouble brewed simultaneously in another quarter. I had taken to writing articles. I even wrote a few guest columns for the *Daily Mail*, with illustrations. And then came one that I had written for *Summer Pie* on the invitation of a friend who was on the editorial staff. It tripped me up, and it really was not my fault. It was a quite naïf essay, nothing more, which was entitled *Glamour*.

'Glamour,' said I, 'is precisely that virtue of remaining tantalisingly beyond one's reach.'

And a few inches further down I wrote, 'the teasing thing about glamour is that the nearer one gets to the source, the feebler its rays. It has no gold standard. At one time to sit in any theatre waiting for the curtain to go up was in itself a thrilling experience. But when I became an actor the enchantment wore off. Though I sat in the stalls a part of me would stray behind the footlights. The scene revealed was no longer of an intangible glamour world; it was a thing of size and hessian, of painfully nervous and conscientious human beings struggling for their lines and sweating under their grease paint.'

I went on to say that by contrast I was still acutely sensitive to the glamour of any type of entertainment that was still foreign to me, citing the ballet, the opera and the Music Hall as examples of glamorous activity. In other words familiarity caused glamour to evaporate.

'It should follow,' I continued, 'that the movies can no longer do to me the thing they used. And up to a point this is true. *It is true that I find precious little glamour in British pictures*. There might be more than one reason for this, but the reason which fits my argument is that I know when I see such a film what has happened to that strip of celluloid every inch of the way.'

I went on to specify a number of funny and/or exasperating things that had happened in the course of my own movie-making which made it difficult for me to see the end product as an object of glamour, although there was still a hint of it in some Hollywood films which were so eminently foreign to us living in Europe. You just had to think of Lena Horne or Fred Astaire or the smooth charm of a Frank Capra comedy or even of Carmen Miranda and Betty Grable.

Any editor would have been justified in tossing the article into the waste paper basket because it was boring and obvious, but there was a surprise repercussion which no one could have anticipated.

While we were still in Germany I received from The Association of Ciné Technicians a letter signed by its president, Anthony Asquith, in which he stated that my allegations were unfair and that the technicians would be quite prepared to set British films against the list of 'Glamour' that I gave at the end of my article. Furthermore I was informed that copies of the letter had been sent to the trade press, the Ministry of Information and the Board of Trade.

I was guilty, it seemed, of having made the single statement, 'I find precious little glamour in British films', ruthlessly plucked from its context. From Asquith's letter one would be justified in assuming that none of the Ciné Technicians had read the entire article, least of all the imbecile who had initially tabled the charge against me.

Then came an equally surprising letter from the British Film Producers' Association which threatened that definite action would be taken against me if there were any repetition of articles or statements derogatory to British Film Production. I noticed that, although it was clear that Mr. Rank had had nothing to do with the authorship, the letterhead claimed him as the president of the Association.

When we had recovered from the initial impact of this Alice in Wonderland development we put our minds to the problem of how best to do a little stirring. I knew that J. Arthur Rank was supposed to be a decent sort of bloke. But that did not prevent me from resenting him. Okay, he was a millionaire miller. To that he had devoted his life. And if he had earned his money supplying the *best* flour and the *best* bread he deserved our respect. There were nowadays many people who could tell the difference between bread and blotting paper, let them be the judges of his milling. It was none of my business. Movie-making *was* my business and it seemed a shame that money from bread gave a man the right to move into movies. I knew that diversification was something that our generation had to live with but the knowledge did not cheer me.

And another thing made me mad at him. It is more than likely that sudden, virtually unpremeditated success in our line of work has an unsettling effect. It is easy to see what it does to a young actor who plays the leading role in a television series that is renewed year after year, or to some of the young rock stars. When the victim is someone like myself who has been slogging away at his job for over ten years and feels that he has been consistently neglected by the Mr. Ranks and by those who constitute the top echelon of the Producers' Association, he goes berserk in a slightly different style. The previous offenders now suddenly start paying him court and offering him important jobs and inflated salaries, but is the victim grateful? No, he would like to kick their teeth in. He does not do any such thing, he is politeness itself, but there is no denying that he *feels* hostile; at least this one did. (I have friends who even now, given the conversational space, will put up a strong defence for J. Arthur and his programme for the British film industry. First they will remind me, in the manner of Jimmy Carter's disciples, that he was a truly religious man, though in place of a Baptist, we had a Methodist. Secondly J. Arthur was encouraging and financing a great many independent producers and giving them unlimited artistic freedom. And third and most important, his films were intended to earn the dollars which the country so much needed at the time. In spite of this I would still choose the anti-Rank brief.)

Pamela and I had more or less decided to have David Rose fix up a nice Hollywood contract with his company, Paramount, but I was at the same time receiving offers from British producers who had distribution contracts with Rank, so I decided to annoy J. Arthur by giving him the impression that I was turning these offers down and heading for America because I had been so hurt by the way the Association of Ciné Technicians and the British Film Producers' Association had treated me.

I wrote a long and predictably pompous letter to Mr Rank anticipating by almost forty years the predilection of Mr Henry Root, the retired wet fish merchant. I reached the following climax on about the third page:

The letter (from the British Film Producers' Association) actually contains a threat that in the event of repetition of my conduct (i.e. the free but perfectly legal expression of my opinion) *action would be taken*. As legal action is out of the question I presume that this must refer to a projected blackballing. No sort of concerted action has ever been achieved in the past to my knowledge, as its members have represented rival commercial organisations. But perhaps the existence of a virtual monopoly has emboldened the Association so that now it feels strong enough to attempt quite illegitimate means of bringing to heel those members of the industry who voice opinions which are distasteful to them.

I feel that a timely warning should be given to both these Associations lest they abuse their powers . . .

And so on for another page or so, and ending with:

I am sending copies of this letter to the Producers' Association and the A.C.T. And as the latter have drawn the attention of the trade press, the Board of Trade and the Ministry of Information, I feel that they too should receive copies.

Yours sincerely, J.M.

Referring to the letter from the Producers' Association of which he was president, Mr Rank graciously replied to me: 'I have no knowledge of this letter as it was sent to you whilst I was in America. I have a good deal of sympathy with your point of view and I shall look forward to talking this matter over with you when you get back from Germany.'

The contents of the two letters that I had received and of the one that I wrote to Rank were aired in the trade press whose reaction was not unfriendly. The final absurdity was an announcement that on the occasion of the Cinematograph Exhibitors' Association's forthcoming meeting the first matter to be discussed was a request from the Producers' Association asking for the support of the C.E.A. in banning films in which I appeared, should I choose to repeat my so-called derogatory remarks about British films. In the event, the Producers' Association withdrew their request before the C.E.A. meeting took place. In the opinion of 'Tatler', the nom de plume of a columnist in the *Daily Film Renter*, the request 'would certainly have been contemptuously rejected . . . make no mistake about that'.

I wondered at the time which member of the A.C.T. had been so illiterate as to have made the original complaint. I was told it was a writer, whose name I have now forgotten. But a *writer* of all people!

The 'Mason Incident', as it was referred to, led to quite a lot of publicity in the national press which I would have appreciated had I been at that time more properly career-minded. One newspaper quoted me as having said that Mr Rank was the worst thing that could have happened to the British film industry. I suppose that I must have said it, though I cannot remember into whose ear I dropped this pearl of wisdom. If I had indeed expressed such a sentiment I would not have gone quite so far since I knew lots of individuals who, given the wealth with which to purchase equivalent control, would have been more than a match for J. Arthur. Our newspapermen were all treating him as if he were a knight in shining armour just because his public relations office *said* he was. And many of these newsmen were as old as I and should surely have known that others much better qualified than he had tried to create a big market for their wares on the other side of the Atlantic and had failed disastrously. I had the feeling that our hero, once he discovered that the actual production of films, as opposed to distribution and exhibition, was a hard nut to crack, would let us down. But I tried to keep my opinions to myself. No one likes a smart guy. And anyway I knew that very shortly I would automatically bring the press down on my head, if we were to carry out our half formed plan of moving, at least temporarily, over to the United States later in the year.

Carol Reed was my favourite director. Before *Odd Man Out* I had never worked with him but in every one of his films that I had seen there was great warmth and understanding. The director with whose work Carol's was most frequently compared was Alfred Hitchcock, presumably because one thought of them both as having a taste for thrillers generously laced with comedy. Indeed Hitchcock very rarely strayed from this line of work. The suspense film was his speciality right from the start of his career as a director whereas in all the films by Carol Reed that I had seen prior to my engagement in *Odd Man Out* the only common ingredient had been an affectionate sense of humour.

I mentioned in the previous chapter that Reed had an important position in Gainsborough Period III when the productions emanated from the Islington Studio. There he made the first three of his films that I saw, *A Girl in the News*, *A Girl Must Live* and *Bank Holiday*. None of these could be called a thriller. And the next was a serious drama from a novel by A. J. Cronin, *The Stars Look Down*, which offered us a great deal of heartbreak against a background of coal mining problems. When Gainsborough Pictures closed down in Islington and set up shop in Shepherd's Bush during the phony war, Carol made his enchanting film about William Pitt the

Younger, and enlisted the most sought-after leading man of those years, Robert Donat, to play the part of Pitt and add to the enchantment. Then came *Kipps* with Michael Redgrave, also at Shepherd's Bush. Then to Denham for *The Way Ahead*, a masterly film which was designed to boost morale and brief us on the progress of the war. This had the benefit of some extremely stylish writing by Eric Ambler, while the principal acting was lightly and convincingly rendered by David Niven, who in this and in his next film *A Matter of Life and Death* * (Michael Powell) was at the top of his form.

Thus I had admired Carol Reed only from a distance. Though he was the director with whom of all the directors in the world I was most keen to work, I never thought of this as a target within my range. And then suddenly out of the mouth of Al Parker came casually the all important news flash that Carol was to make a film of F. L. Green's book *Odd Man Out* and that he wished to have me play the leading part.

The film script had been skilfully assembled by Carol Reed and the author himself. It told with great poignancy and humour the story of a member of an 'organisation' which was understood to be the I.R.A., which at that time was practically dormant. In our story the members of the Belfast Chapter of the Organisation seldom organise serious capers. The young man who is looked upon as the leader of the group, Johnny McQueen, has escaped from prison while serving a sentence for gun-running and has been hiding out in the hills. He is thought by his friends not to be in good enough shape physically or nervously to carry out even the minor payroll robbery which has been planned as a source of money for the widows and children of men who have been killed 'in action'. Johnny nevertheless leads the expedition and his two companions are the ones who lose their nerve and start to panic when the alarm bell goes off a moment after they have effectively

*Released in the United States as *Stairway to Heaven*

214

held up the accounts department in the chosen factory. While hurrying to the getaway car he is involved in a struggle in which an office worker is killed and Johnny is shot in the shoulder. He attempts to jump on to the car but the panic-stricken driver accelerates so violently that Johnny is thrown off into the street. He picks himself up and runs as far as he has the strength, then hides in an air-raid shelter. A fellow member of the organisation locates him and makes an unsuccessful rescue attempt and Johnny is once more alone on the road, looking for a place to shelter or a friend to help him. Throughout the late afternoon and night the loss of blood causes hallucinations and increasing weakness. From time to time help seems to be forthcoming but in almost every case for purely selfish motives. When his strength is almost gone the girl who loves him tries to get a passage for him aboard one of the ships in the dock. She leads him staggering towards the ship but by then the coppers have located him and are closing in. The girl fires a gun in their direction and draws an answering volley which kills them both.

The subordinate characters supply the texture of the story as it progresses. The man's need and the girl's self-sacrifice constitute, strictly in terms of action, a compelling love story. The scenario was a wonderful skeleton which would be given flesh and blood by the technicians and actors and which would be animated by Reed's directorial genius.

Among the flesh and blood suppliers were Bob Krasker, the lighting cameraman, Ralph Brinton, the set designer, Roger Furse, the painter who supplied the canvases which at certain moments had as much importance as the actors, and William Alwyn who gave us the music. There was a relentless underscoring of Johnny McQueen's dying march through the streets of Belfast in the last part which it was necessary to pre-record so that I would never escape from the beat as I played these scenes.

And there was a beautiful cast of actors of whom the most outstanding were Robert Newton who played the drunken, rough and crazy painter who wished to capture on canvas the truth that would be revealed to him in the eyes of the dying man; F. J. McCormick who being struck by the notion that since the Pope is known to be 'quare and rich' he might negotiate the sale of Johnny McQueen with the parish priest, Father Tom; and the actor who played Father Tom himself, W. G. Fay. Though Newton and McCormick were perhaps the most spectacular, at a recent running of the film I could not help feeling that Fay was the truest of us all. And this too I must qualify, for there was a girl who played Kathleen in whose performance the same quality of truth simply expressed, could be seen. Kathleen Ryan was this actress.

But it was Carol Reed's film. Not being a critic I cannot attempt to define its perfection. I can only say that his approach to the filming of each individual scene was the most stimulating and at the same time the most relaxing of any that I have known. I say 'approach' because I am sure that he would not have allowed me to refer to it as 'a technique'. It was just the common sense application of the experience that he had picked up on the road to *Odd Man Out*. He had started as an actor. It is not by any means essential for a good director to have started as an actor, but it helps. The main function of a director is not to figure out from which angles a sequence may best be photographed, nor to figure out which lenses should be used; these are the functions of a cameraman, but it is just as well for the director to develop these skills in case his cameraman is not very bright. No, his main function is to conspire with the actors to create a true happening, to see that there is a common understanding of the value of each sequence and to see that it is expressed with complete credibility as if happening for the first time. Then let the cameraman decide how best to record this happening. It goes without saying that both director and cameraman in consultation with the set designer have a clear knowledge of the essential basic angles which can be used in each succeeding set just as when shooting outdoors it is essential to have advance knowledge of the direction in which the sun will be shining, but I am assuming that the director we are talking about and his actors are not of the sort that will run amok.

Reed also had the virtue of absolute unpretentiousness. He was unaffected by technical gimmickry. I have already mentioned that Hitchcock, a grand master, could be seduced by the fifteen-minutes-without-a-cut vogue. Other directors fall in love with their zoom lenses, extravagances of cutting or the dubious virtues of the hand-held camera. Carol Reed favoured a steady camera so that the spectator would be totally unaware both of camera movement and of cutting.

There was something that puzzled me when I recently read some comments on *Odd Man Out* that were attributed to the critic and screenwriter James Agee who attained cult-figure status among serious film lovers. He said at one point, 'The story seems merely to ramify too much, to go on too long, and, at its unluckiest, to go arty.' He is not specific, and I have wondered just what it could have been that struck him as being arty. Technically the weakest items in the film were the photographic special effects which were used to illustrate the fugitive's hallucinations. Perhaps these bothered him since they provided the only moments in the film in which anyone was likely to see the wheels going round. He also accused us of having all but failed in the early reels 'to communicate the revolutionary edge that is so well got in F. L. Green's novel'. Fair enough. It seemed to me however that when writing the script with R. C. Sherriff and Carol Reed, Green became more interested in the moral attitudes than the revolutionary, the theme being unequivocally stated in the course of Johnny McQueen's third hallucination. Enthroned on the dais of the painter's studio he sees the paintings come down from the wall and form a semi-circle in front of him. They are all portraits and among them he sees the parish priest who instructed him when he was a boy. But this is not one of the paintings but Father

217

Tom himself standing among them and trying to convey some message, reminding him of the importance of something which he has long ago taught him.

You see the look of puzzlement on McQueen's face as he tries to figure out what the message can be, then a look of understanding. The message is evidently contained in the passage from St Paul's first Epistle to the Corinthians, chapter 13, which he now stands up to recite. 'Though I give my money to feed the poor, and have not charity . . . I am nothing.' Yes, he has been a loyal member of the organisation, he had done his duty but he has forgotten the one important thing; he is without love.

I used to think that *The Fallen Idol* was Carol's best film but now I am not so sure. It has always astonished me that a film in which I myself played a part should perhaps find a place in a list of ten best films if ever I were obliged to submit one.

Early in 1946, David E. Rose came to our house to see us. I have to be careful not to leave out that 'E' because there was another well known David Rose at that time who was an American musician. People would say to me, 'How could you possibly not get along with David Rose? He is such a nice guy and such a good composer!' I am sure that most people thought of David E. Rose as a nice guy. We ourselves did for a long time.

He had just returned from one of his trips to California, where we had instructed him to see what sort of contract Paramount were prepared to offer me. So he had discussed the matter with them, he told us, but they had not shown much interest in the proposition. We expressed some surprise because from other sources we had heard so many accounts of the triumph of *The Seventh Veil*. He said that he had been a little surprised too, but the truth was that Paramount was an old-fashioned company, behind the times, and that he himself had for a long time been thinking of leaving them for this very reason. But, said he, the reason that he had come to see us so promptly after his

218

return was that he had thought of an alternative scheme to put before us. Why should not he and I go into business together, form an independent production company? He would take care of the finance, I the artistic side. He had mentioned my name to several top directors in Hollywod, who had all shown great interest in having the opportunity of working with me.

It never occurred to us to question the validity of his report. We thought that what he said made a lot of sense and immediately gave him the go-ahead to pursue the matter. I felt flattered. My self-esteem soared. No run of the mill contract for me. Oh no. An independent producer, no less, that was what I was going to be.

Our ignorance of Hollywood made us believe everything that we were told about the place, good or bad. We assumed that what Independent Production Company meant to us coincided exactly with his own definition, which we were to learn later was not precisely the case. The way we saw it was that he would 'find money' which would take care of the needs of the company as and when those needs would arise, this would be his contribution; and at the same time we would supply the scripts or at least those for the first two or three productions. We did not know that unspecified 'up-front' money was one of the hardest things to find, nor that it was far from what Rose had in mind. For starters, we thought that we would not only supply my own services but one of Pamela's published novels that she always thought would make a terrific film. This was one called *A Lady Possessed* which was published later in the United States with the title *Del Palma*. It was actually the one I least liked of her four novels but since it was obviously one that was calculated to appeal to women rather than men I assumed that her intuition would see us through.

When Spyros Skouras had visited the house about six months previously we had talked about film subjects quite extensively, and we should have taken this conversation as an important lesson in Hollywood thinking. But of course we were too full of ourselves to pick up any useful hints. Skouras had mentioned two subjects in which he had recommended that I be offered parts, *Forever Amber* and *Anna and the King of Siam*. We knew that the first of these was the kind of romantic twaddle that the Ostrers would have bought in the Gainsborough heyday, one in which the leading woman would appear in practically every scene with a series of husbands, lovers and aspirants. Unthinkable. As for the other subject he was not even suggesting me for the part of the king, which surprised me in view of the fuss he was making of me. I was to be the Prime Minister. I asked what actor he had in mind for the part of the king. He said they had not chosen one but they were looking for a sort of young Charles Laughton, foreign of course. I concurred, thinking that he meant oriental or, at a pinch, a Mexican or a Czech or a Greek. One learned later that he regarded English actors as equally foreign, hence the eventual casting of Rex Harrison as the king. I never saw the film but I am sure that Harrison was very good, thus endorsing the Skouras thinking. I said that the most important thing was to find parts for which I was ideally suited and which I could therefore play effectively. And I ventured the opinion that the films that were taken from best-selling novels were usually less interesting than those based on stories written specially for the screen.

'Small pictures?'

'Well yes, they could be. No harm in that.'

'Ha! You make the same mistake as all of them!' said he in richly scornful Greek American tones, 'Just like Jean Gabin!'

'Jean Gabin?'

'Yes, we offered him the best films on our programme, and what did he insist on doing? That little nothing *Moontide*!'

I remembered that Gabin had indeed gone to Hollywood a few years previously and that the only film I remember his having made there was this disappointing film with Dietrich.

'Do you mind telling me,' I said, 'what were the big projects that you offered Gabin?'

'Not at all. I remember that we offered him *How Green was my Valley* and *The Rains Came*.'

'Ah,' said I, nodding my head ambiguously.

When David Rose talked about film subjects he used the term 'an attraction'. Two stars appropriately teamed plus a demanding and effective story constituted an attraction. In a later stage of Hollywood history we used the term 'package'. Agents were to form the habit of putting together packages on the strength of which money could be raised. I realise now that Rose's 'attraction' could have achieved the same results. This aim was consistent with his behaviour pattern from the beginning of our talks, which lasted altogether over six months.

After one of his trips to California he said that some of the people with whom he had spoken, directors and others, were disinclined to believe that he was on the level when he told them that we had the intention of making films in partnership together. He thought that it would be a good idea if I wrote him a letter, nothing official, just a casual note in which I referred to this common intention, so that he would be able to flash this letter next time he went to California so as to convince people that he was on the level. So we went round one afternoon at teatime to Claridge's Hotel where he was staying and chatted about our plans for a while with Rose and a solicitor of his. Then out came a short letter on Claridge's Hotel notepaper which he had typed and which represented what he had in mind and I signed it and that little thing was done.

For much of the time during these six months I was busy working on the two films *The Upturned Glass* and *Odd Man Out* and Pamela and I were not giving a great deal of thought to the projects which Rose and I were intending to produce together. But we were beginning slowly to comprehend that Rose's plan of action was quite different from our own. With some show of satisfaction he would report that he had conducted promising discussions with Spitz and Goetz. Who? Spitz and Goetz. Who are they?

They have taken over at Universal. So? We might be able to do a very favourable deal with them. At *Universal*?

Even from this great distance it had been easy to recognise the low quality of the product which was at that time being splashed out by Universal. We could never understand why, at this stage of the game, Rose should even be talking to Spitz and Goetz. At another time he would mention the discussions that he had had with Eagle Lion. With whom? Eagle Lion; they've just concluded an agreement with Rank. With *Rank*? And so on. It was all very confusing. I was not yet in tune with the American system. I still thought of producers as men like Marcel Hellman who would make a few trips to the City of London and come back with a suitcase full of money with which to make a film, or like Gabby Pascal or Filippo Del Giudice, an Italian with sufficient taste and initiative to launch productions like *In Which We Serve* and Olivier's *Henry V*. But here was our man attempting to start something going by chatting up Spitz and Goetz and Eagle Lion.

As the six months rolled by we came to the full realisation that Rose and ourselves were drifting further and further apart, but we did not know how to handle the situation. Were we to say casually, 'Sorry David, but seeing that we don't seem to see things exactly eye to eye, how about we forget about the whole thing. Okay?' It did not seem quite right somehow, perhaps because we were beginning to realise that our own ignorance and naïveté were partly the cause of our difficulties.

And during the same period Rose had evidently arrived at similar conclusions. The only difference was that he *did* know how to handle the situation. In September at a time when we were vaguely toying with the idea of travelling to the United States, come what might, he rang us up to announce yet another of his returns from California. Could he come out to see us at once? – Is it important? – Yes, I think it is very important. – Okay.

We faced each other around a table. He took from an

envelope a fat printed document. It was a contract.

'Look at it,' said he, 'it is a terrific contract which I have negotiated for you with Paramount. A contract for ten pictures.'

'I see,' I said. 'And I am to produce these pictures?'

'No, this is strictly a service contract for you as an actor. There is no actor at Paramount who is guaranteed the same freedom and personal authority as I have got for you in this contract.'

I had not wanted a contract as an actor and made it clear that I would not accept it. It seemed clear, in these circumstances, that there was no hope of our getting together. This being the case, and Rose having no authority to act as my agent, it seemed appropriate that we go our separate ways. But Rose now surprised us by claiming that the letter on the tasteful Claridge's notepaper which I had signed constituted a contract. A lengthy argument ensued in which both parties expressed their views with a rancour not by any means confined to Rose and myself, since Pamela was never the one to hold back.

Not long afterwards Rose was off to California again and he took appropriate steps with which to reinforce his threat. He registered his intention to enjoin me from working for any producer other than himself. I was therefore liable to be served with such an order the moment I set foot in California. My lawyers told me that whether I were actually served with such an order or not, there would henceforth be 'a cloud on my title', a nice phrase, though not very comfortable to live with.

We could at this point have changed our plans to accord with the new situation and just stayed in England which would have been a sensible thing to do. Even when I have made palpably silly decisions I do not remember ever having gone into reverse. I have never had much difficulty in making them, for I believe that at any given time there is one decision which has to be made, and at that time it was the decision to go to America, even if commonsense might argue that from a purely materialistic viewpoint I would have been better off if I had remained in England.

So, having decided to go, it became a question of what to use for money, since the exchange control which then ruled our lives prevented us from exporting any sterling that we might have. So we made a snap decision to spend the winter in Bermuda where we could live on our sterling until Rose should be taken care of – we had no notion how. But before we had taken any practical steps to carry out Plan A (Bermuda) a change of circumstances encouraged us to develop Plan B (New York) which was the one we eventually adopted.

The author of this latest change of circumstances was Alexander Korda, who was now said to be about to take another stab at the British film industry. At the beginning of the war he had transported his unfinished film *The Thief of Baghdad*, together with his brother Zoli who was credited with its direction, to California, where it was completed and became a healthy source of revenue. He was also known to have made on a tight budget a touching little film about Lord Nelson and Emma Hamilton. For anyone who was not a member of his family or immediate entourage it was impossible to guess what his financial standing might be at any given moment, for he had the air of one who did not stint himself, of a cat, let us say, who had swallowed a number of canaries, some of which he might have trouble digesting. I liked the man.

Now he offered me a contract. I told him that I had decided to go to America.

'That's all right,' he said, 'we'll make it for six pictures, three to be made in the States and three in England.'

'The first has definitely to be made in the States.'

'Agreed.'

Then I told him that I was liable to run into a spot of David Rose trouble. I told him the story.

'Did you sign a contract with him?'

'No. But it looks as if he will try to make out that a short personal note that I wrote to him at one time constitutes a contract.'

'Do you have a copy of it?'

'No, but I remember what was in it.'

So Korda suggested that I get together with his lawyer and tell him all about it. He was, he said, a very good man and if anyone could give us a sound legal opinion, it was he.

He then negotiated the highly satisfactory details of the contract with Al Parker, and pending the opinion of his lawyer, the deal was set. And there was one especially attractive detail, I should be paid an *advance* of fifty thousand dollars the moment I arrived in New York.

Korda's lawyer opined that Rose's contention would hold up in court on neither side of the Atlantic. And he recommended that both Korda and I have no misgivings about going ahead with the proposed contract.

So this was Plan B which we now somewhat clumsily activated. We made arrangements to install Roy Kellino and his second wife in our house. It was sufficiently close to his place of work and they not only liked the house but she had big ideas about interior decoration, and it was all going to be great fun for them. The Kellinos undertook to have certain earmarked items of furniture sent on to us if and when we should eventually settle in an unfurnished house.

But more important still, the Kellinos could be trusted to look after the geese. These were three geese who had been living in the back field when we bought the house. We developed a great affection for them, though I cannot speak for the leader of the trio whom I took to be a gander. He liked to play a game that was almost identical with one that had been very popular in our family when we were children. The child who was 'it' would stand at the end of the lawn or nursery with his back to the others and his eyes closed. While he was in this position the others would stealthily move towards him, always ready however to become motionless again the moment he swung around and looked towards them. If he caught one of them moving that person was 'out'. The others stayed in the game and edged forward whenever the one who was 'it' turned his back. The aim was to get close enough to touch him before being caught moving. When you touched him you became 'it'. It was much the same with the gander. When I had brought them their food and was walking away towards the house, I would hear him pad-padding after me. But I never caught him moving. When I turned round he was always standing stock still. On the other hand he never became 'it', because he never got quite close enough to grab me – if indeed, that was his intention. The game was called Grandmother's steps.

So that was the house taken care of. We had a maid called Gladys who was a good cook. When we asked her if she wanted to come along with us, she gave the matter some thought, then said no, she would be too scared. We then asked Violet Taylor of Cookham Dean if she was free to come, bringing her cat of course. – 'Yes, yes of course. Don't go without me.'

I employed a dresser at the studio who now found himself promoted to valet-houseman or whatever he might choose to be called. And he in turn had an acquaintance who would be glad to work his passage with us, just so he got the chance to emigrate. Add the transportation manager, Monaghan, and we became a party of five. Add one dog belonging to the second houseman, and five cats. People who read about our exodus in the press were surprised most of all by the fact that we also took with us a second hand American Army ambulance. That was my idea. We had so little notion of what the future would hold for us in the States that my imagination often led me in strange directions. In England I had some money which I would have to leave doing nothing in a bank. In New York we would have no money except the promise of the advance from Korda. But you never knew, there might be some snag. We certainly would not have a car with a Left Hand Drive. And then perhaps there might be some quick means of disposing of the David Rose threat and we might wish to drive to California. I was not the first to toy with that drive across

America fantasy and while I was so employed a second-hand ambulance began to seem indispensable.

It was a very odd feeling, setting off like this. But I did not feel seriously destabilised so long as we were on British soil which of course included the *Queen Elizabeth* into which we climbed on arrival at Southampton.

None of us had ever sailed in a big ship, least of all the cats. Bad weather was predicted and Pamela and I were permitted to have the cats in our stateroom with us. They took the journey horizontally as did we and with an almost constant nausea, though the small quantities we ate we all managed to keep down. I crossed the Atlantic several times later but nothing would match this first crossing in the *Queen Elizabeth*.

PART TWO

Nevin 1917 *(left to right)* Rex, Colin, James

With Margaret Lockwood in *The Man in Grey*, 1943

My parents, 1955

In *Rommel–Desert Fox*,
with Leo G. Carroll as von Rundstedt, 1951

In *The Man Between*, 1953

With Sue Lyon in *Lolita*, 1961

With John Gielgud during *Julius Caesar*, 1953

At Almeria, 1967, with Portland who is drawing
Patrick Lichfield as he took this photograph

13/New York

The weather improved slightly as the enormous ship approached the American Continent. The thing had been built at a time when it was a matter of major importance to all the companies that sailed passenger liners across the Atlantic that their latest model be the fastest if not the biggest and so win the Blue Riband which was worth such an acreage of publicity in the newspapers that the sale of tickets soared to ever new heights.

The *Queen Elizabeth* had been scheduled to make its transatlantic debut in 1940. But this had to be postponed until after the war, throughout the duration of which it served as a troopship. The service prospered so well in the immediate post-war years that the company was able to make a full repayment of the money which had been loaned by the government for the building of the sister Queens, Mary and Elizabeth.

During the crossing I was not in a condition to make a tally of the good features of our Queen, the Elizabeth. Before stepping on to the ship I had thought how nice it would be to use its squash court. But once we had set sail I could not imagine that she could ever ride steadily enough to allow the wretched players to keep their feet. It could only have been mentioned in the brochures as a come-on for a few sportive ignoramuses like myself. Smoothness was inconceivable. The worst thing was to be kept awake at night not by the regular creaking such as one might expect but by the ear splitting and heart stopping kraAA ... KKK which could only mean that the backbone of the

231

monster was coming apart and that thereafter it would be a crescendo of whistles and gongs and sirens summoning us to the lifeboats.

But towards the end of the fourth day one stopped worrying about the monster's spinal column and could even take short promenades without fear of nausea.

The sky was just beginning to clear as we approached New York. The sun remained discreetly veiled as we stood on deck waiting for the Statue of Liberty to break the horizon. And there she is! The ship is now travelling with a well balanced, respectful air, and the lady takes forever to glide towards us and recognise the new bunch of immigrants. Of course I was only pretending to be an immigrant but I was busily replaying all those scenes of real immigrants that I had read about, all of them wearing the old-fashioned gear and the long faces of the persecuted.

Once we had passed the Statue the sun came out and the mood changed. The ship dawdled up the East River and there was a man called William Dieterle beside me. He was a German film director who had been resident in California since the early days of the movies. We had only just met, and he was happily and almost proudly identifying the tall buildings for my benefit. For special praise he singled out the recently constructed Rockefeller Center. This was something he really thought that I would like. And indeed I did.

The English picture papers had informed me that it was obligatory for arriving and departing actors to pose for the photographers on the ship's rail. But surely nothing like that would be demanded of an ordinary, unpublicised male? It was much worse. Ultimately we were cornered in some sort of a lounge by about thirty reporters. I had no prepared story to tell them. I had not come to work, I was not under contract to any movie company; about my future their guess was as good as mine.

They suspected at once that I was concealing facts which could be whipped up into a piping hot story. It was up to them to extract these facts. They assumed mistakenly that I was under contract to J. Arthur Rank because a whole series of films in which I appeared had recently opened in New York, indeed at least two of them were still running. All of these were films introduced by the gong-bashing former heavyweight champion by reason of the individual production companies having been swallowed by Rank. I found out later that my embarrassment was being aggravated by someone in charge of Rank publicity in New York, who, being unable to arrange interviews with me for the promotion of the Rank films, was copping out on the grounds that I was 'uncooperative'.

So publicity-wise I made a poor start. I really had nothing to say except perhaps to express an admiration for the Rockefeller Center and to protest that it really was not at all eccentric to cross the Atlantic in company with five cats and a small sheepdog.

During the preceding year and a half we had become the devoted pen-pals of an American couple called Peter and Ann Robbins who had volunteered to make all arrangements for accommodation and other needs of my party of bewildered Europeans. They were the only ones we had warned of our coming, so how did our every movement come to be a matter of public knowledge? We decided that there must exist in New York a sort of jungle telegraph system, like the tom-toms of Africa, and it was by this medium that the fans found out that we were to stay at the Plaza Hotel and later, when we attempted to take an exploratory walk in the streets, the swarms would likewise be alerted before we had reached the end of the first block.

At the hotel, more surprising than the actual appearance of the fans was the fact that there was nothing to stop them from taking the elevator up to our floor and banging on the door of our suite. Monaghan was used for scaring them away. He also answered the telephone when he was around and, in view of the fact that we had no acquaintance in New York other than Mr and Mrs Robbins, and did not wish to participate in publicity nor accept invitations from the unknown, he had limitless opportunities for saying the word NO with varying degrees of emphasis.

He said NO for example to a Mr Wilson who wished to interview me. I believe that being an American from Pennsylvania, he knew of this man and handed him a reasonably polite turndown but this did not prevent Earl Wilson – for it was he – from making a series of rather sour cracks at my expense in his column in the *New York Post*.

But better still he got repeated calls from the legwoman of Louella Parsons and of course he kept saying no. I had heard of Louella Parsons – who hadn't? – but once again there was no reason for me to want to meet her. Although I had never been keen on the publicity round and had done very little of it in England I was beginning to realise that when I started working in films again I would be expected, now that I was in these strange United States, to make myself available for interviews and develop a suitable smile for the photographers. But not now, please.

At that time, as some of us are old enough to remember, radio was *very* big. People used to listen to their favourite radio programmes almost to the same degree as nowadays they fix their eyes on their favourite television series. Late Sunday afternoons there was a series of half hour programmes, one right after the other, which were required listening. Nobody whom I came to know in the next couple of years could bear to miss them. First came the harsh voice of Walter Winchell delivering gossip and news flashes with as much finesse as a pneumatic drill. Next came half an hour of Louella Parsons with her version of current events in Hollywood. The last of the three was someone I had never heard of called Jimmy Fidler, who gave the same sort of material as Louella except that anyone who became a regular listener could easily detect that Louella's information was derived from the top echelon of Hollywood press agents and her gossip from sources very close to the horses' mouths. We assumed too that it must have been very degrading for Jimmy Fidler to have to break off at regular intervals to deliver his sponsor's message personally – it was for Arrid Underarm Deodorant – whereas the messages of Louella's sponsor were read by an underling.

Now on our very first Sunday in the United States we turned on the radio in the hotel suite at the magic hour and listened with appropriate awe to the voice of Walter Winchell. But Louella Parsons was an even bigger hit. Throughout her half hour she talked about nobody else but me! We could not believe our ears. And what a lambasting she gave me. From various sources, including obviously the P.R. man for the Rank films, she had gathered a few facts and a load of gossip with which she attempted to build an impressive case against me. She came out with the same sort of not very harmful smears that had been ranged against me in the English press and which added up to the incontrovertibly damning evidence that I was in one word, *unco-operative*. Also it came out that I was swelled-headed, but it was clear that swelled-headedness was not nearly as bad as unco-operativeness, of which it was practically the worst thing that an actor could be guilty.

I do not believe that there is anyone still living who could claim to know the full Louella Parsons story, but clearly she was a mouthpiece of enormous value to the masters of the big Hollywood Studios; not only did she loudly advertise their product but she could always be relied on to bring recalcitrant actors and actresses to heel. If I had been a Hollywood actor who had in some way slighted her, refused to be a guest on her programme or caused the word NO to be said to her legwoman, she would have insulted me on her programme in the full expectation that I would come crawling to her and ask to be forgiven.

Incredibly, exactly the same thing happened on the Louella Parsons Show the following Sunday. Once more she carried on about me for almost the entire half hour. My first thought was how boring it must be for all the Hollywoodites with their ears glued to their radio sets who would have preferred to hear all about themselves, and, if anyone was to be insulted, let it be their Hollywood friends, for God's sake, rather than this interloper from abroad. After that the sin of pride asserted itself for a moment, for no one could deny that I was getting nationwide attention. And finally I had a comforting thought. My relations with this influential lady were at rock bottom, they could sink no lower, they could only improve.

The legwoman made two or three more calls but got the same negative reaction. If ever I were to dissipate that cloud on my title and be once again free to make movies, we decided that we would boycott this Louella Parsons. We understood that she and the other woman, Hedda Hopper, were deadly rivals. At our meeting with her, Hedda Hopper had been polite and friendly and her chat had been entertaining and her badinage acceptable. So if we ever had any titbits of personal news to dispose of, the obvious thing to do would be to toss them to Hopper.

The advance money accruing from my arrangement with Alexander Korda had materialised. He had also given me the name of the New York lawyer whom he urged me to consult about the David Rose affair. So at my earliest convenience I introduced myself to this gentleman whose name was Charlie Schwartz, as well as to his partner Louis Froelich who would plead if and when the matter came to court.

Schwartz proposed that he prepare a counter-suit with which to hit Rose when he next set foot in New York. Rose's own complaint which had been registered in Los Angeles could not be served on me until I set foot in California which was by no means my immediate intention. Rose was still commuting frequently between Los Angeles and London. Therefore if we kept our intentions secret, we should have no difficulty in serving him before he had a chance to serve me. We would apply to the court for a 'Declaratory Judgement'. Rose and I and others would testify and tell our stories, the judge would figure out whether or not a binding contract existed between the two of us. Although Schwartz foresaw no difficulty in serving Rose promptly and effectively, he made no promise of an early date in the courts in which there was a constant backlog of cases to be heard. – 'And when the case is heard the judge will hand down an instant decision?'

'Not necessarily.'

Not the most gratifying prospect. But I had carelessly got myself into this fix, so I must live with it. Fortunately I had never taken my career with grim seriousness. All right, I could not have been more serious about the theatre and the cinema just as I was about architecture and the other arts, but career was something else. Career was something one associated with a blinkered ambition. No, I was not in a desperate hurry to move on. This was our first taste of New York, so let's see if it lives up to its reputation.

When the decision had been taken and Rose had been successfully served and these powerful lawyers harnessed at who knew what might be the expense, I met more and more people who said, 'Why don't you just settle with the man?'

However we were not prepared to handle our affairs in such a cynical manner. According to our reading of the affair Rose had done me wrong. Our friends would say – Just let the man have part of your salary for your first two or three films, and maybe let him have his name on the credit titles as Associate Producer or something. He'll settle. You'll see.

But no. Pamela and I were far too indignant. We may have thought that we were acting on a point of principle. And we were, but more important was the thought – we'll be damned if we let him get away with it.

The nice Robbinses found us a furnished house to rent in New Canaan, the town in Connecticut where they themselves lived. We wanted to plant our luggage and our staff and our cats and the dogs in the country. It was a lovely house that they found and we at once fell in love with New Canaan and the surrounding countryside but we did not stay there long because something funny happened to the water supply and we had to abandon it. We stayed there just long enough to register the magic of a New England Christmas.

Not long afterwards we moved our chattels to a somewhat larger house in Greenwich, Connecticut. But since we were totally incapable of adjusting to the commuting life we also rented an apartment in Fifty Seventh Street. This turned out to be one of the more extravagant periods in my life. During the time that we spent in New York which added up to about fifteen months we had temporary footholds in New Canaan, Fifty Seventh Street, Greenwich, Riverdale and Sutton Place, some of these overlapping.

One day at the intersection of Fifty Seventh Street and Fifth Avenue a heavy set man with a pronounced English accent stopped me and introduced himself as Rex Evans. I had not met him before but I knew his brother Laurie very well, and I now learned that Laurie had written his brother to say that we were coming to New York and might need to contact Rex if we got ourselves into any difficulties and needed help. That was very nice of Laurie, I said, but actually we were doing as well as could be expected.

'Are you planning to do a play on Broadway while you're here?'

'No. Why do you ask?'

'Just that I read a play recently which I thought was pretty good ... It was about King David.'

'King David? Oh, that's very intereseting.'

'I know the person who owns the rights. I'll get her to send you a copy.'

At any other time I would not have said that it was necessarily very interesting that someone had read a pretty good play about King David. But it so happened that shortly before I had left England a book by Duff Cooper had been published which dealt with King David. Carol

Reed and I had both read it and had discussed it as a film project. What had appealed to both of us had been Duff Cooper's presentation of David as a master of public relations, more specifically his handling of relations between his god, himself and his people. It had been a humorous and well observed study of leadership.

We read the script at once, not because we were much taken with the idea of doing a play, least of all on Broadway, but Pamela had also liked the Duff Cooper book and we couldn't wait to find out if the playwright would treat the subject in anything approaching a similar vein.

The play was called *Bathsheba* and the author was Jacques Deval, a French playwright noted for his comedy writing. His most successful play outside France had been *Tovarich*, although this is sometimes credited to Robert Sherwood who adapted it for the English-speaking market.

Deval's treatment of the David/Bathsheba story was told with considerable humour, indeed it could fairly be described as a comedy in spite of a shift to a more serious mood in the Third Act.

Its style was somewhat reminiscent of Robert Sherwood's in that there was no attempt to antiquate the dialogue. On the contrary the characters all spoke in the modern vernacular which was sometimes used as a laughter-provoking device. Thus when Uriah is describing the conditions of his military service to a fellow officer and wishes to identify the girl who is his slave, he says that he has been 'issued' with such and such a girl, a term which Americans tended to associate with service in World War II.

The Old Testament story according to Deval did not stray very far from the version given in the Second Book of Samuel. We learn in both versions that Uriah, the Hittite, was one of David's thirty men selected to command the army in the field. General Joab, under whom he is serving at the siege of Rabbah, informs him that Uriah's presence is required at the court of the king. David has indeed sent for him because he has made love to Uriah's wife, Bathsheba, and made her pregnant. He is giving Uriah the opportunity to sleep with his wife so that the paternity of the child may be convincingly attributed to Bathsheba's lawful husband. However David's plan appears to have been foiled when he learns that instead of bedding down with his wife during his two nights' leave, Uriah has chosen to billet himself with the palace guard.

The scandal of a royal adultery being too fearful to contemplate, David sends Uriah back to the front with a sealed letter to Joab instructing him to station Uriah in the front line where the hardest fighting will take place, then to withdraw his support so that Uriah will inevitably be killed.

I found the play quite attractive and asked Rex Evans who owned the rights. He said that he was not quite sure if Sylvia Friedländer still owned them but he would call her up and find out. A few days later this lady contacted me and said that she would love to do the play and let's start the ball rolling. I never made it my business to find out what arrangements she had made in order to recapture the rights, all we were to know was that the play was to be presented not by Miss Friedländer alone but in partnership with Max Becker who was Jacques Deval's agent.

After the out-of-town opening Sylvia Friedländer told me that Rex Evans had claimed a 'finder's free' in view of the fact that he had recommended the play to me. Sylvia had agreed to shell out to him a percentage of the producers' take.

The producer of a play is not the same animal as the producer of a play in England where the term is applied to the man who stages the piece, who directs and who therefore in America is called the director just as the man who does the equivalent job in the film world is universally referred to as the director. Although they told me that there were monsters aplenty among the producers of plays in New York, Miss Friedländer was certainly not one of them. She behaved impeccably throughout the life of *Bathsheba*.

I had no misgivings about the play but I had several about myself. Not wishing to be imitative I wanted nevertheless to exploit the comedy values in our piece with as much assurance as – say – Alfred Lunt had shown in *Reunion in Vienna* or *The Guardsman*. And I felt very keenly that I needed all the help I could get from the director. I explained these feelings of mine to Sylvia as soon as we faced the problem of choosing a director. I insisted that above all we find one who was good at handling comedy. I thought that she was rather surprised by my emphasis on this point.

'You don't mean somebody like George Kaufman?' she said.

Actually I had never seen anything that Kaufman had directed but, when I thought of some of his plays that I had read, I did not think that his line of comedy would be at all out of place. She said that she thought that he leaned too much towards the farcical, nevertheless we could discuss it if I liked. I would very much have liked to meet this gifted man but he was just about to embark on an important project of his own, so we got no further with that little notion. And all the others which seemed at all promising ended up the same way. The availables were men I had never heard of and whose credits were unremarkable.

One day Sylvia made a spirited recommendation of Jed Harris, who was a legend. I knew that his record on Broadway had been remarkable; for a period of about five years everything that he touched had turned to gold. Hal Prince would be an approximate present day equivalent. But to New Yorkers those who are acknowledged to have skill and who have the good luck to turn up nothing but trumps through three or four seasons become legends. Jed Harris was a legend. 'You may not think that he is right for this but you'll not regret meeting him,' said Sylvia.

So she brought him to meet us. He was a man of satanic

good looks. Some might dismiss him as ugly if they were intimidated by the air of craftiness and mystery that he transmitted. He had slim feet neatly shod, a slim figure darkly suited, a pointed blue chin and penetrating black eyes.

He had read the script and did not in any way criticize it or put it down. He insisted that the first thing I should think about was my appearance, how I was going to identify with this David physically, what make-up I should wear. I did not agree with him that this should be my first consideration but I stayed mum because it seemed to me that he was much too deep and inscrutable to be likely to show interest in my thoughts on this topic which were pragmatic and shallow. First as an actor I had never been what might be called make-up happy, at any rate since that occasion at the Old Vic when for want of anything better to do, I manufactured a Billy Bennett moustache to wear as the butler Merriman in *The Importance of Being Earnest*. Secondly, I knew that the immediate problem would ultimately resolve itself into a simple question of Beard or NO Beard. I should naturally insist on wearing a beard while the producers, yes, even the understanding Sylvia, would probably try to pressure me into playing the part clean-shaven since they were exhibiting not so much an actor as an exotic phenomenon from the movie world. Dark eyes like Jed Harris's might be advantageous but the exact style of the beard that I would favour was not surely a matter demanding instant decision.

However there was the one matter that I had to bring up to Mr Harris, my need of guidance and help in the area of comedy acting.

'Comedy?'

'Yes, comedy. I mean there are certain scenes where the comedy has to be played with great subtlety, and I don't have much experience in this line.'

'I'm sorry, I don't know what comedy you are referring to.' He was pointing his dangerous eyes at me. I was becoming rattled and I reached for an example and came up with one that was not perhaps the wisest choice.

'Well you have the situation of a man, any man, who has been fornicating with another man's wife and has made her pregnant, so now he is desperately trying to arrange for the husband to sleep with his wife so that everyone will accept the child as legitimate. But the husband . . .'

'And you mean that this is something to be laughed at?'

'Well you have to admit that there is an unavoidable comic undertone to this situation. And I just wondered . . .'

'There is stark majestic drama. I can't imagine how you could think . . . But we shall have lots of time to talk about all this.'

Not with me there wouldn't. I had already had enough of this man. He was Svengali. I knew that I had seen him before somewhere. His nose was straighter than it had appeared in du Maurier's illustrations, but it was the same man. And I knew that when we got going he would with the greatest of ease extract a performance from me that would be his and not mine. Putting myself into the hands of Svengali was not on my agenda.

When he had gone I told Sylvia that much as I had been impressed by the legendary figure I'd as soon take on Jersey Joe Walcott.

The meeting with Harris had brought up an interesting question. Knowing, as we all did, that the Jewish people had a sense of comedy second to none, in how many of them were we going to find, when the comedy concerned the father of their nation, that sense of comedy was suddenly to be switched off?

So we were still looking for a director and since dates were being made at the out of town theatres it became imperative that we find one and get the show on the road. We settled for Robert Gordon whose principal achievement had been a highly successful left over Army Show.

Then came the auditioning of actors. I had assumed that established actors would be asked to do no more than step into the office and have little chats with Gordon and myself on the strength of which we could decide who would be right for which role. Not at all. I found to my amazement that all who were thought suitable, irrespective of their standing, were expected to audition on stage. Indeed they did show up on stage at our bidding, and read some of the lines if called upon to do so. I felt very bad about this, supposing that they were being put through this nerve-racking ordeal simply because I was a foreigner and could not be expected to know any of the actors and actresses they were suggesting. Wrong again. I was told that this was normal procedure. Normal or not, I found it embarrassing. But we put the cast together and got down to rehearsals which were uneventful and did not dispel my feeling that I was going to have a tough time achieving the comedic aplomb which I craved.

The schedule called for one week at Princeton and two weeks in Philadelphia before taking the plunge at the Ethel Barrymore Theatre in New York.

As King David in Bathsheba

I was already enjoying myself as I always do when I am involved in a strange adventure. Nothing desperately strange had happened so far. But that could change. Meanwhile it was refreshing to be away from the city and into an oasis of academic serenity. Princeton was rather pretty and on the slopes around the town there was a picturesque patchwork of melting snow. The lights were rigged without hysteria, and a perfectly smooth dress rehearsal brought us neither depression nor exhilaration.

Then came opening night, and this did both. I heard some welcome chuckles before I made my first entrance. Lines like the one about the slave girl having been 'issued' and others like it were evidently getting the kind of reception that the author had intended. And during my first scenes not only did I feel I was being liked but, better still, all the laughs that I had worried about were coming easily. It was a great feeling. When the play was halfway through Pamela and I were both floating on that feeling of bland confidence that comes when one's efforts to entertain are going down really well. There were passages in the second act which were being received with more and more enthusiasm. And the audience seemed to make the proper adjustment to the serious mood of the third act. I really thought that we were in a hit. There was terrific applause at the end and a gratifying number of curtain calls.

And the author? The author was sitting at a point of vantage in the wings, from which he had watched and listened throughout the performance. His head was in his hands. He was in the depth of depression. He had not expected the audience to laugh.

So were we in a hit or not? After the show our dressing room became the scene of instant post mortem. It became clear that only Pamela and I and one or two of the other actors had felt the exhilaration of victory. Deval alone was the victim of total depression. Robert Gordon and Sylvia had been pleased enough during the first act but during the interval they had checked with the author and at once realised that they had a problem.

Deval did not participate in the post mortem since he had made his feelings clear enough. So it became an increasingly heated discussion between Robert Gordon and myself. He had never revealed his personal interpretation of the play, having concentrated entirely on the physical problems of staging it. And even now he was not forthcoming until I began to make my proposals about what should be our procedure from this point on. Both Gordon and Sylvia had picked up from members of the audience a recognition that Deval had not made his intentions clear, no matter how much they had enjoyed the fun. So I said that it was up to us to make *our* intentions clear with or without Deval's help. At any point where the comic possibilities had not been properly exploited we should find the means to do so. The converse could also have been argued, that is to say that at any point where Deval's serious intentions had not been strongly enough stated something must be done to stress them. But it was clear that this was impossible without a considerable rewrite, for we were playing the play in a perfectly straightforward manner and look what happened: the people laughed. It was not as if we were pulling funny faces or in any way knocking ourselves out to get these laughs.

It seemed that Gordon did not wish to adopt my policy of making it clear to the audience that the comedy was intentional and it was up to them to hold themselves in readiness for a more serious third act. But he did not say with any clarity or conviction what policy he *would* hold still for. I found myself becoming not so much angry as sorely tried. I cannot think of any occasion when I have felt so deeply irked; so much so that I finally said to myself – What the hell, I'll play this for anger. I hate myself when this happens because it really amounts to an act of bullying. And I hate other people when I suspect that they are doing the same thing. But I balled out Robert Gordon, and in the end he quit.

246

Sylvia allowed that throughout our week in Princeton we should repeat the performance that we had given on the opening night and that if I found any passages which could be clarified or strengthened, I was welcome to fix them. As for her, she would talk further with the author and maybe discuss our problem with playwright friends in New York who were sometimes willing to lend their services as 'play doctors'.

I had heard of plays which the authors had wished to be taken dead seriously but of which the audience had insisted on making fun. *Arsenic and Old Lace* was said to have been one such, and there had been an excellent example in England in 1934 called *Young England*, a stoutly patriotic melodrama in which murky deeds were perpetrated in the environment of a Boy Scout camp. The author had been a retired scoutmaster and at every performance (at the Victoria Palace) he sat in one of the stage boxes and glowered at those of us who insisted on laughing.

But ours was a different situation altogether. The laughter in our case was not at our expense, it was in sympathy with what seemed to them to be skilfully written comedy. I never heard of a like experience. I was not at all dismayed because, although I was doing my level best to make a success of it, I had been prompted in the first place by the need to find a good way of passing the time until my law case should be heard. Also it offered experience in the American theatre which I had read so much about and which, with all the ups and downs and conflict and romance, was clearly a type of adventure not to be missed. And now it was all happening to us. They had even started to talk about play doctors, an essential ingredient of the adventure.

After the second night's performance Sylvia came round and told me that she had had a conversation with one of her acquaintances who had seen the show and whose understanding of the play seemed to coincide with my own. He was a young director named Coby Ruskin. Yes, said I, I would very much like to meet him. So this was arranged and before we knew it Coby Ruskin became our new director and we worked a heavy schedule throughout the rest of the week in a combined effort to make the whole show sharper and at certain points funnier. When we opened in Philadelphia the following Monday the audience would recognise our intentions as soon as the curtain rose. We all liked working with Coby, who was loaded with energy and bright ideas.

All we knew about our prospects in Philadelphia was that the theatre was booked solid for the two weeks that we were to play there. We were going to dazzle them.

But a peculiar thing happened. Their response was deadly. Where was that warmth? That laughter? In the first interval the more experienced members of the cast, Tom Chalmers and Horace Braham, tried to comfort us by assuring us that Philadelphia audiences were always like this and we were not to worry. Were they likely to warm up later? Probably not.

During the second act I worked very hard, trying to make the play ten times livelier than it had any right to appear. No response. I peered into the darkness of the auditorium and studied the faces, trying to find one that looked as if it might belong to a human being. I saw a lot of jewellery, I noted the conservative elegance of the ladies and gentlemen occupying the more expensive seats, but I did not catch a mobile or receptive face. I felt that I was being drained of all the zest which I had switched on at the beginning of the act. I felt so depressed in fact that I could hardly repress the urge to step towards the footlight, hold up my hand and say to them – I am terribly sorry that you put yourselves to the trouble of dressing up and coming to the theatre tonight. Because it is quite clear that we are quite incapable of entertaining you. I can see that you are all bored stiff, I apologise. And now I suggest that you all go home quietly. You will be reimbursed for the money you paid for your tickets.

Of course I did nothing of the sort. I just carried on and I am sure that there was not a single member of the audience who picked up the least flicker of my despair. They did not pick anything up. It must have been the worst house I ever played to. And it was packed; I heard of no cancellations during our two weeks.

Nightly we tried to create some magic on the stage, and by day we worked with Coby and tried to persuade ourselves that the new life that was being pumped into the show would not remain unappreciated. We also listened to the play doctors. Yes, Sylvia persuaded two of her playwright friends to pay us a visit. The first one was one of the Chodorov brothers, it does not matter enormously which of the two did us this honour, because whichever it was failed to prescribe plausible treatment. But then Marc Connelly did not come up with any bright suggestions either. But it was nice to have him around for a couple of days because he was a man who was rich in strange facts and wise saws, which he liked to scatter around among whatever company he chanced upon. A theatre, he told me, was like the human circulatory system, in which the blood must flow unimpeded from the actors on stage to the furthest or slowest member of the audience and back again. With a perfect circulation life is assured.

Sylvia was also trying to keep up with Deval's shifting moods, and towards the end of the first week she reported that he had adopted an awkward stance, saying that all laughs must be eliminated, otherwise he would not allow his play to open on Broadway. She and Coby had tried to talk him out of this, but his mind was made up, his patience was exhausted, he had compromised enough. Compromised? He had not changed a single line of dialogue for us. Playwrights in America are well protected by their Guild but did he actually have the right to withdraw his play when no one had altered the script? No one seemed to know the answer to that one and anyway the main thing was to keep going; any suggestion was worth trying. So with much gritting of the teeth we fell into line and made an honest effort to kill those laughs.

249

It was a very interesting experiment. We managed without much difficulty to get rid of the small stuff. A line which had been received with a laugh when thrown away we would now read somewhat deliberately or vice versa. There are ways of getting rid of surface laughs but the real difficulty arises when it is a situation laugh. And the biggest laugh in *Bathsheba* proved to be utterly uneliminable because it was not only a situation laugh but one that was, though Deval might not know it, very skilfully prepared.

To my knowledge Deval had never before written a play as serious as he believed *Bathsheba* to be. He was a comedy writer and he had developed the skills of a comedy writer, such as the one which is displayed in the following scenes.

1. General Joab conveys David's message to Uriah, the Hittite, to the effect that he must return to the home front and report to King David. He wants the young man to make a good impression on David, so he warns him that the King, in order to assess the characters and qualities of the men around him, is liable to 'test' him in conversation.

2. When Uriah is admitted to the King's presence for his interview it happens that David has just concluded a conversation with a Greek slave who is new to the palace and who has been describing to him certain events leading to the Fall of Troy. David now passes some of this information on to Uriah. He mentions that the principal cause of the Trojan War was the adulterous relationship between Helen who was the wife of the Greek king Menelaus, and a Trojan prince named Paris. Uriah is much struck by the story and he asks David,
'And what did they do to Helen after the war was won?'
'Oh', says David, 'she went back to Sparta with her husband, Menelaus.'
Uriah is amazed and says to David,

250

'You mean she was not punished?'

'Evidently not.'

Now there is a considerable pause, at the end of which Uriah gives a quiet chuckle.

'Ah!' he says, 'You are just testing me! Of course they punished her. They stoned her to death, didn't they?'

Hebraic law stated unambiguously that the punishment for a woman taken in adultery was death by stoning.

'No', says David. 'Her husband forgave Helen.'

3. When Uriah's leave is over and David learns that his nights were spent in the quarters of the Palace Guard and that there is now no hope of organising a cover-up for the illegitimacy of Bathsheba's expected child, he comes up with a bold plan to effect retribution for his sin. He will abdicate and name Uriah as his successor. But first he must make a full confession to Uriah.

Uriah prepares to give his undivided attention to what David is about to tell him.

David tells him that when Uriah was away at the front he saw Bathsheba bathing and lusted for her. He then took her to his bed and fornication took place; and now she is pregnant with his child.

When Uriah hears this he is speechless. But after a prolonged pause he shakes his head and smiles.

'Ah', says he, 'you are testing me!'

Now that has got to be a laugh. And even if the great Jed Harris had directed the play he would never have found a way to get rid of it, short of altering the text.

So the play was proved incorrigibly laughter-prone. Not being quite sure of the legalities of the situation I assumed that Deval would now refuse to let us open on Broadway. But he changed his mind again, and when I asked Sylvia what was his reason for this, she told me that without a Broadway opening he would have no hope of selling the film rights. Strange thinking. If ever a story was in public domain, that was surely the story of David and his Bathsheba. And the only original contribution that Deval had made to the telling of it was the device which had guaranteed the laughter which perversely had so displeased him.

So we were permitted to roll happily along, no longer disturbed by the austerity of Philadelphia. They were not so bad when you got used to them; indeed to judge from the reception accorded to us by the unbroken series of full houses, one would have been justified in thinking that they liked us.

During the matinée performance on our second and final Saturday in Philadelphia a bizarre event took place. The young man who played Uriah, the Hittite, and I were halfway through our conversation about what became of Helen of Troy. The prompt corner was on stage right and in order to fix my eyes on Uriah I had to look in a lefterly direction. Behind him, just back of the proscenium arch in a dark area which had hitherto been empty there now appeared the figure of a man in a dark modern suit and bow tie. Semi-consciously I took this to be Coby Ruskin who when dressed formally favoured a bow. But wait a minute, I thought, the man is now walking onto the stage. Perhaps Coby has an important announcement to make, like 'Ladies and Gentlemen, I want you to remain in your seats and not to panic. A small fire happens to have broken out back stage, so . . .' Up till this point my conversation with Uriah continued unbroken, but now I thought that it was time for me to refocus my eyes and find out what Coby was up to.

It wasn't Coby. It was a young man I had never seen before and he was looking at me. He took two more steps in my direction, then stopped. I felt obliged to say – 'What the hell are you doing here?' Very deliberately and loud enough for everyone to hear him he said 'Mr Mason, in my opinion, sir, this play stinks!'

The audience was spellbound.

'Get the hell out of here,' I said. And I seized him by the

scruff of his jacket and pitched him towards the wings on the left of stage. Since he did not reach this target in a single movement I grabbed a pitcher which contained orange juice from the table in front of me and tossed it at him. It was wide of the mark and almost hit Pamela who happed to be standing in the wings preparing for her next entrance. Finally the stranger tottered beyond the audience's eyeline. But I could feel that there was now movement among my friends backstage. Horace Braham, who had been standing near the prompt corner on Stage Right, now startled us all by lifting his *galabiah*, the easier to dash across the stage in full view of the audience in order to arrest the offender. Several others had embarked on the same mission unseen by myself and the audience. There were minor scuffling sounds and then silence. To my eternal shame I had to take a prompt. I would like to have been able to report that my cool never left me and that I was able to pick up the dialogue precisely where we had broken off. But at least we got a round of applause when we started up again.

When arrested by my colleagues the young man was taken beneath the stage and cross-questioned by the stage manager. The culprit, it appeared, was suffering from nervous fatigue occasioned by his military service and receiving psychiatric treatment, while the girl friend who accompanied him to the theatre was by way of being an actress and had unsuccessfully applied for a part in our play.

The play did not run for my usual three months, this one was a three-weeker. The critics on the whole gave us a thumbs down. The only individual who was consistently singled out for praise was the set designer, but I found that with the New York critics this was par for the course. For the sake of my colleagues and especially of Sylvia Friedlander I was sorry that we had not pulled it off, but I do not remember having been deeply hurt personally by our reception. Right up to the end we enjoyed the show simply because the audiences seemed to like it. The Ethel

Barrymore Theatre had been the scene of a long line of failures, but ours was to be the last of that line. For not long afterwards, while we were still living in New York, came a play by Tennessee Williams. It was called *A Streetcar named Desire*, and what a winner that was!

The very first professional job I did in New York had happened before the play, in fact only a couple of weeks after our arrival. It was a radio play. And radio, as I have said, was very big at that time. The most highly reputed regular dramatic show was the Theatre Guild of the Air, just as the Theatre Guild which spawned it was the most highly reputed theatre management, and this in turn had been the brain child of a successful patents lawyer named Lawrence Langner, a very august figure. The Theatre Guild of the Air offered adaptations of successful plays, and the one for which I was hired was *Morning Glory*, a play about the kind of serious stage folk who not long before our own time had been treated with enormous respect by writers and society alike. The exquisite Penelope Dudley Ward was to play opposite me. The occasion was memorable only because these radio events were taken with such grim seriousness. While I was rehearsing for *Morning Glory* they thought it might interest me to be present at the broadcasting of the previous week's programme. There was no question of taping their programmes or in any way pre-recording them. They were broadcast live. That alone was enough to give the actors stage fright. But to make things worse there was always an audience, and in the case of these lofty programmes, a huge one. So we sat in the audience and watched fascinated while Lynn Fontanne and Alfred Lunt read their way page by page through the Broadway hit that they were re-creating. Poor Lunt was so nervous that his hand trembled visibly as he turned the pages. His nervousness was transmitted to the audience and returned to him with interest.

And this was precisely what I went through the following week. What made it perhaps worse was that I had always been inclined to stumble when reading aloud and I was still suffering from the initial impact of the exaggerated attention accorded to me by the wild fans of New York. And when we had finished the show they outdid themselves. It was my first and only experience of having a channel carved for me through an enormous crowd by a detachment of police who then had to link arms to hold them back while Pamela, Penelope and myself threaded our way to the car.

But after this one disquieting experience radio was rendered a sheer joy to me by a very special phenomenon whose name was Fred Allen.

In the American Forces Network that operated in Europe during and after the war we seldom heard the voice of Fred Allen. Bob Hope had already become popular as a movie star and his voice was the one most eagerly sought by British listeners who tuned in to AFN, where we now learned to love others who had made less of a mark in movies. One of these was Jack Benny and it was largely through his repeated jokes at Fred Allen's expense that we first learned of the latter's existence. But there could not have been more than a couple of occasions at the most when I had actually heard his voice before we arrived in New York. As if to offset the unpleasant impact of Walter Winchell, Louella Parsons and Jimmy Fidler came then the refreshing twinkle of the Fred Allen Show.

It must have been McCaffrey who insisted that we switch on at a certain time so as not to miss it. He was insistent, it seemed, because there was something about this week's show that made it obligatory for us, of all people, to be listening.

An agent had introduced himself the moment we stepped ashore, claiming responsibility for having arranged for my appearance on the Theatre Guild of the Air. Since I wished to accept this assignment I could hardly avoid letting him handle it for me but during the course of our relationship he failed signally to measure up to the standards set by my exemplary agent in London, Mr Parker, so I made it clear that I had no intention of retaining him as my representative after the current engagement, and I made haste to find a replacement.

I found William Xavier McCaffrey and, insofar as an agent/client relationship will permit, it was love at first sight. He was an Irish American about ten years my senior with comprehensive experience of New York showbusiness. In earlier years he had been a 'booker' for the Radio Keith Orpheum Vaudeville Circuit. Vaudeville had shifted into radio just as later what was left of it would shift into television. McCaffrey was the right man for me. He had the added virtue of being attached by marriage to a small blue eyed dynamo of German extraction called Margaret who was the private secretary of that pillar of NBC, John Royal. Whether or not it was McCaffrey who insisted that we tune in to Fred Allen on that distant occasion, it was certainly he who took care of my ensuing relations not only with the Fred Allen Show but with all further radio engagements and the short lived *Bathsheba* as well.

The initial Fred Allen Show that we had been told to listen to was another of those shocks that came right out of the blue. The principal feature on the show was a parody, if you please, of *The Seventh Veil* performed by Fred Allen himself and Oscar Levant. The latter, who somewhat resembled me facially and who was basically a concert pianist, had recently found a niche for himself in radio on account of his ready wit. It seemed to me that for *The Seventh Veil* to be parodied on the Fred Allen Show was an even greater compliment than to be singled out for abuse on the Louella Parsons show. Even better was the fact that Allen asked me to be a guest on one of his subsequent shows, and so it came about that, shortly after the débâcle of *Bathsheba*, at a time when some gesture was needed with which to massage my ego, I encountered American radio in its happiest form.

About five years ago I was appearing on a television talk show at the NBC Studio in Rockefeller Center in New York. The man in charge of Sound Effects, whose name was Agnew Horine, said, 'I don't know if you like to collect things like this, but you can have it if you want. But if you are not going to keep it, I shall be glad to hold on to it myself.' And he handed me a dog-eared copy of the script of a Fred Allen show on which I figured as his guest. I thanked Mr Horine and assured him that it would be one of my most prized possessions. I have it before me now. They are very formal documents, these radio scripts. A strict format was essential because it made things easier for everyone, the writer (in this case Allen himself), the regular audience and, most important of all, the sponsor who was paying for the programme and whose messages had to be indelibly spotted. This being only a half hour show and a highly prestigious one, only three commercial spots are indicated. Allen was for ever including in his scripts some rather savage little anti-sponsor jokes. The sponsor was the boss and sometimes good Fred Allen jokes, not necessarily the slanted ones, found their way on to the cutting room floor. In this script I find the following stretch of dialogue on the second page.

Portland Hoffa (his wife): ... It gives me great pleasure to present a man who, thirty minutes from now, will be out of work – He's Fred Allen.
(*Applause*)
Allen: Thank you. Thank you. And good evening Ladies and Gentlemen. And, Portland, I heard you mention that this is our last programme.
Portland: Yes.
Allen: This is the last programme the vice-president in charge of snipping can cut the end off.
Portland: Do you think we'll be cut off tonight?
Allen: Who knows? In case we are I think I'll announce now that we'll be back October 5th.

The format demanded an introductory dialogue between Fred and Portland. At the end of it Fred would announce that he was about to take his habitual stroll down 'Allen's Alley'. This meant that he would knock on the doors of his

257

four regular stock characters and pose to each of them in turn a question arising from news events of the moment. Having collected man-in-the-street opinions from his Southern Senator Klaghorn, his New Englander Mr Moody, his Jewish Mrs Nussbaum and his Irish Mr Cassidy, Fred yielded to the halfway commercial spot and to an offering by Al Goodman and his orchestra. Then we would have another short conversation between Fred and Portland which led to the introduction of the guest of the week and something of an interview with him and finally to the big comedy sketch.

We, the devotees, adored these shows, which continued to entertain us until television had established itself so firmly that all the popular entertainers were obliged to face the test of visibility. Fred Allen never came through in a big way on the new and ravenous medium but maintained his reputation as the wittiest handler of words in show-business until he was snatched by an early death in the year 1956.

We were big spenders during our time in New York. It was not only the high rentals that we were paying but we never held back from the more expensive restaurants and night clubs. Sherman Billingsley's Stork Club, which had become number one glamour spot during the preceding decade, shared the lead with the '21' Club. Both were places where celebrities could be spotted and were made much of by the respective managements since they acted as bait for the wealthier socialites. The same could be said of the El Morocco where the clientele could clutch each other on the dance floor besides eating and laughing and shouting at each other. Toots Shore's, where there was no dancing, appealed strongly to those who liked their celebrities to be ball-players and boxers and the more Hemingwayesque movie stars. We kept going to all of these places and also to the nightclubs where much talked about saloon entertainers did their acts.

When six months and a great deal of Korda's 'advance' had slipped away with a rapidity that could not be checked by an occasional radio fee or the short lived income from a Broadway failure, we looked with increasing concern for alternative remedies.

Pamela had made arrangements with Dutton, the publisher, to bring out one of her novels, but neither of us expected it to be a best seller. It was the one which seemed to be her favourite and which, entitled *A Lady Possessed* in England, Dutton preferred to call *Del Palma*. The one which I considered her best book, *The Blinds are Down*, was thought by the publisher to be too down-beat.

Further contributions to our funds came from a few articles that I wrote, a couple for the *New York Times* Sunday Magazine Supplement, a short story for *Esquire* and further articles for movie magazines and one, which was to cause some embarrassing fall-out, for *Cosmopolitan Magazine*, one of those big shiny jobs which, I have always assumed, lie around in ladies' beauty parlours.

But we found what we were looking for, a sizeable piece of money which eventually enabled us to make ends meet. Only just meet, for it was still going to be a long time before I could do any serious earning. The object that we now stumbled upon was the body of *I Met a Murderer*.

The executives of the distributing company, who had originally kidnapped the film, made contracts for its exhibition in the United States. But these contracts had long ago expired and all that we had to do was to pick up the remains and start over. There was a dupe negative and some prints and we made a new deal with a new company who were willing to make an advance payment against our income from both the theatrical and the television exhibition of our film. It was to be some years before we bought a television set of our own and thus we missed the very frequent confrontations which would have hit us had we owned one during the first years of our new deal. At this period television stations had unlimited air time at their disposal but never a hope of laying their hands on a Hollywood film. And the only form of series that had yet appeared was one in which desperate actors were for ever making lightning changes from suit to suit and set to set to arrive on their marks a split second before the red eye of the camera was upon them.

The hot and humid summer of 1947 found us in a house in Riverdale. It was not far from the Hudson River and if a breeze was to be found anywhere we had supposed that this would be the most likely area in which to be freshened by it.

On the contrary we remained hot and sticky for the duration of our lease. There was of course no air-conditioning but we did not mind that. What we minded much more was the fact that our law case had not yet reached the courts. At this rate we might be stuck here forever; if ever I reached Hollywood I would be a forgotten man. Oh well, it was not so bad here in New York. We would just carry on with our new life style, such as it was.

The climax of our New York life spasm was our courtroom appearance. At the time of the hearing Pamela and I were hopping mad. We felt deeply injured by David E. Rose and almost as deeply by his lawyer who had been present when I put my name to that fateful little note on the tasteful blue stationery of Claridge's Hotel in London. Had both us of caught a dose of paranoia? Having now had over thirty years to think about it, I am inclined to say *No*. One of Pamela's ambitions was to win a gold medal as a thunderbolt tosser, and Rose was a suitable target. As for me, there was some evidence in the British Press that I saw myself as one who was persecuted by Mr Rank and producers in general, and even by the pressmen themselves. Does this point to paranoia? It points, but with a flaccid finger. *No*, I have played paranoids on the screen and dug myself deep into the part and I know that what I found there was like nothing I ever experienced myself.

When at long last the Mason v. Rose case was heard, it was in the United States District Court S.D. New York. The case is reported in '85 F. Supp. 300', whatever that means, and is fairly dull reading. It describes the affair as follows:

> Action by James Mason against David Rose for a declaratory judgement wherein plaintiff sought a declaration that a certain writing signed by the parties did not constitute a valid contract, and defendant counterclaimed for an injunction to restrain plaintiff from violating his obligations under the writing.

Then it plods through all our testimony and all the precedents cited.

Judge Knox heard the case. He was suitably Norman Rockwell-ish in appearance and nutty brown in flavour. I absolutely trusted him. Nevertheless I experienced a totally new kind of fear which consisted of two parts regular old stage fright, one part the notoriety panic that had oppressed me ever since my arrival in New York and one part a fear of the law. This last part was the worst because it amounted to a fear of the unknown. One met many people in New York who insisted that the law was bent and that in New York no one had a hope of getting a fair trial. I did not want to believe this and was reassured by the flavour of our Judge.

But the hearing went on for such a long time and there was such an endless outpouring of surprising evidence emanating from Rose and his lawyer that it seemed almost as if Kafka had taken a hand in the mis-en-scène.

The defendant's number one pitcher was a certain Richard B. Persinger. He had no difficulty in making me sweat. And here again it was all a matter of appearance and flavour. Appearance in this case was the reverse of Norman Rockwell: small, blond, pale and with X-ray eye-glasses. Flavour: acidulated. And it was not as if he asked me any very embarrassing questions. All I needed to do was to tell the truth as it had happened to me, but no matter whether the questions came from Judge Knox or Mr

261

Persinger my mouth remained curiously dry and the right words had difficulty getting into line.

We had done what we had to do. But we were not through with it. There was no way of knowing how long it would take His Honour to reach his decision and hand it down. We would just have to sit it out. We could go back to England, but we did not even entertain the thought. Another possibility would have been to see what Bermuda was like. But in those days the sensible projects were not always the ones we chose. We were now programmed to move only in a westerly direction, for good or for ill.

After that the months dragged slowly by. The winter that followed happened to be intensely cold. For quite a long time the snow in Sutton Place reached the level of the roofs of the parked cars. Everyone was finding fault with the sanitation department for not clearing it up; Mayor O'Dwyer was being given a hard time by his critics. The Mason group was discovering that they would rather be almost anywhere other than in New York. As the New Year came and turned the snow into slush we started planning our escape. Charlie Schwartz warned us not on any account to show our faces in California; if we did, there remained the possibility that Rose's lawyer could serve us with his original suit and then appeal to the New York courts to set aside the agony that we had gone through because Rose's suit, having been registered before my own, was therefore entitled to a prior hearing. We got the message, but the itchy feet persisted.

After this warning we did not discuss our situation with any of our friends but between ourselves we never stopped. We had heard a lot about Arizona, how warm it was, how clean, how dry the air; just the place to recover from almost any physical disability you could name. What was to prevent our stopping off there, acquiring a western tan, doing a little painting perhaps and sitting it out in comfort while our friend, the Judge, continued to work on his version of *James Mason versus David E. Rose*? Not as sensible a choice as Bermuda perhaps, but it would serve.

So, already deep into the New Year, we set off.
Monaghan and the staff and the shepherd dog went ahead
to California where a temporary house for us would be
located while Pamela and I and the cats sat it out in
Phoenix. Everyone told us that the place to stay in
Phoenix was the Arizona Biltmore which was in fact a very
well run hotel. It sat in spacious grounds where with
sufficient patience one could have had a grapefruit fall
into one's hand. We did not need to do that because here
and there a ripe looking specimen would be already on the
grass beneath a tree. We lay on the grass beside one. We
should have let it lie because when peeled it was
exceptionally sour. Nevertheless the atmosphere was
idyllic.

We stayed in Phoenix for only ten days, by the end of
which time Monaghan had found a furnished house for us
in Beverly Hills, which turned out to be a faultless choice.
To preserve the covert nature of our operation we travelled
by road, knowing that anyone who arrived by rail in
downtown Los Angeles, or who even took the precaution
of getting off the train at Pasadena, could seldom avoid
being spotted by the ever vigilant local press.

The house was in Cove Way in Beverly Hills. It had a

nice garden. The weather was agreeable. Sitting on a rather small terrace in front of the house, which was to become my semi-permanent condition in the weeks that followed, I overlooked a quiet road beyond which rose the extensive grounds of the neighbouring rich. Jutting from a slope over there was a tennis court supported by sturdy columns. Tennis courts, I learned later, were less plentiful than the stranger might suppose. Though there is wealth there are also hills, as the name of the city suggests. Hollywood is even hillier. I was to learn later that the man of wealth who had built his tennis court on stilts on the other side of the road was David Selznick, the big shot, and that the zonk of racket hitting ball was not infrequently sounded by Katharine Hepburn. That gave me something to think about; not much, but something and every little helped, for I was now a sort of prisoner.

14/Beverly Hills

It could be said that anyone who shows up in Southern California with intent to pursue a movie career becomes 'a sort of prisoner' if he doesn't watch out, but when I said that I had turned into one I meant it literally. If I were seen shopping in a Beverly Hills supermarket the news could reach the ears of David E. Rose before the evening was out and next day a process server could materialise on my terrace. So I settled down without complaining.

I asked our publisher friend at Duttons in New York if he would be interested in publishing an account of our first year in America, to which he replied that the prospect did not thrill him but suggested that Pamela and I write a book about cats, since an infatuation with cats was the image that had stuck to us like flypaper ever since our arrival in New York over a year before. I construed this as a form of encouragement, even though I was already rather tired of this thing they had about cats. So we liked cats. What was so strange or even interesting about that?

When the writing was not coming well, I would spell myself with a few hours of painting, but there were no serious writing blocks and I never became stir crazy. I was running out of money though. And it became an interesting race: Which would be the first to pass the winning post, the judge's decision or my last nickel? I happened to win that event for I was still solvent when the judge's decision reached us. But now it became a race between the last nickel and the arrival of my first Hollywood paycheck. Halfway through the writing period I took the risk of breaking my cover. Very surreptitiously we made contact with the agent whom I had chosen to represent me as soon as the barrier should be raised.

McCaffrey and other friends in New York had insisted that I would not be able to get along without an agent in Hollywood and they all had a good word for Abe Lastvogel, one of the top men in the William Morris office, which was second only in size and influence to the one I already knew of called the Music Corporation of America (MCA). During the postwar carpetbagging operation conducted in Europe by some of the Hollywood agents and producers, an officer of MCA, intent on acquiring a piece of my action, had approached Al Parker and offered to buy his agency. Though Al was not interested in the idea he kept the man talking because he wanted to know just what was in his mind. Al listed the clients with whom he had contracts.

'And of course you have Mason, don't you?'

'Oh yes, Jimmy is my oldest client.'

Then the man spoke of his great admiration for me and

Al answered appropriately and this exchange went on for some time until Al felt obliged to say, 'I don't have any written contract with Jimmy, I never did have. You see, we are old friends.'

Whereupon his visitor mysteriously lost interest in the proposed purchase of the Al Parker Agency. He said that it had been nice talking to Al and he hoped that they might meet again some time.

And then, when everyone knew that a state of war existed between David Rose and myself, MCA took on my adversary as a client. This may have been a perfectly innocent gesture but I took it as proof that MCA was sure that Rose would get the better of me by settlement or in the courts and would have a piece of the resultant 'partnership'. There was yet a third mysterious happening and my interpretation of it could be taken as evidence that I had indeed picked up a small dose of paranoia. Shortly after the two earlier events, a man who could be described as a very close friend of myself and my wife, was enlisted on to the staff of MCA.

So I covertly invited Abe Lastvogel to come and see me in my hideaway. He was a short sturdy man with a benign face. Officers of the Morris Office were notoriously short. This gave rise to many inside jokes by popular comedians. Abe's benign face was surmounted by ripply mid-brown hair; he looked not unlike Dr Kissinger except that the latter is an inch or two taller, his hair is darker and his voice more guttural. But I could see that I was going to like Abe and described to him the kind of work I was hoping for. I detected a flicker of disappointment when I told him that I had no intention of signing a long term contract with any of the major companies although I recognised that in certain circumstances I might feel obliged to sign a three- or even a six-picture deal as I had done in England with Gainsborough Pictures in order to get the name part in *The Man in Grey*. I learned later that one of his close friends was a big shot at MGM called Bennie Thau and that he would have liked nothing better than to gift-wrap

267

me in a long term contract and deliver me personally to this Bennie Thau with one of his benign smiles.

Soon we, too, had something to smile about. Judge Knox gave his decision. In it he stated that no contract existed between myself and David E. Rose. Although the evidence produced in court seemed to indicate that I had *acted* as if Rose and I were partners, it failed to prove the existence of a binding contract. The letter on Claridge's notepaper which I had signed could not be construed as such because there was no mention of a 'consideration' on Rose's part.

To some extent Pamela and I felt somewhat let down because it would have been nice if the judge had echoed our hopping mad feelings about our antagonist and had used his decision as an opportunity to castigate him. But our suit was, after all, for a declaratory judgment, not punitive damages, and the decision gave us just what we had asked for.

Freedom meant we could now explore the town, reactivate old friendships, establish new ones, and, above all, look for a job. And we knew now that this was going to be rough. Not only was the gingerbread distinctly less gilded than it had been eighteen months previously, but I was still determined to exercise fastidiousness in my choice of work.

Even before I had sailed for New York some quite attractive projects were offered to me which I had been obliged to turn down on account of the cloud on my title. One of these was a romantic costume film to be made by Preston Sturges for whose comedies I had enormous admiration. He wrote telling me that he was going to film *Colomba* by Prosper Mérimée, who wrote the novel on which the opera *Carmen* is based. It led to an interesting correspondence and in California to something approaching friendship with this man of genius. Another introduction by correspondence was to the screenwriter and director Dudley Nichols, who wanted me to be in his *Mourning Becomes Electra*. In New York Walter Wanger came at me with another costume romance and it was hard for me to convince him of the seriousness of my legal predicament. Although I became friendly with Wanger in California I was not displeased when I saw the finished film. It was a mess. Poor Van Heflin had inherited my part and opposite him romped Susan Hayward. The making of *Colomba* was also a big disappointment, I was assured both by Faith Domergue who played the heroine and by Max Ophüls who directed it for at least part of the time. Sturges had gone into partnership with Howard Hughes and was not at all himself, though being himself could also be rather strange at times. For *Colomba* he had promoted himself to the role of producer which did not suit him.

I never got to see *Mourning Becomes Electra* but my reliable friends assured me that it could have been a mite too stodgy for my taste. At any rate I had no cause to regret that these offers had come when I was immobilised by the law. I was lucky really, because if one of them had come to me just now when I was hurting for money I would undoubtedly have snapped it up, to repent later. Now that I was on the spot I realised more clearly than I had before that having virtually cut myself off from the major studios, I had to look to the independent producers for work, and there were not many of them, and most of them were small fry. The exception was the giant, Sam Goldwyn. But then there were giant freelance actors who would continue to satisfy his requirements, such as Ronald Colman and Gary Cooper.

It developed too that I had already, though inadvertently, given myself a bad name in Hollywood. This was an interesting phenomenon. I mentioned earlier that one of the articles that I had been busy writing during the year in New York had found its way into the pages of *Cosmopolitan Magazine.* In ladies' hairdressing salons and dentists' waiting rooms and perhaps elsewhere I had built up quite a nice little reading public for myself with this article, which was entitled *Why I am Afraid of Going to Hollywood.* It set out to be nothing more than a description of Hollywood socio-professional rituals based on the reports that had come to me from acquaintances who had made the Californian Grand Tour. I poked innocent fun, as I thought, no one having told me that the Hollywood settlers were among the most sensitive people in the world, especially those who had settled for the movie industry.

So as the result of my *Cosmopolitan* article the word got around that not only was I known to be unco-operative but that I was already smearing Hollywood *before I had even set foot in the place.* My American readers missed the point of what I had written just as the boys in the A.C.T. in England had missed the point of what I had attempted to say in my *Glamour* article. In the present case the title underlined my point. I was saying – the hair-raising stories I have heard about the place explain 'Why I am afraid of going to Hollywood.' Nothing wrong with that, I would have thought.

But I had made things worse for myself by answering questions put to me by newspapers *after* the appearance of the *Cosmopolitan* article. Sometimes I had even made sly little jokes, and that is always a big mistake. I marked that up as a lesson learned, but it is one that still slips my mind sometimes with disastrous consequences. It was in such an interview rather than in the original article, I think, that there had been a reference to the strict protocol observed in the placing of movie celebrities dining at Romanoff's Restaurant. Something like this is bound to happen in any successful first-class restaurant, but the problems presented inevitably reached the level of farce when Romanoff had to cope with the highly competitive movie stars, wealthy wives and widows who abound in Beverly Hills. Here again I put my foot in it. What I had said about this was innocent enough, but it must have looked bad in print in whichever Los Angeles newspaper picked it up, because it triggered another of those bizarre reactions to which I was becoming accustomed. I was castigated in, of all places, a leading article in the menu of Romanoff's Restaurant.

Whatever sort of restaurant would print what amounted to a gossip column in its menu? It could only happen in the Beverly Hills 'in' restaurant of the moment. Well, now I suppose it could happen anywhere since there is hardly a community on our planet to which Hollywood has not spread its culture. But at that time it seemed quite a breakthrough.

For me it was another attention-getting event, but it did not speedily bring me offers of work. But it would be a long time before the sybaritic life to which we were now exposed would begin to pall, and I was not yet completely unemployed for on my terrace during the daytime I was still making sketches for the cat book which we had just finished.

One day a script entitled *Caught* was delivered to me. The writer was Arthur Laurents and it was based on a story by Libbie Block called *Wild Calendar*. I was invited to play the part of the heavy who was a fictionalised version of Howard Hughes, the eccentric multi-millionaire. Having read the script and admired the quality of the writing I rang Abe Lastvogel and told him that I did not want to play the Howard Hughes part because I was determined to smash my villainous image and offer myself in the guise of a sympathetic leading man. I went on to say that there was a rôle for a nice guy in the script and, if the part had not already been given to another actor, that was the one that I would like to play, even though it was clearly not so effective as the Howard Hughes.

Abe passed the message on to the producer, Wolfgang Reinhardt who, of the two sons of Max Reinhardt, the famous German stage producer, was the one with an air of studious gentility. Gottfried, on the other hand, was the brother who had inherited his father's louder and more aggressive qualities.

271

Wolfgang Reinhardt came to visit me at my house and told me that not only was Max Ophüls going to be our director but that they were still not satisfied with the final sequences of the script. But there were reasons for this, he said. The Producers' Code was raising its awkward head again. *Wild Calendar* told a story of a nice little woman who had been to a charm school and now found herself taken in matrimony by a domineering and unfeeling tycoon. By way of escape she takes a job as receptionist in a doctors' office. One of the doctors is the nice guy of the film and after a while they fall in love with one another. Rich guy continues to treat her appallingly and supply more than enough cause for divorce by the standards of 1948. But the rules of the Production Code did not permit the wronged marital partner to take the initiative in a divorce action. Only the bad guy could do that and since the Howard Hughes character in our story was not likely to volunteer his services as a defendant in a divorce suit nor had been given cause to sue his wife, Arthur Laurents reached an impasse. In cheaper, more lurid films such a problem was usually solved by the *deus ex machina* bringing sudden death to the nasty husband and rewarding the loving couple with a marriage licence.

Nobody expected this sort of cheating to be used in a serious project like ours. But it was reduced to something very similar to that in the end. Arthur Laurents invented a scene somewhat resembling the one in *Citizen Kane* in which Kane runs amok, smashes a roomful of period furniture and *objets d'art*, but in our case he had the Hughes character run amok in his rumpus room, appear to have a heart attack and get hit on the head by a collapsing pinball machine. The girl and the nice guy then bundle the injured man into an ambulance and escort him to hospital, carefully refraining from holding hands. Obviously the two of them heartily wish him dead, as does the audience, but the writer remains true to the Code.

When Reinhardt told me of this I realised that we had quite a problem. On the other hand I was delighted that

Max Ophüls was to be the director who would help us lick it. In spite of the problem, I was glad to find that I was to contribute to a serious project. Not solemn, not stodgy, but serious in the best sense, that is to say a project which all the participants might handle to the very limit of their talents without compromise. Barbara Bel Geddes, who had an excellent record on Broadway, was to play the girl, and now that I had rejected the role of the heavy, it would be played by Robert Ryan.

The casting of Robert Ryan presented a problem which proved to be only a minor one. He happened to be under contract to RKO Film Company which at that time was owned by Howard Hughes. We had all assumed that, when he and his stooges realised that our bad guy was something of a portrait of Hughes, he would get mean and not only veto the casting of Ryan but also find a way to sabotage the film. But he reacted with an unexpected mildness. All he demanded was that obvious similarities between himself and the character in our film, such as the nature of his business interests and style of dress, be eliminated. The script had indicated that our villain's normal footgear was to be white sneakers. This of course had to go, since it was common knowledge that Hughes was seldom seen without them.

The necessary adjustments were made and we were all set to go. Or so it seemed for a moment. Then came over the phone the voice of a rather anxious Wolfgang Reinhardt, announcing that he was coming round to see me right away. The new problem? Max Ophüls had shingles and the attack was serious enough for him to have withdrawn from the film. He was to be replaced by a young director unknown to me, named John Berry. I did not especially want to be directed by someone of whose record I was totally ignorant. There are always young men around about whom agents and producers will say – you're going to see a lot of this guy. They were saying that about John Berry, but it did little to cheer me up. In order to reassure me Reinhardt said: 'But you're not to worry because he is going to have the head of the Habima Players as his dialogue director.'

The very thought of a dialogue director was startling. If a dialogue director was to be someone who coached the actors in their dialogue, who wanted that? The interpretation of dialogue was a matter which exclusively concerned the actors and the real director. I had heard that so-called dialogue directors were sometimes employed merely to run the actors through their lines and make sure that they knew them, but the head of the Habima Players could scarcely be fobbed off with so modest a chore. I expressed my dismay forcefully. If John Berry was the sort who would *want* to have the head of the Habima Players direct his dialogue, then he was not the director for me. I made it clear that I was not in any sense knocking the Habima Players *per se* but the existence of a split directorship could be a serious hazard.

A few years later, the director Robert Siodmak described the intense frustration that he suffered when his leading actor was receiving instructions from a private coach who was actually present every day on the set. When Siodmak was talking to this actor he felt that he was never in direct contact with him because the actor would promptly hurry over to his coach for a second opinion. He had never been so frustrated in his life. He wanted to hit him.

In an attempt to pacify me, Wolfgang Reinhardt said that, even if Ophüls had directed the film, he would also have had a dialogue director because his knowledge of English could not always be trusted. I sighed and let the matter rest. I was not going to refuse to work with John Berry, because I was already committed and my contract did not specify that Ophüls would direct. Besides I needed the money.

With a feeling of some disappointment I settled down to studying the script and thinking myself into the role of Dr Quinada, the sympathetic pediatrician. Then, in less than a week, came good new. Ophüls was going to be sufficiently cured to direct the film after all. If there was a dialogue director on the payroll he was obviously instructed to keep well out of my way, for I never saw one throughout the shooting of the film.

So we made the film. We worked well together. An important member of the team, whom I had not met before we started shooting, was the editor Robert Parrish who had recently shared an Academy Award for his work on *Body and Soul* and was later nominated again on the strength of *All the King's Men*. My latent hostility to producers showed itself at one point. There was a scene in which Dr Quinada, the pediatrician, seated at his desk in the office, is given a report on a patient's condition by the nurse-receptionist. He takes it in and seems to be thinking about what she has said for a moment or two, then suddenly he stands up, picks up his bag and moves to the door. He has considered the symptoms, put two and two together and has recognised an emergency. Max chose to shoot this in medium long shot, that is to say that when I stood up, my full figure, including my feet, would be in the frame. Then he panned me to the door. It was not a situation in which you needed to see the actor's face especially; in this case it was the action that told the story. Max asked me if I felt that I needed a close-up, I said no. What could I do with my face that was not adequately told in the full shot? He was happy because, he said, there was nothing that he hated more than what he described as 'the rabbit shot'. He meant whenever a surprising event took place conventional movie-makers always felt obliged to cut to a close-up of one of the actors registering 'surprise'. So we did not cover what we had done with any further set-ups. But the next day, as we had half expected, word came from the producer's office to say that a close-up would be needed. Max and I were both disappointed. I suggested that we just take no notice of the message because surely a shrewd director's choice of set-ups should clearly indicate the manner in which the sequence should be cut together.

Max said that he would talk to the producer about it. And he did. And he did not give in until the end of the following day when he figured that he had expended more than enough energy on something that was not more than an academic point. And after all, he said, our cutter was a man of taste. He himself was a survivor and he had learned a long time ago that to put your foot down rarely got results. Though we had failed in this case, talk was the thing.

I did not choose to attend any of the private runnings of the film when it was completed. Ideally I liked to look at a film I was in only after it had been shown to the public and the critics.

A sneak preview was arranged at some theatre in Pasadena. The purpose of such showings was to assess the public's likely reaction. They could get a good indication from the manner in which the preview audience filled in the cards, or so it was thought. The questionnaire on these cards would invite each member of the audience to put a check mark against the word which expressed their rating of the film, e.g. excellent, good, fair, poor, too long, disappointing etc. The efforts of the principal actor and director would be similarly rated, and finally there would be a space left for each individual's 'remarks', if any.

Usually sneak previews were arranged to test reaction in three or more different locations but in the case of *Caught* the cards so uniformly rated the picture 'excellent' that the producers decided that the one preview had unambiguously declared that the film was going to be a terrific hit. The name of the company that made our film was Enterprise and up to now their record had been disastrous. 'With this film we'll be able to recoup our losses', was the buzz that went around the studio. Our spirits were all lifted by the promise of success. Arthur Laurents said 'Wouldn't it be marvellous if this film were never released and we went on being feted like this forever?'

But when the moment of truth arrived we were an instant failure. It opened at a carefully selected theatre in New York and practically no one showed up at the box office.

My Hollywood career started with a straight run of five failures, which might well lead the film buff to suppose that my taste guided me unerringly to projects which were artistically unadventurous and financially hazardous. Though I have no alibi and it was myself and no one else who set the course that led me to this archipelago of non-success, it was not exactly a matter of taste. On the one hand I shrank from being type cast or of becoming the long term thrall of a major company; on the other I wished to involve myself in film-making of every variety and ultimately to become my own producer and my own director or writer as well when it might seem beneficial to the end product. Obviously I could not become my own producer overnight; first I must rise to a position of some power, and this could only be done by appearing in one successful picture after another. Though it may be hard to believe, this was my aim throughout my career in Hollywood. Each choice that I made was in fact the best offer available.

I was asked to play one of the principal parts in *Madame Bovary* which was to be made by MGM. Robert Ardrey had supplied them with what I thought was an excellent script but there was something about the set-up that drained my confidence. Unwisely I allowed myself to be persuaded to play the part of de Maupassant in a Prologue and an Epilogue which Ardrey had invented.

The three others of this lamentable group were *Reckless Moment*, *East Side West Side* and *One Way Street*. On the plus side, *Reckless Moment* offered me once again the pleasure of working with Max Ophüls and introduced me to Walter Wanger and his wife Joan Bennett who became good friends. Similarly *One Way Street* led to a friendship with the Italo-Argentinian director Hugo Fregonese. The stories of the three films were weak and old fashioned.

The next film on my list was one that self-evidently raised its head above disaster level, although this statement might be challenged by statements issuing from the MGM Accounts Department. The film was *Pandora and the Flying Dutchman.*

Meanwhile something infinitely more rewarding had taken place on the domestic front. This was the arrival on November 25th, 1948, of the beloved daughter. Our lives were transposed into a new and exultant key. A curriculum now included care and feeding of child, studying the works of Dr Spock, sanctification of Dr Leon (Red) Krohn, the obstetrician, acceptance of rulings laid down by Dr Harold Bernstein, the pediatrician, show of interest in other people's children (not always sincere), attempts to reconcile cats to the arrival of new and attention-demanding pet, discussion of possible names for child, arrangements for christening, selection of god-parents, and so on.

It happened that shortly after the birth we bought a big house and moved into it. This extended our curriculum still further and also our housekeeping bills. The two housemen had found jobs and moved out but we still had Violet. Now we needed some sort of a helper for her, and a gardener to cope with the extensive grounds, and of course a nurse for the first months. Pamela was insistent that, as soon as the child became walkable, there were to be nurses no more because she herself would take every care of the growing child. She had the single-mindedness of a mother who has encountered childbearing after the first flush of youth has passed by. No strange hand or voice was to bring up or influence *her* offspring. Her devotion never flagged.

The christening took place at Holy Trinity Episco-palian Church in Beverly Hills. The godparents turned out to be Mrs Fred Allen (Portland Hoffa), Joan Bennett and Monaghan, who in California was our oldest friend around. We had already decided to call the child Portland, because we were so fond of Fred Allen and his wife. Actually we had chosen the name even before we knew the child would be a boy or girl – 'Let's hear it now for the fifty-eighth President of the United States, Portland Mason!', (Applause) or – 'The Award for the best performance by an actress ... Portland Mason!' (Ap-

Portland

plause) would both sound good. And as we drove down to the church Portland Allen asked us if we had thought of a second name. For Americans second names seem to be almost obligatory, and also I suppose that she thought that the child might at some future time wish to escape from such an unusual name as Portland. We could not think of anything we specially fancied, and so at the last moment Portland suggested we call her Portland Allen Mason. The suggestion was instantly approved, although Allen was hardly likely to recommend itself as a name behind which she might later wish to seek refuge. So shortly afterwards in the church the girl became Portland Allen Mason.

A celebration took place in the big house during the evening of the same day. It was not a large group because at that time we had not collected a great number of friends. Among them was Preston Sturges whom I admired and who had entertained us in his house and had been several times to ours. While we were having some dinner during this celebration Preston, who was sitting beside me, said, 'James, I arrived rather late as you know and all of you were already in the church. But in the path leading to the church there was a small group of men who looked as if their feelings had been hurt in some way. They looked very upset as they stood there. Had something disagreeable happened before I arrived?'

I explained what had happened. Although truly I always wanted to be friendly and cooperative with the press, I thought that public figures – or whatever we were supposed to be – should on certain occasions and in certain places be allowed a degree of privacy. I figured that a christening was a very private affair and I had instructed Monaghan to say to any member of the press corps who might ring up before the event to find out where it was going to take place that it was to be strictly private and that he had been instructed not to give out any information. Well, they must have got the message because I do not believe that anyone approached us or tried to take photographs as we entered the church. Pamela and I and the godparents and the minister were ranged around the font and the service was just about to begin when I noticed a strange man entering through the West Door, which had been left open. He was carrying a press photographer's camera with a flash attachment and he came directly to where I was standing. Lowering my voice, I said, 'Are you a press photographer?' He said yes. I said, 'Get the hell out of here!' I spoke very quietly but I must have looked very fierce because he turned and left at once.

This was evidently the disagreeable happening that had caused the photographer and his buddies to look so upset. Now that I had confirmed Sturges's deductions he took it upon himself to pontificate somewhat. He told me that he had the habit of observing events with the eyes of a playwright and he was extremely sensitive to the least show of emotion and could usually assess the cause. He had been saddened, he told me, by what he had seen outside the church and he hoped that I would not mind if he told me that there is always a way of handling such situations and it was up to me to find it. It was not the man's fault, he said; he had been given certain instructions by his editor and it was up to him to bring back the required photographs.

As a matter of fact I *did* mind Sturges giving me this lecture but I let him go on. I was not going to make things worse by having a useless argument with my guest on such a happy occasion. Naturally he had seen the event objectively, whereas I was an involved protagonist. And no matter how high an opinion I had of his playwright's eye, I had more than a suspicion that on occasions when he was involved personally his reflexes acted just as promptly as mine had. Neither the episode itself nor Sturges's lecture made me feel especially guilty. To say 'Get the hell out of here' when standing beside the font seemed to me no worse than to say it on the stage of that theatre in Philadelphia.

Let me add that though this incident would hardly

support the claim, I have always thought of Sturges as one of Hollywood's few men of genius.

Another visitor who came to our new house soon after we had moved in was Albert Lewin, who had invited me to participate in his project *Pandora and the Flying Dutchman*. At MGM he held an exalted position. Aside from his range of skills as a film-maker, he had also functioned unofficially as Irving Thalberg's personal investment counsellor. A tiny man physically, he was smart, but amiable. When he came he brought salt and a loaf of bread with him, a custom with which I was not familiar. He noted the large hall, the grand staircase, the large salon, dining room and library. His blue eyes twinkled as he said, 'Irving Thalberg used always to be very pleased when any of his stars bought himself a big house, because it meant that he would need to keep working!'

I had paid for the house with most of the salary from my third film. Most of my salary from the second film had paid the fee of Charlie Schwartz, the New York lawyer, and this was more than the price of the big house. The salary from *Caught*, the first film, was supposed to look after our living for a while. Then there was always income tax and so on.

The script of *Pandora and the Flying Dutchman* arrived long before Al Lewin had succeeded in organising a set-up for its production. But he seemed to have no doubts about his ability to do so. The man at MGM for whom he had originally worked and whom he held in such high esteem, Irving Thalberg, was long since dead, and now Lewin seemed to occupy a position among the principal executives, though not very clearly defined. More than anything he was a high ranking trouble shooter who gave his opinion on all the important scripts and the films when they were completed; if a film was in trouble he gave his advice on how it could be saved. But all I knew about him before I read the script was that he was one of the high-ups at MGM and I was naturally wary. None of us could deny that many films of high quality had been turned out by this factory but the more one heard about it, the more disagreeable it sounded and the more justification for thinking of it as a factory. When I had taken the job in *Madame Bovary*, an MGM film, I had not been asked to give options to the company for further films because the role had been one that appeared only in the prologue and the epilogue of the film. But I had been taken by Benny Thau to meet the big chief himself, Louis B. Mayer. It was, I supposed, like being taken to meet Mussolini. No, not Mussolini perhaps because meetings with Mussolini have been described many times by the unfortunate individuals who had been obliged to walk the full length of his immensely long hall, losing confidence with every step they took, to the formidable little man seated at his desk at the far end. No, one did not have to walk very far in the office of L.B. Mayer, which was more like a small courtroom. His desk was raised on a dais and to one side there was the flag of the United States and at eye level round the room were framed portraits of his racehorses. He greeted me with a formal display of cordiality and gave me the kind of talk that a ruling monarch might give when greeting for the first time a newly appointed foreign diplomat. He knew that I was British, so his talk touched on the desirability of good Anglo-American relations. One's fears of Hollywood were borne out by an encounter such as this. Van Heflin, whom we had met with his wife, when we were in New York, had become one of our close friends and he had a fresh gripe about the studio every time we met. He was under a long term contract to MGM.

Consequently it was a big surprise that among the life at the top could be found such a cultured innocent-seeming person as this nice Al Lewin. He was extremely well read, a fact which displayed itself perhaps too clearly in the pages of his script. He also had a great knowledge of the visual arts and had a fine collection of surrealist paintings. I was very happy that it took him such a long time to put together the film because it gave us all the more time to improve our acquaintance.

For him there was no urgency to get moving because, being a member of the Hollywood establishment, he was immune to the virus of insecurity to which independent producers were normally prone. MGM permitted him to take off and make a film of his own at pre-arranged intervals. MGM were probably given first refusal of his films, but cannot have been under obligation to distribute all that he made, since, if so, they would have insisted on having ultimate approval of his script and of the final cut of them all. And I am sure that it would have spoiled his fun if he had anything less than total control.

His first and best film was *The Moon and Sixpence*, faithfully based on Somerset Maugham's novel of that name which in turn was based less faithfully on the life of Gauguin, the post-impressionist painter. His cast included two of the best actors who ever graced Hollywood movies – Herbert Marshall and George Sanders. It often happens nowadays that some film that was made in the forties or fifties makes its appearance on television because the name of the star who heads the cast is listed as one of the immortals and you find that the only thing that makes the film still worth watching is a supporting performance by Sanders or Marshall or one of their ilk. And their ilk is a very exclusive club.

I had seen this film and liked it very much and was confident that Lewin would do something interesting with his new work. He had only written and directed *The Moon and Sixpence* and his other film of distinction *The Picture of Dorian Gray*; now he was going to be the producer as well, but that should not be a handicap for a man of his experience. He set up a company with a man called Joe Kaufman, which they called Dorkay. This found the money for any dollar expenditure there might be and made an alliance with the English company Romulus to take care of all European costs. The exteriors of the film were to be shot on the Costa Brava in Spain and the interiors in Shepperton Studios in England. Romulus was a production company owned by John and James Woolf.

It was a project full of promise, to which, regrettably, it did not live up, although I have met many people who spoke of it afterwards with lavish enthusiasm. Members of the public, that is, for those who took part in the making of it were more restrained, and the English critics were quite cool. The critic for whom I had most respect, C.A. Lejeune, said for instance, 'Conspicuous in its confident assumption of scholarship and in its poverty of taste and imagination. James Mason correctly interprets a man who obviously needs a rest after being chivvied about the world for two or three centuries.'

If there was a relationship between the girl in our film and the lady who figured in Greek mythology, I was never able to spot it. Our Pandora was a beautiful American girl who has many love affairs, but actually never falls in love until she meets the Dutchman who is indeed the character from legend. For the purposes of his film Lewin relates that his Flying Dutchman, having murdered his wife, whom he suspects of infidelity, and made things worse for himself by committing monstrous blasphemy, is condemned to roam the seas indefinitely, but is allowed to conduct the life of a normal human being for six months every seven years. His sin will be expiated only if he can win the love of a girl who will die for him. Upon this rather arbitrary foundation Lewin constructed a romantic spectacle featuring Pandora's high-handed treatment of her glamorous suitors who include a suave British racing driver and a jealous bull-fighter.

Although this does not look very good on paper, I remain of the opinion that it could have been something quite marvellous. Indeed there are many who thought that the film we made had a lot of magic to it. Unfortunately it suffered from one grave handicap, of which I became aware as soon as I started my work.

We arrived in Sagaro on the Costa Brava some days after

the rest of the actors had already started work. I was shocked to discover, as soon as we had settled into the luxury hotel where most of us were to be lodged through the period of shooting, that the other actors were speaking of dear Mr Lewin, my friend, as if he were some sort of monster. To Nigel Patrick, who played the racing driver and was Lewin's most articulate critic, and to the entire English contingent Lewin was bad news. I went to sleep thinking that the whole lot of them must be suffering from a bout of anti-Americanism. The next day I went to work and was in for a bit of a surprise. I found that I was being directed not by the nice Dr Jekyll but by Mr Hyde. I exaggerate of course, but it was enough of a personality change to give me quite a jolt. His stature may have had something to do with it. Many of my friends are small, but Lewin was the only one who had director status.

And being a director is the next best thing to being a generalissimo. As soon as I saw him at work I realised that to make his own film every so many years meant much more than just an escape from his cage at MGM or the opportunity to express himself as an artist: for him it was a matter of putting on the mantle of authority and making people jump. He did not bark his orders. He was a cool führer. Unfortunately for him he was also a deaf führer. Although he wore a hearing aid he missed much muttering by the malcontents around him and he often printed shots in which the actors had not even said their lines correctly, not that this amounted to a major disaster because in any event all the scenes that we shot outdoors would anyway have to be recorded in the studio. Pictorially the set-ups he chose were good, it was the pace of the scenes that hurt. Directors of the modern school have discovered that speed is a great coverup for weak material, and that an illusion of even greater speed can be effected by zany cutting. Seeing our film in its final form was like being asked at one's leisure to study a series of beautifully composed still photographs. Jack Cardiff was the cameraman and he did a great job. He gave us an Ava

Gardner on the crest of her great beauty. For some spectators no doubt the slow tempo of the sequences in which she appeared was not unwelcome.

It was tedious work. For me one day it became worse than tedious. A love scene was to be shot on the beach, day for night. That means that you shoot the scene in broad daylight and by dint of inserting a special filter the cameraman can make it seem like bright moonlight. All very convenient for everyone except the actors. It was not one of your modern erotic scenes but Ava and I had to do a lot of gazing meaningfully into each other's eyes. What with Cardiff's line up of Brutes (the biggest lights of all) grilling us from one side and the Spanish sunlight from the other, it was a painful exercise. Even when the camera was not attempting big close-ups we felt pretty stupid trying to find the mood with our eyes tightly squinched. Ava's eyes, being sensitive as well as green, suffered even more than mine. When they watered we had to pause while they patched up her eye make-up. I chose to have a bit of a set-to with Lewin. I suggested forcibly that he salvage the long shots that he had already shot, but that for the medium range shots and above all the close-ups he must arrange for a facsimile of a small section of the beach to be constructed in Shepperton Studios where the important content of the scene could be attempted under advantageous conditions. I won the point, but at the expense of some self-respect because I was conscious of having gone beyond the line of forcible suggestion and moved into the area of bullying movie star for a moment. I did not like that. Indeed the whole project had become a disappointment, for it is usually the preparation and the actual making of the film that I enjoy and the end product is comparatively irrelevant. Maximum seriousness could not be achieved when working with a Lewin because having limited directorial talent he had a low threshold of achievement. *His* achievement ended with his writing, whereas we, the frustrated actors, reached for something beyond the writing. What I am saying is that I was not at all pleased with the job I did and I am copping out. I just wished that Lewin and I could resume the happy relationship we had enjoyed in the days before Spain.

While working towards the completion of our film at Shepperton Studios I sometimes found the atmosphere on the stage which we occupied a little oppressive, and on such occasions I would mosey over to another stage and take a look at another group who seemed to be having a much livelier time. They were shooting *The Mudlark* in which one of the stars was Alec Guinness whom I knew only very slightly at the time. But the director was from Hollywood and I knew him quite well. This was the ever popular Jean Negulesco. When I went on to this stage I would do so only in the sneakiest manner imaginable because I just wanted to watch what was going on from among the shadows. Least of all did I want any of the actors to become aware that they were being observed. But one day I found that they were shooting a big scene with plenty of extras which was supposed to take place in the House of Commons. I moved in closer than usual so that I could see what was going on. Before I knew it the doors of the stage were shut and the red lights went on signifying that they were on the point of shooting a scene. I looked for an avenue of escape but Negulesco spotted me and called out 'Jimmy! Come here. No, don't go away. Come here and sit down. We are just going to shoot Alec's big speech!' In order to avoid making a scene as much as anything I moved over to the chair to which he was pointing and tried to look as if I wasn't there. Then the cameras rolled and the scene started. Guinness entered and took his seat on the Treasury Bench traditionally occupied by the Prime Minister, then immediately stood up again and started his speech. He was playing the part of Benjamin Disraeli and his speech must have occupied fully three pages of script. At the end of it he sat down, Negulesco said 'cut' and the scene was over. There was a round of applause from the film unit, a phenomenon which sometimes happens when an actor has played a long or especially tricky scene.

Negulesco stood up and called to Guinness in a loud voice, 'That was marvellous, Alec! Quite marvellous. You couldn't have done it better. You deserved all that applause. Even James Mason who is sitting here was applauding. He thought it was marvellous too, didn't you, Jimmy?' I nodded my head vigorously in Guinness's direction hoping that he would notice the subtle apology which I tried to insert into the gesture. My God. I was never more embarrassed in my life! From that moment on I have made it a point of honour to enter a sound stage on which other actors are liable to be at work only in the case of an extreme emergency, and I cannot imagine just what that would be.

The producer of *The Mudlark* was Nunnally Johnson and in fact, my intrusions onto his sound stage were only partially prompted by the boredom which was then infesting my own stage. I had a special reason for wishing to meet Johnson and I intended to have Negulesco introduce me.

' I had at the time been fascinated by everything that I had read in newspapers and periodicals about Field Marshal Rommel. And now a book had been written about him by Brigadier Desmond Young. It was not yet available in English bookstores but I was hell-bent on getting myself a copy because I privately fancied the idea of perhaps obtaining the film rights and promoting an independent film based on the Rommel story. But I soon learned that the rights of Desmond Young's book had already been sold to 20th Century Fox and the production assigned to Nunnally Johnson, whose record of achievement as a writer in Hollywood was one of the more impressive. *The Grapes of Wrath* was his best known screenplay.

Negulesco effected the introduction and in no time at all we became very good friends. Pamela and I saw a great deal of Nunnally and his wife Doris, until the time came for him to pack up and go back to Hollywood where post-production, i.e. cutting, scoring etc., of *The Mudlark* was to take place. I had told Nunnally before he left of my interest in the story of Rommel and he had said that he would mention my name when he got around to discussing the casting of the film with the studio boss, Darryl F. Zanuck.

For our part we stayed on in England for what turned out later to have been not the best of all possible reasons. It was a question of converting Pamela's novel *Del Palma* into a film by a bold experiment in independent production. Hindsightedly it is possible to question the wisdom of nearly every decision that we made.

The production plan was based on the premise that we still had some frozen money in England, which would be sufficient, we figured, to pay for not less than half the cost of the film. We would shoot our half in either France or England and return with half a film tucked under our arms to Hollywood where we would have no difficulty picking up the rest of the necessary finance.

We enlisted the service of two established friends. June Havoc was to play the leading lady. Her husband, Bill Spier, was to write the script and direct. Bill Spier had been an eminent radio director, none better. At one time an entrepreneur had offered to finance and produce a short series of radio dramas for me. We had made a false start with another director but, finding that he was not easy to get along with, we replaced him with Spier who had been recommended by McCaffrey. He really was extremely good and had great confidence as a radio director, but we were disappointed with the screenplay he turned in. Pamela and I wrote an authorised version.

We then discovered that it would be impossible to shoot in France, where the unions and other authorities had laid down rules designed to encourage and safeguard a healthy renaissance of the French film industry. So we would have to shoot in England.

But here again the A.C.T. took a sensible stand which we should have anticipated. They would recommend granting a work permit to a foreign technician – in this case a director - only if his credits in major motion pictures were internationally recognised. Well, that took care of Bill Spier, who, we promised him, could do his share of the directing in the section of the film which we would later shoot in America. Meanwhile we would fill in with a British director who took the form of Pamela's number one husband, Roy Kellino. I, as the producer, was rather distressed to find, when shooting commenced, that June Havoc was not too keen on taking direction from Kellino. It was not that she had anything against him but she was reacting to her disappointment that Spier had been jettisoned. So, since a producer is entitled to do anything he chooses during the shooting of a film - he can move a piece of furniture or an ornament or touch up a woman's body make-up - without causing the crew to walk out on him, I felt that I was entitled, nay in this case obliged, to do a little directing myself. A reluctant directorial trio is what Spier and Kellino and I became.

The original inspiration for this story came from the discovery, in the attic of a house that we had rented, of a load of bric-à-brac discarded by a previous owner, things like old restaurant bills, theatre programmes, account books and even a few letters. Pamela invented a woman whose husband has rented a house just outside London in which to convalesce after a breakdown. She too finds bric-à-brac in the attic, first builds up a picture in her mind of the previous owner and then identifies him correctly as a recently bereaved popular entertainer. She thrusts herself into his life, and for a while he reacts with a sort of gratitude since she seems to have such unexpected sensitivity about his background. But then she believes that she is possessed by the poor man's dead wife, and it all becomes too much for him, just as it was for the critics who later commented on our effort.

We used Olleberrie Farm, our old house, as a background for certain sequences in the film. And before visiting the house for the first time after a break of three and a half years during which Kellino and his second wife had lived there, Pamela and I had a dreadful fear that we would once more fall in love with it and want to buy it back from them and live there again. But we were spared. We found that the Kellinos had, for reasons best known to themselves, cut down some of the most lovable trees which, so far from threatening damage or causing excessive shade, had enhanced the beauty of the place. The great elm tree dominating the semi-circular lawn. Gone. The tall white-blossoming wild cherries so appropriately dancing attendance on the smaller shocking pink prunus. Gone. They had even made an unsuccessful attempt to improve the studied disarray of a sunken garden by concreting the bottom of its little pool and stocking it with goldfish. Heartbreaking.

Back in California our first task was to find the money with which to shoot the interior sequences. Abe Lastvogel was the man to help us. But when I called the Morris Office I learned that he had been in New York for some time and was expecting to remain there for two or three more months.

'What's he doing there?'

'He is packaging television shows. It's becoming terribly important, you know.'

Mindful of my contract with the Morris Office I realised that now was the time to make use of the services of Johnny Hyde, since it was clearly stated that Lastvogel and he were the only members of the organisation entitled to handle my affairs. However Hyde proved to have suffered a heart attack and was in hospital; he was not expected to resume his work for at least six weeks.

'Sammy Weisbord.'

'I beg your pardon?'

'Would you like to speak to Mr Weisbord?'

'I guess so.'

Well, I believe that Sammy Weisbord did his level best to sell our unlikely bundle to United Artists and other companies that were known to consider the projects of independent producers. But he lost me completely when he seriously suggested to me one day that we kiss goodbye to our investment in *The Lady Possessed*, as the film was to be called, and just write it off as a loss. I daresay that, if we had been smarter, we could indeed have written it off as a loss when the time came around for filing our statements for the Internal Revenue Service. But I was almost as bad as Pamela when it came to pig-headedness. This man Weisbord was actually advising us to *give up*! That was not at all the kind of advice that I wanted, so we did not invite him to make any further efforts on behalf of the film.

Several friends suggested that we try Herbert Yates at Republic. But we were not in a hurry to do this because Republic did not have a very good name. It came under the heading of Poverty Row. Yates had his own distribution company to handle his product and was thought to have made a heap of money. For reasons best known to themselves, John Ford and John Wayne were making some films at the studio during this period; in fact on the occasion of one of my visits, Yates was so good as to introduce me to Ford who put on a some-of-my-best-friends-are-Englishmen act for my benefit. Yates married a champion skater named Vera Hruba Ralston and starred her as an actress in a number of his studio's productions.

Reluctantly and almost furtively we made a deal with Yates who undertook to finance the balance of our film to the tune of two hundred thousand dollars. So we went ahead and finished the film. One of the pleasures of doing so was to renew my acquaintance with the Hungarian comedian Steve Geray, who had worked with me centuries ago in one of my very early films *The High Command*. The wise Al Lewin had cast him effectively in *The Moon and Sixpence*. And I was happy to find a part for him in *A Lady Possessed*, only to be informed when the time came that his salary had to be paid directly to the Internal Revenue Service instead of to Steve. I tried to figure out a way around this directive, but I did not come up with any foolproof technique.

Having completed the film we went to the expense of hiring Russell Birdwell to stir up publicity for us when the time came around for its release. Birdwell was perhaps the best known public relations genius of his time and had brought off some sensational stunts, especially when he handled the publicity for Howard Hughes's film *The Outlaw*. He had made the most of its star Jane Russell's big breasts and hired skywriters to decorate the blue skies of Southern California with a pair of enormous circles with dots in the centres of them. In modern parlance this could be described as the 'logo' which he established for the film. Of course we did not pay Birdwell as much as Howard Hughes had done, and did not therefore expect such sensational results. But we hoped for *something*. We learned a lot about him and about the principles of his craft. It was he who pointed out to me something which had never occurred to me. Since columnists were always on the lookout for brief items with which to fill their space you could usually make them extremely happy with a bit about some celebrity having won an award. And if you could not coax an existing society or periodical into giving an award to one of the stars you represented then you just invented one.

But he did not invent one for any of us. The film first emerged in San Francisco, so he had us go up there for a day to be interviewed by a couple of newspapermen. Herbert Yates himself was helpful to the extent of arranging for Pamela and myself to be given the Keys to the City by the Mayor who happened to be a buddy of his. But by and large the press coverage we achieved was minimal.

A funny thing happened at about the same time. We went to a theatre in Beverly Hills to see a movie called *Red Badge of Courage*. It was based on a story by Stephen Crane, whom I admire, and directed by John Huston, so it could not be all bad, we figured, in spite of all the talk of problems and disappointments connected with it which was making the rounds. And indeed it was interesting if not enthralling. But it had been savaged in the cutting room and its running time was now little over an hour, by orders from on high.

There were very few people in the house. Soon after the film started I could not help noticing that at the other end of the row on which Pamela and I were sitting were two men, one of whom never stopped talking. Since we had a preference for watching movies in silence, the sound of the running commentary from the other end of our row got on our nerves. I said to myself, 'If this guy does not shut up, I shall walk over to him and point out to him coolly and quietly that other people in the audience prefer to hear the dialogue coming from the screen without distractions. So will you please keep it down?'

I held out as long as I could. Then I decided that the moment had come for me to move along the row and say my piece. There were no others seated in the row and I made the distance in record time. Then I heard myself say something like this: 'For Christsake will you SHUT UP!! You're talking so bloody loud that we can't hear a bloody word of what they're bloody saying.' My delivery sounded strangely harsh. The man stopped talking of course and looked up at me as I crouched over him. He said 'Oh. Hello.' And now I recognised him. It was William Saroyan, with whom I could claim some acquaintance. I mean I had met him at parties. So I said, 'Is that you, Bill? You ought to be ashamed of yourself, making such a goddam noise.' And I slapped his face. Not hard. Not enough to hurt. Just enough, I thought, to stress my complaint. This did not lead to a serious commotion. But the people in the immediate vicinity could not help tuning in, and among them I noticed a man who had the air of an assistant manager. He was coming towards us as if he felt that he should protest to one or the other of us. I waved him aside and returned to my seat. I quite liked the film though it seemed to be lacking in urgency. I would have liked to have seen it before they cut the hell out of it.

Presumably it was indeed an assistant manager that I

had seen and presumably he had not kept the story to himself because it received enormous attention in the press. This was really ironical, we thought. Pamela and I had just been knocking ourselves out to earn some publicity for *A Lady Possessed*, and nothing, but nothing found its way into the papers. And then this silly scene takes place in the Beverly Hills Theatre – the one that looks like a mosque – and all the world is told about it.

So much for *A Lady Possessed*. From time to time we received statements from the company detailing the receipts from the showing of the film and the charges that had been made in each area for the handling of it. For instance we were surprised to find that there had been considerable charges against it in Rome/Italy, but no evidence that it had actually been shown to the public. And the Italians will sit through practically anything. We complained about this to our more experienced friends and asked if they thought we should 'demand to see their books'. They would not advise it, they said, pointing out that if we insisted the company would eventually send round a truckload of returns from all the cinemas where the film had played and the salary alone of the accountant we should need in order to check them would run into thousands of dollars.

Sometimes in the case of friends who share the disappointment of having made a dramatically unsuccessful film together, the friendship takes such a beating that it comes unstuck. But in the case of Bill Spier and his wife our friendship with them was actually reinforced rather than weakened. That was one good thing. Also we could mark it all up to much needed experience. I was a slow student but I was beginning to learn.

In my travels I have always got the impression that no matter where I went there was substantial evidence that *Pandora and the Flying Dutchman* had been popular. But maybe the British distributors did better with it in their areas than MGM in the Western Hemisphere. How else may I account for the fact that, though my contract had guaranteed me a percentage of the profits, never did a nickel reach me? But the film was widely shown and well received in Hollywood. And I was aware that my professional standing had risen a point or two. At any rate the people at 20th Century Fox thought it worth their while to consider me for the role of Rommel in the film *The Desert Fox*. It was regarded as an important project and I knew that several actors were in the running. There was an able actor under contract to 20th Century who looked like a dead-set winner to me. This was Gary Merrill who had seemed awfully good to me in a film called *Twelve o'clock High* and, to make his chances even better, he looked like Rommel and was of about the right height. In the event, I not only got the part, I got a success under my belt.

*The Desert Fox** was a film into which we could all put our hearts. Nunnally Johnson constructed an excellent screenplay and Henry Hathaway directed the film with vigour and good taste. Before I started to work I had known Hathaway only to the extent of a brief introduction in his office at the studio. He was on the point of leaving for the desert where he was to shoot some of the action scenes which did not concern me. While he was away I read whatever additional literature I could find about Rommel and the German High Command and in one of the viewing theatres they ran for me all the obtainable news reel material. Then I would watch the rushes of the work that Hathaway was sending back from the desert. This was in a sense my first experience of Hathaway at work. The very first scenes that were projected showed the manner in which Desmond Young himself had been captured by the Germans. As a prisoner of war he had met and talked with Rommel and it was the favourable impression that Rommel had made on this occasion that gave him the incentive later to write the book. The scenes I watched had been shot with sound, although there was

*Released in England as *Rommel – Desert Fox*

very little on the sound tracks that could possibly be used in the finished film, and so Hathaway was shouting his directions throughout, very much, I imagined, as the directors had done in the days of silent movies. Desmond Young was playing the part of Desmond Young and was doing as well as an amateur could be expected to do under the circumstances, and Hathaway was yelling at him like an all-in wrestling fan. The voice came over high pitched and bristling with obscenities. He was not being mean to Desmond Young. It was just his way.

The bad news about Hathaway was that everyone was afraid of him because they did not wish to receive a tongue-lashing; the good news was that the stage where Hathaway worked was an oasis of silent industry. The crew did their work on the principle of fire and fall back. When each man had made his mechanical adjustment, whatever it might be, he would fall back into a silent obscurity. Only those whose functions demanded their presence during the actual shooting of a scene were permitted to remain in the immediate vicinity. The property men feared him most of all because having been a property man himself he made no allowances for imperfection. The disgruntled used to say that he was mean to the humble working man or the bit actor and affable with the stars. It is true that the majority of those who received a rocketing were humble working men or bit actors, but only because they deserved it. His assistant director did his best to enlist a crew made up of perfectionists like Hathaway himself and on *The Desert Fox* there were only two men whom he balled out to my knowledge. One was a bit actor who always arrived on the set appreciably later than the leading actors and the other was a featured actor who was plumb lazy. As for the selection of stars, he seldom allowed himself to be over-ruled by Zanuck, the head of the studio, because he knew the ones who could be trusted to work always at the top of their bent. So these were not the kind of people with whom he would be likely to quarrel. He said to me once as he saw me leaving the set at the end of the day:

298

'Do you go to see the rushes?'

'Er – yes.'

'Why?'

'Well – er, one is always liable to find that one was doing something awkward or silly without being aware of it. Pulling a face of some kind ...'

'Bullshit. You know what you are doing. You've had enough experience. You want to know why you go and see the rushes?'

'Er – yes.'

'You go and see them because you hope that it will look better up there on the screen than it felt when you did it on the stage ...'

And he went on to say that it was just the same with directors. The ones who watched the rushes were the ones who hoped – unconsciously perhaps – that it would look better on the screen. John Ford never looked at rushes because he saw what he was shooting and he knew which lens the cameraman was using. Nor did he, Hathaway, look at the rushes, for the same reason.

I knew that he was right. It was true that I rarely knew if I had done it right, but I was not likely to know any better if I saw the rushes, because I had not yet learned about acting what I was to come to know later.

Of course Hathaway's ruling would not necessarily apply to the new directors because they invite so much improvisation of movement and dialogue that you can never be quite sure which take ended up looking good.

Hathaway told me that when the craze started in Hollywood for taking extensive travelling shots with the camera moving every which way on a crane, he took command of a crane and made tests with it for a whole week. A director named Edmund Goulding had made a big name for himself at 20th with this style of work. But Hathaway found that it was not for him; he could say what he had to say more effectively with a camera which scarcely moved.

People have often asked me if we filmed in the part of

Africa where the battles had taken place. Many people must have been misled by the introduction into our film of scenes from a British wartime documentary by David McDonald, which 20th Century had purchased for this specific purpose. The reconnaissance carried out by the studio's Art Department revealed that a place called Borego Springs in the Californian Desert offered scenery which was a perfect match for North Africa. So that is where we did most of our exterior scenes.

In spite of my prejudice against any sort of long term contract I had to sign on in order to secure the part of Rommel for myself. But it was only for two years and I had a certain say in the selection of parts. Not a very strong say, but better than no say at all. I seem to remember that I was allowed to reject the first two parts that they offered me but was obliged to accept the third – one of those deals. As it happened I never was confronted with a difficult choice and there was not a moment's indecision about the first offer that came to me soon after the release of *The Desert Fox*. This was for a film to be made from the book by L.C. Moyzisch, called *Operation Cicero*, about the singular achievements during World War II of a real-life spy whose code name was Cicero. Zanuck did not wish to market the film with a title containing the name Cicero because he believed that to a United States movie-goer the name could only refer to a suburb of Chicago which had been well known as a hot bed of gangsterism. And he himself came up with an alternative title, *Five Fingers*, which to him signified greed.

An Albanian valet was employed by the British Ambassador in Ankara during the war. Evidently the Ambassador never entertained any doubts about the fellow's trustworthiness. He was useful and companionable, that was the important thing. The Ambassador liked to play the piano and, since the piano at the Embassy was not of the best, he would have his valet accompany him to the radio station where there was a superior instrument. Sometimes he would encourage the valet to sing since he had a nice baritone voice. But there was no room for scenes like this in the film which concerned itself almost exclusively with Cicero's exploits as a spy.

He learned the combination of the Ambassador's safe and photographed the top secret documents he found there and sold them to the Germans. Over a considerable period Cicero sold thirty-five top secrets including the plans for 'Operation Overlord', the Allies' plans for the invasion of Europe, but the Germans, although paying him a good price, never profited by them because they were never convinced of their authenticity.

Michael Wilson organised out of this remarkable story an excellent screenplay, which was made even better by the witty embellishments supplied by Joe Mankiewicz whom Zanuck finally appointed as director although Hathaway had done most of the preparation. During this period Mankiewicz could do no wrong. Two years running he had taken the Oscars for best director and best screenplay, thus for *A Letter to Three Wives* and *All About Eve* he scored a total of four Oscars. Our *Five Fingers* was such a good film that I need only say of it, that the most original performance came from Oscar Karlweis who took the role of Moyzisch, the author of the book, who ironically became the butt of the Wilson/Mankiewicz humour. One catches the film quite frequently on television and I still admire it; in fact it is one of the few films in which I appear which can be relied on to hold my attention throughout. I must qualify that. I would not hold still for it if it showed its face on an American commercial network since I am allergic to commercial breaks. In Switzerland, where I now live, there is no such handicap and French dubbing is exemplary.

Hollywood, which attracts ten times more technicians and artists than it can possibly use, also attracts crises, each of which causes the studios to cut down their staffs and aggregate the ratio still further. The crises are also widely publicised because the fear that they engender will make everyone accept reduced salaries less grudgingly.

The annual receipts from the films made by 20th Century Fox were declining, there seemed to be no denying that. Zanuck, who enjoyed the best possible relations with directors and writers, had been making a number of movies which were beyond the easy grasp of the average movie-goer. Although *The Desert Fox* and *Five Fingers* did as well, if not better, than the other normal ratio black and white films that were being made at the studio, it looked as if the honeymoon was over for serious films aimed at a more discriminating audience. Nothing but colour would do from now on, and experiments were being made with lenses that would change the ratio of the image thrown onto the screen so that the widened and magnified effect would kid the audience into thinking that *better* movies were being made. One of the most devoted revolutionaries in this movement was Spyros Skouras, the head of 20th Century. Zanuck was merely the head of production whereas Skouras was the utter head. No one was ahead of Skouras except possibly the banks.

In three or four years, television had grown into an all-consuming, all-threatening monster. That had cut deeply into movie profits. But something else happened during this same period that gave quite a jolt to Skouras and his peers. The Labour government's Chancellor of the Exchequer, Hugh Dalton, introduced what the Americans referred to as a 'confiscatory tax', which was in fact a 75% ad valorem duty on all foreign films. This resulted for a short period in increased British film production to which the public did not react with enthusiasm and, since fewer American films were imported, they felt deprived and the government was obliged to revert to the status quo ante.

But while this ugly situation lasted, I picked up a lot of uneasy vibrations on the 20th Century lot which convinced me that it would no longer be the best place to look for my type of movie. Indeed although there were options for further films at 20th Century I was now not at all sure that they would pick them up. And I slid into one of my low periods.

Pamela and I made an unsuccessful attempt to get into television production. The greatest artistic achievement that found expression on American television was the live Anthology Series. It existed at its best during the early years when every show had to be transmitted live and it lasted only until the sponsors discovered that an anthology programme, a different play with a different cast every week, was useless for selling products since it lacked 'sponsor identification'. The most effective means of merchandising was to ensure that the same performer came through each week with the same sort of show. The identification of Dinah Shore with Chevrolet cars still persists even in my mind. Dramatic fare had to be forced into the same pattern. Hence the dreaded series. David Soul and Paul Michael Glaser were the same cops week after week and Telly Savalas became *his* kind of cop. I mention comparatively recent examples because I never watched this sort of entertainment enough for a lasting imprint to be made by any individual dramatic or 'sit com' series. (Notable exceptions: The witty *Get Smart* and, of course, the exploits of Lucy Ball.)

During this critical period, the live anthology was still alive. We thought we might make an anthology series on film. So we wrote or caused to be written four half-hour scripts to serve as a sort of 'pilot'. As soon as the right people saw these we would have no trouble in setting up a deal to make an entire series. Kellino would direct most of them, it was thought. Kellino? Yes, the same one who figures earlier. His second marriage had gone sour. Since there were no great opportunities for him in London, Pamela and I both thought that we should try to launch him in the United States. And actually we succeeded in doing just this. He quickly embedded himself in the television medium, and since the anthology format was never totally extinguished, there was a lot of work for him and a lot of TV film director awards for him to earn.

We registered total failure with the series that we had planned for ourselves. Three of the films we strung together and marketed as a single feature movie. One of them, with the direction of which I was credited, we marketed as a supporting feature. It was called *The Child* and introduced the young Portland. She performed most attractively and earned some good reviews for herself in England.

In our household we held off buying a television set for a long time. We always had more than enough to do without our attention being distracted by the thing. Finally we gave in because we were bound eventually to have a professional relationship with the medium. And we happened to have in our salon the ideal place to install a set. It was a Mediterranean style fireplace made of busily moulded stone. Not very pretty. Nor hitherto very useful because, having a heating system which did all that it was called upon to do in the cool weather, we had no inclination to light a fire. A cosy fireside atmosphere seemed out of place. So that is where we put the television set and surprisingly, we still held off lighting a fire.

For some time Portland was the only person to whom the set had any use, and so, in order to keep the room habitable while she was enjoying it, I had a long cable made with a plug on one end and earphones on the other. The cable went from the set under the carpet across the room, to where the earphones hung on the wall behind the long sofa directly opposite. When colour came in we bought a set, put it beside the first one and attached a similar cable, again with earphones to hang alongside the others. Any child/grown up combination could be entertained by this arrangement. The technical grown-up who had some damned favourite programme he wanted to watch was promptly planted on the sofa with plugs in his ears, and sat there like a fool smiling at jokes or scowling at sob stories which we couldn't hear while Portland sat beside him wearing all the expressions which *her* programme occasioned.

I had avoided taking an active part in live television shows longer than most of my colleagues, because my experience at Alexandra Palace in London had taught me that it was a medium to be feared. But I finally gave in when an excellent ninety minute programme was allowed to erupt in the CBS studio in Los Angeles. The producer of this show, Playhouse 90, was Marty Manulis and it displayed the early directorial skills of such as Marty Ritt, Johnny Frankenheimer, James Roy Hill, Bob Mulligan and Sidney Lumet. With this last I worked on two ninety minute dramatic shows which were much the same sort of operation though emanating from New York. It seemed that Lumet had signed a pact with himself never to work in California. Had he perhaps been bitten in his youth by a Warner Brother? Something like that, I supposed. The first was an excellent production of Robert Shaw's bizarre story *The Hiding Place*. That is the one about the Nazi official in a small town during World War II who personally arrested two RAF officers, whose plane had been brought down, and kept them locked up in his cellar instead of turning them in. Then when the war ends he chooses not to break the news to them but rather to maintain the status quo. At the end he is struck by a convenient heart attack while attending a neo-Nazi get-together. Whenever I see Dick Cavett he likes to remind me that he was the junior member of the neo-Nazi group who loosened the official's collar. If I wanted to big-note myself, I could say to people that I knew Dick Cavett when he was a bit player.

The second show that I did for Sidney Lumet was the *John Brown's Raid* about which I have written earlier. It was less than enthusiastically received. I was surprised, when I saw it, that in its final shape it lacked the smooth intelligible continuity of the original script. But it could have failed for any number of different reasons. My impersonation of John Brown for instance?

This show was made later than the other events I have been describing. I can fix the date with unaccustomed precision. We were shooting in Harper's Ferry when John Kennedy and Richard Nixon were conducting their televised debates during the Presidential Campaign of 1960. I know this because the make-up man who had been working on my face was suddenly snatched away because one of their faces was thought to be in greater need of his skills. He was a good make-up man and therefore I must suppose that it was for Kennedy that he was snatched. Nixon's contribution to the debates was most notably his blue jowls. Some said that his five o'clock shadow lost him the debates and the election. Just think. If it had been Nixon who snatched my make-up man, the recent history of the USA might have been quite different.

15/Shepperton

In 1949 and 1950 a new format was introduced in England consisting of three or four separate stories strung together to form a single feature. Sydney Box successfully presented some of Somerset Maugham's short stories in this manner. This inspired the millionaire Huntingdon Hartford to assemble a little two-story film in Hollywood that was put out under the title *Face to Face*. One of them was Stephen Crane's *The Bride comes to Yellow Sky* played amiably by Robert Preston and Marjorie Steele. I obtained a sixteen mm. copy of the film and kept showing this section to the movie-loving daughter Portland who was crazy about it. The other section, in which I figured, was no less good but more sombre, being based on Joseph Conrad's *The Secret Sharer*. What I liked about this project was the director, John Brahm, who had the skill and the patience to render convincingly a seagoing yarn within the limits of a single small stage in a remote and no-account studio.

Then came *The Story of Three Loves*, a three-headed threat. This was an MGM package consisting of three love stories, directed by three directors and featuring seven or eight stars of varying scintillation. Moira Shearer and I were the protagonists in a story about an impresario and a ballerina who was the inspiration of his biggest hit. In a later encounter he makes her dance it again for him so that he may sketch her movements and recapture every golden moment, unaware that she is perilously tubercular. In the event he dances her to death. Not much of a story, but I liked Shearer very much and admired her as she danced for us take after take of what Frederick Ashton had choreographed to the music of Rachmaninov's variations on a theme by Paganini. Also it was fun to encounter Gottfried Reinhardt, the loud obverse of his brother Wolfgang, who had produced *Caught*. Gottfried worked with gusto and MGM had been his home ground for many years. As a producer he had given us Garbo in *Two-Faced Woman* for instance, though perhaps he would be happier if I mentioned *Command Decision*. He was the best of company and his wife, Sylvia, the best of cooks.

I did not in these days find myself spiralling upwards by any means, but I had at least reached a slightly higher level than in my early Hollywood films. Now, at its worst, it would be a matter of facile assembly work as in *Botany Bay* and *The Prisoner of Zenda*. Everything was so well organised in these factories that there was no audible griping. The producers may have been given a hard time by the studio bosses but they did not hand it on to the lower ranks. The electricians and stage hands were well paid and enjoyed a high standard of living and were so keen to get home at night that they did their work with a smooth efficiency, sometimes even at the double. On *Botany Bay* I made the interesting acquaintance of John Farrow, the director, who may well have been the only papal knight I ever ran into. I played the part of a ship's captain who was given to acts of cruelty and Farrow was able to give me some useful hints.

There was a similar atmosphere on the stages of MGM where we shot *The Prisoner of Zenda*, easy and lush. The good things that this offered me were the happy reunions with Deborah Kerr and Stewart Granger. For the latter the task of playing two characters for the price of one was not an easy one, and I recall that on one occasion, after completing a long and difficult take, he asked the director Richard Thorpe if he might be allowed to do just one more because he thought he could do better, Thorpe refused, saying,

'You can't improve things to an extent that represents value at the box office. In my experience I have found that if you print the first take which has a reasonable tempo and in which all the actors say their lines in a way that's completely intelligible then there is no point in retaking it.'

To Granger this represented an extremely depressing attitude. Granger in this case was the perfectionist and Thorpe the Hollywood professional. Perfectionism, though not exactly rampant among the current directors, was being practised in certain elite circles into which it was for Granger and myself to insinuate ourselves. To a degree I succeeded in this for it could be said that Joe Mankiewicz was a perfectionist in his fashion, and his circle I now crashed for a second time, he being the director of *Julius Caesar* with the abundant advantages of the MGM production machine and some of its disadvantages.

I never could figure out the relative powers of Louis B. Mayer and Dore Schary who at this time had all the earmarks of a production head. Did Schary have the same sort of authority in his rather solemn sphere of activity as Arthur Freed enjoyed in the musical sphere? If the reader is desperate for an answer he will have to find an MGM survivor and put the question to him. Gene Kelly perhaps?

Anyway it was Schary who activated *Julius Caesar*. John Houseman was to produce it and Mankiewicz to direct it and it might be supposed that between them they would have uncontested authority. Yes, but the studio machinery once set in motion also generated some power of its own and each departmental head had an academy award dangling before his inner eye. The average director would gratefully absorb their plans and the system would contribute to an overall efficiency, but it made it extremely unlikely that the average production would then emerge with an individual style. And Mankiewicz, though far from average, did not quite manage to impose an individual style upon his *Julius Caesar*. This may have been occasioned by the heterogeneous casting but much more so by the heavy foot of the Art Department. Nevertheless, it passed as a classy production in spite of its faults, of which one was me. At least so I was convinced.

I had very much wanted to play the part of Brutus, partly because I had played it successfully at the Gate Theatre in Dublin those many years before; also because I regarded Brutus as the anchorman of the play and did not wish to see the part go to one of the other actors I knew to be on Dore Schary's short list. At one time, either during the shooting of the film or later, Gielgud said that he thought it might be fun sometime for the two of us to do the play again but with him playing Brutus and me playing Cassius. Indeed I would like to to that, though I cannot see Gielgud ever being able to justify Caesar's line, 'Let me have men about me that are fat'.

Clearly Shakespeare had never heard the rumour that Brutus was Caesar's son, otherwise he would never have so firmly stressed the enormous respect in which Brutus is said to be held by the fellow conspirators. An abundant respect for ancestry, social standing and surely age too would be needed to offset his deficiency as a pragmatic thinker. Lean and hungry or not, Gielgud could have shown the qualities that command respect much better than I.

Having played a part in any film which deserves to be taken seriously I very often wish for the chance to do the whole thing over again. In some cases, as in *Julius Caesar*, I would settle for doing even a single sequence over again. Having fretted about it for some twenty-five years I am convinced that I could now make something even of the 'It must be by his death' monologue.

I thought at the time and, having caught it again on television, I still hold that the only impeccable performance by a member of our cast was that of Edmund O'Brien as Casca. And at the beginning there were misgivings even about his eligibility. Here was a man who had established himself as an actor of style before he appeared in his first movie. We saw him as the poet in the Charles Laughton version of *The Hunchback of Notre Dame*. After this the producers and the casting directors could see him only as someone with class, and it was exceedingly difficult for him to gain acceptance as a gangster or G-man or any of the rough characters that proliferated in what were called 'program pictures' at that time. But ultimately he assumed the tough guy so indelibly that Mankiewicz had the greatest difficulty in persuading Schary and the rest of the top brass that Eddie could play Shakespeare to the manner born.

Mankiewicz's first choice for the part of Mark Antony was Richard Burton who had not yet invaded the United States as a film actor. But he had made a great name for himself at Stratford-on-Avon and at the Old Vic. Indeed he was under contract to the Old Vic when Mankiewicz made a bid for him, but the contract was binding. There were many who did not share Mankiewicz's quiet assurance that Brando would prove himself as a Shakespearean actor. But they were confounded. It is the character of Cassius which dominates the first third of the play just as Antony dominates the central section and Brutus the last. With Gielgud as Cassius there could be no misgivings about the vitality, the style and the credibility of the first section at least.

Juxtaposed with John Gielgud, I must admit I felt depressingly feeble, particularly in the vocal department. He spoke with such richness and authority and was charged with such emotion, while I who had been mumbling my way through one movie after another, now had a voice which was deplorably lacking in mobility and range. One thing that I did about this was to accept with alacrity an invitation, which came from Tyrone Guthrie, to play the following season at the Shakespeare Festival in Stratford, Ontario.

But here I must reintroduce a character who dropped out of the narrative several chapters ago, Alexander Korda.

As a result of the imposition in England, as I have mentioned, of what the Americans called the 'Confiscatory Tax', several British producers who had developed a knack of finding finance for their production on either side of the Atlantic now lost it. One of these was Korda, who had undertaken to star me in a series of films the first of which was to be made in America. I had been given the right to approve the subject matter of these films and the choice of director, leading lady etc. It was a real star's contract. Now clearly he could not satisfy those requirements but he did not want to write off the contract as a total loss. Besides he had certain other assets and possibly he could wrap some of these up to form a package so appealing to me that I would not wish to insist on the precise conditions that he had promised.

Unfortunately the ploy did not work. He owned the film rights of a book by Daphne du Maurier called *The King's General*. He could also offer as director his brother Zoltan who lived in California. A screenplay based on the book had been prepared by Zoltan. This was sent to me and duly read.

I liked Alex Korda very much and I heartily wished that he had come up with a proposition which I could accept. I also liked *The King's General* as a book, but it was not a good script. Though I hardly knew Zoli I was prepared to believe that he was a very nice chap but as a talent I had always thought of him as the Harpo of the brothers. Alex wanted me to get together with Zoli and work it out. But we seemed to me to have reached an impasse. Besides, since the background of the story was the English West Country at the time of the Civil War, it would need to be made in England. Alex clearly did not wish to mention that the so-called 'confiscatory tax' had made it impossible to launch a film in the United States since that would have been an admission that he could not honour his contract. So very sensibly he tried to marry me off with Zoli, and when that failed he made another move which it was much more difficult for me to handle. He had given me an 'advance' of fifty thousand dollars which we had spent in New York. He now claimed that this had not been an 'advance' but a 'loan'. There was an exchange of lawyers' letters of which the last that I received from his lawyer assured me that if I did not at once repay the loan 'steps would be taken'. He could not take any steps while I remained flat-footed in California, but it was not my intention to remain there for the rest of my life, although at that time I was determined to establish myself as an indispensable star in California. And while I remained there I was not in a hurry to concede to Alex that the fifty grand was a loan when he knew very well that it was an advance against the salary that his contract would oblige him to pay me. If I had been a litigious person, that is one who actually enjoys lawsuits, I could have countersued for breach of contract and claimed at least the salary for our first film. But, no, thank you. No more lawsuits.

I believe that Alex got quite a kick from his lawsuits. At the time of my legal conflict with David E. Rose he had assured me that it was a great mistake to take one's lawsuits too much to heart. He said that at one time he had been involved in a suit with Sidney Bernstein, an old friend. Seeing him one day in the Vendôme, that nice restaurant opposite the entrance to the St. Regis Hotel in New York, he had approached him with his customary smile and outstretched hand, only to be cut dead by Bernstein. He characterised Bernstein's attitude as downright childish. I think that he played his lawsuits like games of chess. First he had moved a pawn in the shape of his brother Zoli. When I ignored this as a move of no significance, he moved out one of his bishops which suggested the possibility of a serious gambit. I would have to move judiciously.

Meanwhile another problem was thrown at me. The film *The Desert Fox* had been released very successfully all over the world except in Russia and other countries where dictatorships still flourished. But there were ex-servicemen in England, veterans in the United States and members of the returned Soldiers' League in Australia who were affronted. And they had good cause. We had assumed that Rommel was as decent a man as a career soldier can be, as decent as Eisenhower, for instance, and had therefore treated him sympathetically in the film. To do so was construed as an insult to those who had fought so gallantly against him. 20th Century Fox played it craftily. On the one hand they publicly recognised the justice of their complaints and on the other hand they read it as an open invitation to indulge them with a sequel which would glorify the ultimate victory of the Eighth Army over Rommel's Afrika Corps.

So, written into the script of their new project *The Desert Rats* was a solitary sequence in which Rommel would appear. Given that Rommel has suffered a slight injury, he receives treatment in a German hospital tent where a wounded British prisoner of war is also being treated. They indulge in brief conversational sparring. Not much of a scene, but the casting department thought it appropriate that I play the part since I had already been identified with the Rommel character in the earlier film. I did not want to play it because it was a trivial scene, certainly not one of the leading parts, and did not warrant a starring salary. There was only one consideration that made me lean the other way. In *The Desert Fox* all the characters had been German and therefore it had been wisely decreed that we make no effort to alter our own British or American accents. In *The Desert Rats* on the other hand all the characters except Rommel and a German doctor were British and Australian, so the actors who played Rommel and the German doctor would have to play with German accents. I figured, if I did not accept the role, the casting department would be well advised to offer it to a German actor. I did not care for this item because such a German actor would most likely seem much more authentic in his portrayal of Rommel than I had been in *The Desert Fox*, an invidious comparison which I should avoid.

The *deus ex machina* in this little drama took the form

of the well known attorney Gregson Bautzer, who in his time has represented everybody in Hollywood. Everybody who *was* anybody. That he had represented me in two or three little matters I had regarded as a distinct status symbol. It was no surprise at all that Alex Korda enjoyed the same distinction. It was characteristic of Bautzer that he should find three loose ends and plait them neatly together as he now proceeded to do. You might say that he was Alex Korda's knight who put me into a fool's mate. Thus I accepted Bautzer's solution, namely that I should accept the so short rôle of the German-speaking Rommel, while my salary, such as it was, would be paid by Fox not to me but directly to Alexander Korda.

But the nicest result of Bautzer's handiwork was that it led directly to Shepperton Studios and a period of pure contentment. While Pamela and I were rashly planning to make the film *A Lady Possessed* we had, as I have said, thought first of doing it in France. And during the short period that this fantasy lasted I asked my then mother-in-law, who had lived in the South of France and had many French or French-speaking acquaintances, to find me someone who spoke French and would work for me as secretary and/or dresser. Although we had quickly dismissed the French scheme my mother-in-law insisted on introducing the French speaker she had found. He was a very nice man called Frank Essien, whose father had been an immigrant from what is now Ghana. He had invented a fairly serviceable shorthand of his own, typed well and in every way could be said to know his way around. In the event of French production I was going to brush up my French conversation with him and there were occasions later when I was able to profit by his familiarity with basic French. When I first employed him he became my dresser/secretary and reported every day at Shepperton Studios while we were shooting *Pandora and the Flying Dutchman*. At this time Korda and I were virtually at law with one another, that is to say he was threatening me with his bishop.

I became aware that at Shepperton Studios Zoli Korda

was preparing to make a film of *Cry the Beloved Country*, an African story. I said to myself: 'Aha. Frank is black and an experienced performer. There must be lots of parts which he could play in Zoli's film.'

So I sent him along to see the casting director who was finding actors for the film. When he came back he was laughing his head off.

'What happened?'

'The casting director, who was very nice, telephoned through to Zoltan Korda's office and told him she was sending me in to see him. He greeted me quite nicely and asked me what I had done before, and I made it as short as I could. But then I made my big mistake.'

'Mistake?'

'Yes. I told him that I was working for you. And he said' – uncontrollable laughter again – 'and he said, "Any friend of Mason is an enemy of the Kordas!" And he threw me out!'

Yes, Zoli had the reputation of being the emotional one.

So now, three years later, I am back in Shepperton Studios and actually working on a film which is being produced by Alex Korda with whom I have recently terminated my legal contretemps. I am entering the main building and before I can recognise who has attacked me so rapidly a small dark-haired individual has thrown his arms around me and planted the statutory number of Hungarian friendship kisses.

'Oh, I am so wonderfully happy that we are all friends again. This was such wonderful news that you and Alex have made up and are working together again. Welcome back!'

It was Zoli of course. The date of these hugs was the 10th March 1953. I can be so precise because I have salvaged two or three discontinuous diaries which I kept spasmodically at the time.

We had left Pamela and the young Portland behind and crossed the Atlantic on the SS *America*. I took Monaghan with me to keep me out of trouble. After Le Havre and

316

Paris we hit Hamburg in February and flew to Berlin the same day. The film, to be directed by Carol Reed, was a story which illustrated the tense relations between dwellers in East and West Berlin at that time. The protagonist was a German who lived by his wits in both sectors, hence the title of the film: *The Man Between.*

This was long before the building of the Berlin Wall and John Kennedy's revelation that he was 'ein Berliner'. The 'Crisis' involving the air-lift had taken place in 1948–9. Stalin died just before we started shooting our film in Berlin. The story which we attempted to dramatise took its colour from the conditions which existed immediately prior to his death. One particular feature which we certainly did not wish to discard just because Uncle Joe had died was the ubiquitous display of monster billboards throughout East Berlin, all bearing identical portraits of the dictator. People who lived in East Berlin simply could not get away from him. Stalin's successor Malenkov did not rate this treatment, presumably because his face must have been almost as unknown to the Russian and East German populace as it was to us, and they could hardly expect an unknown face to scare the living daylights out of a mass of people, no matter how huge the poster.

It was clear that we could shoot the exterior scenes of our film only in the Western sector even though many of them were supposed to take place in the Eastern. Therefore our art department was obliged to erect the monster posters of Stalin in the Western section, which was quite a shock for the casual Berliner who had not read in his local newspaper what might be expected from us. Almost all our shooting was done at night and consequently such shocks were usually sustained by the drunkard tottering out of his bar at three o'clock in the morning. There in front of him, thirty foot high, would be the floodlit portrait of Stalin. Had he invaded already? Or had the drunkard inadvertently drifted into the Eastern sector? Carol Reed was not unduly put out by reports of violent scenes resulting from recurrent shocks of this nature because he was haunted by another embarrassment. There was an inescapable police chief who never stopped bending Carol's ear in an effort to prove how useful he was being – a terrifying looking man like the caricature of a plain-clothes S.S. man which we always had managed to insert into our wartime movies. Carol was painstakingly polite to him.

The action of our story was derived from the rash of kidnappings that had taken place in Berlin during that period. Every so often we would read in our papers that a scientist had been snatched and taken to the East, or a banker or a blackmarketeer. So in our story there is a plot to snatch the character played by Hildegard Knef, who was supposed to be married to the character that I played. The kidnappers mistake a perfectly innocent English visitor (Claire Bloom) for the Knef character, snatch her and lock her up securely in the East. My character, whose name was Ivo, has common business interests with the kidnappers, but he is not without a small particle of chivalry and makes it his business to restore her to the West without compromising his friends. There were at that time check points on all the roads connecting the sectors and the operation required a familiarity with the city comparable with that of a skilled taxi-driver and also in this case some initiative and courage.

There is much more to the story than that. In fact it was full of interesting detail and intrigue although the screenplay was in some areas clumsily constructed, to the detriment of its commercial success. I could not at the time have put my finger on what was wrong with the structure, but a few years later I learned the secret of suspense not from Hitchcock, the certified master of the genre, but from Andrew Stone, another director. My education took the form of employment in two of his films, *Cry Terror* and *The Decks Ran Red*.

In 1953 Berlin was still in ruins. Of course sufficient rebuilding had taken place to allow the population to live and practise their trades in a manner approaching

318

normality. But many of the buildings were just a heap of rubble. In the East things were much worse and in certain places along the border between East and West where there was an unusually large amount of undisturbed rubble one could still pick up the smell of decaying flesh. They referred to this as Naft Stalin.

There was a lack of young people in Berlin. The prospects for them there were negligible because it was not a place where capital was being invested. West German entrepreneurs and bankers could see prosperity ahead in other cities, but for business men, as for the young, Berlin was definitely not the place. The middle-aged must make what they could out of it, but their livelihoods and futures were heavily dependent on the future policies of their Eastern neighbours. And this in a peculiar way made it an exciting place in which to find ourselves at that time. The hard-working optimistic Berliner living in this insecurity evinced a dour humour that reminded me of wartime Londoners.

My scrappy diary reminds me that when I first saw Carol Reed he was 'glittering with enthusiasm and benzedrine'. Before my arrival he had contrived to work with two separate crews for night and day shooting because he wanted to knock off all the scenes that could be done with doubles only before getting involved with Knef and Claire Bloom and myself. Without the benzedrine in such circumstances he would have collapsed. He had said to me once when we were making *Odd Man Out*:

'Making a film is like going down a mine for eight weeks.'

For him and for very few others that I have known, directing was a total commitment.

This was one of the very rare occasions when I have really enjoyed night shooting. There was very little daytime shooting by comparison. It was always bitter cold at night but I was supplied with an unusually splendid mobile dressing room, which, to judge from its furnishings, must surely have belonged to some prominent circus performer. It had heavy mahogany furniture and a stove that tended to send me to sleep in the early hours if I didn't watch out. Pamela and I always carried some coffee-making device when travelling (I had not yet learned the dangers of coffee). And so on this occasion my friend Mankiewicz had lent me an electric coffee pot together with a heavy transformer in case I found a different voltage in Berlin. My then agent, Charles Feldman, had insisted that I could not withstand the cold Berlin nights without his minklined topcoat which he insisted that I borrow. I wanted to comply with his insistence so that he would not feel hurt, but finally had to recognise that it was so heavy and so grand that I did not think that I could live with myself so accoutred. So I left it for him in Beverly Hills.

And it needed a lot of persistence on my part to put the Mankiewicz coffee pot to its proper use. The caravan was fed with electricity by the film unit's generator. The coffee pot would not respond and there were endless discussions between the German electrician and his mates from which I picked up the new words Durchstrom and Wechselstrom (direct and alternating current). The German wanted me to forget about the Mankiewicz device in favour of one that he proposed to lend me. Then the British electrician got into the act and in a matter of days the problem was solved. I was supplying myself with Wechselstrom-coffee at 110 volts without a transformer. The scrap of disconnected diary is rich in such trivia. I am glad I found it because it brings to light the nostalgia which this European engagement was effectively appeasing.

Working in England on *Pandora and the Flying Dutchman* had given none of the feeling of a home-coming. The work itself had not gratified and there had been too many newspapermen around who felt it their duty to write about me as one who had abandoned England in favour of Hollywood, who had bitten the hand that nurtured him (J. Arthur Rank's) and, perhaps worse still, had done nothing in Hollywood except appear in five dud films.

But now the atmosphere was completely different. Everything in England was looking up. The curtain was rising on the new Elizabethanism. This was the year of the Coronation, only a few days before which Pamela, Portland and I had to sail back to the United States. The two of them had been with me for six weeks, but the peak of the homecoming experience had happened before they arrived. Under Sunday, 5th April, Easter, I find the following:

... British Railways luncheon not as bad as cracked up to be (Grapefruit, stewed ham, cheese, tasteless coffee. 9s 7d). Weather variable, light sky, heavy storm clouds and rain. Such a cloud immersed Wakefield when I arrived, making it slaty, shiny, grim. Dad and Muv met me in good pre-war looking Rover and took me a long way round to Rex's house (in Brockholes) for tea.

This was my first sight of the West Riding since 1938, a gap of at least fifteen years.

Genuinely moved by the scenery. Denby Dale. Cawthorne. Trees hunched against the heavy weather, huddling in copses, sheltering in tiny valleys, beginnings of spring buds, heavy beads left by the rain, bright green lichen. The country houses square stone boxes, the heavy blockhouses of lodgegates. Little isolated neatly dressed people walking. The drama of Cawthorne Park ripped open by outcrop coal mining. (They say now that the earth gets neatly replaced, the topsoil carefully on top again and once more arable.) Dad seemed to have only vaguest idea of where roads he took would lead him. Muv backseat driving confident she knew the road better. Probably did. Dad won't let her drive now, to her great disgust. She had never actually damaged a car, only scared the bejesus out of Colin and Dad. Skelmanthorpe, another name we pass through, then Farnley Tyas, Woodsome, Almondbury. Rex's house in Brockholes somewhat less forbidding than had remembered. Rex goes out to feed his pups in antique hat and army groundsheet slung around him. The Spartan house hardly changed. Val (Rex's daughter) plays quite well on the upright piano imported from Croft House. The pictures of couples of Beagle pups. The bumper tea, bread and dripping with marmite, the bread and jam, rock cakes, cream sandwich cake, fruit cake. Halo the happy mother cook. The room where Rex makes furniture and Christopher (Rex's son) has designed and built a layout for his model train. Drive through Honley, Berry Brow, Armitage Bridge, then up through Gledholt to Croft House. The black velvet sandstone buildings in town with the face of the stone flaking off and causing effect like bark of a plane tree. No railings or front-gate (war scrap). Colin returned from Scarborough hockey festival with battered ankle. Sat and talked till late. In drawing room and dining room all furniture and pictures unaltered, even curtains mostly the same. Dining room: Refectory table, square Liberty style, chairs, black ornate Dutch mantelpiece, fancy brass clock. George IV gentlemen drinking print, ancestral miniature. 'Taffy was a Welshman' etching, pewter on dresser, glass in corner cupboard, dark red relief pattern dado, Meissonier etchings. Strange black Cromwellian armchair and Sam Kay's Windsor Hall: 'That's Bully' by Cecil Aldin, old guns and swords, electric heating unit bar (new), glazed walnut doors to vestibule, front door of bright green and stained glass, thin latchkey, the great arched bathroom door with stained glass triton. Tambourine Harry and deer heads. Drawing room: Armchairs and sofa of patched Liberty print, good period mahogany bureau containing drawers full of photos, glazed oak bookcases, 'Moorland and Mist', photos over fireplace, Rex and Col in uniform, Geoffrey Gaunt, drawing of great grandfather, early photo of his friend Dr Simpson, little heat throwing fireplace, old sampler primitive design lions, cats etc., draught excluding curtain on door.

Monday, 6. Sleep in spare room, intense cold of sheets. Edith brings early morning orange juice. Edith is thirteen stone, short, with red button nose, heart of gold. Then we ramble through the bathroom, strong room and the 'den' where we have breakfast.

... Galoshes to walk round garden with Colin, shows me his trimming of the trees. Walk to Lindley Clock Tower. Tells of Dad's present status, little business but would lose car and perquisites if he retired.

Then he drove me to Wakefield. He told of trouble with the headmaster of the school where he taught. Colin had trained his bullnosed Morris car to chug driverless after him across the playing fields and was pleased with this achievement. His headmaster was not amused. This was a disappointment to me because I had known him at Cambridge and had credited him with a sense of humour.

My brother Rex, instead of having lunch each day with the top brass in the Mill where he worked, would run up to his house to see to the needs of the couple of beagle pups he would be looking after. Every year he would be responsible for a fresh pair. A short run with them, a feed for the pups, a snack for himself and back to the Mill. My father regarded this practice as unbusinesslike but it made sense to me.

The somewhat Spartan house, referred to above, in which Rex and his family lived, was beside the little church of which he was a pillar, a conscientious church-warden; when the visiting parson was prevented by inclement weather from materialising Rex filled in for him. Into the pulpit he would bound and improvise a thoroughly sensible sermon. Also he was the regular bellringer.

When the three of us were boys, a business friend of my father said to him:

'Well, Jack, you've got three grand lads. What will you do with them when they grow up?'

'I shall let them choose for themselves.'

'Ay, but there must be things you'd *like* them to do, Jack.'

'It's all the same to me so long as they're happy. But . . .'

'But what?'

'I was going to say there are some jobs I'd rather they kept out of.'

'Such as?'

'I'd not like one of them to be a schoolmaster. I've no time for them. They're a mealy-mouthed lot. Nor a sanctimonious parson, I wouldn't like that either. Mmmm.'

'What else?'

'I was going to say an actor, but that's not likely to happen in my family.'

I never heard this story until long after I had become an actor. I was the first to enter one of my father's shortlist of least loved professions. The second was Colin when he quit the rag trade to take up schoolmastering. And Rex came as near as one can get to parsonhood, short of actually taking holy orders. Ours was a forgiving father if ever there was one.

The last entry in the scrap of diary that I have been consulting was dated May 29th. I was sailing back to the United States on a neat little ship of the Cunard fleet, but the inefficient diary fails to mention its name. But we get two professional references.

– Read the script of *Prince Valiant* at last. Ha ha. Also re-read Joe Mankiewicz's treatment of *The Barefoot Contessa*. Doubt if he will have script ready to start shooting in September.

Joe had indeed asked me to read the script of his next

project because there was a part in it that he wanted me to play. But the character was not only relatively unimportant but impotent, and a madly competitive actor, which is what I was at this stage of my career, does not wish to play the part of an impotent Italian Count even if he is supposed to symbolise the decadent culture of Europe. I was competitive because I was not getting anywhere very fast. I had not made first base. The first step towards the acquisition of the power to control my own destiny was to win enormous popularity among the ticket buyers by putting on the macho image, with which the male ticket buyer would wish to identify. There was a formula for the macho star which could almost have been invented by Alan Ladd since he adhered to it so assiduously.

A hero is as tall if not taller than anyone else on the screen.
He is intrinsically chivalrous to women, although an occasional slap or hit is permitted when required to save hero's face.
Nobody draws a gun faster than hero.
Nobody tops his shrewd observations or jokes.
He is neither impotent nor a cuckold.
He protects the underdog.
He wins.

George Arliss was familiar with this formula. All the star stars of the golden pre-war years respected it. Important exceptions are the comedians who of their nature are required to come off much worse than we, the ticket buyers, would in similar circumstances.

So Mankiewicz was not going to enlist me for this new venture of his, especially since the Count would be juxtaposed with a formula macho played by Humphrey Bogart. Now if Joe had offered the impotent part to Bogart and the Bogart part to me, he'd have had my acceptance in a flash.

Mankiewicz had at last rid himself of his contract with 20th Century Fox. For years he had resented the fact that he was not the complete master of the films he made, that Zanuck was the man who handled the shears and could make minced celluloid out of Joe's masterpieces if he so chose. It was Joe's opinion that Zanuck had done precisely that with a film which started life as *Dr Pretorius* and ended with the Zanuckian title *People will Talk*. And it was this experience that had prompted Mankiewicz finally to cut loose.

Now Zanuck in his turn was being bitten by the bigger flea on *his* back. Spyros Skouras, the bigger boss, had already caused the studio to produce films in Cinemascope. These were ever so big and ever so wide, in fact critics both inside and outside the studio referred to the shape of this image as the letterbox ratio (about 4½:1 I would estimate). They started with an indifferent Biblical epic, *The Robe*, to which the response had evidently been sufficiently encouraging for them to press on and make more and more of these curious monsters. Producers and directors in the employ of the studio did not know what to make of this shape. Obviously they could not introduce closeups, they supposed, and it would give the audience a series of terrible jolts if cut with any rapidity from one shot to another taken from diverse angles. From now on, it seemed, spectacular subjects should be chosen and staged very much as in a live theatre. To make matters worse all these films would be processed in the studio's own laboratory, hopefully called 'De Luxe'.

I still had the remains of my own brief contract with the studio and had not been able to imagine in what sort of a project they would wish me to take part. Well, here it was, in my lap as I sailed sleepily across the ocean in a ship pointed towards the United States. Yes, it says in the diary that I felt sleepy all day.

By the time we came to shoot *Prince Valiant* a lot of the

bugs had been gotten out of Cinemascope, and Henry Hathaway shot the scenes with roughly the same technique that he would have employed before the revolution. The film was loaded with action scenes which tended to roughen Hathaway's temper. His vocal cords took a lot of punishment, as did the ever-present cigar. There was every kind of work for a regiment of stunt men who did not always take kindly to Hathaway's urgings. The material for the film was drawn from a popular and firmly established strip cartoon. In it Prince Valiant, son of a Scandinavian king, was forever getting into scraps with every sort of medieval bad guy. For the purposes of our film he became the page of one of King Arthur's knights of the Round Table. The principal bad guy took the form, believe it or not, of one of these very knights who have always been thought of as a body of men whose honour and loyalty were beyond suspicion. Ah, but as soon as this knight lifted his visor the audience could well become a prey to serious doubts. It was me.

I believe that this was Robert Wagner's first film. At any rate he was lacking in experience. He has now become confident and popular and almost a super star, but at that time he was loath to raise his voice, which was consistent with the character of the young Prince Valiant as it had been firmly established in the King Features syndicated throughout the United States. But there was one sequence in which Hathaway was quite rightly insistent that the princely voice be raised.

While performing some errand for his knight, Sir Gawain, Valiant runs into a group of rogue Vikings, led by that formidable actor Neville Brand, who quickly get the better of him and are in the act of trussing him up when a rider on a dark horse bursts out of the adjacent boskage. The rider has his visor down. Ah, thinks Val (as all the nice guys in the picture addressed him), this must be the sinister black knight of whom I have heard tell. The rider now raises his visor and reveals that he is Sir Brack, a knight of the Round Table. Val puts two and two together and concludes that Sir Brack *is* the sinister black knight. The rogue Vikings treat the black knight as an old friend. So Val says the one word,

– Traitor!

It was a long time before Hathaway bullied Wagner into raising the princely voice to a satisfactory pitch. Bullied is of course the wrong word, though a complete stranger who had never seen Wagner or Hathaway before might have been excused for thinking that an act of bullying was taking place.

No, Bob, for Chri' sake, this guy is one of the *Knights* of the round *Table*. And now you find out that he is nothing but a louse. Now come on, Bob, let's hear it. *TRAITOR!!*

Traitor.

Cut ... now Bob. This guy, Sir Brack, is a terrific guy. You've always kind of worshipped him. This other knight, the one you work for, Sir Gawain, he's not in the same *League* as Sir *Brack*. So you can imagine what a *Shock* this is. I want to hear you really snarl that word at him. *Traiturrr.*

– Traitor!

– That's much better Bob. Now let's have a little more volume ... etc.

And so it went on endlessly. And Hathaway could really snarl that word.

The same hypothetical stranger who knew neither Hathaway nor Wagner might have thought that another act of bullying was taking place as he watched Hathaway directing scenes with Sterling Hayden who played the part of Sir Gawain. I watched with some discomfort because, intent on minding other people's business, I had insisted to Hathaway that Hayden was the right man for the part. And now here was Hathaway seemingly distressed and Hayden looking hot and mad. I had seen him being hugely impressive in several widely different roles, and in one of them he had played a keen, dedicated scoutmaster type, which had convinced me that he was right for Sir Gawain. The discomfort went on for quite some time but at the end of the day I realised that basically Hayden was a cucumber. In the best sense. Cool. I, having top billing, got the footprints, but Hayden's was the only good performance in the film.

I can't pretend that the making of this film gave me much pleasure. The best that I could say for it at the time was that the 20th Century Studio was not far from the house in Beverly Hills where we lived and that we had recently constructed a tennis court, which was where I liked to be most of the time.

I suppose that there were some ticket buyers who thought that they were getting more for their money when they saw a film in Cinemascope. At any rate 20th Century was now stuck with it and the other studios tried to pretend that by widening the screen they were miraculously increasing the value of their merchandise. MGM offered 'Wide Screen' which was less revolutionary than the others. 'Panavision' was subsequently introduced at Paramount and had more lasting qualities. Though the ratio was not widely different from the old norm, the precision was so extraordinary that it is still the most wanted system.

The development of these gimmicks added enormously to the cost of production. The screens were so vast and the depth of focus usually so impressive that backgrounds could not be vaguely hinted at nor deftly back projected as in our dear old black and white films; now the backgrounds had to be spelled out in detail, and this meant that huge film units had to travel all over the world. Not that I had any cause to complain. I liked to travel.

Prince Valiant was given a proper Hollywood première at Grauman's Chinese Theatre, which was now one of a chain called Fox West Coast Theatres controlled by one of the brothers of Spyros Skouras. Until I am contradicted I shall insist that this was Charles Skouras rather than George, and thus give him credit for ordering me to leave an impression of my feet and hand prints in the forecourt of that renowned theatre. I had always supposed that it was only the feet of the *enormously* famous that were imprinted on these flag-stones, and now I found that I was to be so immortalised merely because I had top billing on a film which the Skouras brothers were desperately trying to inflate. A bit of a let-down I thought – I mean for the public and the Hollywood idolaters – no let-down for me, since I would happily have grabbed any distinction offered to me.

Spyros Skouras was enormously popular with the Greek Community in Los Angeles, because he was credited with having paid for the erection of a lavish Greek Church, which to my eternal regret I never visited. He was popular with me because I happen to like Greek feta cheese, and in the dining room at 20th Century Fox I could always find it. Skouras, being the boss, had installed a Greek caterer named Nick. So when I ordered my Anne Baxter salad every day (coleslaw and shredded chicken) I would see that a lump of feta cheese came with it.

As with Louis B. Mayer and Dore Schary, so with Spyros Skouras and Darryl Zanuck – I would never have been able to answer a test paper concerning the precise limits of each man's authority. Surely Zanuck was the executive in charge of all film production, and yet it was Skouras who was blamed for the introduction of Cinemascope, and a few years later another aberration entitled *Cleopatra* was claimed by no one but Skouras. I do not know what Zanuck's official title was, but I have reason to know that Skouras was President. (Unless he kept changing his title.)

If once again we may flash forward, this time to the year 1959, we come to Khrushchev's visit to the United States and more specifically, to Los Angeles. He was a rather popular figure, though no one had yet invented Détente. He had become popular by sheer force of personality. When he was being aggressive he seemed to be aware that he was still a figure of fun. Most people still had memories of Senator McCarthy and Richard Nixon and would not wish to be caught being over-friendly with a Russian; there was still a long time to go before such a friendship was to be permitted by the same Richard Nixon. But on the occasion of the luncheon given to Khrushchev in the dining room of the 20th Century Studio an appreciable friendliness characterised our greeting. I attended because I was again a 20th Century Star, and there was a welter of stars from the other studios and important executives. Three items stand out in my memory. One was that poor darling Judy Garland, with whom I had made *A Star is Born* about five years previously, was going through one of her very fat periods. Next there were the mysterious dark looks and muttered exchanges that rippled along the row of seated Russians. We learned later that these were occasioned by Mrs Khrushchev's keen disappointment upon learning that there would be no visit to Disneyland. The third was the post-prandial entertainment laid on for the visitors. The studio happened to be shooting Cole Porter's *Can Can* at the time of this luncheon. So someone had decided that a musical number with lots of Can-Can dancing would be just the ticket. The Russians were reported later to have been deeply offended but since I was not on speaking terms with any of them I never knew precisely which aspect of the entertainment had shocked them. I myself was not deeply impressed by the costume department's contribution, but would the Russians have been better pleased if the performers had worn the authentic costumes favoured by the clientele of La Galette? On this occasion the nice Frank Sinatra surprised us by introducing the show in a strangely take-it-or-leave-it manner – almost as if he had sworn a private oath that no one would catch him being polite to those S.O.B.s.

But the most memorable item was Spyros Skouras's after-luncheon speech of welcome. At least one had to suppose he intended it as some sort of welcome. He rambled on in a very boring way about the virtues of the United States. No one wished to criticise him for his tributes to their country, but he was so boring that

American members of his audience kept hissing at him with the friendliest of intentions,

'Sit down, Spyros!'

Finally he excelled himself. He told us at immense length that the United States was such a fair minded democratic haven that a little Greek immigrant named Spyros Skouras had been able to climb the ladder step by step until he finally became the President of 20th Century Fox. (Renewed hissings of 'Sit down, Spyros'.)

The Russians took the speech patiently and politely. They were a healthy looking bunch of men, much more relaxed than our lot. Khrushchev's speech was very well received, at least up to the half-way point. He seemed to have a good sense of humour, refrained from pointing out to Skouras that this little Russian nobody had climbed the ladder step by step until he became leader of the second most powerful nation in the world, and in every other way showed unfailing politeness to his host. But at the half-way point he segued into what was obviously his prepared speech, and now *he* became the bore. He did not brag about himself as Spyros had done, he bragged about his country's achievements in the realm of motion pictures. He lost his audience completely at this point because – and I don't know if he realised this – for most of us it was virtually impossible to *find* a Russian film, for unless you went to Acapulco, Mar Del Plata or one of the other film festivals, or unless you were one of the small body of Academy members who volunteered to work on the nominating committee for Foreign Language Films, you would never see one. To most of his audience the films that Khrushchev bragged about were unheard of, so he too lost his early advantage and was remembered as the second worst after-luncheon bore.

Hopping back now to the aftermath of *Prince Valiant*, I played a lot of tennis and spent happy times in the pool with Portland and we did a lot of painting together. Sometimes we would work together on the same canvas or piece of paper, with amazing results. She was old enough now to take a keen interest in some of the movies. *Prince Valiant* did not grab her especially but both the films that followed in quick succession commanded her keen attention. These were *A Star is Born* and *20,000 Leagues Under the Sea*.

I had been aware for some time that Judy Garland and her husband Sid Luft were planning a remake of *A Star is Born*, a story which had been filmed twice already. The first one which starred Lowell Sherman, was called *What Price Hollywood*. The second and more famous had Fredric March and Janet Gaynor and was a superb little film, an unpretentious and credible Hollywood story. And now came Judy and Sid armed with a new scenario by one of the top playwrights of the time, Moss Hart, and a healthy looking contract with Warner Brothers. I thought, when I heard about it, that it would be exactly my cup of tea but I was right in supposing that I was by no means the front runner for the role of Norman Mayne, the movie star on his way down. I know that the part was offered to Humphrey Bogart. I can only suppose that he turned it down because his career moved along so smoothly and easily, since he must have been the world's most popular movie star during the few years before he died and there was a plentiful supply of those rough/smooth sweet/sour madly masculine roles that he played, and in Hollywood no one would expect *A Star is Born* with Judy Garland to be a smooth or easy ride.

I know that Cary Grant was another to whom the part was offered. In fact he reached the point of participating in at least one story conference with the Lufts and George Cukor, the director, before it dawned on him that he was wasting their time. There were probably others but in the end it came to me and I grabbed it smartly before it slipped away. The feeling in Hollywood about the project was very negative. Judy told me later that Arthur Freed, who had produced a long list of excellent musicals at MGM, had said of her to Luft in the presence of one of her friends, 'Those two alley cats can't make a picture.'

Judy had made a sort of bad name for herself because in a commercial town like Hollywood reliability is the big thing. And Judy had developed as a child star at MGM the unfortunate habit of taking uppers and downers, nothing half so bad as what the young stars inflict on themselves today, but yes, she took things like dexedrines to sharpen her up in the mornings and some sort of sedative to help her sleep. She was a party-goer, almost too eager, some may have thought, to join whoever was at the piano and sing along, while the hostess made sure that her medicine cabinet was safely locked.

An important downfall had taken place when, cast in the part of Annie Oakley in MGM's projected *Annie Get Your Gun*, she had allowed unpunctuality to get the better of her and been replaced by Betty Hutton. After a difficult period she had been restored to a position of strength by Sid Luft who was a kindred spirit. They were both mavericks and he had given her the confidence that had at this point been taken away from her. Professionally her restoration found its expression in an entertainment at the Palace Theatre in New York which Luft mounted for her. *Judy at the Palace* had been a sensational success and it was on the strength of her new fame that the Warner Brothers contract had been negotiated.

But there were no great expressions of joy about the Lufts' projected film. One would hear people say,

'They're supposed to start shooting next week, but Judy'll never make it.'

So it was ironical that I, whose reputation for punctuality was impeccable, was the one to hold up production for the first couple of days. My inner ear went on the blink causing a chronic dizziness. If I turned over in my sleep I would wake up with a sensation that I was about to tumble out of bed. When I felt I was getting a little better I started taking anti-seasickness pills but I remained unsteady for a long time. I was quite happy to be feeling unsteady when I started to work at the studio because it happened that the first set was of Norman Mayne's bedroom and the only sequence to be shot in it concerned his waking up in the middle of the night after having been put to bed a few hours earlier in an extremely drunken condition. I could now 'use' my dizziness. But in any case most of the sequence was discarded because it did not work as well as Cukor had intended. Cukor had a habit, aided and abetted by his friend, George Huenighan Huhne, of relating his films or parts of them visually with the work of some painter. In this case George had thought of the drunken Mayne waking in the night as a nightmare by Henry Fuseli (a.k.a. Johann Heinrich Füssli). The window drapes in the room were to take on the look of nightmare girls. I had not learned of this until I ran into a strange looking girl in one of the corridors at the studio. When I commented on her appearance she told me she was playing the part of a curtain. She seemed to think that this explained everything. I don't believe that this particular elaboration even made it as far as the 'rough cut'.

George continued to be refreshingly inventive throughout the production and kept adding flourishes and codas to many of the sequences when the time came around to shoot them. A good example was his treatment of a sequence which dealt with a conversation between the studio boss (Charles Bickford) and Norman Mayne. Cukor staged it as if it took place while the lights were being rearranged between one set-up and another during the shooting of a swashbuckling programme picture. Mayne is dressed becomingly as a pirate. The somewhat downbeat conversation concluded, the assistant director of the pirate saga tells Mayne that they are now ready to shoot. Mayne accepts a cutlass from the property man and, in the company of a hundred or so extras and a seasoning of stuntmen, leaps into action.

Unfortunately I never saw the first cut of the film which reached the stage of being publicly previewed and lasted over four hours. Those who saw it say that the film played better in this marathon version than in any of the shorter ones which followed. The first time I saw the film was during its initial run at Grauman's Chinese Theatre, now reduced to two and a quarter hours. So I missed not only a lot of Cukor's gratuitous flourishes but also many delightful scenes which had been uprooted from the first half of the show simply because they were not essential story-telling links. At the time when the film emerged, the habit of offering the public three and a half or four hour films broken by a midway intermission had not yet been established. I believe that *Gone with the Wind* was the only film to have been accorded this special treatment. In any case the Warners opted for putting this one out at a comparatively modest length, without intermission. Actually they had in the middle of the film an enormously long musical number by Judy called 'Born in a Trunk,' which induced a feeling in the audience that they had now *had* an intermission and that, after it, they must pay attention again as if it were Monday morning. The material itself was fine and would have hit a terrific rating as part of a television special or a Long Play record, but in the middle of a film I thought it was a liability. At the showing that I attended in Grauman's Chinese there was at the conclusion of the 'Born in a Trunk' number a general easing or restabilising of the buttocks which occupied the seats around mine and I heard a voice mutter, 'It's going to be a long film.'

That was because the tension had been snapped. I do not know who made these big decisions, Sid Luft or Jack Warner, but it was an odd point at which to choose to insert a blockbuster musical number. In the story Norman Mayne's career is rapidly declining while his young wife's talent is beginning to be exploited. At some risk the studio boss has finally given her a leading part in a musical and all the top brass of the studio have gone down to the preview which is being held in Long Beach – or some place in that area. From a story-telling point of view this is a tense moment, the characters in the story are anxious to learn if little Vickie Lester (née Esther Blodgett) will make it. On the other hand it was totally unnecessary to prove to the audience that our Judy Garland was a star. We had been loving her for years. Therefore, I told myself, all the film needed at this spot was a few feet of Judy belting a show-stopping number. The obvious thing for Jack Warner to do was to ring up Louis B. Mayer – assuming that they were on speaking terms – and, having broken the ice with a couple of locker room jokes, say something like,

'Hey L.B., I'd be very grateful if you could find me a few feet of some Judy Garland musical number that they couldn't find a place for in one of your musicals. Nothing important. A finale of some sort would work best.'

I had to keep reminding myself that I was neither Jack Warner nor Sid Luft, nor even Louis B. Mayer. Maybe some such conversation *did* take place. However, many people appreciated the long interruptive 'Born in a Trunk' number and the almost equally lengthy New Orleans number towards the end of the show. There was another that I personally could have done without. Vickie Lester comes back to her home after working all day at the studio. She finds her husband in the dumps because he has had nothing better to do all day than practise putting golf balls into a tumbler and has received the final movie star's humiliation at the hands of a boy who has come to the house to deliver a parcel. Instead of addressing him as Mr Mayne, the boy says,

'Sign here please, Mr Lester.'

So in order to cheer him up she performs for him a mock facsimile of the number she has been working on at the studio. It was quite a long one. And all that the actor playing Norman Mayne had to do was to laugh, smile and chuckle for about five minutes.

It seems almost as if I was full of complaints and disappointments concerning this film. Quite the contrary. I was having a wonderful time. The only thing that bothered me at all was something that was beyond the power of anyone to fix. And maybe others did not recognise it as a problem. Judy was essentially a witty, lively, talented, funny, adorable woman. And her talent worked the greatest wonders when she was acting the fool in a sad or alarming context. It would have been a great thing for all of us if someone in power at MGM or elsewhere had pushed her in this direction, or if she herself had had sufficient self-discipline or been more of a bully girl to bring this about for herself. Over and above her musical talent she was as funny as Lucille Ball, another lady of genius, and could have been as heart-breaking as Chaplin at his very best.

This is probably only one man's opinion, but it explains my disappointment at failing to find in the final cut of the film some of the early comedy scenes that had been so touching. As a matter of fact there is no such thing as a final cut in the case of this film because it continues to be shown all over the world both in theatres and on television screens. If there is no pressing appointment to stop me I will always watch it when it shows up on my nearest television set. When I was taking a walk with Portland on the side of our local mountain in Switzerland we stopped in at a café for a cup of tea when the voice of Judy singing made us turn towards a corner of the room where a small black and white set was lodged. When she stopped singing another voice took over her share of the dialogue. Both she and I had French speaking voices attached to us and Portland and I sat through it spellbound to the end. I have seen it again a couple of times since I married Clarissa and last time we saw the French version I noted that it ran for not more than an hour and forty minutes. The uprooted sections were mostly musical.

Judy was not always reliable, in fact there were some days when she would not really be fighting fit until after the lunch break. Yes, there were quite a lot of mornings when she would arrive late at the studio and consequently, to give Jack Warner and others the impression that we were hard at work, I would be required to do an inordinate number of 'driving' shots. I mean simple shots of me driving the Mercedes or the Lincoln Mercury in or out of the studio, in or out of the grounds of the house supposedly occupied by the Maynes, among the Hollywood hills, in downtown L.A., along the Pacific Coast Highway, etc.

The higher-ups tended to forget that they had undertaken this operation knowing full well that Judy did not have a reputation for reliability; they forgot that prizes are not won nor audiences bewitched by an exercise in reliability. Hathaway used to say that to bring in a film under schedule was not going to make it a hit. Producers and directors strove to come in under schedule because they were afraid of the studio boss. To get something as unique as Judy's talent, some patience and certain sacrifices were needed. If the film went over budget only a very small fraction of the overage was due to Judy's erratic time table. When I think of it, my God they were well off! Judy was by no means a temperamental star. 'Temperamental star' is usually an euphemism for selfish and bad tempered, and a temperamental star of this sort can be a *real* time-waster. I have worked with some. And they are more rampant now than they used to be. But this was not Judy.

George Cukor and I and Sid Luft are the principal survivors of this operation. Gone are not only Judy herself but also Jack Warner, Moss Hart, Harold Arlen, who gave us the good music, and the actors Charles Bickford, Jack Carson and Tommy Noonan. Cukor is at the head of a short list of directorial elite with whom I worked in Hollywood. Most of his elite contemporaries have been (quite unfairly) superannuated, and perhaps Cukor survives because he was always totally faithful to the spirit of the subject matter that he planned to convert into film, whereas some of the others might be accused of singing the same song too frequently. The sage of Hollywood he may not be, but a very active sage.

During those early days when I started to work with him I found it rather hard going. He was nervous in the

339

same way that practically everyone on a sound stage is nervous on the first few days of a new movie. I was feeling not quite on the top of my form because of the lingering dizziness, and here was George talking at me, talking, talking. I was trying to assemble myself in the pattern that I had prepared and at the same time to incorporate the drift of his suggestions. Although I hope he would agree that we did in fact communicate and share our ideas effectively, in the long run I was left with the regret that I could not do just what he had wanted of the character in the first place. I fancied that the Norman Mayne whom Cukor had in mind had all the colours of John Barrymore, whereas I was putting together an actor who resembled much more closely some of my own drunken friends. In fact this was the best that I could offer him. Stylistically a Barrymore figure might have been preferable but I had never liked what I saw of Barrymore.

It is a pity that incriminating evidence about actors of the twentieth century is available in the form of old movies. I mean dramatic actors, for the standards of acting acceptability have changed so violently since the early days of movies that those one-time favourites now look perfectly terrible. Only the comedians – and not all of them – survive. In the 21st century the only winners from our present lot will be Peter Sellers and Mickey Rooney.

In most of our lives this film meant a great deal. The Hollywood Establishment saw little virtue in it, but elsewhere it had some good reviews, though not raves. It was by no means a commercial success at the time. But now that it is revived so often I think we may call it a retarded success.

When the film first came out the people of Hollywood knew Judy as a person who had trouble written all over her. But now there are people all over the world who rate her among the two or three great popular singers of our century, an irreplaceable treasure. Now we can be grateful even for 'Born in a Trunk'. And, while we are at it, thank God for Cukor.

During these years I practically ran the gamut of the Hollywood agencies. I was best served by Charlie Feldman's agency. Charlie himself was a man of whom it was easy to become very fond. He was a generous warmhearted person. Although he was loaded with charm experience has taught me never to refer to anyone whom I like or trust as 'charming'. I no longer use it as a term of approbation. Eventually I left the Feldman Agency but not until I had enjoyed the relationship for a number of years and until both Charlie and one of his principal officers, Ray Stark, had become producers.

Shortly after the completion of *A Star is Born*, I received an offer from Walt Disney to play Captain Nemo in his up-coming live action film of *20,000 Leagues Under the Sea*. The script was quite good. But the making of a live action film was a comparatively new department for Disney, and I was afraid that there would be too much of a Children's Hour quality about it. For a long time I held off because I could not, in the old-fashioned Laughtonian sense, find my key. I was like Gerry Ford trying to make up his mind whether to run for presidency again in 1980. I kept pretending to say yes without actually saying it and I exploited the fact that Ray Stark of the Feldman Agency needed to work out some tricky contractual points. He was in a position that for anyone but Ray Stark might have been mildly embarrassing, that is to say he was working for two clients with conflicting interests, Kirk Douglas and myself, each of whom demanded top billing. Also I suspect that anyone else but Ray Stark would have allowed me to drop out and suggest to Disney that he find another boy to play Nemo. But he held on gamely and kept suggesting all sorts of trick billing clauses which hopefully would so confuse Kirk Douglas and myself that we would each feel reassured that we had come out on top. But I knew that this was a lot of double-talk and that if I finally thought that I could play the part interestingly I would have to step down in favour of my rival Kirk, who would be playing the part of the comedy harpooner. So I did both of these things. Kirk got his top billing and I found my key. Then as a face-saver I suggested that Disney allow me some extra concession. Said Stark,

'Like what?'

'Oh, well, er . . . I thought of something that we might call The Portland Clause.'

'Yeah? And what's that?'

'Well, how about you insert a clause which obliges Disney to lend me each week any feature films of his that I choose to ask for?'

'In 16 mm?'

'Yes, of course. And if there is no feature that we want to see then we would make it any half dozen short features. Would he go for it?'

'I'll try it out on him.'

Disney seemed to think it was an excellent notion. So I went ahead and made the film.

And Portland and I got to know all our favourite Disney films practically by heart, and cut by cut. Also we both went down to the opening of Disneyland together which happened during the year after we had finished making *20,000 Leagues Under the Sea*. My, it was a hot day.

I thought that the film we all made was quite splendid and I am sure that unlike most of my films it has made mountains of money. It still holds up, as they say, and every four or five years it is exposed to a new bunch of kids who think the world of it. It is another film that I like to see again, given a suitable opportunity. I saw it once dubbed into German and it became better than ever. Not only did they give me a marvellous deep gravelly voice, but they fitted one to Kirk which exactly matched his teethplay.

People generally assume that it must have been enormous fun making this film. But I have to say that it was not especially so for the actors, particularly for Paul Lukas and myself. It must have provided a lot of fun for Kirk who not only, with Peter Lorre, did some location work in Jamaica, but himself had to learn to strum the guitar and sing a dotty song, exchange jokes with an attractive, well-trained seal and end up suing Disney because the latter had taken some home movies of Kirk on the day that he visited the Disney home and rode on the Disney miniature railway, and then subsequently included these scenes in one of the Disney Television Programmes without benefit to Kirk.

Paul Lukas and I, on the other hand, had no such fun; it was routine studio work. I don't even believe that the film provided enormous fun for our extremely skilful director, Richard Fleischer, since – let's face it – it was neither an actor's, nor a director's film, it was a producer's film. To Disney himself was the glory and the team responsible for meticulous preparatory work shared some of the fun. The one I remember best was Harper Goff who played banjo in *The Firehouse Five Plus Two* and created half the wonders of Disneyland.

Richard Fleischer

When the film was complete, there was a special showing at the studio for the entire team who made it. I took Pamela and Portland to see it and at the end Portland was really mad at me for my intolerable habit of dying in almost every film of mine that she had seen. I took her criticism seriously and made a list of my demises up to that point in my career.

Fire over England	Sword thrust
I met a Murderer	Shot and drowned
Secret Mission	Sniper's bullet
Fanny by Gaslight	Pistol duel
They were Sisters	Heart attack
The Wicked Lady	Pistol
Odd Man Out	Pistol
The Upturned Glass	Suicide leap from cliff
One Way Street	Bandits
Pandora and the Flying Dutchman	Suicide pact by drowning
Desert Fox	Suicide by poison
The Man Between	Rifle shot
Julius Caesar	* Edmund Purdom
Botany Bay	Spear from Aboriginal
Prince Valiant	Broadsword
A Star is Born	Walk into the sea
20,000 Leagues Under the Sea	Shot and drowned

* I apologise to Edmund Purdom for referring to him as a deadly weapon. I did so only to remind me to mention the following splash of typically Hollywood colour.

And since that time:

Torpedo Bay	Sunk by Italian submarine
Fall of Roman Empire	Arrow
Lord Jim	Cannon loaded with gold
Genghis Khan	Chopped up, put in sack and dragged
Cold Sweat	Machine gun
Kill	Rifle
Child's Play	Leap from roof
The Mackintosh Man	Pistol shot
Frankenstein	Hoisted to mast-head and struck by lightning

344

11 Harrowhouse	Suicide by poison
The Marseille Contract	Shot while dancing
Mandigo	Shot by slave

Since then I have gone straight.

Unlike *A Star is Born*, our film of *Julius Caesar* was well received by the Hollywood establishment. I supposed this was because there were well known big names connected with it and it reached for, though failing to grasp, the golden ring of a culture rare in Hollywood entertainment.

There was a general feeling of oh-how-great about its reception. The big people saw it either projected onto their own screens in their homes in Bel Air and Holmby Hills or else in screening rooms at the big studios. It was in one of the latter that Jerry Wald attended a screening of *Julius Caesar*. Jerry Wald was a busy and well-liked Hollywood operator. Some credit him with having been the model for the opportunist hero of Budd Schulberg's *What Makes Sammy Run?* He wrote screen-plays and produced successfully, and once partnered Norman Krasna, who was also a prolific writer-producer, in running the RKO Studios when they were owned by Howard Hughes. One way and another Jerry Wald was always on the go.

On the occasion of this screening everyone in the little theatre was completely held by the film right to the bitter end when Romans are being killed all over the screen. Penultimately Cassius (John Gielgud) goes and Brutus (J.M.) says good-bye to his old friends and loyal officers. One of these is a small part officer named Strato, played by the handsome Edmund Purdom. Strato is the last to leave, and Brutus says to him:

Brutus: I pray thee Strato, stay thou by thy lord:
Thou art a fellow of good respect;
Thy life has had some snatch of honour in it;
Hold then my sword, and turn away thy face,

While I run upon it. Wilt thou, Strato?

Strato: Give me your hand first: fare you well, my lord.
Brutus: Farewell, good Strato. – Caesar, now be still:
I kill'd not thee with half so good a will.
(runs on his sword and DIES)

Jerry Wald never missed a trick. Like all the go-aheads in Hollywood he would be quick to corral a promising young arrival. So, no sooner had Strato obliged Brutus by holding the hilt of his sword while Brutus fell upon it, than Jerry Wald was out of his seat, his hand a-grab for the nearest telephone. He said to his aide at the other end of the line –

'Get me the name of the guy who just killed Jimmy Mason.'

Shortly afterwards the handsome Purdom became almost as famous as John Travolta and stamped his footprints outside Grauman's Chinese.

Also there was for me a purely personal sequel to *20,000 Leagues Under the Sea.* Jules Verne, don't let's forget, has during the last century given much joy to French schoolboys and a great deal for them to think about so . . .

In the year 1961 I happen to be making a film in Tahiti. When not actually working I am likely to be found in or upon the lagoon directly opposite Punaauia. I enjoy fish-watching and paddling around in a pirogue which is a small dug-out canoe with an outrigging which prevents it capsizing.

So one day there is quite a strong breeze causing little wavelets to break over the gunwhale and fill my canoe with water. But it will not sink entirely because, after all, it is nothing but a piece of wood with a person in it. But we do sink about up to the level of the hair on my chest, so that the act of paddling is now rather awkward. The breeze also prevents me from making a landfall at the point where I started. I have to navigate my craft to a point about a kilometre to leeward.

I see that there is a small boy on the beach who has

spotted me and studies my approach keenly. Then he backs up to the side door of a little house and calls to his mother. When he has got her attention he says in a voice loud enough for me to hear,

'Vienci, Mama. C'est Capitaine Nemo qui arrive dans son sous-marin!'

And I wasn't even wearing a beard.

16/Stratford, Ont.

In 1953 we learned that in a small town in Ontario, Canada, which happened to be named Stratford on Avon, they had contrived to organise a Shakespeare Festival, that the great man of the theatre, Tyrone Guthrie, was its artistic director and that the eminent Shakespearean actor Alec Guinness had been enlisted to play in the first season. The event had been a triumph.

But even if it had not been a triumph I would have accepted Guthrie's invitation to participate in the second season with equal alacrity. Guthrie was one of my heroes and, as I have mentioned, my experience with the filming of *Julius Caesar* had suggested to me that as an actor I needed to be broadened and loosened and stretched. I would need to rehearse for five weeks for appearances in Shakespeare's *Measure for Measure* and the *Oedipus Rex* of Sophocles. And the entire engagement would keep me in Stratford for almost five months. Pamela did not take kindly to the project.

Anyway, I went ahead when the time came. I flew to Detroit and bought a new Ford car which was of a surprising coral colour. In this I drove to Stratford in Ontario. I met all the people involved and listened several times to the story of the theatre's beginnings. There can hardly be anyone in the Province of Ontario, perhaps even in the whole of Canada, who has not heard of Tom Patterson, the man who had the dream. If you live in a town called Stratford and are interested in theatre or public relations it seems a fairly straightforward dream to have had. But it was not so much the originality of the dream as his persistence in selling the idea to the local men of influence, both civic and commercial, that made him take on the look of a patron saint. He had developed his idea no further in practical terms than to suggest an outdoor production of *A Midsummer Night's Dream* with a team of local actors. But he discussed his dream with the town councillors and important business men and such persons as he could find who could claim to have had experience in Canadian theatre. Luckily for him there was a lady called Dora Mavor Moore who had pioneered theatre in Toronto and was well connected theatrically, being a cousin of Dr James Bridie, the Scottish playwright, who had flourished in the thirties and forties. She also was a friend of Tyrone Guthrie and introduced Patterson to him. Community Theatre happened to be Guthrie's passion and it was no problem at all to get him to fly to Canada and give them the benefit of his advice.

Guthrie told them that Community Theatre should be promoted seriously or not at all. Nothing amateurish, nothing half-hearted. All the theatrical resources of Canada should be harnessed, but it should not even stop at that; in order to attract attention and gather support they should, if only for the first few seasons, enlist suitable international stars. He sent for Tanya Moiseiwitsch and had her make plans for the ideal theatre that he had envisioned for a Shakespeare Festival. But if they could not immediately scrape up enough money for this fancy theatre, or if they wanted to make a racing start while the idea was hot, let them use a circus tent for the first two or three years.

So that is what they did. It was a Guthrie-Moiseiwitsch landslide. The tent alone which we used was a miracle of ingenuity. The front of house and backstage sanitation were permanent structures and there was a concrete foundation for the areas where the seats would be and for the stage itself. The tent was supplied by a company in Chicago, and when it arrived each year, it was accompanied by its master Skip Manley and his small staff. If ever a man knew how to handle a tent it was Skip Manley. The stage was a beautiful two storey all-purpose structure which had been designed by Moiseiwitsch, nudged helpfully by Guthrie. It had been taken down at the end of the preceding season and re-assembled for ours, which was the second season, and was to offer *The Taming of the Shrew* as well as *Measure for Measure* and *Oedipus Rex*. Alec Guinness and Irene Worth in *All's Well that Ends Well* and *Richard III* had been the big attractions of the first season.

With the exception of Guinness, Worth and myself the entire casts of both seasons were genuine Canadians. I lie. There was another notable exception who was a tower of strength, Douglas Campbell, who had triumphed as Parolles and Hastings in the first season and was tremendously impressive in the three plays of our season. He had a magnificent voice which he could toss into the furthest fold of that damned tent. Yes, and there had also been the English Michael Bates in the first season. And Guthrie should also be given credit for having hauled Canadians, Frances Hyland and Douglas Rain, back from England for the Stratford Festivals.

The auditorium was like a large round biscuit out of which one bite had been taken. This bite was the raised two storey stage, which could be entered on three levels from the rear or from the mouths of two tunnels facing the front of the stage, and from the back of the on-stage balcony. It was enormously convenient and the players had the constant feeling of being wrapped around by the audience whom they could address in almost any direction, no matter where they stood.

I played no part in *The Taming of the Shrew* and consequently could watch the performance as often as I wished. Each time I chose a seat in a different part of the auditorium and each time I was able to pick up different details in the wonderful team-work that Guthrie had evolved with the help of his actors. I liked everything that Guthrie thought up for this production. Had I been a critic on a knocking spree I would have had no difficulty in finding targets. For instance, adopting a purist attitude I could have knocked Guthrie for presenting the play in the costumes and style of Western America circa 1910. But it enriched the entertainment. One might say of some Shakespearean character, 'He's the kind of guy you'd see roaring round the town in a spanking new jalopy,' or, 'He never has a cigarette out of his mouth.'

It works very well as a device for making recognisable a whole gallery of portraits. The familiar props were all there, even down to the spanking new jalopy.

Our critic might say that he would like to have seen Petruchio played as the boastful bully of tradition. And I am sure that he would have found a lot of support for this view. But Guthrie was not the man to miss an opportunity to experiment. He had too far to go. He had too many communities to visit all over the world and in his perennial study of classic theatre to take new soundings. One of the communities where he had previously produced *The Taming of the Shrew* was Helsinki. And here something had happened quite by accident, which he found so intriguing that he had decided to do the same thing again somewhere but this time do it on purpose. In Helsinki the personality of the boy who played Petruchio had made the spectator think that Petruchio was not in fact a bully boy at all, but that he was an ambitious young man with an understanding of psychology; one who by acting the bully boy found a place for himself among the top people in his adopted town and an attractive, if wilful, wife into the bargain.

So now at Stratford he was to see how much further he could go with this accidental slant.

It worked in the first half of the play but not in the second. The Canadian actor William Needles, who played this specialised Petruchio, was extremely good and made the first half much funnier than usual, but the second half more unattractive. In the second half Petruchio bullies Katharina, wears her out, contradicts her, brings her to heel by treating her like a dog, all of which makes some sense when you are offering a Petruchio with a naturally sadistic bent, but when you had a Petruchio who is putting on an act it really does not work. But then I have never seen a production in which the second half did work.

To me the play is little more than a cynical skit on marital relations. A few years later than this, when the National Theatre had been securely established in London but was still enjoying the cosy environment of the Old Vic, those in command decided that it would be interesting to do one of Shakespeare's comedies with an all male cast, as they were in fact performed in Shakespeare's day. The play they chose to do was *As You Like It* with Ronald Pickup playing Rosalind. Unfortunately I did not have the opportunity to see this production, but it gave me an idea about *The Taming of the Shrew*. Surely, I thought, of all Shakespeare's comedies this was the one that would justify an all male presentation. It is like a stag party send-up, a sketch for a smoking concert, a roast, and, taken in this spirit, the second half could be almost as funny as the first. Funnier!

Be that as it may, Guthrie's production was so full of lively invention, it would have had to be an especially sour critic who would have wished to knock it. Mind you, sour critics do exist. For anyone who is not involved they can be fun to read.

The most triumphant and memorable production of the 1954 season was that of *Oedipus Rex*. Although Guthrie had the greatest admiration for Laurence Olivier as an actor, he had not accepted the manner in which the play had been produced when Olivier had appeared in it so successfully in the 1945/46 Old Vic/New Theatre Season. That had been a realistic presentation. Though obviously a success - largely if not exclusively because of Olivier's presence - it was in Guthrie's opinion a totally wrong approach. He could bring himself to present a Greek play to a modern audience only by approximating as closely as possible to the condition in which it was originally produced. Each of the classic Greek plays was one of a trilogy. The subject matter came from the Greek myths which dealt with the exploits of the ancient heroes and stressed their relationships with the Gods of Olympus. A trilogy of three such plays was performed as part of the rituals prescribed for certain days of the religious calendar. Thus the spirit in which those plays were accepted by the audiences of those days was totally foreign to what we regard as theatre. The experience of attending a trilogy at that time could perhaps be compared with the combination of Passion Play, Eisteddfod and a suggestion of some unspecified sporting event. It lasted a long time, you took your family, your cushions, your picnic lunch. There was 100% audience participation in the solemn and stylised unfolding of the heroic tales.

Our tent theatre was the perfect setting for Guthrie's venture. We already had the wrap-around audience. Guthrie involved them very closely with the actors, especially with the chorus, in the case of *Oedipus Rex* a dozen citizens of Thebes who are there all the time forming and re-forming into groups in the central area and on the broad steps leading up to the all purpose stage setting. Another device for audience involvement was an inescapable but not too oppressive assault by incense. The actors wore the cothurni which increased their height by eight inches and huge half-masks. I had them rig up a sort of crane in my dressing room so that my heavy robe could be lowered onto me from above.

Our author, Sophocles, became the favourite play-wright of the Athenians when he won his first Festival victory in 468 B.C. and beat the previous idol, Aeschylus, whose plays had been more formal than those of Sophocles. The characters in the plays of Sophocles were also much more human than those of his predecessors, though the telling of the story remained highly stylised.

The story of Oedipus unrolled itself with the resonant and slow-moving formality of a High Mass. Laius, the king of Thebes, having been told by an oracle that he would be killed by his own son, gives orders that his newly born child be exposed on a remote mountainside, his feet bound with a 'spancel'. But the child, henceforth called Oedipus because of his swollen feet, is rescued and brought up by a shepherd. When he grows up he is involved, while travelling, in an altercation at a crossroads and slays his father without knowing it.

Meanwhile a monstrous sphinx has become another traffic hazard in the neighbourhood of Thebes, posing riddles to travellers who enter or leave the city and devouring them if they fail to come up with the right answer. The regent, Creon, who is the brother of Jocasta, the widow of Laius, offers the kingship and Jocasta's hand in marriage to the first person who solves the Sphinx's riddle. This is Oedipus. He marries Jocasta, who is in fact his own mother, and begets a number of children by her. Later a blight falls upon the land, and, to find a means of overcoming it, Oedipus sends Creon to consult the Delphic Oracle. On his return Creon reports that he has received instructions to drive out 'the defiling thing that has been cherished in this land'. This statement by Creon comes at the very beginning of the play during the course of which the 'defiling thing' is identified as Oedipus himself. He learns for the first time that the man he slew at the crossroads was his father. Distraught he puts out his own eyes. And Jocasta kills herself.

The audience gave us a standing ovation. I know that this is a gesture which has become devalued in present day New York, but at that time and in that place it meant something. Though the ovation was in recognition of Guthrie's work and had little to do with my husky contribution, it was exhilarating to be part of a production that so regularly stirred an audience.

Our *Measure for Measure* made less of an impact although the play worked well on our permanent set and there were some excellent performances from the Canadians, and Campbell outdid himself as Pompey.

The family scene throughout this period was less encouraging.

I came to Stratford a little ahead of Pamela and Portland and rented a nice enough house which was probably built shortly before World War I. Pamela did not endorse my choice. Nor did she have any need or desire to make friends with my colleagues or the governors of the theatre. She had a point. There would not have been much to interest her in Stratford while I was working in two plays out of three. She suggested that, if I wanted them to stay, we let the house go and take a suite in a hotel in London, Ont., which was some distance away. But after the plays had opened there was something Pamela had to attend to in California, so they were away for a fairly long time. I know what it was now. Ray Stark, being the son-in-law of Fanny Brice, had thought that her Baby Snooks act might yield a television series, performed by a real child rather than an adult comedienne. So Portland was to be tested. The tests were made but the idea was not taken up, and later Stark had the smarter idea of turning his mother-in-law's life into a musical play. Hence *Funny Girl*.

So I became a commuter, with one rather happy consequence. It might be said that the good thing about London, Ont., was that it was a large enough city to allow a licence to be issued for a night-club. In Stratford at that time there was no place where one could legitimately go for a drink after the show. My whisky was served to me from a teapot in the Chinese restaurant. At London on the other hand there was a good place called Campbell's where I could find a snack and a drink and the Oscar Peterson trio. Yes, the great Oscar Peterson himself, who happens to be a Canadian.

Traffic at the box office demanded that the season be extended for two weeks. This caused a professional conflict for me and I had to leave before the others.

I had to come away from Stratford a little before my departure was due. In spite of my remote living arrangements I developed affectionate ties with everyone back stage. But somehow I came away without having developed a close acquaintance with any of the governors or the people who had launched and supported the theatre. And they certainly had not got to know much about me. As an earnest of this the Board gave me a curious going away present. During the entire time that I was in Stratford I had never once smoked. They gave me a silver cigarette lighter. Well, almost silver.

I remember all the circumstances of my departure from that nice theatre, together with a lot of irrelevant detail. Since both *Oedipus* and *Measure for Measure* had to be repeated a few more times in the last two weeks, an accommodating and distinguished young actor named Donald Davis took over the parts of Angelo and Oedipus. Elspeth Cochrane, the stage director, volunteered to drive 'Pretty Isabella' back to California since I seemed to be in such a hurry. Pretty Isabella was the name, wrenched from the text of *Measure for Measure*, that Elspeth had given to my coral coloured Ford car. My final drink-up party is recalled totally. But why was I in such a hurry to get back to California?

The answer to that question evaded me for a long time. It did not want to stand up and be counted. But I am sure now that it is into this slot that I must place a certain wretched item named The Lux Video Theatre.

The man in Charlie Feldman's agency who was looking after me at this time was Jack Gordean. When I had told him about my proposed Canadian adventure he had expressed his opinion that it was rather careless of me to tie myself up for so long since the film offers would be coming thick and fast now that I had figured so prominently in *A Star is Born* and *20,000 Leagues Under the Sea*, and the word had been so good about both of them. I let him assume for his peace of mind that if a gigantic film offer were to come my way I could extricate myself from Canada – snap – just like that. I had no intention of allowing any such thing to happen, and I was beginning to realise that my own prognostications were much less sanguine than other people's. And I was almost always right. I was so right in this case that I had to wait over a year for my next film offer, which was something called *Forever Darling* which was to occupy me in June and July of 1955. And it was not really what I would have called acceptable; I only took it out of a sort of desperation.

I was learning that for an actor Hollywood is not necessarily the place to hang out. That is why you see so many Hollywood actors pretending that they are something else. If they are unsuccessful actors they pretend that the stockmarket is so much more fascinating, or real estate, or rock collecting, or even owning a corner drugstore or a part of a racehorse. If they are successful they want to be mistaken for sages, prophets, political thinkers or founder members of the smartest cult in town. I had come to Hollywood to be an actor. If I had been a shrewder Englishman I would have come to Hollywood to be a tailor, a hairdresser or a bookmaker. But it was done now. I had a big house and I should at least turn in a respectable income each year, which was unlikely if I chose to spend half a year acting in a tent in Canada.

So during the five months that I spent having a good and improving time in Canada and reading from time to time some trashy film script that had been sent to me, I was on the look-out for something that might bring in a little money, serve as a distraction and save me from saying yes to the offer of one of the trashy film scripts. It came in the form of an invitation from a man called Cornwall Jackson to become the host of a newly invented television series, that was to be called The Lux Video Theatre. Cornwall Jackson was the West Coast boss of J. Walter Thompson, one of the biggest advertising agencies in the United States.

I had a solid contract for the whole season, a matter of thirty-nine weeks, and I was not being asked actually to read any of the commercials; the most I would have to do would be to slip in a line like, 'And now for the benefit of those housewives who wish to have an easier time on wash day ...', then they would flash to a previously filmed commercial. I would have the right to fiddle with the interview material as much as I liked with a view to making it sound 'just like myself'.

As for money, they were to pay me enough to make everyone reasonably happy though not exactly what I would call a handsome salary. So I decided that they could expect, in return for this salary, only so much work as I would supply on the one day when I was required to be present at the studio. I would not study my lines on any previous day, I would allow them to come to me as we kept running through the performance on the day of the transmission. And I was not being mean or unco-operative or lazy, I truly believed that I could thus do a perfect job.

I failed. The first two weeks I got by without incident. I got the impression that everyone, including Corny Jackson, was disappointed with my performance as a host, but they were not down-hearted. But I really made a mess of the third show. During the last act I was hit by a sudden fear that I had not adequately memorised the dialogue that would be required of me in the final interview. I was dressed in a suit that was intended to suggest a degree of informality, and I had been provided with a lightweight lectern which supported a well bound book, like one in which people somewhat older than my generation might have kept souvenirs of their wedding day.

Monaghan sometimes came to the studio with me and there he was on this occasion brewing himself a cup of coffee. I asked him to run me through the lines of this interview. I was still busily running through the lines when I heard the feverish voice of Walter Grauman, the floor manager, reverberating in the corridor outside, – 'Mister Mason! MISTER MASON!!'

Oh God, I thought, I was going to be late for my appearance at the lectern. So out into the corridor I dash, onto the stage and straight to my lectern, which I grab so desperately that the top segment of it collapses and spills the ornate book onto the floor. I pick up the book and replace it on what is, I hope, the readjusted lectern top. I have previously left it open at a page on which I have jotted three or four key words calculated to help me through the interview. The book is now open at a page on which are scribbled the key words for the previous week's interview. No, they are not on the following page. Straighten up and look relaxed. The camera is staring at you.

Words came slowly. Fortunately the actual interviewee appeared almost at once at my side. And what a friend she turned out to be. It was Thelma Ritter, who had given us so much joy in so many 20th Century Fox films. And now she was proving herself as unflappable as she had always appeared in the roles that she played. She put me back on the track as if I were a derailed locomotive. I hope that I thanked her properly.

The show was over and I walked away from my lectern and made for my dressing room. I tried to look relaxed and devil-may-care in spite of the severe looks of everyone I passed. When I picked out the severe looks emanating from the producer I shrugged and said to him airily, 'Okay, so next week let's have a teleprompter.'

The introductory comments with which I had led into the first three shows concerned themselves with the author of the work we were presenting, the Film Studio which had given us the moving picture from which we had adapted it and the prominent members of the cast. But the format of the fourth play differed. When the host had spoken in his customary manner about author, Film Studio, cast etc., he had to participate to a limited extent in setting up the story itself. That is to say, his off-screen voice described the circumstances and the actual scenery amongst which the drama was to take place. On screen there were five or six scenic shots while the voice droned on. This was an important difference.

The teleprompter was a fairly new invention. One or more of these gadgets were placed above or beside the camera so that an actor or news reader could read the words which were written large on an endlessly rolling and well illuminated band of paper. I did not need to use my teleprompter during the rehearsals, it was to come into play only when we were transmitting. I should mention that these plays of ours were broadcast live, they were not taped. The presence of the teleprompter now made me genuinely relaxed. I had nothing to worry about. I thought.

But when the moment came for us to transmit, the camera cued me with its red eye and I looked good-naturedly and confidently in the direction of the gadget that was to relieve me of all my worries. *The rollers did not turn.* I could not believe it. I was flabbergasted. I daresay some interesting expressions chased each other across my face. But I talked without interruption. The kind of block that makes one forget what one has to say is set up only by the nervous build-up which on this day had been removed. I had no difficulty in finding the words without benefit of teleprompt. But then I reached the point at which I had finished the on-camera introductions and my off-screen voice was to continue with the description of the background of the drama which was about to unfold. When the red eye of the camera that had been photographing me was switched off I completely forgot about the descriptive passage that was to follow. I had only one thought in my mind. I was going to look round until I spotted the guilty party who was responsible for the non-functioning of my teleprompter. Ready on my lips were the words with which I was about to reproach him. They were, 'Fine fucking machine!'

Then miraculously I became aware that my microphone was still open and I was due to start describing the backgrounds. In a sense I was saved. But in another sense an opportunity to become immortal was snatched. People would have said, 'James Mason? Oh yes. He's the man who said "fucking" on the Lux Video Show. He's famous.'

Television in the United States has now become the biggest advertising gadget in the world. On my recent visits I have been made aware that to the mass of people nothing in the world actually *exists* unless it has been plugged or discussed on the box. Being a foreigner I do not like to be caught talking or writing about Network Television because it would only give me a bad name and, being in the entertainment business, *I need* the box to let people know that I exist. I mean I need the talk shows for their advertisement value and I recognise that movie movies are fast disappearing and that we all now have to project our dramas on to some form of television screen, whether it be a regular old-fashioned free-as-air network operation or pay television or cable television or the cassette which is flung up and bounced back from a satellite or a new fangled disc which you play like an L.P. But I don't need to read commercials, thank God.

You'd think that if you caught a well known actor reading a commercial it would be a sign that the poor fellow was hard up. Not so. I was always amazed in the old days when I saw that it was being done by Hollywood's wealthiest. Bing Crosby for example was a well-known Croesus. And yet when we were sweating our guts out on one of those Playhouse Ninety shows it gave us no pleasure to see that the intermission was turned over to Crosby plugging a gas company in return for, among other perquisities, an installation in his new house in Palm Springs.

I take this opportunity to confess that I have betrayed my principles three times. Once I was talked into doing a commercial for Gillette razor blades, on the grounds that it would be used as an interruption during the World Series which everyone in the United States would be watching. This was one up for Russell Birdwell. The second was for Motorola Television. Pamela informed me that all I would have to do was to make an appointment at Universal Studios and be photographed doing a ten second spot, and we would be given the best colour television that RCA was then manufacturing. I pointed out that we already had a colour television set.

'But we need one for upstairs.'

'Ah yes, of course.'

It certainly sounded like a bargain. So I took myself up to Universal Studios, and this is what I had to do.

The camera would catch my head and shoulders looking somewhat off-camera. I would then turn and, looking straight at the camera, I would first smile and then say – See me at my best. See me on a Motorola!

I felt as Oedipus must have felt when first confronted by the sphinx. It was that sort of a challenge. The telespectator had practically never seen me. I may at that time have made some feeble guest appearance on a Jack Benny or Bob Hope Show, but I don't think that I had intruded even to that extent. My exposure must have been limited to the running of some old and tired English film like *I Met a Murderer* or *The Mill on the Floss*.

Thus the text they had given me clearly made little sense. The dedicated telespectator would know me only as an actor whose movies, when sufficiently aged, sometimes appeared on the box. But there was no point in discussing the issue. To the director and his crew I was just another face that had to be put through the prescribed routine. It was a simple job, so let's knock it off.

Simple? The first problem was the smile. It so happens that I cannot place a smile upon my face – snap – just like that. I could find many people to testify that they have seen me smile in private life. I can also smile when I am inside a character when I am acting. But this Motorola smile was something beyond my range again. It is on just such an occasion that someone will say,

'Just be yourself.'

But what sort of a self was this person who flashed a smile when he turned to a loaded camera and then had the gall to say, 'See me at my best. See me on a Motorola!' without shrieking with laughter?

I sweated a lot. A make-up man kept patting my face with a powder puff wrapped in tissue. I tried, to the tune of thirty-three takes. I laughed my way through the first twenty-five or so. Then I worked my way through the rest with a grim determination. I cannot imagine what my smile looked like. Finally the director issued instructions to print the last two takes and gave up. I had noticed that he was showing signs of boredom.

I got the television set but I cannot believe that they ever used my ten second spot. None of my friends caught it. I saw a number of others performing the same text, some established television performers, some just movie actors like myself. I was full of admiration for the ease with which they flicked on that smile. Laraine Day, for instance, gave a stunning performance.

Skipping ahead momentarily to the year 1964, I perpetrated my third and final commercial reading effort because I happened to be genuinely short of money. Pamela and I were divorcing each other and I was living under the strain of something called 'Temporary Maintenance'. My affairs were now handled by the Hugh French Agency and the son of the house, Robin, told me that a certain San Francisco advertising agency had offered ten thousand dollars – I could use it – if I would do a commercial for Thunderbird Wine. I said,

'Yes, if I can okay the text.'

They agreed. I then corresponded with the agency and took some pleasure making idiotic suggestions, some of which were accepted. For instance, 'This wine is like nothing you have ever tasted.'

I was feeling guilty for having accepted the job and was taking it out on them. The advertising agency with whom I was communicating may have been the originators of the slogan, 'Have A Happy Day', which is what the telephone operator said when I called. The logo on their stationery consisted of a drawing of a smile accompanied by these same words, which I suppose one might say, caught the mood of the ever-expanding population of California. I then took some pleasure in telling the agency that if they wanted to film the commercial during the period they had specified they would have to send their crew to Cadaques in Spain where I would be filming. Agreed. I was staying in the Rocamar Hotel and I made arrangements with the management for the work to be done in a banquet hall which opened off the main lobby. It was the best we could offer.

The camera never reached its destination. The roads approaching Cadaques are narrow and unfriendly, unlike the town itself which is adorable. But at that time no provision was being made for the kind of tourists with whom the coastal areas of Spain are closely associated. It was like a little art colony patronised almost exclusively by the French. This was one of the few periods in my life when I actually took some pride in the automobile in which I kept driving around Europe. It was a good looking Alvis and it took a lot of punishment on the rough and sometimes precipitious roads that led to Cadaques.

The car containing the Have a Happy Day crew and equipment, turned over. The crew were unhurt but the equipment went over a precipice. Fortunately the day chosen for our happy event was a Sunday and so they were able to borrow equipment from the company for whom I was working. (It was a film called *Les Pianos Mécaniques*.) It was not easy, because the Rocamar Hotel catered for more tourists on a Sunday than on working days. Even when we managed to keep them out of the banquet room the sound recording was a problem.

About a month later Have a Happy Day contacted me and told me that there was nothing technically wrong with the sound recording, only that my voice did not sound quite so happy or enthusiastic as they would have wished. Could they make a rendezvous with me in London which would allow them to post-synchronise my voice and give the whole thing more of a lift? I said, 'What about my appearance? Did I look all right?'

'Oh yes. Everything else was fine . . . Have a happy day.'

'You too.'

A date was made and I did what they wanted. But they had been wrong about my appearance which proved to be almost as down-beat as my voice. The only point in my going on at such length about this escapade is that the result, which I saw later, was terribly funny. The post-synchronising had been done in the easiest conditions that salubrious Soho can offer. There was no longer the stress that went with a Rocamar Hotel bulging with Sunday business, and consequently my voice was as chipper as that of a contestant in a BBC guessing game. So that what you got eventually on the screen was a jolly eruption of idiotic sales talk oddly issuing from a glum actor. I had several happy days but I doubt if I sold much Thunder-bird.

To get back to 1955, the year of Lux Video, I was slightly involved in another event that is a member of the advertising family, the award-giving ceremony of the Academy for Motion Picture Arts and Sciences. Let me say at once that I am not one of those who knock the Academy awards. On the contrary, they provide one of the most popular television spectacles in the world. I cannot quote figures and I assume that within the United States the Academy show cannot quite compete with the World Series, the Presidential Elections and the play-offs of other spectator sports, but outside the United States it must surely have been the most popular show on record, though recently the interest may well have flagged.

The way it is told, the presentation of the awards was at first an occasion for mutual back slapping and comparatively informal jollity among the top Hollywood people. First there was a banquet then the presentations. Leg pulling and fun were not excluded because it was essentially a domestic affair. But I am sure that even in the beginning there must have been some little Birdwell brain in there who recognised the true value of the occasion. By design or by accident it became a merchandising weapon of the highest calibre. Throughout the twenties, thirties and forties, when the compulsive response of moviegoers was as pre-dictable as the year of the Wildebeest, Hollywood's own evaluation of the stars was no laughing matter, it was a supreme court decision.

An Oscar-winning film instantly doubled its market value. And in the days of the big studios a variety of pressures were understandably exerted during the voting season. The salaries of the Oscar-winning stars in those days would not necessarily soar, because most of them were contracted to the big studios and their salaries would increase strictly according to the escalations specified.

Since the collapse of the big studios the winning of an Oscar has had a magical effect on an actor's salary. In the old days the 'Trade Mark' on a piece of movie merchandise was the name of the company that turned it out. The public knew that the name MGM, Paramount, etc., guaranteed satisfaction even more than the names of the stars. But now in order to attach a Trade Mark that will suggest quality the independent producer can only rely on the names of his stars. And a player who is associated with a hit picture or who wins an Oscar or is even nominated for one is thus elevated to superstardom. The whole scene makes a fascinating study.

Both Judy Garland and myself were nominated for Oscars as a result of *A Star is Born*. If one or both of us had won, it would have done a lot for the gross receipts and we ourselves could have asked for a raise if and when we got another offer. Judy was in Cedars of Lebanon Hospital when Oscar time came, expecting a child. She and Sid seemed convinced that she would win, so much so that they allowed CBS to erect a scaffolding outside the window of her room, the better to peer inside and photograph her when the good word came through.

I was less sanguine. I love winning prizes, and an Oscar would have been a great treat for the oneupman in me. But since Hollywood had shown no great excitement about the film, it would be very strange, I figured, if a Hollywood cross-section, the Academy Members, were now to honour us.

The top people in the Academy were said to have been disappointed in previous years by the absence of some of the best known nominees. This year our friend Johnny Negulesco had been put in charge of the entire stage show which incorporated the actual presentations and, to make those top people happy, he had designed the stage show in such a way that all the nominees would be actively involved; they would make little speeches, sing little songs, tell funny stories or simply introduce themselves to each other.

Johnny had included me in this dazzling programme and he told me when and where I should be required to rehearse. Without a flicker of hesitation I said that I would be there. But I was lying. I had no intention of being either at the rehearsal or at the show itself. But I did not wish to discuss his programme nor to argue with him; it would have put us both in a bad humour. The Oscar Show is always a little better if things go wrong, so I had no need to feel guilty about letting them down. In the unlikely event of my winning there would be someone connected with the production who would be only too happy to bound up onto the stage and accept it for me.

The rules of the game insist that no one learn in advance the names of the winners, with the possible exception of an accountant in the employ of Price Waterhouse, whose tongue has been used to seal the envelopes. It is assumed that what the audience most like to see is the crestfallen look on the faces of the losing nominees when that envelope is opened and the name of the winner read out. In 1955 the television camera still had a problem with white shirts, so anyone who thought that he had a chance to be photographed in close-up would wear a blue shirt with his Tuxedo. It was true that when the camera played on the faces of the losers there would always be one or two who would pretend that they did not care. They took it as an acting exercise, but the smiles on display were uniformly sour. But I was not a good enough sport to put on the blue shirt and play this game. Betty Bacall, whom I happened to see somewhere during the following days, said that I was a cad. She was right, of course.

But I still maintain that it is a terrific show and gives people a lot of pleasure all over the world. There are those who become very frosty on the subject of these awards and argue that they have no validity as a means of judging quality. They take the whole thing too seriously. I remember reading a quote in the newspaper attributed to Dyan Cannon when she was speaking of her relations with her ex-husband, Cary Grant. She said that on Oscar night he was so emotionally involved that he jumped up and down on the bed abusing the nominees he feared might win. Now that is the proper spirit. Also it is a great occasion for laying bets. In that year the best actor and actress in leading roles turned out to be Marlon Brando and Grace Kelly.

But I was really sick to think that poor Judy was prinking herself up in that hospital expecting that any minute the red eye of the CBS camera outside her window would light up and make her Queen of the May.

In 1955 my film acting career reached the point at which I found myself playing the part of Lucy Ball's guardian angel in *Forever Darling*. During the two or three preceding years Lucy and her husband Desi Arnaz had been accepted showbiz champions by reason not only of the enormous popularity of their television programme but also the skill and technical originality with which it was made. All the settings involved had been lined up on a sound stage and in them the acting team performed as in a theatre. The real laughter was recorded while several cameras photographed the antics on stage. Lucy was such a brilliant comedienne that I always rated her the best actress in the United States. She is certainly one whose shows will still be worth re-issuing in the twenty-first century. In saying this I am not putting down the ladies who have been so impressive recently in more sombre material, e.g. Jane Fonda; it is just that with comedy comes joy.

Having apologised to Jane Fonda, I now apologise to Lucy Ball because, when asked by interviewers which of my films I would most happily consign to the incinerator, I developed the habit of saying *Forever Darling*. Let me explain, if I can. First of all it was based on a not very original or interesting script, though it did at least provide Lucy with the opportunity to do some funny bits. And, as I have said elsewhere, all film footage featuring Lucy Ball should be mounted in gold. But what made the film odious to me was that in it I rendered a performance, which, of many low grade performances recorded on celluloid, was probably the worst.

Although I am not trying to excuse myself, I should warn aspiring actors that the part of a guardian angel is one to avoid. That is, unless the angel is treated as a figure of some sort of fun. The director of this film was Alexander Hall. I did not precisely blame him for my failure, but by dint of his association with it he inevitably ran into some disfavour in my mind. Many years later I learned that he had directed the low budget MGM film which everyone adored, called *Here Comes Mr Jordan*. So he must have been a pretty good director. Not only that, but the actor who played Mr Jordan, another guardian angel, Claude Rains, must have been an even better actor than I took him for. I have no cop out. Guardian angels are not for me.

But it was a pleasure making the film. I enjoyed the company and we had the additional bonus of shooting in Yosemite Park for a while. Since I had no very exacting work to perform, I could devote myself to the study of the sequoia, the plantain and the redwood and all those other stalwarts, and look for bears.

Much better than all this was the arrival on June the twenty-sixth of a son, to whom after some delay we gave the name Alexander Morgan. Alexander the Great and Alexander Korda for dreams of Empire and Henry

369

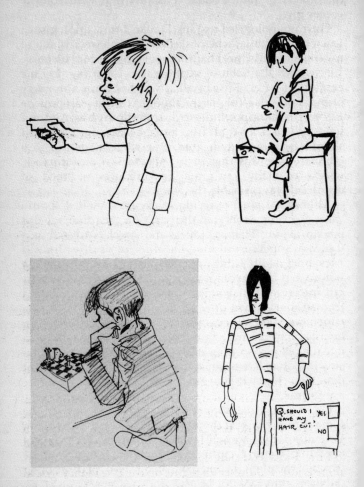

Morgan

Morgan, the Pirate, and J. P. Morgan for more commonplace buccaneering.

Unlike Portland, who had been looked after exclusively by her mother during the pre-school years, Morgan had a devoted and infallible nurse, Martha Miller, who kept her eye on him until he was six at which age he had already taken up gun-slinging and became a tremendous bore because people never stopped giving him toy guns with which he would shoot us all down. Open the door to be greeted by a burp gun. He was still at it when he and I were both working in a film called *Hero's Island* on the island of Catalina. Neville Brand was another actor in the film and, being the second most decorated American soldier of World War II, was even more aggravated than the rest of us by Morgan's eternal bang-banging.

Assuming one of his more alarming expressions, he said to Morgan, 'Never point a gun at a person unless you intend to kill him.'

There was very little gun-play after that. Flashing ahead another six years or so Morgan was into music for a couple of years. As a member of his audience I enjoyed this period very much. He had a little group with whom he would get together and try out numbers which one or other of them had thought up. He had hitherto been threatening to become an actor. I thought that he could do much better for himself, and that this musical interest might well lead to a general gratification.

I told him that if he were inclined to pay attention to his lessons, become interested in books, go to college and study law, it would be a cinch for a smart boy like him to become President of the United States, if the idea appealed to him. But I said that the idea that a friend of mine, let alone a son, should set his sights on the Presidency would certainly not appeal to me. On the other hand music was the only creative art which guaranteed not only an enjoyable showbiz life, but also a just reward. I mentioned ASCAP.

During his late teens he observed that, while his sister

Portland had a lot of talent but no ambition, he had ambition but no talent. This did not seem to bother him, partly because he was aware of the exaggeration. The talents were there but they had not yet been pigeon-holed.

17/Grenada

In 1955 Darryl Zanuck, the big man of 20th Century Fox, made a major decision which affected not only his own life but also the lives of his friends and the lives of his friends' friends. I, for example, was a friend and client of Charlie Feldman who, in turn, was a friend of Zanuck.

Charlie told me that he had discussed with Zanuck an employment contract for me with 20th Century Fox. I was to be hired not just as an actor but as a triple threat: producer, director, actor. Did I want it? It sounded very nice. Yes, I did want it.

But I could not figure out how Charlie had managed to swing this on my behalf. I now have a theory but unfortunately neither Charlie nor Zanuck is available for verification. Zanuck at that time was tired of his life as production chief in the 20th Century Studio. He wanted to go to Europe and produce important pictures for the organisation, but independently. He wanted to become the big international maestro, something like Jack Warner who spent much of his time in a grand house on Cap d'Antibes, but with a touch of Diaghilev added. André Hakim would teach him to speak French for starters.

It was noticeable that, before he launched this new career, he made some generous deals with old friends in Hollywood to keep them happy during his absence. One was obviously Charlie Feldman. Charlie was a great one for buying the film rights of plays and books and hiring writers to develop these as film projects. Zanuck bought at this time about a dozen of these for an impressive sum. I, being a client of Charlie's, also benefited. And there were others much more important than I, to whom lovely deals were handed out which might have been difficult to explain by an application of the rules of supply and demand.

It was a time of change. Strange things were happening at all the big studios as a result of the Anti-Trust Legislation which had the effect of divorcing them from the theatres which they had owned. Darryl Zanuck's whacky behaviour was a symptom of the general disarray in which the big studios found themselves. Palace revolutions, mysterious changes of policy, selling off back lots, the merging of majors, the disappearance of the feudal bosses, and the recognition of the agents as a master race – these could be chapter headings for a short history of Hollywood following Zanuck's convenient exit.

It was convenient for me in my undemanding way and presumably convenient for Buddy Adler who was to become the new boss as soon as Zanuck had packed his bags.

But Zanuck was still very much there when I checked in and so remained for the first months of my contracted service. My only stipulation had been that I would accept the contract only if and when I was definitely assigned to a project as producer. Zanuck welcomed this condition and had a quick come-back when I went to the studio to talk things over with him. He said,

'I have often thought of remaking *Jane Eyre*. It was one of our big successes.'

'I'm amazed.'

'It made a lot of money, didn't it, Lou?'

He looked to Lou Schreiber for confirmation. Lou said, 'Oh, very big.'

I do not know what Schreiber's job was called officially, chief of staff, executioner, hatchet man, fixer? He was the executive in charge of keeping Zanuck happy.

I told Zanuck that I was surprised that his previous *Jane Eyre* had been such a success. I was very careful of what I said because it would not have been politic to tear one of his big hits to pieces at our first meeting. I said that it was a pity that the later sections had not retained the excitement and quality of the opening scenes, something very gentle like that.

The opening scenes had indeed been excellent. Henry Daniell made a terrifying Mr Brocklehurst and Peggy Ann Garner played the young Jane very touchingly. But everything went to pieces after that, including the musical score by that clever composer Bernard Herrmann. The scenes from the book had been injudiciously chosen, and the writer had made no visible attempt to supply a third Act.

I asked Zanuck to let me think about it for a couple of days, and added that if I could think of a satisfactory formula for a fresh adaptation I would be happy to take it on. I really looked forward to discussing the story with him because Zanuck had a reputation for being wonderfully helpful and sympathetic with writers and directors. But it was not to be. I told him a few days later that I had found my key for the treatment of the story. So he told me to choose a suitable writer, have him put on the payroll and go to work. On the one hand I was slightly disappointed that he did not want me to tell him about my key, and on the other hand I thought that perhaps it would be as well not to discuss it in case he try to talk me out of it.

I interviewed a number of writers and selected one who had recently done well with a stylish play on Broadway. But she did not pick up the savour of Charlotte Brontë and we wasted time, money and paper. Zanuck now counselled me to try my luck with an Irish writer, John Byrne, who had written a play which appealed to Zanuck and had been rewarded with a contract at the studio. This meant that he was already on the payroll for a less than enormous fee and I might just as well use him up and see how he responded to Charlotte Brontë. After a couple of days I knew that the arrangement would work.

Meanwhile I was given the go ahead to see what I could do with *A High Wind in Jamaica* by Richard Hughes.

This is a great novel, but it always got the better of those who tried to shape it up for a film. Charlie Feldman had owned the film rights but never developed a worthwhile script, and if he had done so he would have got a better price for it from Zanuck, for it was one of the parcel of books and film scripts that the latter had bought from him. I worked with a good writer called Edward Hope on this project and finally we turned in a script which was a trifle longer than we had originally intended, say 180 pages which by the standards of serious scriptwriters is nothing to be scared of. It was a well written script and I expected to be summoned by Zanuck to discuss the final sequences which were a very delicate affair and could be handled in several different ways. But he surprised me. I received a curt message saying that he was not interested in reading the script until I had reduced it to a more readable 130 page maximum. One of the other producers at the studio who had been studying Zanuck for a number of years assured me that he had been happy to buy the property because the title *A High Wind in Jamaica* held promise of a Caribbean swashbuckle loaded with Errol Flynn. I was disinclined to accept his theory.

I made no effort to shorten the script because I knew that Zanuck had finally got around to packing his bags and that his mantle of authority would shortly be assumed by Buddy Adler, with whom I could maybe discuss the project later.

There was a Zanuck coterie which consisted of those whom he invited to his house in Palm Springs where croquet was played. As a Hollywood cult croquet was at that time played not extensively but big. The recognised masters were Zanuck, Sam Goldwyn, Negulesco and George Sanders. Into these areas Pamela had not established a bridgehead. But I got to know one semi-social facet of Zanuck since I had now been welcomed into the executives' dining room.

Friends at Paramount had told me that the atmosphere in their executive dining room was entirely different from ours. Luncheon at Paramount, they said, was a truly social event with the kind of bonhomie that one would find in a men's club. Talk of world events, local news and gossip, football scores, broads. It was not like this in our dining room. When I told Nunnally Johnson that I was now a staff producer at Fox, he told me that, while enjoying all the perquisites, I should never make the mistake of actually producing a film. I got the impression that many of my table companions held the same views. But they were better adapted to the table play. I cannot remember anything that was discussed in our dining room except the Dow Averages, the ups and downs of the shares that each individual owned or had just sold, the latest oil strikes and the affairs of 20th Century Fox. They were an amiable bunch of men and they all seemed to know by experience that this last item of conversation must be handled only in a very positive manner. Films currently in production would be discussed positively and, of course, all past productions that had been successful at the box office, but those that had been unsuccessful somehow were never allowed to intrude, that is until they qualified as antiques. I heard Lou Schreiber, for instance, make several laughing references to failures of long ago. Lou, incidentally, became in the dining room a straight man for Zanuck. In the manner of Ed McMahon vis-à-vis Johnny Carson, Lou would whack the table in approval of Zanuck's jokes. I never got close to the real Zanuck, although during this period he treated me with the utmost consideration. He would say things to me like, 'Jimmy, we were running this rough-cut yesterday and the girl in it is beginning to look really great. You ought to take a look at her. She may be just what you are looking for. Get them to run it for you.'

He went to France before a firm decision was made about *Jane Eyre* – unfortunately, because I still had the feeling that, given a chance, I could talk to him. And I could never satisfactorily talk to his successor. At the time when I started to work on the project, it had been assumed that I would play the part of Mr Rochester and that we would hunt for a girl, who was not necessarily a star, for the part of Jane. Ideally our prey would have been a nice little mousy English girl, but I had not spotted a Jane Eyre in any of the English films I had seen lately. And I did not close my mind to the possibility of finding an acceptable American girl who could do the trick. In fact I had my eye on one who had recently been in a small Western film that had been made at our very own studio. She was a girl from Louisiana called Joanne Woodward. She could act and look mouselike at the same time and I ventured to suppose that she could be persuaded to speak with an accent that Phyllis Bentley and fellow members of the Brontë Society would happily endorse.

But it was not to be. Another crisis had further ruffled up the composure of our big men, and so one day I heard Buddy Adler say to me, 'We have sent the script of *Jane Eyre* to Audrey Hepburn's agent. He has had it some time now. Things being the way they are, we'll go with the project only if we can get a big female star into it. After all it is not going to be a cheap picture. If we can't get Audrey, I guess we shall shelve it for the present.'

I did not even attempt to argue with him, because the argument was right there in the script just as it was in the book, and our presentation of Jane on the screen must be true to the book. Useless to point out that Audrey Hepburn just happened to be the most beautiful woman in movies. A head turner. The whole point about Jane was that no one noticed her when she came into a room or left it.

Of course I should have paid more attention to Nunnally Johnson's advice and just had a good time in my office, reading books, writing letters, conducting interviews, but no, I was determined to make something. I showed Buddy Adler a piece that had appeared in the *New Yorker* magazine under the general heading 'Annals of Medicine', and he gave me his okay to go ahead with the project. We called it *Bigger than Life*.

I interviewed writers and settled on Cyril Hume and

Richard Maibaum to do the script. The Annals of Medicine in the *New Yorker* always concerned actual medical cases meticulously documented. They made compulsive reading. The one that I chose concerned a schoolteacher who was not making quite so much money as he felt he needed, so he took an evening job as a taxi despatcher. Since he suffered from severe arthritic pains, he consulted a doctor who prescribed cortisone, which alleviated the pain and gave him a feeling of well being. The doctor rationed the dosage because he knew of the dangerous side effects, but the schoolteacher found that the prescription could be filled concurrently by several pharmacists if he handled the matter shrewdly. So he went plunging into all the side effects one after the other, starting with the euphoria and ending with the paranoia. His euphoria was punctuated by periods of depression. He tended to treat his wife with contempt and his son with a devotion which became so severe as to be sadistic. Finally the son, dismayed by his father's fitful behaviour, attempted to destroy the cortisone tablets. Convinced now that the son would grow up to be a criminal, the father planned to kill the entire family. It almost ended in tragedy.

Our script having been accepted, copies were circulated among all the departments that would be involved logistically. I recognised the need to have the film made in Cinemascope and for the De Luxe laboratory to handle the processing. If I had had more weight to throw about I would have tried to persuade them to let the film be shot in black and white so as to avoid the lurid colouring that was at that time the speciality of this lab. With black and white we could have aspired to a documentary reality. But I knew that nothing on earth would make them relinquish the Cinemascope format at that time. Any shade of blue came out so fiercely when treated by De Luxe that I figured that the only thing to do was to eliminate it completely, allow it on to our screen only in the form of the inevitable Californian sky.

The greater part of the films that were made at our studio followed the traditional big studio routine, that is to say it was only when the staff producer had developed a script to the satisfaction of himself and the studio boss that a director was approached. In this respect the modern routine is quite different. The initiative is now usually taken by a free-lance director or by an independent group which has as its nucleus a director or a superstar. One would think that the new routine must be superior, but it does not necessarily work out that way because the initial launching of the project becomes the main task and, once that has been done, the scripting is sometimes neglected.

Ours, let's say, was an old-fashioned operation and the film was generally regarded as a failure. But it was not a failure *because* it was an old-fashioned op. It failed for several good reasons. It was a little ahead of its time, suggesting as it did that an easy acceptance of miracle drugs, even those endorsed by the A.M.A., could land us in a heap of trouble. Secondly the colour and the Cinemascope detracted from its credibility. And thirdly I made a big mistake in allowing myself to play the central character. I had been an international star for over ten years and, in spite of my determination to play all sorts of different roles, I was stuck with a certain image which was solidly entrenched in the mind of the American moviegoer. He saw me as a foreigner (some had read that I came from England, others knew me for my appearances as a German or an Irishman) and as one who was mean to people. (I had been mean to Stewart Granger and Alan Ladd, not to mention Ann Todd who had appeared to relish the treatment.) So I should not have cast myself as an ordinary American small town school teacher.

Although the production was a failure and was thus not likely to show up as a subject of discussion in the executives' dining room, something happened during the course of production which makes it worth recording as one of my more bizarre experiences.

The director I chose was Nicholas Ray and my choice

was approved by Adler and Lou Schreiber. I had admired a number of Ray's films but it was his handling of *Rebel without a Cause* which persuaded me that he was the right man for our little film. As soon as he checked into the studio I went down with him to have an introductory confab with Adler. As we were leaving he said,

'Oh, there's a little thing I'd like to talk to Lou Schreiber about. Do you think I could go and see him now, Buddy?'

'I'm sure that will be okay. I'll call him to let him know you'll be dropping by.'

So along we go to Schreiber's office. And Nick Ray made what I thought was a surprising request. He gave Lou the name of a young Englishman whom he wanted to use as dialogue director.

'English?'

'Yes, but he is enormously talented and I am sure he will be able to help us a lot.'

'Well ... Okay, we'll have to get permission from Washington and I don't know how we will prove that he is indispensable. But don't worry, Nick. I'll get Frank McCarthy to take care of it right away.'

Frank McCarthy was the executive who took care of all home and foreign relationships, everything to do with censorships, permissions, licences and – what proved to be especially important in the case of our film, clearances from important public bodies such as the American Medical Association. He was a big man, this McCarthy, having been a personal aide to Eisenhower during the war, retiring with the rank of General. Later he produced the very impressive film about Patton.

As we went back to my office, Nick explained that the young Englishman, Gavin Lambert, was the editor and film critic of a magazine called *Sight and Sound* which catered to the tastes of discriminating moviegoers. But what had impressed Nick most of all was the little black and white feature film which Lambert had recently made on location in Morocco, on a shoestring and entirely his own initiative. Realising that this did not adequately explain the need to employ Lambert as a dialogue director, he said that as a younger man he had been taken on as an apprentice and enormously helped by Elia Kazan and as a result he had always felt it was his duty, in the event of finding someone with outstanding talent, to help him in a similar way.

We did not communicate very well, Nick and I. He was a great one for lengthy pauses. He made it quite clear that in his opinion our script needed more work but I could not get any specific suggestions out of him. And this accounted for much of our pause play, with me waiting for him to break his silence about the script. Would he like to meet the writers Hume and Maibaum and brief them about the improvements that he had in mind? No, he definitely did not want to talk to them. And so on.

He opened up considerably, so far as general conversation was concerned, when Gavin Lambert arrived from London. Everything rolled along splendidly so long as we avoided talking about the script. Then, suddenly, one day he told me that he thought that we should ask the eminent writer Clifford Odets to do an overall re-write. I said no, I did not think that was at all a good idea. I pointed out that he, Nick, had claimed writing credits on some of his previous films, as indeed had I; and we ourselves could surely tackle whatever was bothering him. I thought that we already had the material with which to make a good film. I learned later that he had made the same suggestion to Adler who presumably had backed me up since there was no more talk about a general re-write and we got down to shooting the film.

A subsidiary reason for my anti-Odets stance had been the conviction that a first class writer, on being given the go-ahead to re-write an existing script, would inevitably go back to square one and give his own personal rendering of the whole story. The average Hollywood writer would make sure that he re-wrote everything down to the last comma, if only to make sure that he be given the entire writing credit. I would not of course expect such an attitude from Odets, it would be strictly the artist in him that would oblige him to do the whole thing over. I was certain that our film would be a success or a failure judged solely on the content of our story and not on the quality of the writing. 'Therefore, let's do it, Nick. Let's not procrastinate.' Later in his career Nick developed procrastination into a fine art.

Our rather modest budget would not allow us to shoot certain exterior scenes 'Night for Night'. Shooting at night is always expensive, involving as it does increased labour and lighting costs and the wastage of time, caused by switching from a daytime schedule to a night time schedule and back again. So we had to shoot these scenes 'Day for Night' which works well only under certain specific conditions. In our case, with the added liability of De Luxe colour, these scenes were bound to look very nasty. But apart from this Nick and I had few worries. A couple of times a week Nick would say to me at the end of the day,

'Er ... I think that one of the sequences that we are supposed to do tomorrow could be improved. So I'll get together with Gavin and we'll see if we can come up with any ideas. You have no objection?'

'None at all.'

I have never known the script that would not welcome an improving hand. If anyone comes up with a good suggestion, whether he is the director or one of the actors, or the property man, I say God bless him. We had to submit any substantial alterations, which we might happen to make, to Adler's office at least a day before shooting them because with a delicate subject like ours his approval and Frank McCarthy's and in some cases even the A.M.A.'s had to be obtained.

So now we come to the penultimate day of shooting. Nick comes to me towards the end of the day and says,

'Er ... James ... This last sequence has always worried me just a little. I think maybe we can improve it.'

'I feel the same way about it.'

'Trouble is ... I have to attend the running of a film tonight ... Rather a long one ...'

'That's easy. While you are at the running I'll have a session with Gavin. And when you are free, Gavin can carry on with you. How about that?'

'That might work all right.'

So that is how I leave it. Nick is a tall man, with an impressive forehead and a handsome if somewhat dilapidated face. He is accident-prone, a weakness that gives rise to some droll stories. He is said to have been standing on a street corner in New York waiting to cross over when a taxi, in taking the corner rather too closely, managed to get one of its door handles or other projections hooked under Nick's belt buckle and dragged him for an entire city block. In some ways he resembled that character in Al Capp's strip cartoon, Li'l Abner, who is easily recognisable on account of the small cloud of bad luck that is always featured about his head. However there are no accidents nor unlucky incidents during our film, only the surprise is to come next day.

Nick greets me with a new kind of troubled look on his long face. He says – without any pauses,

'The darnedest thing happened last night, James. Gavin picked me up when the running was over and we went straight around to Clifford's. It was late, and Clifford had already taken his sleeping tablets.'

'Oh.'

It is now my turn to hold a pause while I get this lively denouement under control.

'... Hmm ... So?'

'So I have made some arrangements and I think it will be all right.'

'Arrangements?'

'Yes. I've arranged to have a table and chair set up behind a flat in the corner of the stage. He'll be able to work there this morning while we are shooting the sequence that does not need the re-write. We'll have lunch together and discuss his idea for the last sequence and, if it's okay, we'll go ahead and shoot it in the afternoon.'

The man is talking to me as if I am a party to the midnight script conferences that have been going on. A question that still remains unanswered is does Clifford Odets get paid for his night's work? All the rest of us profited by his generosity, for the little improvements, which I had been attributing to the Lambert-Ray combo, were all worth while. Many of them may indeed have been Lambert or Lambert-Ray improvements. It never occurred to me at that time to enquire how frequently Nick had been picking the master's brain.

Lunch with Clifford. In the previous sequence the school teacher, at the peak of his craziness, has passed judgement on his allegedly lazy and unfilial son and has cited the example of Father Abraham who had no hesitation in taking a knife to his son Isaac when God so commanded him. The boy is saved in our case by the intervention of the sports master (Walter Matthau) who knocks the father unconscious.

We have established that the father is taken to hospital and further knocked out by heavy sedation. Now comes the wake-up scene, which up to this point has been rather feebly and unconvincingly written. Clifford's contribution is especially valuable to us because the audience knows that the story is over and will only be kept in its seats if we come up with something that is really worth listening to on its own account.

Clifford's success is due to his shrewd handling of the teacher's subconscious. The wife is there by his hospital bed, waiting for him to recognise her and come to himself. Suddenly he becomes sharply awake and intent on telling her his dream. Clifford has played the Abraham connection. The teacher says that he has been talking to Abraham Lincoln in his dream and it is so touchingly put into the words of Clifford Odets that all seems to be well, both for the characters in the story and for Messrs Ray, Lambert and Mason.

But there is one nasty moment. Soon after lunch I am

sitting in a small portable dressing room which is parked just outside the door of the stage on which we are working. Inside Nick is rehearsing a re-written section with Barbara Rush and Walter Matthau. My door is open and suddenly I see three men marching purposefully down the sidewalk towards the door of the stage. They are Lou Schreiber, Frank McCarthy and Sid Rogell. This last character is the studio manager, whose job is to look after the physical running of the plant. I could never figure why he was a member of this marauding detail. Lou's presence I could understand because he wanted to arrest us all, and Frank was qualified to plead the case against us – whatever we had done. They were moving fast, clearly intent on mischief, so I bounced out of my box and stood in their way.

'Where are you going?'

'I understand,' said Lou, 'that Nick is shooting some material that has not been approved. He can't do that. You know perfectly well that you can't go ahead ...'

I then went into one of my shouting acts – well almost shouting.

'You're not going on that stage,' I said, 'they're working in there. Nick is rehearsing a very difficult scene, and I won't have him upset. We will listen to your complaints later, but not now. You can come in here and discuss it with me if you want.'

Somebody should have said to me, 'Who do you think you are?'

But they chose not to pick up that cue. To my surprise they dispersed. At least Rogell dispersed, having no doubt realised that no problem existed here for a studio manager. He had just been supplying additional bulk. Lou looked red and flustered and repeated his original charge with a variety of different inflections. Then he too disappeared and I was left with Frank McCarthy who, though far from relaxed, at least knew what he needed to keep saying to me. It was all on account of the A.M.A. On several occasions he had had to tell me about little things in the script which

386

might ruffle the surface of our good relations and bring out the bully in them. And now he was particularly embarrassed because we were doing it on a day when Buddy Adler was away. He made it sound as if we were purposely taking advantage of the boss's absence.

I managed to persuade him that there was absolutely nothing in the new material that had the least medical significance. I described the scenes to him in detail and apologised for my inability to press a copy of them into his hands, but Nick happened to be using the only copy right now on the stage. So everyone ended up reasonably happy.

Nick had been a close friend of Marilyn Monroe, who happened to be approaching the final scenes of a film called *Bus Stop* on one of the adjacent stages. Since at the end of our last day of shooting we intended to serve drink to all our crew Nick suggested we ask Marilyn over. So she came and it was nice for us all because she was an amiable lady. Only when she was working might one find her difficult. And even on this brief occasion I caught a glimpse of this other Marilyn. She came over to our stage before we had shot our very last scene. I was lying in the hospital bed, beside which a doctor was standing. A nurse entered and offered the doctor a selection of instruments on a tray. That was it, just one of those connecting shots. When it was done, Nick said,

'Hey, I've got an idea. Wouldn't it be funny if we took a shot of Marilyn carrying the tray instead of the nurse?'

A number of the boys laughed their approval.

'It will be a terrific laugh at the rushes,' said one of them. Another said,

'They'll think our rushes have got mixed up with *Bus Stop* rushes. Ha ha ha.'

'Okay,' said Nick, 'turn them over ...'

Action.

A child would have understood what we were up to, but not Marilyn. Instant panic took over.

'Oh Nick,' she said, 'tell me what you want me to do! I can't do it, Nick! Tell me!'

387

'Cut,' said Nick.

He hugged Marilyn and comforted her and then said that he did not think it was such a funny idea after all, so let's not do it. Come on, Marilyn, what do you want to drink?

Nick always had very good relations with the Festival mob, the people who administered, organised the programmes for and wrote about the International Film Festivals. Of the European events the Hollywood favourite was then and still is the Annual Film Festival at Cannes, because it is so frenziedly commercial. In 1956 the major studios were not really on speaking terms with the Venice Festival, the organisers of which insisted on choosing the films to be entered from each country themselves rather than letting the Americans, for instance, decide which films they wanted to send. But the Venice people still sent their prospectors over to the States and extended invitations to individual producers or directors. Nick knew one or more of the Festival people and ran our film for them. They liked it and consequently I found myself leading my family group on a vacation-plus-business trip to England and Venice. This was some sort of triumph for me because my three year itch was playing up and I had begun to fear that I would never see another beach again except those at Santa Monica and Malibu. Even on this expedition I did not expect to plant my toes on English sand or bruise them on English pebbles, but the Lido Beach was surely something to look forward to.

I had once hoped that my career would be caught in an updraught. But if this was going to happen at all it was clearly going to take its time. In fact the modern rocket-like ascent to fame and fortune was less common than it is now with the mobilisation of the successful television and Rock music as effective launching pads. In those days the main body of us Hollywoodites did not rapidly spiral upwards or downwards, we sort of stood still until suddenly overcome by inertia. To avoid this fate I made every effort to maintain an active spiral but settle, if necessary, for the horizontal. I would spiral horizontally in every direction, starting with Venice.

Pamela was knocked out by her first sight of Venice, but that was about the extent of it. She mentioned smells. Martha Miller proved to be an uneasy traveller. And Morgan was too young to catch on to what Venice was all about. Portland and I had a consistently good time. People had insisted that September was not the best time for Venice. It was still burdened with tourists, they said, and the Film Festival brought the wrong sort of people. And if you were sensitive to smells they tended to be worse at the end of the summer. But we were not aware of these shortcomings since the greater part of the day would be spent on the Lido Beach adjacent to the Excelsior Hotel. Yes, there were a lot of international newspapermen, but there was a lot of space and if, as sometimes happened, an English newsman was still stuck with the idea that our alleged permissive rearing of Portland was still a matter of import to his readers at home, we could always take to the water with or without the aid of the ever available pedal boats. Or we could swim out to an old hulk that was anchored a decent distance from the shore and stop off for elevenses of exotic seafood. It was a real holiday, something we did not have in our adopted California.

Rather mysteriously, when the sun went down, a bugle sounded on the Lido, a signal that we must now vacate the beach. Though not wishing to contravene the law of any foreign country, I believe that Portland and I did so once or twice. It was especially nice on the beach at that time. On one of these evenings, having walked along the empty strand for about half a mile, we went to the end of a little jetty. There we paused and looked around. Now there were two teenage Italian girls on the part of the beach that only minutes ago had been empty. Each had a stick and was writing with it in the sand. Then I noticed that two men were approaching and had turned onto our jetty. We were trapped. At least I felt that I was trapped, being conditioned by the ever present fear of being accosted by a farflung correspondent from the *News of the World* or *The People*. They were certainly approaching us with intent. They stopped and introduced themselves. The better looking of the two young men was the young Count Volpi. Oh dear, I thought. One of the best known features of the Venice Festival at that time was the ineluctable Volpi Ball. As soon as we had arrived at the Excelsior Hotel we had, like everyone else who was thought to qualify as some sort of star, been snowed under with invitations. Among them was one from Countess Volpi to her fabled Ball. We had ignored almost all of them, especially this last item because it was the kind of event to which wild horses could not have dragged us. All that splash and glitter and the resultant photographs grinning from the pages not only of *Gente* and *Oggi*, but from shiny magazines world wide. I was desperately unsocial in those days. Pamela was social but on more of a Kaffee-klatsch level.

So I had not even answered the Countess's invitation and here was the young Volpi tracking me down on the deserted beach to coax me into reacting appropriately to his mother's quasi-command. He seemed such a nice young man that I wanted my negative reaction to be so compelling that his mother could not take it out on him as the bearer of bad news. He was also extremely polite because he accepted my prosaic excuses with the utmost courtesy. We were tired, I said. True. And we had no suitable clothes. Not quite true, but graciously accepted. So the young men made off at a good pace, and Portland and I more slowly. I was particularly anxious to read the messages that the girls had left in the sand. One had written,

NAPOLEONE.

The other had written,

DEAN.

This referred of course to the idol James Dean who was about to die in an automobile accident.

And *Bigger than Life*? It was very well received. They had a very nice Italian title for it, *Dietro lo Specchio – Behind the Mirror*. I was never enormously pleased with our own title, although I thought of it myself. The original title of the *New Yorker* article was *Ten Feet Tall*, but another group had sneaked in ahead of us with *A Man is Ten Feet Tall*, so we had to think of something else.

I mentioned earlier that for the ultimate failure of the film in the USA and the United Kingdom I partially blame my decision to cast myself in the role of an average American schoolteacher. Now for the average French or Italian moviegoer this criticism was invalid, our voices generally having been dubbed. And even the critics do not as a rule seem to be bugged by the nice distinctions between British and American images. At any rate they gave us excellent reviews, even the high priests of *Cahiers du Cinema*.

So back to California and to my office in the studio. During my absence *Bigger than Life* had been released in the United States and mauled by some of the critics who, not being familiar with the *New Yorker's* Annals of Medicine, assumed that the story was exaggerated. The release of the film was not reinforced by a heavy advertising budget. In keeping with my observations about the shop talk in the Executives' Dining Room the top brass at the studio failed to mention the film in conversation with me, whether inside the dining room or out. But members of the crew spoke of it with great warmth as of some happy period in their past lives.

I did not succeed in grabbing the interest of Buddy Adler for any of the new subjects I proposed. Under my current contract I made, as an actor only, one other film. And having resumed a freelance status I was to make two more before my eventual getaway. I mean the getaway from Hollywood; for I was never in a hurry to get away specifically from 20th Century Fox which was a studio where I always felt comfortable and where I liked the people. And the catering. It was inevitable, though, that an excess of oil-well table talk should finally drive me back to the main dining room, my Anne Baxter salad and my feta cheese.

It was not long before the new Zanuck came back into my life. He was changed only in the technical sense that he was now handling one film at a time instead of an entire programme. I had heard nothing of his life in Europe other than a description by Joe Mankiewicz of a Zanuck dinner party in a Paris restaurant which he had attended, and which featured one of Zanuck's early attempts to order the dinner in French. When we met again it was on the Caribbean island of Grenada. Zanuck, who had his son Richard with him, looked refreshed and almost blithe.

The project was *Island in the Sun,* based on Alec Waugh's best-selling novel about fictional black/white relations on one of the West Indian islands, then still governed by the Colonial Office in London. The plot presupposes that the head of a wealthy and important family on our island has some black blood in his family line although this is not generally known. It is known, however, to his ambitious son, Maxwell (my part), and has an unsettling effect on his disposition. So much so that he murders a man whom he suspects of having had an affair with his wife. And on top of that he is attempting to conduct an election campaign against a black union leader which he knows he has little chance of winning. He loses on all counts. So the central story is not very satisfying except for fans of Harry Belafonte, who plays the part of the union leader.

A great deal of the film was devoted to random romances. I cannot do better than quote from a synopsis which I found in another publication. It says,

Boyeur (Belafonte) is having an affair with Mavis

Norman, a white woman (Joan Fontaine), and Denis Archer, the Governor's aide (John Justin) is having an affair with Boyeur's ex-girlfriend, Margo Seaton (Dorothy Dandridge). Maxwell's sister, Jocelyn (Joan Collins), fears that adverse publicity about the family background may prevent her marrying the Governor's son, Euan Templeton (Stephen Boyd).

Since it is hard for a writer and a director to stir up the audience's interest in half a dozen stories at the same time, they were in this case accepting a severe challenge. However we must bear in mind that, for commercial movie makers, miscegenation was practically virgin territory. Zanuck had taken bows for touching anti-semitism in one of his films, and, in something called *Pinkie*, he had also touched on the race problem. So he must be forgiven for dwelling on the interracial sexplay in our effort, uninteresting though it may appear in the cold print of the above synopsis. To me as a spectator only two images remain firmly in my mind. Just as during the shooting of *A Star is Born*, when there was nothing else lined up for the director to shoot, he would fall back on yet another shot of me driving the car in or out of Warner Brothers' Studio, so the director of *Island in the Sun* would fall back on yet another shot of a melancholy Belafonte walking away from camera. That was one oft-repeated image. The other persistent image is an exchange of dialogue between Joan Collins (Jocelyn) and Diana Wynyard, who played Mrs Fleury, her mother. Jocelyn, knowing – as she thinks she does – that there is black blood in the family, feels that this may be thought to constitute a let or hindrance to her being joined together in holy matrimony with Euan, the Governor's son. Her mother is in an unique position to reassure her on this point. The stretch of dialogue went something like this:

Jocelyn:	I didn't know about my Jamaican grandmother.
Mrs Fleury:	Is that the only reason you're refusing to marry him?
Jocelyn:	If things were different.
Mrs Fleury:	They're not different – but suppose they were, would you give anything to marry him?
Jocelyn:	Yes.
Mrs Fleury:	Don't worry about marrying Euan. You have no negro ancestor. My husband isn't your father.

On the occasion when I saw the film in a public theatre, this line got a terrific laugh. They probably sent it back to the cutting room with orders to eliminate the laugh. I do not know whether or not they succeeded.

In spite of the devotion applied to the making of the film by Zanuck and his director Robert Rossen, the result was not recognised by the critics as any sort of masterpiece though I dare say it did well enough at the box office. Rossen had an excellent record as a film maker (among his earlier films were *Body and Soul*, *All the King's Men*), but having been somewhat victimised by the Senator McCarthy gang, he had been out in the cold for a couple of years.

The good thing about being involved in a film with such a fragmented story line was that, for the actors at least, there was lots of spare time. I should add – *if* you are on the island of Grenada, which I happened to think the loveliest place I had ever known. I am not saying that I would necessarily want to settle there for the rest of my life, but if anyone asks me – in all your travels which is the loveliest place you have ever known? – the answer comes pat. Grenada.

We were there in November, so that we came in for the tail end of the rainy season, but this did not put our

394

shooting schedule in disarray. There would be a short, sharp tropical splash and within ten minutes everything would be dry again. Only some of the ladies' outfits and the more delicate of the men's needed to be protected. The tourist season, such as it was, was after Christmas, and at the time the Grenadians did not put themselves out to attract visitors. They seemed to have the kind of economy which, up to a certain ceiling, took care of everyone and did not encourage untoward progress, to use the word in its pejorative sense. Though its exports included cocoa, cotton, bananas and lime oil, its speciality was nutmeg and mace. Thus it was known as the Spice island.

In 1955 Hurricane Janet had destroyed a large percentage of the nutmeg-mace trees, which normally took twenty years to mature, but the islanders did not seem to be unduly downhearted, being richly endowed with humour, tolerance and serenity. This is of course the superficial judgement of a traveller who was devoting all his energies to having a good time and doing as little work as possible. Therefore if my judgement is way off target I hope that any Grenadans who may read this will forgive me.

On the day after our arrival, when we were all installed in the Santa Maria Hotel, the local people effortlessly put on for our benefit an unique after dinner entertainment. The lady who seemed to be their cultural leader gave us a brisk lantern lecture illustrating the attractions of the island and a very brief history. Then suddenly there was the sound of a steel band and through every entrance of the big hall came the singing bouncing populace. It was Caribbean Carnival time in miniature. Round the tables, in and out of the entrance the celebrants danced in the lurid costumes which they had run up for their regular springtime carnival. There was never anything more exhilarating. The band played the marching song that had taken the prize at this event, along with the recent Calypso hit from Trinidad, *Mama looka Booboo*, and the much older *Jean and Dinah*. Finally there was the Limbo dance which none of us had ever seen or attempted. Rum played its part in the evening too, but no one was discernibly overloaded.

Two or three times a week the same steel band, which was called Gasspo, played at the Beach Club which was a little more than half a mile from the hotel. Its spell was magnetic. Not only were you drawn like a zombie to the Beach Club as soon as you heard the distant music, but it held you in its spell until they decided to call it a night. The Club was a not very new building situated at the far end of the Grand Anse, a long beach gleaming white if the moon was up, being made up of weathered fragments of white coral. Perhaps even more magic than the nights and the dancing and the steel drums was the moment when the sun went down. You were already in the sea because that was what you did as soon as you had finished your work. The sun having made its exit, the sea, the air, the sky, everything became still, the only sound a lazy splashing of feet and hands. And when the sky had darkened to the correct shade of violet blue up came that glorious Caribbean moon. When at last you came out of the sea it would be time for your favoured rum drink. There was a Scottish doctor in the bar of our hotel very often. He could have been placed there by Robert Louis Stevenson. He said that the thing to do was to drink your rum standing up. And he could take a fair number of drinks in that position, as could some of our lot. The only drunks were in downtown St George's where you might see several, using such loud voices on each other in and around the little bars where they sold the white rum, that it was impossible to tell if they were really angry or just jocular.

The only members of our gang with whom I seem to have spent much time were the actor John Williams and his wife Helen, not only because I liked them so much, but because he and I were written into the same scenes in the film and therefore had the same days off. But I got to know quite a lot of the local people who were kindness itself. I remember watching the sun go down on a seascape

396

towards the north of the island. I saw then for the first time what Homer had in mind when he referred to the wine-dark sea.

One day one of my friends said,

'You know, the Mayor is mad at you.'

'How can he be mad at me? What have I done?'

'It's about something you wrote to Louella Parsons.'

'Something that *I* wrote to *Louella Parsons*?'

Into St George's then to find a Mayor, who tells me what it is all about. What had happened was this. Being a conscientious correspondent, I had written home to Pamela on my first morning at the Santa Maria. I had at that time nothing better to tell her than that I had slept little during the night because the rain was hammering down on the corrugated iron roof outside my window, and that the only locals to whom I had so far spoken had such a funny dialect that it was hard to understand what they said.

Unbelievably, Pamela had found herself in conversation with Louella and had spilled the contents of my letter. So the following day readers of Louella's column throughout the world were told about the funny accents and the corrugated iron roofs. I was very cross naturally because I had regarded my letters home as confidential documents. I did not wish to have to censor them for fear of leakages and possible misconstructions, but there was nothing I could do in this case but to admit my contributory guilt and apologise deeply. The Mayor was a very nice man, and sophisticated, as were most of those I met.

An aspect of Grenadan life that made it specially appealing to this foreign visitor was the absence of any effective black versus white prejudice or vice versa. Since virtually everyone on the island had some black blood in them the basic colour prejudice did not exist. The few genuinely white people who worked in Government House looked no more white than half the people you would see in the street. It may have got this way because in

397

the old colonial days it kept changing hands, Spanish, English, French, English, French, then not inextricably English until 1795. I believe that in this way it avoided a really determined exploitation by any of the colonial powers. To France is generally attributed the discredit of having liquidated the Carib Indians, but on the other hand there is at least an attractive legacy, which expresses itself in terms of architecture and life style, reminiscent of the Midi, which is definitely one up for the French.

In contrast to this, it was difficult to detect a cultural heritage on the island of Barbados, Britain's oldest colony, that the short term visitor could be proud of. I mention Barbados because that is where the *Island in the Sun* unit had to go for certain backgrounds that were not available on Grenada. We were instantly aware that this was an island with a heavy sugar cane curtain. And the twentieth century settlers and the tourist traders referred euphemistically to the more luxurious resort hotels and restaurants as 'Clubs'. This meant that if someone who was racially undesirable asked for a reservation he was asked to show his membership card. It was a not very subtle method of restriction. Admittedly the system was by then already on its way out; presumably it made a rapid exit when independence showed its face.

Although the Grenadan tug will never loosen, I am told that one should not go back to a place where one found some joy. So I shall ignore the tug but continue to wonder with concern how things have been affected by political metamorphoses that our papers have told us about. When independence struck, there was the West Indies Federation in 1958 until its dissolution in 1962. Grenada then tried to form a new federation with other Windward islands and the Leeward islands and Barbados, but ultimately stood alone. Then one read about the deification of Eric Gairy. One even saw a television interview with him by the irrepressible Alan Whicker. I saw Gairy making a speech in the market square of St George's in 1956. He was a true demagogue.

Soon after the war he had organised a farm workers' strike which caused such a ruckus that the British sent a cruiser to the island to pick him up and keep him out of harm's way while they worked out a solution for the economic troubles. At least Gairy said it was a cruiser. He managed to introduce a reference to the incident into the speech I heard, and they told me that it had become his theme-song. It was handy for him to have a martyrdom story to which he could refer when his rating was slipping. But he spoke well and his inside jokes about political rivals got roars of laughter. Later, when he had become supreme union boss *and* Prime Minister, I assumed that he had it made for life. But it seems not to have worked out that way.

Whatever the future of this special island, I try to draw comfort from the thought that the nature of any given community governs its own destiny. And as for ideologies, my favourite quotation is from Alexander Pope:

O'er forms of government let fools contest.
What'er is best administered is best.

18/Tahiti

At one time during the years that followed I suffered from a protracted sickness. Bob Parrish wanted me to get out of bed so that he could start shooting the film we wanted to do together. It was an acerbic anti-Mafia tract called *The Brotherhood of Evil.* But I would not stir because I knew that I would not pass the obligatory medical examination for insurance purposes and I did not wish to compromise my insurability. For some strange reason I was considered indispensable for the Godfather-type role and the project was cancelled. Not surprisingly, rumour had it that Bob and I had reneged from the film because intimidated by the Mafia, which would have made it a much more exciting incident than it actually was. By and large this was not a fruitful period.

Also I should mention, since I have neglected to say much about my marriage, that its fabric was becoming so threadbare that it now kept threatening to fall apart.

In the preceding chapter I found myself mentioning an incident involving our old friend Louella Parsons. Anyone who happens to have an undying interest in the Hollywood ogres of the period may well be saying,

'But I thought the Masons weren't *speaking* to Louella Parsons.' We weren't. Or hadn't been. Ever since she greeted me to the United States with her regular Sunday keel-hauling, we had kept our distance and handed all our guff to the opposition lady, Hedda Hopper, whose words encircled the world by courtesy of Colonel McCormick and his *Chicago Tribune* syndication machinery.

But this situation could not last forever because once we had settled down in Beverly Hills it became clear Hopper was ten times the bitch that Parsons could ever be. She was perfectly polite to Pamela and myself and we allowed her into our house. But whenever I read her column she was saying something vile about people I liked or respected: She was vile to Rex Harrison, and she practically went to war against Charlie Chaplin. So much so that I would say that she, more than any other individual, was responsible for Chaplin's shabby treatment at the hands of the United States Immigration Department.

Joan Bennett was a friend of ours and one of Portland's godmothers, therefore a person to be championed and protected. Joan was mad at Hopper for throwing some mud at her husband, Walter Wanger. She confided in Pamela that, by way of demonstrating her low opinion of Hopper, she had purchased a live skunk and had it sent to her by express messenger. But now Joan was worried about the skunk. She was afraid that Hopper's well known inhumanity could be directed to skunk just as easily as to man. Pamela got the message. Before breaking off relations with Hopper she would give her a casual call and say that there was a rumour going around that someone had given her a skunk. Was it true?

So she did that and ended up by saying that we had a friend who had always wanted a skunk and asked if we could have it. The skunk lived with us for a day and a half – it had been deodorised while we made a hundred telephone calls trying to locate an authentic skunk-fancier. A very attractive animal he was.

That was the last civil conversation that was conducted between either of us and Hedda Hopper. We now gave our patronage to Louella Parsons, who was not a bad old slob. A few years later she lost coherence and was taken to a quiet place where she survived for several years. They say that they gave her a disconnected telephone to play with so that she could imagine that she was conducting endless conversations with the stars.

Why is it that Hollywood deaths seem so specially gruesome? Because we all – public included – think that we have known those people so well. Preston Sturges, whom I *did* know quite well, and who survived until 1959, said that when he wrote his autobiography he would call it *The Events Leading up to my Death*. But mostly his jokes were less black. He said much that was human and wise. He caught me going into one of my diatribes about producers. This was soon after I had arrived in Hollywood and was still judging everything by standards established in England. Though in fact I had worked with at least two sensible producers there, the word conjured up old scraps with the ones who had driven us round the bend.

Sturges said to me, 'But, James, even if producers are as ignorant and inconsiderate and opportunistic as you say, you should accept them that way and not treat them as a constant burden. What would a game of golf be like if it was all fairway? It is the sand traps that make it interesting.'

I thanked Sturges for his good advice. But I do not insist that this is what made me tolerant. It was age, experience and constant mingling with the breed of producers that had evolved in Hollywood. The staff producers at 20th Century and MGM worked as inconspicuously as electric clocks. One of my first Hollywood films introduced me to another type of staff producer, just as well organised, but not always so quiet. This was Leonard Goldstein.

His twin brother Robert held down a job with Universal's New York Office. When you asked what Robert Goldstein did, any wag would reply, 'He spits for Goetz and gets for Spitz,' Spitz and Goetz being the new bosses of Universal.

A more realistic reply to the same question was, 'He's the kind of man who, if you've lost your latch-key at two o'clock in the morning, has a friend who is a locksmith.'

Strangers bound for Universal Studios in Hollywood would be seen onto the train in New York by Robert Goldstein and greeted on arrival by his spitt'n image. The twins enjoyed the shock value of this routine. Leonard Goldstein, the one who received you in L.A., was a producer at Universal and I don't hold it against him that he employed me in nothing more interesting than *One Way Street* which was not at all a typical Leonard Goldstein item. He was at his best when drooling over some incredibly perfect attraction that he was putting together. He'd say: 'I got an idea that you won't believe, it's so great. I mean, I have to pinch myself to make sure I'm awake, it's so fantastic!'

Some of Leonard's original notions did in fact make a fortune for Universal. Rightly or wrongly I credit him with the success both of *Ma and Pa Kettle* and Donald O'Connor's with *Francis the Talking Donkey*. And it was from him that I first heard the expression Tits and Sand to describe the sexy films about Sheiks which they were fond of making at Universal in those days.

Leonard was an example of the kind of enthusiastic producer who enjoyed his work and whose head rattled with fantastic ideas. I liked these men, even if I did not always go for their ideas. One eccentric enthusiast whose ideas I *did* go for was Andrew Stone. I heard of him first when I was developing all those scripts at 20th Century. He had made, on a very low budget, a film which dealt with the same story as did another film which was extremely expensive and had Spencer Tracy and Humphrey Bogart playing the leading parts in it. Andy Stone's film featured a young Johnny Cassavetes and was called *The Night Holds Terror* and the expensive one, directed by William Wyler, was called *The Desperate Hours*. Both set up a situation in which a wanted criminal on the run hijacks a suburban villa. The family who own the house become his hostages, for he is armed. *The Desperate Hours* had first been a Broadway hit and obviously only a major company could afford to buy the film rights, such desirable material did it seem to be for a suspenseful film. But the better film was Andy Stone's. Clearly Stone was a master of suspense, and I wanted to meet him. An introduction was not necessary however because he simultaneously asked me to play the leading man's part in his next film, *Cry Terror*.

This was the picture in which Andy introduced the idea of placing bombs on airplanes. It may not have been his original idea, since he had a rare collection of *Police Gazettes* from which he drew material for his films. In this case, let us suppose, he had read about the criminal who was the first ever to place a bomb on an airplane. His script begins with the management of an airline being informed that there is a bomb on one of their planes. No threats, no ransom demanded, but the FBI, having been alerted, finds the bomb and detonates it. A television repair man watching the TV coverage of this event recognises the bomb as his own handiwork, a prototype made for a wartime friend to help him get a manufacturing contract with the armed services. The next stage of the bad wartime friend's plot is to have a second bomb made which he will threaten to plant on another of the same airline's planes unless they pay him a ransom. The first bomb had been for advertising purposes only. The bad guy holds the repair man and his wife and child at gunpoint and uses them to further the increasingly complicated plot. Actually it was a very well worked out screenplay, and I was not in the least surprised that I was expected to play the bad guy. If I had been a little smarter I would have accepted, since it was a much better part than that of the nice guy. But I was still trying to kick the bad guy habit. C. A. Lejeune wrote of it in the *Observer*: '. . . James Mason, Rod Steiger and Inger Stevens appear in it, but not noticeably for their own good.'

But it was distributed by MGM and did very well in the United States, where the critics were not at all sour.

In spite of the thankless role I was playing I got a great deal of pleasure from this assignment purely on account of the strange new techniques that Andy had developed. The credit titles on an Andy Stone film included the items:

Producers: Virginia and Andrew Stone
Directed and written by: Andrew Stone
Editor: Virginia Stone.

Trick number one was to construct a story from real events described in the *Police Gazette*. Trick number two was to shoot the film on real locations and in real buildings. If you played these two tricks correctly the result could not fail to be stark realism, was Andy's theory. He was the pioneer of shooting in live sets; later the practice was forced upon other producers by the rising costs of studio rental and of set construction but it was Andy who showed them how to do it. Virginia Stone cut the film in cutting-rooms that they had built behind their house. Post-synchronisation was rarely needed because Andy made sure that his sound recordist could record usable sound no matter how difficult the circumstances. It was only when it came to the musical scoring and the ultimate dubbing process (mixing of tracks) that Andy needed studio space.

One of Virginia's contributions towards producing was to knock on the doors of those in whose houses they wished to shoot and arrive at suitable terms. Not only houses. In this film for instance there were shots of the plane with the bomb on board. It was up to Virginia to find a co-operative airline. As soon as she mentioned the word bomb she would be shown the door, though they knew there would be no question of using the airline's real name. She was a persistent lady, and also a good cutter. They pursued this very personal picture-making pattern for ten years or more with varying results. I don't believe they ever bettered *The Night Holds Terror* and *Cry Terror*, though they ultimately hit it rich with their *Song of Norway* in the worthy cause of which Andy set aside the *Police Gazette* and took his extensive musical interests out for a picnic.

I made a second film with him which was not highly

esteemed. But I enjoyed working on it perhaps even more than on *Cry Terror* simply because most of the work on this one took place on an old and scruffy Liberty Ship which had been absorbed by one of the Greek mercantile lines. Yes, feta cheese was available, as was also an endless supply of sweet muddy, Greek coffee. I learned to say

ὑγιειά χαρά παίδια

The film started life with a fairly respectable title but ended up as *The Decks Ran Red*.

Being now veterans of two films in common, Andy and I took to lunching once a week at Romanoff's to exchange news and gossip and evaluate each other's up-coming projects, if any. The last of these lunches took place just before I was off to Europe to make a film. In reply to my query about his projects he said that there were several very good ones which he was mulling over, but all with certain drawbacks.

'For instance, did you know, James, that there still exists a prolific slave trade in Africa and the Near East? I could work out a very good story line.'

'And the drawbacks?'

'The only drawback that I can see is that if you are an unbeliever and you are caught at one of their slave markets it is an offence punishable by castration.'

This seemed to both of us to be the kind of challenge which it would not be wise to accept out of sheer bravado.

The director of my next film *North by North West* was Alfred Hitchcock and there is very little that I can add to the rapidly growing corpus of Hitchcockiana that his life and work have inspired.

He was a man who asked for and expected no help from anyone other than the technical aides with whom he set down the blue prints, meticulously prepared, well in advance of the shooting stage. The principal aide was his writer and to greater and lesser degrees his cameraman, his editor and his art director. But it is bad luck that an increasing number of actors feel that they have to be 'creative' and that it is their right and duty to make 'choices' which affect the staging of sequences and even the text. For the likes of them, Hitch had no use. He did not require his actors to be creative nor to extend to him the benefit of their choices. He had cast them because their records had shown that they were capable of playing the roles which had been unambiguously delineated in his script.

He also had a very clear view of the value of the stars he employed. Although his own name was of enormous market value and he would have been permitted by his financiers, if he had pressed the point, to do without the additional names for his marquee, he knew precisely how much those names could add to the box office gross. He told me for instance that the name of James Stewart on an Alfred Hitchcock film could be relied on to bring in one million dollars more than that of Cary Grant. He said this without any disrespect to Grant who, he was quick to point out, would obviously be more valuable than Stewart in other contexts. But he wanted to hit the big markets of middle America, an area of which Stewart was the darling.

He succeeded by cold calculation. Correction. He succeeded because he had an enormous theatrical talent and cold calculation was the manner in which his skills were applied. Though it did not happen on our film, I have heard it said that sometimes he did not even watch a scene being shot. Having received the nod from his camera operator and his sound recordist he would order the scene to be printed and move on to the next. So sure was he of the infallibility of his planning.

Though he devoted his enormous talents to a lifetime of film making he was the man who could say in a moment of crisis:

'Don't worry, my dear, it's only a movie.'

Many people regard *North by Northwest* as the last of the Hitchcock classics. By a classic I mean a film in which the first half hour is action-packed mystery. The audience is trying to make sense of a strange sequence of events. Then suddenly it becomes clear. With this flash of understanding comes the recognition that a menace has been set up, and for the rest of the film's duration the thread of suspense is unbroken. Also it is typical of the Hitchcock classic that the form is everything, the content nonexistent.

In our film the initial mysterioso section of the story has never been bettered, the brilliantly funny kidnapping of the Cary Grant character by reason of mistaken identity. I had been most eager to watch this Grant at work and figure out the secret of his perfect comedy playing. He was earnest, conscientious, clutching his script until the last moment. Then onto his feet and it would just happen. If there were a question in a testpaper that required me to fill in the name of an actor who showed the same grace and perfect timing in his acting that Fred Astaire showed in his dancing, I should put Cary Grant. What about Rex Harrison? Ah. Well, let's say it's a photo finish. There was one sequence towards the end of *North by Northwest* in which Eva Marie Saint and I were to embark in a small private airplane. Hitch, in those overripe pear-shaped tones of his, instructed me somewhat as follows:

'James, when Eva goes towards the plane I want you to stay exactly where you are for a count of three, then start to follow her.'

I allowed that to sink in slowly, and then I said, with a show of concern, 'Yes, I understand what you are saying, Hitch, but the trouble is that I can't tell in advance how soon I shall feel the impulse to follow her. It could be one second or it might be as long as ten seconds. Maybe it will work out just the way you want it but . . .'.

As I continued in this vein I could see that I had him hooked for a few moments. Eventually he had to realise that I was pulling his leg and he broke into a smile. He said, 'Sometimes that sort of thing really happens and, I can tell you, it's no joke.'

He told me that he had been directing Montgomery Clift in a film in Canada called *I Confess* and wanted to make it clear to the audience that the room where the action was taking place was supposed to be in a building which faced the same square as did the City Hall but at right angles to it. In fact they were working in a studio nowhere near the City Hall. In the course of the action Clift was to lean out of the window and look down supposedly into the square. Hitch now instructed him to make a point of looking to his left for several seconds since he intended to insert a shot of the City Hall as from Clift's point of view, and thus establish the topography.

Clift was being asked to assist Hitch on a purely technical level. But it was no good. Certain actors are liable to dig in their heels and respond only to the dictates of The Method. If Clift did not feel like turning his head to the left and pretending to gaze for a count of three at an imaginary City Hall, Hitch would be rendered helpless. Having never seen the film I do not know how this hurdle was surmounted. But I do know that Clift was a magnificent actor, method in his madness, or not.

Most of the serious actors in the United States will admit, when challenged, to being method actors. This does not mean that they necessarily behave in the obstinately self-assertive manner that the word conjures up. It only means that the method promulgated by the Actors' Studio in New York is accepted as a symbol of exalted status. It is true that, as a result of oversell, many American actors regard it as the only true dogma. But fortunately there are also many who recognise that Stanislavsky's method represents only one isolated approach, to which a superstructure of occasionally useful drills and disciplines has been added in recent years; and that the skills of an actor should not be confined to the teaching of one school but, given intelligence and

409

imagination, there should be no limit to his reach, even though his grasp may fall short.

We had a young actor in the cast of *North by Northwest*, called Marty Landau, who was very keen and fresh from New York where, even when out of a job, he had never been out of work. That is to say, he was forever at acting school, to teach or to study, no matter which. His first sequence in the film involved a long exchange of dialogue between Grant, myself and Landau. Actually Landau had very little to say but had been able to persuade himself that it was for him an important scene. He had given it much thought and, with a sense of something already achieved, said to me,

'There is a very clear progression for me in the course of this scene and, step by step, I have planned exactly what I must do with it.'

Hitchcock emerged from his office and joined us on the set. 'Now then,' he said to the secretary, 'which set-up did we decide to start with?'

Having consulted her notes, she replied, 'You said that it would be simplest if we did the high angle shot first, Mr Hitchcock.'

'Ah yes. Well now, this will come about halfway through the scene. James, you're sitting behind your desk and, Cary, you are by the fireplace and . . . where has Marty got to by now?'

'He's been standing by the door since his entrance, but when Mr Grant got up – at the top of the page – you said that Mr Landau was to join him at the fireplace.'

'That's right. So Marty, at this point you'll enter shot from Left of camera and walk behind James in the direction of Cary. But we shall have cut the shot before you reach him.'

And so it was throughout the sequence. The order of lining up the camera set-ups was dictated by Hitchcock's private sets of logistics and took no account whatsoever of Landau's carefully worked out progression.

But it was a well-shot sequence and Marty's

performance throughout the film was exemplary.

During this strange period I made only two further Grade A Hollywood films: *Journey to the Centre of the Earth* and *The Marriage Go Round*. After that I was to make many Grade A international films and do an entire range of jobs that it would be hard to classify but I do not believe that I was in another Grade A Hollywood film until as recently as 1977 when I worked with Warren Beatty in *Heaven Can Wait,* which was a remake of *Here Comes Mr Jordan*. I must stress that the term Grade A has little to do with quality, it refers strictly to the budget. Of the three I have just mentioned *Heaven Can Wait* managed to pick up some quality on its way along the assembly line, *Journey to the Centre of the Earth* less so and *The Marriage Go Round* came out from 20th Century with much less quality than it had when it went in. Before immersion it took the form of a hit Broadway play, very slick and smart, written by Leslie Stevens.

Journey to the Centre of the Earth was an adaptation of the Jules Verne story which had climbed onto the 20th Century programme as a result of much love, devotion and hard work on the part of veteran producer-writer Charles Brackett. The script was excellent and it was not badly served during production. It was well served by able director Henry Levin and among the well known entities engaged to play the leading parts were myself, Arlene Dahl and Pat Boone, who among the early white rock singers was second only to Elvis Presley. Ours was one of the first movies he had appeared in and had the distinction of being the venue for his first screen kiss. The lucky girl was Diane Baker. Arlene Dahl, whom I had barely met before, turned out to be a friendly cooperative lady of considerable beauty. One of my reasons for liking her – and a good reason – was that she did not take it out on me when I could not think of her name when introducing her on the Lux Video Theatre. It was little errors like that that made the Lux men and their fellow detergents despise me so. And while they were doing that, the host of an anthology programme on another network was winning the undying love and respect of *his* sponsors, the General Electric people. This was President Ronald Reagan.

I was a little worried while we were shooting the film because I was afraid that 20th Century were likely to let us down when it came to the special effects. I had experience of the Buddy Adler regime. But my misgivings were unwarranted. The special effects were the hit of the film, especially the scene in which our party, having constructed a raft from giant mushroom timber, is riding the tricky meteorological conditions which prevail down there. Our raft was mounted on a turntable which could revolve or tilt in any direction. The contraption stood in the middle of a shallow tank into which tons after tons of water were dropped from above. To add to the fun they gave us wind machines and lightning effects, while onto a huge screen behind us were projected vistas of unending havoc. The boys did a great job with the raft scene and the film reappears as a holiday item for children almost as regularly as *20,000 Leagues under the Sea*.

Leslie Stevens, the author of *The Marriage Go Round*, having spent some years in Hollywood had acquired enough confidence to promote himself as a producer and director. He believed that films of quality could be made for a fraction of the normal cost if meticulous care were given to the preparation of the script and all technical problems. He scored an initial success with his first venture, a black and white thriller which cost considerably less than a hundred thousand dollars. The second, *Hero's Island*, a pioneer story, which we shot on the island of Catalina in nineteen days was almost very good.

The story concerned a man and his wife, formerly bonded, who chose to settle with their two young children and a helpful friend on an island off the coast of Carolina. Three unfriendly fishermen claim the island and attack the family, killing the father. A castaway lashed to a raft is rescued and undertakes to help the family, but, out of consideration for the mother's religious susceptibilities, attempts to avoid violence. However, the fishermen also find allies in the form of a brutal overseer and his two stewards, and in the end there has to be some spilling of blood. The overseer and the fishermen were well characterised. The fishermen at the beginning could have been mistaken for the Scraggs Brothers in *Li'l Abner*, but later one of them turns out to be a good sort and is allowed to marry the widow.

I have to say that the script was better than the completed film. We shot it entirely outdoors, it looked beautiful and United Artists thought that they had a winner. Box office returns proved otherwise. Those who can claim to have seen it probably caught sight of it between commercials on their television screens.

Between professional engagements I would find myself almost frantically reaching for new pastimes. It was thus that I planted myself on the committees for the nominations of foreign films, short subjects etc. for Academy Award consideration. I taught myself the guitar and made up songs for my own amusement. Although a star, I was clearly not among the top seeds. I intended to hold my position if only with a view to hitting my customary income. But I was not doing much acting, and this distressed me because it was something which I enjoyed. My friends could play bit parts, read commercials, take part in soap operas, do anything they liked without impairing their professional standing, because they had none. I did not want to read commercials or wallow in soap operas but I was sure that there were bit parts that I would have fun playing. In Westerns for instance. Yes, I could invent a new actor for whom no part was too small or too thankless. He would become more and more sought after until he rated feature billing below the title, but never make stardom.

I would create another Gabby Hayes, the popular supporting actor seldom absent from the kind of Westerns that so attracted the kiddies of that era. His name? I settled for Enoch Gates, which was the name of the eldest of the three scruffy fishermen in *Hero's Island*.

The next step was to canvass all of my acquaintance who had anything to do with the production of a Western series. I would take them into my confidence and offer my services for Screen Artists' Guild basic salary under my new alias.

It was such a good idea that I wish that I could claim spectacular success for it. But the trouble was that I knew so few potential employers, and most of them either missed the point entirely or thought that I had dreamed it up as a publicity stunt. Leslie Stevens was the one exception. He now had a production company of his own for which he had created a Western series called *Stoney Burke*, the name of its leading character which was played by Jack Lord. And so he obligingly wrote for Enoch Gates a part which made no great demands and was just what I fancied at that stage of Gates's career. Leslie having, quite rightly, no great faith in my ability to come through with a credible Western accent had reduced my dialogue to a series of mumbles. The part was that of a bum who was found in possession of a murder victim's watch. The bum was hauled along to the police station and grilled. It was then proved that he had come upon the watch quite innocently.

It was a start and I was sure that Enoch Gates could build quite an interesting career for himself as soon as I had improved my accent. I could do it now, given the chance, but at that time I was an actor only two-thirds formed; I was just beginning to catch on. Unfortunately my night's work was somewhat spoiled by the presence of a newspaperman to whom the secret had somehow been leaked. I swear that no one on the unit would have penetrated my disguise, but his man was onto me as soon as I arrived on the set. I tried to parry his questions, vigorously denying that I was in any way connected with this James Mason, whoever he might be, but I could not keep it up. Eventually I confided that his suspicions had been justified but urged him not to give me away. He obliged me at least so far as present company was concerned, and fortunately his paper turned out to be nothing more sinister than a minuscule television guide.

The creation of Enoch Gates represents one of my last efforts to find a fragmentary professional interruption between bouts of tennis. I was now living a slow process of orientation, feeling I had exhausted my portion of Western hospitality and that my place was in Europe. I remember thinking that, when I got there, I might find a spot for Enoch Gates in the Spaghetti Westerns that had recently surfaced in the American market.

During these last years of my Hollywood stretch there had been other side trips independent of my movie career. In 1957, for instance, Pamela and I appeared for a fortnight at the La Jolla Playhouse which was not far from San Diego and a favourite exercise yard for Hollywood actors who were becoming rusty.

An English friend, Dario Bellini, who had collaborated with us on various bits of writing in 1939, sent me a good little play called *Paul and Constantine* which had good parts in it for Pamela and myself. So we made ourselves agreeable to John Swope, who was the administrator of the La Jolla Playhouse, and suggested that he present us there. The play served its immediate purpose, but I do not believe that it was widely played elsewhere because it called for a young actor and a middle aged actor to play the same character at different stages of his life; an almost insuperable casting problem.

In 1958 an even more demanding adventure was launched. The thing to do, we decided, was to find a play not only for Pamela and myself but also for Portland who was clearly a girl with talent. The play we chose was *Midsummer* by Vina Felmar which had played successfully on Broadway with Geraldine Page, Mark Stevens and Jenny Hecht in the leading parts. That production had been a legendary event since the young Jenny Hecht, who cannot have been more than ten years old, found occasion to bite the leading man during a performance and was hauled before Equity and reprimanded. And it was not even a biting part. The child's relations with her parents in the play were idyllic.

In the old days, when it first came into being, summer stock was a blessing for the acting profession because it gave the actors something to do during the heat of the summer when most of New York's theatres were closed. Something to do moreover in nice country towns and holiday resorts. But it had not been quite the same since the coming of airconditioning because most of New York's theatres now stayed open. And coincidentally the summer stock game had become a bit of a racket. But for some refugees from Southern California for instance, it remained a welcome institution. We played only for six weeks in the States of New York, New Jersey, Connecticut, Massachusetts and New Hampshire. Only one other actor toured with us, the rest of the parts were played by local talent.

Pamela and Portland played their parts with complete success. I went on. I say that because I have always wanted

416

to find a good opportunity to use that phrase in that certain sense. It is another quote attributed to John Barrymore by Al Parker. When someone asked Barrymore how was some actress's performance in such and such a play, he said – 'She went on for it.'

Actually I got my most treasured review for that performance. The leading man in the play is a schoolteacher who suffers from an urge to go on the stage. His wife knows of this urge, and for her own sake as well as her child's she fears that he will have to give way to this urge. In the end he does. That is the play. There is a scene in the first act in which the hero's pal, who is a vaudevillean, pays them a visit and the two of them do a time step together. This presented quite a problem for me because I had never shown a flair in any area of dancing. However during the weeks preceding our departure I had taken tap-dancing lessons. And I would practise my routine on the marble floored area at the far end of our living room. It was a checkerboard of black and white squares and it claimed the distinction of having had Rudolph Valentino tango upon it. Having put on a suitable record I would practise regularly with my back to the main living room.

One evening Milton Berle and his wife, Ruth, paid us a visit and, while they were there, Pamela said, 'Why don't you show Milton your tap routine, James? He'll be able to give you some hints.'

This made sense. But it was uncomfortable, like doing an audition. Worse than that, I started to do the routine the way I'd always practised it, with my back to the room. Berle made some joke and Pamela suggested I turn around. But if you are used to doing a thing one way it is impossible to do it in the opposite direction. At least that is what I discovered on this occasion. My act was an unintentional riot.

But I mastered it before we were due to rehearse the play, or rather I mastered it as much as I was ever going to master it. And when we played Boston a local critic wrote a review which made the whole thing worth while. He said (approximately), 'Another thing in favour of Mr Mason's performance is that his time step is far superior to Laurence Olivier's in *The Entertainer*.'

What a brilliant critic, I thought.

I do not think that anyone commented on the inadequacy of my vocal projection on this occasion, partly no doubt because the theatres were small, but also because Mrs Holmes had entered my life.

I was not looking for a vocal coach, but it happened that at one time Pamela had the idea that Portland could use one. Any proper young actress, especially a Californian one, should learn to sing and it is not a bad idea to have the speaking voice acquire some range while she is at it. Portland's voice tended to emerge from the top of her head like a puff of smoke, so I endorsed the idea, although in *Midsummer* she projected well enough. Pamela had by this time become a Television Personality and was constantly interviewing the people who appear on talk shows because they have something they wish to publicise, like a book they have just written or a saloon act that has a local booking. One day she asked a girl who sang exceptionally well what was the name of her singing teacher. The girl said that she went to a lady who was more of a generalised vocal coach.

So Portland started to take lessons from the great Mrs Holmes who turned out to be an old lady. But it did not work out for her because Mrs Holmes insisted that all pupils come to her own house, and this led to transportation problems. Also the lessons were a terrible grind which could be tolerated only by grown-up and very determined people like myself. Mrs Holmes told Pamela that she had long wanted to get hold of my voice because I was not using it correctly. So I took over where Portland left off.

I submitted to the drill for about three years. It was a matter of sitting beside her on her piano stool and uttering the same notes that she thumped out on the keyboard. First she would run you through the vowel sounds, up and down. Then she would get you doing a closed lip sound which agitated the nose. I cannot describe her secrets because she did not confide in me what she was up to all the time. But she passed them on to her daughter in law, Claire Holmes, who may, for all I know, have inherited the piano and carried on thumping. Having at the commencement of the drill reassured herself that vibrations were emerging from the top of my head à la Portland, she worked on them until she could feel with her hand that the back of my neck had picked up the rhythm and until ultimately the whole rib cage was throbbing. It was hard work. She kept boxes of tissues on the lid of her piano and expected her pupils to do a fair amount of spitting even when they had promised faithfully that they would never touch another cigarette.

I was an immensely satisfied customer, and I began to notice a great improvement in the films in which I appeared dating from her tuition. *Lolita*, a film in which I took part in 1960, was one of the first in which the change was clearly audible. At any rate Mrs Holmes and I were pleased.

She tried to get me to recommend her services to Laurence Olivier. I backed away from this notion because, no matter what he was doing to his vocal cords, his voice had always been a splendidly effective instrument. One has but to think of the prodigious basso he manufactured for his Othello. But Mrs Holmes mentioned another voice of which she would have liked to take charge. Did I know President Kennedy? It was *dreadful* what he was doing to his voice! I did not know the man and so I could not help her to take charge, although I agreed that it was a nasty sound that he kept producing.

In the January of 1959 my father and mother came to visit us. My father had been suffering from physical and nervous exhaustion. He still occupied his office in the warehouse in St George's Square. The rest of the space he contrived to rent out, a preoccupation which now accounted for much of the time which he spent in his office. But certain aggravations in connection with his brother George's will had been a great strain on him and the long sea voyage to California via the Panama Canal was prescribed by all of us. But he stayed only just over a fortnight in Beverly Hills. I took him up to San Francisco, which was in fact the only place in the United States which he had wished to visit. He was addicted to seafood and I treated him to an enormous crab on Fisherman's Wharf before seeing him onto a plane to take him back to Europe. The crab was a disappointment, he said.

My mother stayed on for a few additional weeks. But there was disappointment for her too. When I was very young she had heard regularly from a relative in California called Melanie, whose correspondence had planted in her head the idea that California was a land of flowers which bloomed the whole year round. I accepted this until I arrived there in 1948 and found that while the 'Golden State' otherwise justified its name it was not especially florid. True, dedicated gardeners could achieve spectacular results but the average garden did not enchant. There were some good night scents if you were favoured with the company of jasmine, datura or even petisporum, but the soil and the climate did not encourage growth without a lot of human aid. True, there was the Flowering Desert, but it was rather out of the way for most of us and only put on its show for a strictly limited season.

By visiting us when they did, my parents were spared some of the hardships that prevail in a winter of Yorkshire. But what about the flowers? I knew what my mother would be looking for but the established habit was not broken just to please her. The two boring flowers bloomed on schedule. They were – and are and ever will be – the Bird of Paradise (strelitzia) and the poinsettia. Neither made a good impression.

But there was a sudden change for the good. An English friend, Ivan Foxwell, loomed up from the past, with

420

backing from Paramount for a little film which he proposed to make in England and Scotland. He had been talking to me for some time about a literary property that he had acquired, called *The Megstone Plot* by Andrew Garve, but such news I habitually treated as too good to be bankable. But now it had become a reality. Four pairs of hands had gone to work on Mr Garve's book and made it almost unrecognisably and enchantingly comical. These hands belonged to two writers, Roger MacDougall and Paul Winterton, the producer, my friend Foxwell, and the shrewdly chosen director, Guy Hamilton. And I would already have been happy enough with the straightforward thriller that I had read in paperback. It needed a new title to go with the dry humour with which it was to be treated. I suggested *A Touch of Larceny* and since no one objected the title became official. A very close equivalent was even found for the French version: *Un Brin d'Escroquerie*.

Disregarding the excitement that always comes to one about to undertake something downright sensible for a change, the journey back to England alone gave me a tremendous lift. In New York there was already the bright crispness one is sometimes lucky enough to catch in its springtime. In London things were better still. The crocuses were beginning to open in Hyde Park. For people who have been brought up in a country where the seasons make the rounds with a dramatic emphasis, the seasonlessness of a region like Southern California is a drag. It is all right for native Californians of course and not a thing one can argue about. For those who need to stretch out in the sun it is hard to accept the proposition that two feet of snow can be nicer.

London was sustaining the new Elizabethan euphoria with the Beatles, Mary Quant and Harold Macmillan. The work we were doing at the MGM Studio in Elstree was invigorating. The cast was good: George Sanders, Vera Miles and Harry Andrews. George, as I have implied before, was one of the great talents of my generation of

421

actors. He did not have the kind of ambition that actors need to succeed, nor the pleasure in doing the job that is available even when material rewards do not add up to much.

He said to me several times during the period when we first knew each other, 'Are you in demand, old boy?'

I was actually slightly more in demand than he at that time because he had been longer in Hollywood than I had and his early gilt had been rubbed off. But it seemed to me to indicate that he wanted very much to be sought after, though it was not his nature to jostle his way to the top as most of us were trying to do. Later on, though he told his friends that he wanted to be a tycoon more than anything, it seemed that he wanted tycoonship to fall accidentally upon him. His best efforts were devoted to the establishment of a high class cabinet-making business, largely for the benefit of his brother. But though he had great talent in this direction he applied it as unambitiously as he seemed to apply his acting talent. I may, of course, be wrong about him; vigorous effort may just have been overtaken by Hollywood inertia.

The first time I ever heard from him was shortly after our arrival in Beverly Hills in 1948. A call came to the house while I was out; Monaghan took it and told me that George Sanders had rung. Since I had never met George Sanders, I asked Monaghan to ring the William Morris Office, ascertain the telephone number of George Sanders, then ask him if it was in fact he who had telephoned. I had started behaving like this when I first became the big popular star in England and was exposed to the unpredictable demands of my early film fans. If I was not constantly on the alert they would attract me to the telephone by identifying themselves as Margaret Lockwood or Ann Todd. I became twice as cautious in New York where they did very odd things which made me feel surrounded and threatened. A heavy-set girl threw herself on the sidewalk at my feet as I emerged from the stage door of the Ethel Barrymore Theatre, another girl encircled our rented house that hot summer in Riverdale, N.Y., never to be seen again after the disappearance of my favourite cat. Pamela and I were convinced that the girl had stolen him. And there was the one who made a practice of going through the garbage cans when they were put out and making off with any scraps of paper she might find with my handwriting on them. The lawsuit I was contending did nothing to alleviate the feeling of harassment, not did the self-imposed house arrest which prevailed when I first moved to Beverly Hills.

When I finally spoke to George Sanders he expressed surprise at my furtive behaviour and then gave me his reason for calling. This is my reconstruction of what he said:

'I have been told that you are a trained architect. Is that so?'

I detailed my architectural background.

'Good. I am glad to know that the report was correct. I'll tell you what's in my mind, old man. I have been involved in the building of a couple of houses here and I know the ropes. My idea is quite simple. I propose that you and I go into business together. I am the builder, you are the architect. We hang up our shingle as such. Sanders and Mason, or if you prefer it, Mason and Sanders. I tell you, Mason, we can develop a fabulous business. It's ready made; all the wealthy widows will be falling over each other, all wanting us to build them one of our delightful hillside residences. My great friend is Mrs Hilton who can introduce us to all the wealth of Los Angeles. And of course you won't have to do anything, except make a suitable impression on the clients; we shall have a tame architect of our own who will do all the work. How does the idea strike you?'

I laughed. I told him that apart from being a very droll notion, it would give us a lot of fun when we put it into practice. After this Pamela made social contact with him and Mrs Hilton who was to become better known as Zsa Zsa Gabor, a lady who, taken in small doses, was excellent company. You could enjoy her banter on two levels, for it was punctuated with a genuine wit, and, if you chose, you could make fun of her with impunity. I have to add that for those who were *close* friends the impunity was not always available. Not for nothing was she Hungarian.

However my promising business relationship with George tended to get lost under a layer of social froth. At home I set up my drawing board and starting designing the prototype Sanders–Mason residence for wealthy widows. No tame architect was going to snatch this opportunity from me. But then George disappeared to Spain to start work on a film. This kept him abroad for many months. By the time he was due to come back I myself was out of town for a spell. In the event we never got down to business. Our hillside residences remained pinned to my drawing board.

I saw very little of George in later years in Hollywood, and never worked with him until we were in England contributing to *A Touch of Larceny*. I did not see much of him even then. There was only one brief scene in which we worked together. He had taken his script apart and retained only the pages on which there was dialogue that he would need to commit to memory. As he completed each scene he threw away the pages concerned. It somehow depressed me to see him do this because it was symptomatic of his negative attitude to the thing we were jointly trying to construct. Foolish of me to feel that way because it was 'only a movie', as Hitch would say, and certainly not a very important one. Obviously it meant a great deal more to me than to him. Ivan Foxwell had opened a window in my coop and I was responding to the sunshine and the fresh air. When all the rest of the cast had been dismissed I travelled to Scotland with the unit and enjoyed the kind of gorgeous spring which, they told me, was often to be found in Oban and the islands beyond. Work completed, I stopped off to spend my fiftieth birthday in Huddersfield on the way south. I shall be for ever grateful to Foxwell for allowing me these treats.

A couple of years later Foxwell presented me with more sunshine, more fresh air. He set up a film that had to be made primarily in Tahiti followed by some studio work in London. The resultant film, *Tiara Tahiti*, though less good than *A Touch of Larceny*, was a rare adventure for all concerned. On a point of magic, Oban had it over Papeete. But then I am not by nature a sea rover and Quinn's on the waterfront of Papeete is not my favourite type of bar. Also, it should go without saying, Tahiti could not hold a candle to Grenada, although if I had made landfall in the days of Captain Cook and Captain Bligh, I might disagree with that verdict. Bligh first became acquainted with Tahiti when he was serving under Cook. When he came later to transport that cargo of breadfruit from Tahiti to the West Indies, which never reached its destination on account of a certain mutiny which we are never allowed to forget, he confided in his log that the island had deteriorated since his days with Captain Cook. Cook having been one of the first European explorers to visit the island it had still, in his time, been an uncontaminated paradise. Over the last two hundred years everyone who has visited the island more than once repeats in different words the findings recorded by Bligh. Not what it was, they all say.

When Foxwell and I went there in 1960, not only had the mariners of the world worked hard to mar its salubriousness, but there had been added two new threats. One was the recently constructed airstrip, the other was the intrusion, lasting over eighteen months, of a film unit launched by MGM for the remaking of *Mutiny on the Bounty*. They told us that this had seriously disturbed the island's economy. We were a small unit and not very wild, and as a source of social aggravation we could not compete.

A very powerful, romantic film was once made in Tahiti, *Tabu*, co-directed by Murnau and Flaherty. The leading lady was still in Papeete, still enjoying the bringues. Someone found us a copy of that old black and white film. The magic was still there, a little desiccated like the celluloid itself.

I was jealous – I think that is the right word – of those acting colleagues who, when oppressed by similar feelings, would pack their bags and fly to New York and start rehearsing for a stage play. I was more than ever jealous of Rex Harrison who was lifted to the ultimate glory of actordom by his unique performance in *My Fair Lady*. While I was in this mood I happened to go to New York for a few days for a television play and attended a dinner party in the River House given by Dina Merrill and her then husband. There were several gifted performers among the guests and after dinner a very good modern guitarist arrived to entertain us and to supply accompaniment for any of the guests who might be coaxed into singing. Several were easily coaxed. A friend of mine was there who had heard me sing a typical number from my brief repertoire. So he challenged me and I was in a sufficiently good mood not to mind making a fool of myself. The typical number was, as I recall, 'I've Got a Lovely Bunch of Coconuts'. I may even have added 'Ain't It Grand to be Blooming Well Dead' as an encore. Next morning I was preparing to wipe the whole incident from my mind when I received a phone call from a fellow guest, Marty Baum, who was an agent. And it was with an agent's antennae that he had scanned the party.

Said he,

'I was beginning to think that the party was going to be a dead loss when you got up and sang those songs . . . It gave me an idea. Dietz and Schwartz have a new musical which will be going into production shortly, and I thought that while you were in New York you might care to meet them. Have you sung in a musical before?'

'No. And I'm not sure that my voice is . . .'

'We'll get into that later.'

I was immensely thrilled. I met Dietz and Schwartz and I met Michael Kanin who had written the book for the musical which turned out to be based on *The Affairs of Anatole* by Schnitzler. I was asked to meet Henry Greene, musical director at the theatre where *The Music Man* was playing. I got the guitar player from Dina Merrill's party to come along to the theatre and there I auditioned for Greene, who gave my singing voice his nod of approval on the understanding that I would spend time in his studio where he could build up its strength.

From that point on I lived a new and unsettling fantasy. I was to be Broadway's new musical idol. I dug myself so deeply into it that I almost missed the opportunity of doing just the kind of film I was always looking for. Stanley Kubrick telephoned me to say that he wanted me to play the part of Humbert Humbert in the film that he was about to make, in England, of *Lolita*.

I told him that unfortunately I had made up my mind to appear in a new musical based on Schnitzler's *Anatole*, and wasn't that exciting. Kubrick sounded a little surprised but made no effort to dissuade me. I learned later that he had already offered Humbert Humbert to several other actors who had turned it down, so I imagine that at this point he was mechanically going down a list of possibles for the role.

When I told Pamela about this she looked at me as though I was dotty. Since this from her was no new look, I took no notice. But when all my friends reacted the same way, I accepted it as a fact that I was dotty. I knew that I had been leaning in that direction for some time. I quickly contacted Kubrick and thanked God that I caught him before some unworthy rival had inherited the part that I had in fact longed to play ever since I had read of Humbert's strange fancies in Nabokov's great novel.

Kubrick's partner James Harris worked as producer while he himself directed. Ray Stark's company launched the project for them and every effort was made to find the major distribution company which would not only finance the production but would allow Kubrick and Harris to retain total artistic authority. They came quite close to making it with Warner Brothers, but in the small print we discovered words which unambiguously reassured Jack Warner that not only the fate of the film but also its ultimate form were vested in his hands and no one else's.

So the film was to be made for a scanty budget of one million dollars, and – in order at least to have more time to spend it – in England, although the background of the story was patently the USA.

Once committed, I could think of nothing else but the exciting new project. But even though for what seemed an eternity I remained fidgeting in California while the sets were being built in Elstree, I no longer coveted Rex Harrison's glory. In the event, no invitation to sing in the musical dramatisation of *The Affairs of Anatole* ever came to me. The management finally settled on the Italian actor Walter Chiari, for whom I have nothing but admiration. But I cannot say that the failure of this musical caused me any loss of sleep.

Through no fault of its own, *Lolita* marked the end of one period in my life and the beginning of another. It took me to England for a longer period than usual and at the end of it I felt as if a repatriation had actually taken place and that though I went through the motions of life as conducted in California I no longer lived there.

Lolita was one of my very best adventures in film making. Among Kubrick's most striking talents was his ability to choose the right subject for the right moment. I had made his acquaintance when I was occupying that office in the 20th Century Fox Studio where in theory I was forever planning exciting projects and interviewing exciting talents. One of his first films, *The Killing*, had been a perfect example of how to make an inexpensive thriller to a desirable commercial formula without sacrificing originality and technical virtuosity. When I met him he was planning *Paths of Glory*, which was to win him even louder critical acclaim. I noted with increasing admiration the step by step development of a novel describing profligate expenditure of human life in World War I into an equally explicit and powerful screenplay. Predictably the executives of the company which was to finance the film were forever begging him to supply a less painful conclusion to the story, but he refused to compromise. (In the story a French general attempts to take a position held by the Germans, knowing it to be impregnable. Three survivors are arbitrarily charged with desertion and executed.) Instead, he devised a little epilogue to this incident, a bar-room scene in which French soldiers coax a local German girl to sing for them, then, at a word of command, silently rejoin their units. Kubrick plays it, in fact, not as a conclusion so much as any isolated episode in an endless tragedy.

The acting in the film however did not match the quality of the writing, partly, no doubt, because British and American actors are seldom credible when playing Frenchmen. It is only fair to say however that Kirk Douglas was never better. But when we came to the shooting of *Lolita* it was evident that Kubrick had learned a great deal about screen acting since *Paths of Glory*, and this may have been the result of time spent with Marlon Brando while preparing a film which was never made – unless it was reshaped into something called *One Eyed Jacks*, the direction of which was claimed only by Brando himself.

Ultimately Kubrick had to give up on the Brando film because he figured that life was too short. Brando, it seems, was not one to make snappy decisions. But in all other respects Kubrick had nothing but praise for him. Aside from his talent as an actor he had, according to Kubrick, great theatrical intelligence and on the spur of the moment could improvise an entire plot development or an impressive exchange of dialogue.

Whatever the reason, Kubrick had become a director of

enormous sophistication when it came to handling our group. I can think of only one minor criticism. He was so besotted with the genius of Peter Sellers that he seemed never to have enough of him. There was one scene in which Sellers, immersed in the character of Quilty which he was playing, pretended to be an undercover detective for a full nine minutes while poor Humbert Humbert had nothing to do but look uncomfortable. I was Humbert Humbert.

I should tell something of the story. Humbert Humbert ('a salad of racial genes', as he describes himself in the book) is erotically inclined to girls generally to be found between the ages of nine and thirteen. At the beginning of the story he is looking for lodgings in a small New England town and is on the point of turning down the paying guest arrangement offered to him by a middle-class widow named Hayes when a glimpse of her twelve-year-old daughter triggers an instant change of mind. The kind of girl that attracts him is one in whom he detects a precocious sexuality, a species for which Nabokov coined the word Nymphet, now firmly entrenched in the English language.

Propinquity to the Hayes daughter, whose name is Lolita, is ensured for Humbert by a marriage of convenience to Mrs Hayes. Though conscientiously respecting her marital rights, he cannot help thinking of the ever more delightful propinquity with Lolita which would be available if there were no Mrs Hayes. For a moment he entertains the thought of drowning her. But shortly afterwards Humbert's true feelings (though not touching on murder) are revealed to her when she discovers his diary. She runs out of the house in a state of distress which makes her an easy target for a passing limousine.

Throughout the subsequent scenes of seduction and cohabitation with his beloved Lolita, which take place in a series of motels, Humbert is haunted by the knowledge that she makes secret telephone calls and even occasional rendezvous with a mysterious character called Quilty. Sometimes Quilty, who is a merciless practical joker, is introduced in person as a psychiatrist, a visiting lecturer, an under-cover man or what not. Humbert becomes more and more jealous of his phantom rival and when Lolita ultimately disappears, the shock sends him into a nervous breakdown.

One of the difficulties about telling the story was that in the place of a second act there was only a rather hazy résumé of Humbert's subsequent Odyssey, during which a former friend of Lolita's supplies him with a clue as to her current whereabouts. There follows a brief but powerful third act.

Lolita, who he tracks down, is married to a depressingly ordinary artisan and pregnant. Humbert offers her money and every kind of security which she recognises as inducements to reestablish their former relationship. But she never even liked him, she says; the one she loved was Quilty. Humbert goes to Quilty's house and shoots him.

Lolita was one of the very few films in which we actors were allowed a fair amount of time for rehearsal, both before principal photography and immediately prior to the shooting of each sequence. During the first period we discovered that Sue Lyon, who played the part of Lolita, had so conscientiously memorised all her lines throughout the script that they were inclined to come out of her parrot-fashion. So Kubrick very sensibly suggested that all of us pretend to forget the lines that we had memorised and, being fully aware of the aim and content of each sequence, express these in our own words. This had a magical effect on Sue Lyon. She was type cast, being only two-and-a-half years older than the age specified in the novel, and the language that she now introduced into the script and the fact that it came out freshly minted made her suddenly a very vivid nymphet. She was really wonderful throughout the film and, I thought, rather more sensible than the rest of the gang.

Come to think of it though, you could not fault Peter Sellers. He was the only one allowed, or rather encouraged, to improvise his entire performance. The rest of us improvised only during rehearsals, then incorporated any departures from the original script that had seemed particularly effective during rehearsal. Sellers told us that he did not enjoy improvising, but I think that he was referring to the occasional necessity to think on his feet when giving a live performance. He was painstaking and meticulous in his preparation. He had told Kubrick that in order to play Quilty with an American accent he must find a model, since he needed always to be specific. Together they decided that the ideal voice for Quilty was that of Norman Grantz, the jazz impresario.

The sequence in which Sellers impressed me most was when Quilty is shot by Humbert Humbert. Kubrick's set for this sequence looked like the main hall of a Victorian mansion, complete with grand staircase, chandeliers etc. He asked me if I could think of any items that could be introduced which would suggest the bizarre lifestyle of Quilty, its present occupant. I said that a ping-pong table beneath the principal chandelier might look nicely incongruous. But I certainly did not imagine that he would ask us to play on it. Then, in order to suggest that a wild party had taken place the night before, he had the property man distribute wine glasses and tumblers on the table. So when we came to play the scene which now incorporated a game of ping-pong, Peter, while keeping the score, would insert little wisecracks relative to the hits or misses scored by the ping-pong ball as it careened among the glasses.

Improvisation was a dirty word to most producers and to all screenwriters at the time when we made *Lolita*, a mere twenty-one years ago. The authorship of our script was credited to Vladimir Nabokov himself although it was conceded that Kubrick had supplied a modicum of technical assistance. During our period of improvised rehearsal Kubrick cautioned us to keep it to ourselves since he did not want Nabokov to get the erroneous impression that we were playing fast and loose with his dialogue. Which was another way of saying that he hoped that Shelley Winters would keep her mouth shut, since she was the only one of us who enjoyed chatting up newspapermen. Regardless of all her Oscars, awards and citations for other pictures, her work in *Lolita* was her best.

Before the film I had met Nabokov only briefly as he paused momentarily at my table as he was being steered by his host to the other side of a crowded restaurant. I met him a second time after he had seen the completed film. It was at a dinner party for the Nabokovs and myself given by Kubrick at the Four Seasons Restaurant in New York. Nabokov testified that he had admired the film and congratulated Kubrick on having done a number of things which he himself would not have thought of. His enthusiasm seemed to be quite genuine.

Kubrick had in fact departed from the original script in two areas, in his treatment of Humbert's momentary homicidal attitude towards Mrs Hayes, and of the non-existent second act. Kubrick had had constructed in the studio a vast set representing the lake and its surroundings where Mrs Hayes and Humbert and the other 'young marrieds' were wont to disport themselves of a weekend. But he rebelled against the idea of shooting such an important sequence 'Interior for Exterior'. He had the feeling that the contemplated murder sequence could and should be staged in the complex set representing the interior of the Hayes house, if only we could put the pieces together in the right order. I was permitted to discuss the problem with Kubrick every time I met him, and we were greatly helped by the fact that in the book itself Mrs Hayes had at one moment exhibited among other souvenirs of her dead husband his cherished revolver. In switching from the dreaded 'Interior for Exterior' set Kubrick succeeded finally in stringing together an unbroken continuity of scenes starting with Humbert describing confidentially to his diary his transition from Lodger to Husband, and terminating with Humbert in his bathtub, happily smashed, after poor Mrs Hayes has suffered death by limousine. Although Lolita herself had no part to play in it I thought that this was the most skilfully executed section of the film.

When it came to Nabokov's attempted second act, Kubrick jettisoned it, figuring that the only way to treat it was with the aid of an old fashioned Fade-out. Establish that Lolita has done a bunk. Dramatise Humbert's nervous crisis. Fade out. Fade in. Humbert's car is approaching a terraced house in a low rent district in what is recognisably the outskirts of New York (although in fact it was shot near the Great West Road on the outskirts of London.).

On one of the many occasions when, in later years, I passed time with Nabokov in the corner of Switzerland where we both lived, the great man hinted that he would like to see the film made again because the girl we used in our film was too old. I should have asked him a few questions then and there. And this only goes to remind me that when I have questions to pose I should never hang back. The questions in this case were: In a *complete* dramatisation of his book what age should the actress we chose have been? And, with whom had he been discussing a film production in which the actress playing Lolita should have been no more than twelve years old? Now it is too late, because this truly great man has left us, ahead of schedule.

That Nabokov could even for a moment entertain the thought of remaking the film with a twelve-year-old Lolita distressed me because I had previously taken a poor view of those who faulted our film on the same grounds. The first had been Bosley Crowther, the *New York Times* critic. I should have written asking him for further elucidation, but by the time the film opened in New York I was caught in a fresh tangle of personal problems.

Through no fault of its own *Lolita* marked the end of

V. Nabokov

one period in my life and the beginning of another. It had kept me in England longer than usual and by the end of it I felt I was a European again and that California could no longer contain me. In fact on the day after the opening of *Lolita* I was already on a plane taking me to Italy. This was for the first European film that was offered to me since *Lolita* and which I had accepted in a flash.

At the same time as its New York opening a splashy European première was organised for *Lolita* at the Venice Film Festival. Soon afterwards, at a party in Rome given by a lady called Bricktop I found myself almost alone in one of the large rooms of her apartment. A dour-looking individual sat silently in a remote corner. He returned my greeting but seemed in no hurry to set up a conversation. After a long pause he said, 'Did you like *Lolita*?' I said that I liked it very much and hoped that he, too, had enjoyed it. After another pause he said,

'I didn't like it.'

'Oh, I am sorry to hear that,' I said, 'I hope at least that you did not have to pay for your seat.'

No immediate response. Then,

'The French critics hated it.'

'Yes,' I said, 'I read some of their reviews. And I can understand their attitude. They had feared that the French

435

film industry's ascendancy as purveyors of sexy entertainment might be threatened by us. But, finding that Kubrick had treated *Lolita* as a love story rather than an essay in exploitation, they felt that they had scored.'

Another long pause. Had he gone to sleep or left the room? No he was still there, darkly glowering.

'The girl was too old.'

'Ah,' said I, 'it is interesting that you should bring that up. Other critics have said the same thing. I take it that you are a critic.'

'I am a critic.'

'It is a pity that we did not have you around when we were making the film. The right age for the girl who played Lolita was always a problem and undoubtedly we could have profited by your advice. You see, Lolita did not remain the same age throughout Nabokov's story. She was indeed twelve years old when Humbert first met her, but when he found her again at the end, she was married and pregnant and surely not less than eighteen. Now it is much easier for a petite eighteen-year-old girl to pretend to be twelve than for a twelve-year-old to make like an experienced eighteen-year-old. Before I got involved with the film I had assumed that for this very reason we would have to use a clever actress in her late teens and I was delighted to find that they had found a clever girl of fourteen and a half who was equally convincing as the precocious American twelve-year-old and the some-what jaded expectant mother of eighteen. So tell me, since it was necessary to show Lolita at the two different ages, what would your advice have been?'

A long pause. Then, triumphantly,

'You should have had two actresses.'

Many different films could be extracted from a book like *Lolita*. Many people thought that the best thing about the book was its sardonic review of the American Motel. If one of the New Young Directors attempts another version I assume that the sex act will be prominently featured; but,

436

from no matter what viewpoint, I am sure that we have not seen the last of her.

The film that had brought me to Italy was not one of my most distinguished. But I knew by this time that my future lay here in Europe and that it was here that a long line of work and adventure was waiting to be lived. To be shooting a large part of this film in Siracusa was already something. I would meet Venus Kallipygos in the local museum and I would visit the mines where those unfortunate Athenian prisoners of war had been put to work after the disastrous action which stirred in Pericles his most noble oratory.

When I landed at the airport which serves travellers bound for Siracusa I was greeted by a small curly haired individual who looked as if he might have dropped in from North Africa. He proved to be a newspaperman, and he had two questions to put to me.

'Is this your first visit to Sicily?' and 'Is the name of your lawyer . . . Jake Ehrlich?'

I answered both questions in the affirmative. He seemed to be satisfied and drifted away.

I was the one who finally ripped the marital fabric. I had decided to find a lawyer and ask him to introduce himself to whatever lawyer Pamela chose to name, and achieve by patient negotiation a state of divorce. I found my lawyer in San Francisco because I had formed the opinion that all telephone operators and secretaries in Los Angeles were corruptible, especially when it came to obliging such columnists as might now be wearing the shoes of Louella Parsons and Hedda Hopper.

My man did not distinguish himself in the handling of my case. But then I had not handled myself very well in the events that led up to it. He at least can be excused because he did not habitually traffic in divorce cases. He had earned his spurs in criminal cases.

At a later stage in the proceedings, when things were

getting hot, he extracted a promise from me that I would not marry again. About ten years later he died without ever knowing that I was about to break my promise.

Epilogue

In the year 1964 I became excitedly involved in a French/Spanish production that was to be made in Cadaques in Spain. This is the one to which I referred when I wrote about taking part in a commercial about Thunderbird wine in the chapter called 'Stratford'.

Henri-François Rey, the French writer who lived in Cadaques had written a novel called *Les Pianos Mécaniques* about a group of people who were assembled in Cadaques during the summer when the action took place. So we made the film in Cadaques under the eyes of the author. But he did not give us any trouble. His behaviour was impeccable. Eccentric but impeccable. The director was the excellent Juan Bardem.

It was perhaps the most turbulent production in which I ever took part. Never a dull moment. Personally however I was not involved and I carefully refrained from stirring.

There were warning tremors before ever a camera turned, for the leading lady was not in the best of moods when she arrived. She explained this by saying that 'they' had promised to have some of her scenes rewritten before calling her to Spain to start work. Nevertheless, like a good trouper, she was now in Cadaques, ostensibly ready, willing and able to appear before the cameras.

Whether or not our original producer had made errors of judgement, the moneymen in Paris saw fit to remove him in mid-turbulence and send down a replacement who was not only good with film but could handle people with consummate tact. His name was Raymond Froment.

The first scenes in which I appeared were supposed to

take place on a wealthy American's yacht which Ray had dreamed up as something comparable in size and luxe with the black schooner of Niarchos. Unfortunately they could not find such an item and had to settle for an unimpressive substitute. In spite of an equally unimpressive weather forecast we put to sea in it.

My part was supposed to be that of a middle aged Parisian writer, passing the summer in Cadaques with his twelve year old son and over-indulging his tastes for drink, talk and young women. The sequence on the boat illustrated these predilections. Centre deck sat I with a nice looking girl on my lap surrounded by actors and actresses pretending to be jet-setters. It was a long but rather static dialogue scene.

The boat rolled and lurched on the rough sea and I do not believe that Bardem got one complete master shot in the camera before a general sea sickness took over. One by one they dropped out. Bardem changed the angle several times to exclude the casualties. He was soon obliged to come so close that he framed only me and the girl on my lap. But when the colour of her face started to change he pushed closer still and settled for a close-up of the talkative writer who was the only dramatis persona still active. The only other survivors by now were Bardem himself, the camera operator and the man recording sound.

Bardem called a break and planned to wait for calmer weather. But when he suggested that we take advantage of the pause to have luncheon served we discovered that the prevailing indisposition had rendered unusable both cook and galley. This kind of minor disaster can happen on the best of films which involve shooting on location. What was to come was fascinatingly abnormal. But I shall not go into it because I have so far avoided knocking any of my colleagues and I do not intend to stumble at this stage.

Although the conflicts that broke out did not prevent me from enjoying myself I had a special reason for hoping that we would not fall disastrously behind schedule. I had to get to California in time to attend the finalisation of my divorce. The production department had assured me that on the last day of August I would have ample time to drive to Perpignan in the south of France, board a plane for Paris and make a convenient connection with an Air France flight to Los Angeles. But I was getting nervous again.

Frank Essien, my London secretary, was with me on this trip, and we had the greatest difficulty with telephone calls. In fact we had decided that from Cadaques communication with the outside world was a write-off. The best thing to do, we found, was to cross the border into France at a place called Perthus. There was a good restaurant just on the French side of the border from which we had made several telephone calls, as well as dispatching telegrams from the local post office just up the road. The last such mission took place only a few days before my date in Los Angeles and we could not help noticing that the traffic had mysteriously thickened. The line of cars waiting to cross the border from south to north now stretched for almost a kilometre. It was as if the entire population of France crossed into Spain during August and were now committed to being back at work in France by the first of September.

Back in Cadaques I told producer Froment that my carefully worked out timetable was being seriously threatened by the mass exodus of French holidaymakers. He said, 'I have thought of that and I have made a plan.'

No wonder the money men in Paris had faith in this man. Nothing would faze him:

'The owner of the restaurant in Perthus where we all go to make our phone calls happens to be the Chef de Pompiers, the Fire Chief. On the day of your departure he will be here well in advance of the time you plan to leave. He will drive ahead of you to the border. When you come to the line of cars which will stretch for almost four kilometres, you will follow close behind him and when he sounds his siren you will both drive past the entire line of cars on the wrong side of the road directly to the frontier post.'

It was lucky that I had Frank Essien with me. The way Froment had briefed me I had assumed that I was supposed to shoot right over the border in the wake of the Fire Chief. But at the time of my departure I was rebriefed by the chief himself. He would be my accomplice, he said, only as far as the border, and then it would be up to myself to explain the urgency of my mission and justify my mad pursuit of the fire chief's car. A heart attack? Excellent idea. I promptly cast Frank in the role of the victim, although I could have played the part myself since I was not going to be driving the car. A friendly chauffeur had come from Madrid and I had instructed him to drive the car on up to Switzerland as soon as he had dropped us at Perpignan Airport.

It all worked like a dream. I had cast Frank as the heart attack victim because all he had to do was to look comatose. I was the one who had to put the story over convincingly. When it was all over I prided myself on one of my best performances: I had even asked the man to recommend me a local hospital where I could take the patient and painstakingly wrote down the answer, throwing nervous glances at the patient as I did so. So that was my divorce taken care of.

The sequel took place in 1968.

This was the year that Michael Powell and I became co-producers. The film we made was *Age of Consent*, based on a novel by the Australian, Norman Lindsay. Since Michael had already made one film in Australia and since his son Kevin was to be our production manager it was appropriate that he travel down ahead of me to take charge of the physical preparations, which included some of the casting of small parts in the film. By delaying my arrival I almost missed the chance of my life.

On my first day in Sydney, Michael had arranged for a further casting session to take place. We were to look for local actresses to fill three fairly negligible roles and one that I rated as extremely important, though limited to a single sequence.

442

I was very glad that I had made this casting session because, being a great admirer of Powell and having therefore seen practically all his films I was aware that his taste in women was very different from mine. There were not many of his films in which you would spot an actress who warmed up and bubbled. Though perhaps not so cold as many of Hitchcock's leading ladies they tended also to be not so beautiful. Out of the initial dozen young women who presented themselves we were able to pick three who would serve well enough in the three fairly negligible roles, but I could see that it was not going to be easy to find a woman for the part I had rated as extremely important.

It was a good scene she would have to play. The story concerned an Australian painter who had won enormous international acclaim but had ended up painting abstracts and not knowing where to go from there. He had, as it were, run out of gas. So he had decided to return to his beginnings and recover that old urge. He is aiming for a place called Chugaberrime in Northern Queensland and when the plane puts him down in Brisbane the second thing he does is to look up an old girl friend and spend the major portion of the ensuing week in bed with her. We had conceived a sequence immediately preceding this one in which our hero, whose name is Bradley Morahan, is interviewed on local television as the local boy who made good. Our scenarist Peter Yeldham had skilfully entwined these two sequences, that is, while the two are rolling around in bed, the television set, which has been left on, suddenly gives out this recorded interview. The woman wants to listen, to the annoyance of the man who wants only to carry on with what they were doing.

For this part we were looking for the right actress when Clarissa Kaye was ushered into the room where the casting session was taking place. Here for the first time was a woman whose face was a window rather than a blind. Here was a good-natured woman with big expressive eyes, a generous mouth and no pretensions. She had the air of one who had dropped in to pass the time of day and see what kind of people these were who had arrived from overseas.

And this is in fact more or less what was in her mind. I've heard her tell people about this interview many times and it is always a vigorous and colourful account.

She was thirty-six at the time and had done everything that any actress might be called upon to do, except sing in Grand Opera. She started as a dancer at the age of two. She played all the dates available to tiny tots, including the local gaols and the local asylum. At twelve she found that she was a contortionist and became eligible for the circus circuit. Thence she moved into nightclub with a range of song, dance and contortion. These having been spectacularly displayed in a big production of *Kismet*, she moved on to straight drama and was a founder member of the Ensemble Theatre group, for whom she gave outstanding performances in the *Suddenly Last Summer* of Tennessee Williams and other demanding roles. But in doing so she learned that there was a very low ceiling for professional acting in Australia. In fact at that time it was practically impossible to become a full time professional. On many occasions she took jobs behind a bar, just to keep going. She then spent almost two years in America studying under Stella Adler and trying to get a work permit. No go. In America Australians received an even cooler welcome than they had come to expect in England.

It cannot have been very long after this that Michael Powell and I invaded. By this time she had found that if she persisted in being an actress she would be well advised to make up the deficit on the race track. She had several good friends who were in the game and she was an apt student herself.

As she tells it, she came to our casting session not so much to get herself a job as to prove a point. Two actors' agents figure in her account, both ladies. Val was her current agent, the other, Gloria, had represented her before and had now been taken on by our company as casting director. Since the theatre world in Sydney was so limited, competition was intense, especially, it seemed, among the agents. When Clarissa asked Val if she had suggested her for a part in our film she replied that according to Gloria, the casting director, Clarissa's eyes were 'too deep' for the only part that was still available. This did not please Clarissa at all, partly because even if her eyes had been 'too deep', this would have had no bearing on whether an actress could play the part or not – unless it happened to be a film about an eye doctor; and partly because she figured that she had a right to hear this strange verdict from Michael Powell himself.

She assembled all the still photographs she could lay her hands on, from babyhood snapshots to studio portraits and stills from all the plays she had appeared in. Eyes blazing and nostrils quivering she flung the photographs onto her agent's desk and said, 'Show *those* to Gloria! Ask her if my eyes are too deep in any of *them*.'

Val had been in the middle of a telephone call but was so struck by Clarissa's dramatic entrance that she dropped the phone and rushed across the street to Gloria's office to convey Clarissa's challenge. A few minutes later she reappeared with just enough breath left to announce, 'You have an appointment to see Mr Powell tomorrow morning.'

After her very short interview with us she dropped in to see Val who asked anxiously, 'Did they ask you to read a scene for them?' This would normally suggest that the reaction had been good.

'No. I didn't have to read anything. But I got to see Michael Powell, that's all I wanted ... Oh and James Mason was there, too.'

And she was out the door and on her way down the stairs. The telephone rang, and moments later Val was at the head of the stairs shouting after Clarissa who was already out among the street noises and could not hear her.

As she approached her house in Marrickville she could hear the phone ringing inside and had to play the exasperating game of find the latchkey and open the door before the ringing stops. But Val was not in a hurry to hang up. Her client had got the part!

But it was a long time before I saw her again. The rest of us went up to Dunk Isle, on the Great Barrier Reef, and worked there for five or six weeks. Back on the mainland we shot some scenes in Cairns and then came down to Brisbane where I had a rendezvous with an almost naked Clarissa Kaye to shoot the bedroom scene.

Although she seemed bright and relaxed and proved at once that she knew what acting was all about, she had more than a touch of pneumonia on that day. Her temperature was 104°F and in Sydney her doctor was biting his nails down to the quick, having now convinced himself that he should never have let her make the flight to Brisbane.

The Dutch lady, Rita, who was the wife of Dennis Gentle, the art director, and was in charge of first aid throughout the period of our production, assured me rather mysteriously, 'I just want you to know that Clarissa Kaye is no longer contagious.'

We both survived. On this and many other daunting occasions Clarissa Kaye proved indestructible.

We finished the film in a studio in Sydney, where we added one or two additional shots to the bedroom sequence and my next appearance was to be at the airport for the first leg of my return to Switzerland. I said to the indestructible that I hoped we would meet up again in my continent or hers and that meanwhile I would be writing to her. And that is where it might have ended. But there was another stroke of luck.

This is a story that someday I shall get her to write down herself because it needs her style of storytelling. During the following year she did less acting and more punting. The acting was successful but limited to short bursts. For instance she played in a film for television based on *The Drover's Wife* by Henry Lawson and was given a special award for her work. This was the first time that an award had been given to an actor or an actress by the Australian Film Institute. Also she had been cast as Ned Kelly's mother in the film Tony Richardson made with Mick Jagger playing the part of the folk hero.

But there were not many race meetings that she missed. She also happened at this time to own a piece of a race horse, but she had sense enough to regard him as a friend rather than someone who was likely to make her rich.

Her horse figures in the good luck story, and also a little skittish mare to whom she took a fancy, and a well known jockey. The race in which they participated is not one that will go down in the annals of the track as one of major importance, but for Clarissa it meant a tidy sum and for me it meant a whole new life. Her winnings enabled her to take a leisurely trip around the world. After visiting one or two friends in the United States she made a point of flying to Geneva which is close to where I live. We got to know each other much better this time. That is why, every once in a while, I raise my glass and drink a toast to that well-known jockey.

INDEX

Index

453

454

457

DETOUR

CHERYL CRANE WITH CLIFF JAHR

Good Friday, April 4th, 1958. Lana Turner, the movie star, is sobbing uncontrollably. Her 14-year-old daughter, Cheryl Crane, is clutching a butcher's knife. And the bloodied corpse of Lana Turner's lover, Johnny Stompanato, lies sprawled between them.

Now, thirty years later, and after decades of lurid supposition, Cheryl Crane has broken her silence to reveal what really happened on that horrifying night, and the sordid train of events leading up to the fatal stabbing. She tells of her traumatic life in the spotlight, as the daughter of one of Hollywood's much-loved megastars; of her mother's obsession with 'image', her wild lifestyle of violent and drunken outbursts and the series of men, some of whom loved Cheryl, others who lied to her, and one who repeatedly raped her.

'The truth is more shocking than anyone's worst imaginings' *SUNDAY EXPRESS*

0 7474 0342 2   AUTOBIOGRAPHY   £3.99

IN FOR A PENNY

THE BESTSELLING UNAUTHORISED BIOGRAPHY OF JEFFREY ARCHER

JONATHAN MANTLE

Millionaire, bestselling author, ex-MP and ill-fated Tory
Deputy Chairman Jeffrey Archer sounds like a hero of
his own fiction. And, to a large extent that is exactly what
he is. During the making, unmaking and remaking of his
extraordinary career, he has presented to the world a
self-styled image of himself. Nobody – until now – has
checked the facts behind the fiction.

'Archer's life has been told many times but it is usually
told by Archer . . . what Mantle does, which is riveting,
is to tell the story as it actually happened and point out
Archer's rewrites, revisions, inventions and omissions
along the way'
The Listener

0 7474 0442 9   BIOGRAPHY   £3.50

Olivier

ANTHONY HOLDEN

'The most complete book about Olivier . . . benefits
from the quality of the writing and the thoroughness of
the research. Light, bright, incisive'
INDEPENDENT

'The most eagerly awaited and the most monumental
study of the Great Man yet mounted . . . sharp,
unsentimental, up-to-date and fully worthy of its
chameleonesque figure'
TIME OUT

'An important biographer and a major subject. A
substantial achievement'
SUNDAY TIMES

'What we want from a good showbiz biography is
gossip, information and intelligent star-struck prose,
and Holden provides it all . . . this thoroughly
researched and indefatigable biography often seems to
be the history of the English theatre in this century'
THE STAGE

0 7221 4857 7   BIOGRAPHY   £5.99

All Sphere Books are available at your bookshop or
newsagent, or can be ordered from the following address:
Sphere Books, Cash Sales Department, P.O. Box 11,
Falmouth, Cornwall TR10 9EN.

Please send cheque or postal order (no currency), and
allow 60p for postage and packing for the first book plus
25p for the second book and 15p for each additional book
ordered up to a maximum charge of £1.90 in U.K.

B.F.P.O. customers please allow 60p for the first book, 25p
for the second book plus 15p per copy for the next 7 books,
thereafter 9p per book.

Overseas customers, including Eire, please allow £1.25 for
postage and packing for the first book, 75p for the second
book and 28p for each subsequent title ordered.